The Perennial Wisdom

MYSTICS, SKEPTICS, AND PRAGMATISTS

Courtney Schlosser

Professor of Philosophy

Philosophy Department

Worcester State University

2014

ISBN: 1495266176
ISBN 13: 9781495266171
Library of Congress Control Number: 2014901206
CreateSpace Independent Publishing Platform
North Charleston, South Carolina

OUTLINE

INTRODUCTION: FRAMING THE WISDOM OF

PERENNIAL PHILOSOPHY

"So this world has no substantial reality, / but exists as a shadowy pageant or a play." Shabistari
"God has created the world in play....And it is God himself who is sporting in the form of man." Sri Ramakrishna
"All the world's a stage and all the men and women merely players." Shakespeare *(As You Like It)*
"This world, with all its stars, elements, and creatures, comes out of the invisible world...." William Law
"The atoms of the universe may be counted, but not my manifestations; for I (Creator) create innumerable worlds." Srimad Bhagavatam

1. Aldous Huxley and the Perennial Philosophy

Every work of art, philosophy or science has a point of view or framing for its creativity and it is important to make this explicit from the beginning. This book is the result of the Perennial philosophy which, in recent times, has been best articulated by Aldous Huxley in his integrative survey of the great world religions titled *The Perennial Philosophy* (1944). In the same year Huxley wrote an "Introduction" to a translation of the Hindu religious classic, the *Bhagavad-Gita* which means the 'Song of God' from the Sanskrit language. In that essay, he wrote a summary of the four doctrines or premises of Perennialism; and they go as follows:

"First: the phenomenal world of matter and of individualized consciousness—the world of things and animals and men and even gods—is the manifestation of a Divine Ground within which all partial realities have their being, and apart from which they would be nonexistent.

"Second: human beings are capable not merely of knowing about the Divine Ground by inference; they can also realize its existence by a direct intuition, superior to discursive reasoning. This immediate knowledge unites the knower with that which is known.

"Third: man possesses a double nature, a phenomenal ego and an eternal Self, which are the inner man, the spirit, and the spark of divinity within the soul. It is possible for a man, if he so desires, to identify himself with the spirit and therefore with the Divine Ground, which is of the same or like nature with the spirit.

"Fourth: man's life on earth has only one end and purpose: to identify himself with his eternal Self and so to come to unitive knowledge of the Divine Ground." (1)

It is this philosophy which serves as major assumptions and guidelines to much of *The Perennial Wisdom*. At the same time, there is a necessary critique of the Perennialist thesis, to offer a more balanced and nuanced appraisal of this important philosophy from several other viewpoints; and it mostly for this reason that the subtitle *Mystics, Skeptics, and Pragmatists* is intended to create a more inclusive, grounded and holistic view of the Perennial philosophy.

In the ancient philosophies of India, especially the Hindu schools of thought, the principle of *Maya* plays a major role in the forms and manifestations of reality. *Maya* is the dynamic, worldly force of *Brahman,* the eternal God of Hindus, and creates our ignorance of the one reality or Truth. Enlightenment occurs when we realize that knowledge and ignorance co-exist in the real world; and when we truly see this fact, we realize the divine aspect of *Brahman* in this world which is *Atman,* the inner, higher Self of all sentient beings.

The three faces of *Brahman—Brahma, Vishnu, Shiva*—personified for the masses what could only be understood metaphysically and impersonally. These three faces of *Brahman* were interpreted as the actual manifestations of *Unmanifested Brahman* or the most sacred sound of the universe, *Om*, the One Supreme Source that is eternal, infinite and beyond comprehension. *Brahman* manifests in the gross world of materiality through the creative energy of *Brahma*, the inexhaustible and universal Source of all forms, from atoms to galaxies and everything between. The second face, *Vishnu*, is the God who sustains creation, keeps it going, in myriads of way everywhere, for all of time. And the third face is *Shiva*, the great God of destruction and transformation, who dances with glee over the corpses of the countless life-forms of the universe who journey from *one* life-form to another, in the dream of escaping the controlling gravity of *karma*, the electromagnetic force of causality that links everything together on the wheel of *samsara* or birth, life, death and rebirth, in cyclic existence.

The *dream of liberation*, complete, final and ultimate liberation, is the illusion that binds all life-forms to this and every other world. We desire and in desiring, we attach ourselves to existence and Life. The path of *asceticism* or turning away from the world and existence is the path of illusion, dissatisfaction, attachment; and the path of *hedonism* or turning towards the world of the senses, pleasures and forms, also leads to disillusion and the lack of satisfaction. The only path left that leads one away from the dream of eternity or the nightmare of nihilism is that of the way between the extremes of existence and to the experience of *tranquility*. *Nirvana*, the release from attachment to forms of all kinds, is the path away from misery, dissatisfaction, and dreaming, to the absolute freedom of eternal Being termed *moksha*.— Such is the well-known script among the Hindus of the world.

Meanwhile, there are many parallel viewpoints in the Perennial philosophy, which have the same originating Source, sustaining substance and ultimate destiny. The three modes of reality—creativity, sustainability and transformation—parallel the three modes of time or past, present and future; this triadic pattern of existence can be seen everywhere in the forms of the world, which at causal and material levels, are impermanent, contingently related and constantly changing.

In the West, George Hegel in eighteenth century Europe expressed a similar view of reality in his dialectical philosophy of history, culture and the Absolute. In Hegel, dialectics took the form of *thesis, anti-thesis and synthesis,* a pattern of thought that can be seen around the world. In ancient Chinese Taoism, a dialectical tendency can be seen in the transformations of the sixty-four hexagrams of the great *Tao* or *Way* that joins *yin* and *yang* or the complementary oppositions found in nature, civilization and the cosmos.

One can also find dialectical pattern between reason and observation, reason and nature, observation and speculation, mankind and the gods, this world and another world, etc. among the pre-Socratics, Socrates, Plato and Aristotle of Greece; and a similar dialectic of reason and faith, spirit and matter, man and God, life and death, Heaven and Hell, good and evil, etc. can be seen in the rise of the Middle Eastern theologies of Judaism, Christianity and Islam. Modern and post-modern Western Philosophy is mostly a story of the conflict between religion and science, reason and experience, creation and evolution, experience and knowledge, experiment and speculation, man and woman, the individual and society, self and the universe, theory and practice, etc.—dialectically paired oppositions that are only fulfilled or completed with a higher movement of thought and action in the synthetic mode of Being.—At least this is, in part, the thesis of the present text.

Play or the goddess *Lila* (Sanskrit) is an unsung actor on the stage of philosophy and cultural life of the Indian subcontinent and elsewhere. The relative, material world is a result of the divine play of the God *Vishnu* among the worshipping *Vaishnavas* of India. When the creative principle of *Lila* is embraced in relation to *Nitya* or the transforming love of the absolute, then human action and worship becomes fully liberating and enlightened. More generally, play is excess energy like laughter, dance, and imagination and it is a crucial ingredient in the creative process—whatever the field of endeavor. Intuition, the use of memory and imagination, the analytic processes of symbolic thought —these functions and more concerning the life of the mind are of critical importance to human intelligence and reason. (2)

The creative process is central to the growth and development of Perennial Wisdom. Indeed, wisdom arises in the magical zone of insight when we penetrate the surface appearances of things and understand deeper processes. Indeed, the language or symbols that we use in communicating is the expressive medium by means of which we can realize or actualize ordinary knowledge and wisdom. Although we understand that very complex psycho-physiological and neurological regions of the brain are responsible for abstract thought and symbolic expressions, our knowledge of creativity is more like gee-whiz rather than precise science; and as importantly, there is uncertainty about how consciousness or awareness arises from the neural structures of the brain and the nervous system of the body—in the first place.

In truth, there is much more that we do not understand or really know about ourselves and the universe than what we do know—the premises of Perennial philosophy notwithstanding. Perennialism has broad generalizations about key doctrines in the various world religions and other forms of spirituality. It is a useful philosophy for its conceptual scope and power; and most importantly it has the potential for becoming the basis for a new, scientifically informed, progressively oriented, and nonviolently inspired view of human spirituality and civilization.

2. The Language of Perennial Wisdom: Metaphor as Truth

The title of this book, *The Perennial Wisdom: Mystics, Skeptics and Pragmatists,* denotes the necessary dialectic of *believing, doubting and acting* that every knower goes through or experiences in the growth of wisdom. We are born, live, and die in the symbolic universe of the Eternal Now; and our present life-time is but a moment in the eternality of Being or what-is. Although we may seek an unyielding absolute and certainty in our lives, individual awareness represents a single perspective that is grounded in subjective Being and an objective, real world. Indeed, the historical record of philosophy shows that as we approach questions of absoluteness in human knowledge and values, intellectual agreement diminishes as we become distanced from the relative, personal and social world.

Although metaphysics or a theory of ultimate reality conventionally denotes a God-centered universe, I have tried to avoid the language of *metaphysics* and *God* for the emotional baggage, divisive and confusing array of views *associated* with these terms. Instead I have used the more philosophical and impersonal term *Being* owing, in part, to its ancient origin in the vision of Parmenides, the pre-Socratic philosopher, as well as the frequent appearance of this term in contemporary perennial, existential and spiritual literature.

In particular, *existence* is a crucially important term in gaining a historical and temporal perspective of universal Life as well as situating human subjectivity in a life-world that is oriented towards the transforming experiences of life, death and liberation. Unfortunately, the referents of the words and symbols of Being and existence are not as concrete and definite as we would like them to be and often lack the specificity that makes for clear writing and easy reading; however, the existentialists and others have often said in their criticism of the logical analysts, *clarity is not enough* and what is needed is depth—the depth and intensity of experience and meaning.

The danger in metaphysical thinking is the ambiguity, vagueness and uncertainty of any term denoting *absoluteness* or complete finality. Yet it could be very consoling to think that one can know God or similar absolutes of transcendence through reason alone. The usual way that symbols of absoluteness are indicated is by simply capitalizing one noun after another; furthermore, italicized and hyphenated terms are often the tip-off that you are dealing with metaphysics, spirituality or religion.

That said, the premises, symbols and values of Perennial philosophy represent a serious effort to bridge the differences between the established world religions. However, there is nothing to suggest that the symbols and experiences alluded to by Perennialism differ from those of the established religions, mysticism and other forms of spirituality. Hence, there is a real sense in which the Perennial approach to spirituality and religion conserves rather than transforms the established religions of the world by showing their congruence with each other.

Love it or not, we are symbol-using, addictively metaphorical beings who live in the intangible ether of meaning *and* experience; for there is no substitute for the experiences that give meaning and significance to the words we use and the books we love to read. In fact, few things are more real and valuable in our life-world than the neurological system of the body that enables us to use language and communicate with others.

Albeit, the experiences of the body, mind and soul only mask or cover up *the ontological uncertainty of existence* especially when we use words to represent what we believe is absolutely real, true or good. In other words, the *truths that we speak and write, hear and read,* are no more or less an authentic part of our identity as human beings than the unspoken and nonverbal truths of the body, heart and soul. What historically is called the *mind* is a symbolic and experienced byproduct of the brain and nervous system, the totality of our experience, and the language and symbols of our knowledge; thus the body and mind are inseparably, complexly and mysteriously related in our experience and knowledge of the world. And as will be discussed, the soul is the symbolic and intuitively real essence of who we are.

Language especially the language of Perennial philosophy is entirely natural and cultural in origin. Whether anything human or natural and cultural is *divine in origin* is a very controversial question that no use of language can adequately answer or settle, whether it is logical, theological or theatrical in form. However, *The Perennial Wisdom* affirms the existence of metaphysical phenomena, which is necessary if one sets out to be integrative and inclusive of the world's spiritual and religious traditions. Of course this does not solve the metaphysical problem that religions face, but only removes it to a more philosophical, secular and unbiased perspective.

Meanwhile, the phenomenology of personal identity is often created by roles that people play, the language that we use and who or what we identify with. For example, if I say that 'I am a professor of philosophy, a citizen of the United States, a white, middle class male in his last quarter of life' I have created metaphorical images of who I am; and this identity is personal, social and existential. However, if I say and believe that my 'real identity is soulful or divine in origin' it is a quite different matter—a matter of belief or reflected upon faith; and I also believe, which I do, that the *real me* is beyond categories of all kinds— role, gender, race, class, age, etc. and unknown completely even to myself.

We are born into the world entirely ignorant of any language—karma and metaphysics notwithstanding. Our most essential form of higher learning takes place instinctively due to our innate potential for learning a language. And the language that we learn to speak and write like practically everything else about our personal identity is entirely natural, cultural and existential in origin—so far as we know.

Whether or not we can meaningfully speak about metaphysical phenomena like a soul, the free will, or God is a question that cannot be scientifically or even philosophically settled. In other words, language, ideas and human intelligence can empower us to gain knowledge about ourselves, nature and the universe, yet the limitations imposed by nature or evolution upon reason, language and human understanding are evident everywhere. Thus, at the outset, any speech, writing, or argument about *ultimate* meaning, purpose or design of life and the universe, is doomed to merely tentative, approximate and interpretive success.

A somewhat different approach to ontological questions (questions of personal being) and related phenomena is possible. This approach is necessarily cautious, curious and concerned about the human condition; and it is one embedded in the physical, cultural and symbolic universe. *It is this primitive, pre-cognitive and existential sense of the present moment that causes me to believe that the desire to experience, know and say what we feel and think is still worth doing and necessary for our reason and purpose for living.*

Finally, mystical, religious and spiritual language is a highly charged metaphorical and poetic discourse due to the emotional energy conveyed—if nothing else. If one takes language as the literal truth about reality, you have already missed the differences between word, thing and user! A word is only an intentional sound at the level of speech or a symbolic cue at the level of sight and it is not the thing it merely represents or stands for. This truism cannot be said enough since language habits and its patterns of thought and emotion are neurologically wired in the brain and interpreted by the mind.

3. Eckhart Tolle: Popularizing the Perennial Philosophy

One of the many players in the inspiration of this book is the contemporary, popular philosopher and writer, Eckhart Tolle. Several parts of this book were inspired by insights and ideas coming from Tolle's two popular books, *The Power of Now* and *A New Earth.* Both of these books have sales in the millions and they have been translated into many different languages.

Certainly much of Tolle's popular success was made possible by Oprah Winfrey, the famous talk show moderator, who took a keen interest in his philosophy of Now. However, well-established before his collaboration with Oprah, but of course her considerable promotion power did not hurt his fame at all. The wave of Tolle inspired retreats, lectures, videos and other educational and entertainment media has probably crested now (2014), although the themes that Tolle uncovered for popular culture deserve to endure since they are rooted ancient sources of thought and belief in philosophy, religion and literature.

Early in Tolle's popular text, *A New Earth,* he clearly states his view of the perennial Truth in the subsection, "Truth: Relative or Absolute?" And his answer to this question can serve as an initial definition of Perennialism and its esoteric philosophy of mysticism that can be found at the metaphysical core of the world's religions:

"There is only one absolute Truth, and all other truths emanate from it. When you find the Truth your actions will be in alignment with it. Human action can reflect the Truth, or it reflects illusion. Can the Truth be put into words? Yes, but the words are, of course, not it. They only point to it." (3)

Tolle's view of *Truth* is an echo from the ancient Chinese Taoist insight that although we may have words, images, and concepts for what may be ultimate in the universe—the Tao or Way— we cannot know with absolute certainty if we have the right word much less how well they may represent the ultimate Truth. Thus there is an unavoidable *agnosticism or not-knowing* in the intellectual game of Wisdom and Truth-saying that must come into the picture of all metaphysical discussions—if we are at all honest in our use of such words and symbols; otherwise we may fall into the psychological syndrome of self-deception, hubris and dogmatism.

On an existential or personal level, the perennial Truth is the innermost essence of who we are. Tolle states his position quite clearly and emphatically: "Yes, you are the Truth….The very Being that you are, is Truth…. Being, the essence of who you are is what Jesus meant when he said, 'I am the way and the truth and the life.'" As a Perennialist, Tolle relates this saying of Jesus to "the essential identity of every man and woman, every life-form, in fact….Some Christian mystics have called it the Christ within; Buddhists call it your Buddha nature; for Hindus, it is Atman, the indwelling God." Furthermore, when you gain access to the soul or essence of who you are, "all you actions and relationships will reflect the oneness with all life that you sense deep within." And this innermost experience is the love, truth and being that is universal, eternal, and without natural boundaries. (4)

Tolle never explicitly uses the term *Perennialism* in either *The Power of Now* or *A New Earth*. In the Perennial tradition of Aldous

Huxley, Huston Smith, Joseph Campbell, and many others of the twentieth century, there is no doubt that Tolle stands in this same unitary tradition of wisdom—but most uniquely since he has no apparent attachment to or identification with any of the various spiritual or religious traditions from which he quotes. As he freely admits in the opening sentence of *The Power of Now*, "I have little use for the past and rarely think about it" –except perhaps as he uses the stories and concepts in his writings that rather obviously derive from one religious tradition or another. (5)

A personal goal of *Awakening to Perennial Wisdom* is to express and clarify some of my intuitions within the conceptual frame of the Perennial Philosophy. I use the word 'vision' to apply to Tolle's viewpoint more than I do 'philosophy' or even 'thought' since the deepest insights that inform his view of things emanate from an intuitive sense of perennial *Being*—the eternal unifying Truth of everything. And on the subject of *Being*, there are no *ifs, ands* or *buts*, the prominence of *Something Absolute* shines like a supernova star in Tolle's philosophy.

Being, Now and Consciousness are terms denoting metaphysical absolutes—however clearly or unambiguously Tolle represents them. His arguments about these terms of absoluteness are based upon the primacy of *Now* or the fusion of *eternity and time*; eternity is commonly viewed as a vertical member of a cross completed by time and worldly relations, the horizontal member. His conviction (*and my own*) about the dialectical and humanistic connections between *Now, Human,* and *Being* comes from an intuition that there may be no better alternatives or options for adequately understanding our existence *and* place in the universe.

Tolle is a drop-out from academic life at Cambridge University in England where he was preparing to be a university professor. He has been heard to say that the answers to 'Life's most persistent questions' cannot be found in higher education. Like Friedrich Nietzsche and others before him, Tolle seems to have perceived something toxic in the role-playing, ego-posturing and intellectual habits of academic life that is incompatible with creative genius and especially the mystical outlook. Certainly, Tolle is a breath of fresh air in the stale atmosphere of higher education—which thrives on traditional roles, the past and bureaucratic rituals; and although Tolle does not directly take on the establishment in education or elsewhere, the ethical, political and economic implications of his vision are easy to grasp.

4. The Dialectical Pattern of Thought and Civilization

The history of philosophy, religion and education East and West, North and South are a rich source of the Perennial philosophy. The mystical dimension of human thought and civilization can be seen throughout the geographical world in its primitive, modern and postmodern settings. Frequently, the unitary belief is found in relation to a conflicting skepticism and doubt; instinctively, the mind and heart seek a way to resolve the tension between oppositions. In the history of human experience and knowledge, the conflict between mystical and skeptical, believing and doubting, unitary and divisive elements, has existed with individuals and their cultures.

Meanwhile, the dialectical pattern of conflict is a symbolic pattern whereby meaning and purpose emerges from experience. However, the historical evidence of a worldwide, triadic pattern of Unity within human consciousness can be seen in the belief and symbol systems of civilization. Although the evidence for a triadic pattern of growth and development is most obvious in philosophical and theological systems of thought, this phenomenon shows up in many other fields of human interest, effort and culture. *The triadic pattern shows itself most clearly in the idealist and mystical, realist and skeptical, non-dualist and agnostic elements of world thought.*

For example, in architecture, the elements of form and function must obey the physical law of gravity which unifies the structure upon its foundation; in psychology, the conflict between reason and passion, head and heart, higher and lower experiences of the total self seeks resolution, balance and integration in order to make decisions and act harmoniously in the real world; and in cosmology, the experience of Being or the unitary sameness of reality is evidenced in the atomic, chemical and physiological elements of matter at perceptual and conceptual levels of awareness as approximately and perspectivally understood through the wholeness and unity of the universe.

Although the belief in a triadic pattern of consciousness is not a sufficient basis for a theory of the self or the whole of civilization, it is a necessary one since higher Consciousness has become the Holy Grail of a philosophy long extinct but showing signs of rebirth in world cultures. For example, George W. Hegel (1730-1831), the Enlightenment philosopher of Europe, developed a phenomenological analysis of Consciousness that linked the experiences and knowledge of the body, mind and soul with human freedom (Spirit), History, Reason and the Absolute. Arthur Schopenhauer, a contemporary of Hegel, sharply disagreed with Hegel's view of reality, knowledge and human values, arguing that no ultimate purpose or meaning is served by human existence.

Historically, doubt, ridicule and controversy invariably accompany any new theory, symbol or construction of belief and thought among thinking men and women; and this is as it should be in the critical, forward-looking, and progressive movement of civilization and the moral, intellectual and spiritual growth of the *Homo sapiens*. Huxley, Hegel, Tolle and the major religions of the world have all had their detractors and critics—persons who believed and thought differently about their metaphysics (theory of ultimate reality), epistemology (theory of knowledge) and axiology (theory of value). And the debate among thoughtful persons about ultimate meaning and purpose and our place in the universe, will continue for as long as humans do.

When one considers the fleeting, impermanent nature of ordinary existence and the contingencies of individual Being, it is a wonder that anyone can maintain, for very long, faith in the ultimate meaning and purpose of existence. The length of our stay on Earth is very brief compared to the span of the geological ages and no one can know *with absolute certainty* whether any form of personal awareness *survives* the death of the body or for how long; or what the ultimate meaning and experience of Life may be—if anything. We have only many inherited religious systems of belief, wagers, and doctrines of desire and hope, fantasies, speculative theories and narratives about death and an afterlife.

First, all our ideas, feelings and theories of metaphysical certainty are based upon belief, Revelation and authority, in the *mystical* stage of dialectical consciousness. Reasoning or thinking at this stage takes place by deductive processes of thought and are based upon supposed *a priori* or absolute and a-historical forms of Truth –that precedes or exceed ordinary experience. This is the stage of faith, religion and spirituality, as such, and the possibility of genuine insight, truth-seeking and meditative Being first occurs. From acorns, great oaks can grow.

The second phase of dialectics is the *skeptical,* doubting and questioning stage of consciousness; here, any form of certainty is based upon perception, reflection or conception and logical reasoning proceeds by inductive means. At this stage of consciousness, conflict is apparent between the thesis or the first stage of thought and the anti-thesis—second stage—where genuine questioning and thinking begin. This is the stage in the development of individuals and cultures where problems or sources of conflict, anxiety and real obstacles for further growth become visible and the desire for resolution and problem-solving begins.

The third stage of development in the evolution of thought and civilization is that of synthesis where oppositions, conflicts and differences seek and find resolution from tension, anxiety and uncertainty. At a *pragmatic* or real world level of experience, the third stage usually takes the form of action previously conceived as policy directives, plans of action or imagined and desired futures. Whereas idealism or the abstractness of ideas and ideals dominated the first stage and realism or a physical and naturalistic view of the world dominated the second stage of consciousness, the third stage is dominated by an *enlightened form of pragmatic realism* which seeks to reconcile idealism with itself at worldly and practical levels of experience and knowledge.

At the third stage of dialectical experience, thought and action, ordinary or perceptual awareness becomes intellectual, intuitive and spiritual and evolves at a higher level of development towards the Perennial Consciousness. Just as human actors believe that they have fulfilled the promise of an earlier, less developed stage of growth in consciousness, the dialectical movement towards further growth seizes the ground of worldly Being. This is the beginning of a new level of realization at the first stage of freedom and the new beginning of learning, adaptation and transformation towards authentic Being and self-knowledge. Although the past is never fully lost within evolving consciousness, the present moment of place, time and Eternity, is the true grounding of all transformations with the continuum of time and experience. In this context and most others, *meaning* is merely a byproduct, a residual essence, awaiting transformation in the cauldron of experience.

At the start of the third stage of thought and culture, there is only a partial resolution of the uncertainty realized from the mystical and skeptical phases of thought or spiritualism and materialism. This polarizing of thought results in the stagnation of growth and metaphysical despair that is nihilistic if left to dwell inwardly without release or action. But in the throes of metaphysical uncertainty, *not-knowing or agnosticism* is a happy, freeing resolution of opposing views or options; yet it instinctively seeks a completion or fulfillment through action, practice or doing; and in philosophy, *Pragmatic philosophy* continues to offer the best perspective of human experience and knowledge and the development of a higher culture that is informed by intellectual problem-solving and active doing.

The American philosopher, John Dewey (1859-1952), developed his theory of intelligence or intellectual problem-solving based upon a generalized method of scientific thinking which he applied to philosophy, education and society. He believed that scientific problem-solving was the best way of thinking about philosophical issues and he sought to apply his five-fold way of thinking, i.e. 1, problem awareness, 2, hypothesis-formation, 3, taking action on an alternative, 4, examining the results or consequences of such action, and 5, evaluating the ideas and actions taken—to problems in education and other social institutions. Being a major voice in the progressive movement of ethics, politics, and economics in the early twentieth century, Dewey believed that social needs, interest and goals could be most readily met through the application of a scientific approach to conflicts and problems in society.

It is this triadic pattern of human consciousness that can be most clearly seen in the historic developments of the world religions and of the responses to them by succeeding generations of mystics, skeptics, and pragmatists. At the same time, the institutional pattern of development in Judaism, Christianity and Islam followed the organizational blueprint of the earlier Zoroastrian religion of Persia: 1, the central place of sacred Scripture or the *Book*, 2, the Revealed or visionary Truth of one exceptional Founder, 3, a moral doctrine of good and evil with implications for eschatology or a doctrine of Heaven and Hell, 4, external and internal rituals whereby individual obedience is secured involving prayers, sacrifices, moral precepts, rites of passage, and 5, loyalty to a religious, political and military hierarchy and its faithful officials in the secular world. Although this organizational pattern has been threatened many times in every world religion, it has remained essentially the same for thousands of years.

The Perennial Wisdom is an analysis and synthesis of selected themes and elements in the mythic journey of a single, solitary self as it grows, ages and matures on its own uncertain, *heroic path* in the mystery of existence. In this context, the late Joseph Campbell has written extensively about everyone's journey in Life as that of a *hero* in birth, life, death and rebirth:

"There are two types of [heroic] deeds. One is the physical deed, in which the hero performs a courageous act in battle or saves a life. The other kind is the spiritual deed, in which the hero learns to experience the supernormal range of human spiritual life and then comes back with a message.

"The usual heroic adventure begins with someone from whom something has been taken or who feels there's something lacking in the normal experiences available or permitted to the members of his society. This person then takes off in a series of adventures beyond the ordinary, either to recover what has been lost or discover some life-giving elixir. It's usually a cycle, a going and a returning...

"A hero is someone who has given his or her life to something bigger than oneself." (6)

The journey of everyone, a hero in just being born and ever after through the various stages and transitions of Life, is one of continual challenge, loss and gain, a going out and coming back to ourselves. The pattern of travel and the returning home, being alone and with others is one seeking balance, a centering point and gravitational force within the self that provides the confidence and courage necessary for genuine freedom of action; and such conditions result in the growth of wisdom, in time, and through reflection.

"Where we had thought to travel outward, we will come to the center of our own existence. And where we had thought to be alone, we will be with all the world." (7)

Being alone with others, all others, is only one of a myriad of paradoxes discoverable in living; or retreating or turning away from the world only brings you closer to it, inwardly, where it is essentially experienced and understood.

Finally, the topics chosen for development are not systematically arranged but only as they intuitively and conceptually appeared to support the insights of the Chapters. The reader would do well to keep in mind the foregoing *pattern of change and permanence* when reading the text, and the differing contingencies of experience that can be known through human consciousness and its structures, functions, and potentialities. For deeply embedded in the interstices of ordinary consciousness and Being are the infinite potentialities for authentic experience, knowledge and wisdom.

For example, *The Perennial Wisdom* invokes a higher or enlightened Consciousness in many contexts which is informed by the mystical and unitary experience of an individual self or a sacred Presence in the world. This assumption is central to the Perennialist project about the eternal mystery and infinite potentiality of each sentient being. Numerous other interpretations, associations and historical perspectives accompany the mystical view of Consciousness; and it is the quest of the perennial Way to discover, investigate and know ourselves as the embodiment of essential truths and a privileged view of the Light.

5. Contemporary Sources among Humanists and Scientists

In Western philosophy, *Perennial philosophy* can be most clearly traced back to the European philosopher, Gottfried Leibniz of the 16th century; and long before Leibniz's doctrine of pre-established Harmony, there are the Scriptural and mystical writings of the major world religions from Asia and the Middle East. Nothing like a survey of these traditions will be offered in the present text, but only a use of their insights, parables and doctrines that bear upon the topics at-hand.

The Latin term '*perennis*' means 'throughout the year' or 'present at all seasons of the year'. Its botanical reference as 'perennial' plants, trees, and flowers is indicative of the earth's natural cycles in seasonal change, night and day, and its relations to the sun. In philosophy, particularly the philosophy of religion and / or mysticism, Perennialism became known when it was used by a number of scholars and teachers around the middle of the twentieth century to refer to the unitary or mystical experience found encoded in the Scripture or sacred writings of the world religions.

Conservative, fundamentalist and sectarian values within the various religions has prevented anything like a general acceptance of the Perennial vision; but *the vision of a world peace, based upon justice and nonviolence and a common or unifying faith in ultimate meaning and purpose of existence has not diminished over time.* As humanity grows towards a universal Will and higher Consciousness, in present and future generations, it will reflect the realization that humanity is a family of individuals more than it is of nation-states or religions; and that the hope of a truly better world will occur when compassion, nonviolence and caring are the habits and values of individuals, and when real peace, justice and equality are the ways of the world.

The assertion that an identical center or mystical core exists in every religion is questioned and debated by many religious conservatives and skeptics alike. There are other detractors of Perennial philosophy who, for philosophical reasons, reject all religions and everything spiritual because they are not compatible with the experimental or empirical model of science. Ironically, the physical and behavioral sciences are of keen interest to many Perennialists, like the descriptive uses of biological evolution, astronomical cosmology, and social and psychological knowledge of individuals and society—among the many subjects of scientific interest, research and experiment.

Among the long and growing list of mystically oriented scientists are: Max Planck, Gary Zukov, David Bohm, John Eccles, Michael Talbot, Anthony Chew, Stephen Hawking, Albert Einstein, Ilya Prigogine, R.G.H.Sui, Lama A. Govinda, Dali Lama, Paul Davies, Loren Eisley, Frithjof Capra and scores of others who are too numerous to even mention here! Of course, even given the possibility of a Grand Unification theory from the scientific perspective, can the approximation principle of knowledge ever be overcome? Or is such knowledge already-at-hand in the form of our deepest intuitions about universal Being? Indeed, it may be for those whose mind, heart and soul have not been blinded by the dogmas of logical positivism and scientific materialism.

Among the long list of humanistic, pragmatic and progressive Perennialists are: Joseph Campbell, Aldous Huxley, Huston Smith, Allan Watts, Thomas Merton, Frithjof Schuon and numerous others; and there is a growing number of thinkers and doers in all fields of endeavor who use the term 'spirituality' instead of religion to denote something that they believe is *ultimate* in the great here-and-now of universal Being.

Of special interest among the scientific group of Perennialists, are the number of trained scientists, mathematicians and experimentalists who—through the lens of their own highly specialized work—have discovered or are working towards a metaphysical Principle, mathematical Formula or physical Force that is the sublime Unification of the known universe. The translation or link from their work to the real world problems, needs and values of humanity is a perennial challenge.

6. The Philosophical Case For and Against Perennialism

From the ancient times of Greece, philosophy has meant the *love of wisdom* (*philo* means love and *sophia* means wisdom); never mind that *wisdom* is one of the most ambiguous of terms in any language and *love* is no less problematic in usage. Thus, we must trust that our use of abstract and ambiguous words like these will not cover up the truths of our heart, mind and soul to ourselves or others.

Let us briefly re-consider the meaning of Perennial philosophy and its claim of absolute certainty. As we have seen, Perennialism is based on the assumption that there is only One Truth or one unifying Principle of everything. If this is true, how does the One Truth relate to the many lesser truths of ordinary knowledge? Perhaps most importantly, does believing or knowing the eternal Truth change the way that you feel, think and act in the real, changing world? And from a pragmatic perspective, you could weigh the consequences of believing or not believing in the Perennialist thesis of Unity or sublime Oneness, and consider how it does or does not enrich and contribute to your experience and satisfaction in Life—before accepting or abandoning its precepts.

Or you might consider Plato's last, rather playful rendering of perennial Truth from the Fifth century BC:

"Man is made to be the plaything of God, and this, truly considered, is the best of him; wherefore also every man and woman should walk seriously, and pass life in the noblest of pastimes, and be of another mind from what they are at present....And what is the right way of living?... We ought to live sacrificing, and singing, and dancing, and then a man will be able to propitiate the Gods." (8)

Plato's view of God is a somewhat high-minded and happy one that begs the question about the real existence of God or Gods that Plato—ever the writer—ducks. Plato and his mentor, Socrates, used the popular myths of Athenian times to develop many of their ideas about reality, speculating upon their truth or falsity, in Athenian culture. And among the many questions of philosophy that Plato wrote about in *The Republic*—his ideal or perfect society—is that of education: what are the best possible, most ideal conditions for educating persons from all classes, genders and nations of the world for the perfect society led by a philosopher-King!

The modern world has mostly moved away from Plato's elitist view of society, often to our detriment since excellence has too often been replaced by popularity and mediocrity. We have a long way to go to realize the most ideals conditions of society; but so long as there is incremental improvement, there is hope. If we give into despair, we will lose everything.

Plato's mystic vision of the *Idea of Goodness (or God)* is, in historical context, the philosophical basis of the theologies of the Middle Eastern religions, i.e. Judaism, Christianity and Islam. Furthermore, it is the same mystic vision and higher Consciousness that we can see in the Hindu theology and cosmology of Asia, as well as the atheistic philosophies of Jainism and Buddhism. A strong case can also be made that the mystic vision of Perennialism exists in Chinese Taoism especially the texts of the *I Ching (The Book of Changes)*, the *Tao Te Ching (The Way of Nature)* and *Chuang tzu (his collected writings)*. It is also well known that the pragmatic, humanistic and agnostic Confucius was strongly impacted by the mystical, ethical *and* naturalist dimensions of Taoism—as was his most famous philosophical follower and mystic, Mencius.

Arguably, philosophy is a virtually unlimited source of wisdom and passion that is multi-disciplinary, multi-dimensional and multi-national. Whether philosophy can deliver on the mystical wisdom or the One Truth is a personal and educational matter. However, my own view is that it can, otherwise I probably would not have bothered writing this book! That said, it leaves out the larger question as to whether or not the One Truth or Principle of everything is really *true*, and initially, I assume that the One Truth or the existence of a metaphysical Absolute is intuitively true and symbolically meaningful in personal existence. And the same faith in the value of personal existence can become a catalyst for the larger faith in the possible Being that is eternal, trans-subjective and fully liberating.

Is the Perennial Philosophy of Oneness or Unity merely a dream within a larger dream called Life? Or does eternal Being control or dominate the material change that is everywhere evident in the real world of forms? And finally, are such questions about abstract universals even answerable by finite, perspectivally situated beings like us—without ambiguity, qualification and uncertainty?

In the effort to make sense of the *Perennialist* search for wisdom, it has been the bias (bordering on prejudice) of Western philosophers and educators to emphasize Western and European philosophy to such an extent that the Asian philosophies of India, China and the Middle East have been sorely neglected and in most cases, completely ignored. Among other things, this book intends to correct the record and add more perspective, balance and diversity into the views that Western philosophy and higher education have typically or traditionally transmitted.

This intention is only partially carried out in the present text since it is not a systematic or historical account of any one philosophy, religion or related perspective; but it does represent *a pragmatic, existential and humanistic approach to* different philosophies and religions relating to the *Perennialist* conception of wisdom.

In this respect, there are few other philosophies that should occupy the attention of morally concerned persons more than the *humanistic Pragmatism* which originated in American thought and culture during the late nineteenth and early twentieth centuries, with Charles S. Peirce, William James, John Dewey, and Alfred North Whitehead. It is the *critical and constructive spirit* of pragmatic philosophy that the present text is committed to uphold, in the *moral, intellectual and social thematic of Perennialism.*

In *Pragmatic Philosophy,* it is the cultivation of human diversity and democratic ideals that stands out; similarly, its protection of human rights and individual liberty; its love of knowledge in the pursuit of truth wherever it takes one; its appreciation of the entire spectrum of human goods and values, in the arts, humanities and the sciences; its extolling of everyday life in society, not on the basis of the unjust, violent conditions but on that of what is most possible, desirable and workable in society for majority needs and interest and not those of the privileged minority; and its courage to identify and try to solve problems in the face of the uncertainty of existence and the certainty of change.

7. Questions of Meaning, Being and Experience

Of all the questions of a philosophical or metaphysical kind, the *question of immortality* is most significant. *Do we survive death in any conscious or independently existing form?* And of all the fears of humankind, none is greater than the fear of death or non-being and oblivion. Yet it is appalling and galling to think how little if anything real and testable we know about a spiritual or metaphysical Absolute; *appalling* given the certainty that we hear on the religious networks of television and radio and *galling* given the moral condemnation that falls upon one group or other from the religious right, based upon ignorance, prejudice and delusion.

Arguably, the mystical aspect is the most important aspect of any religious or metaphysical philosophy since the Presence of *something absolute* within the self raises the possibility of immortality or the survival of death. Does anything exist in complete or total independence in the universe? Obviously, if we are aware of something, how can it? Or, are all forms of existence merely conditional, relative and completely interdependently related, starting with consciousness itself? Again, on existential or ontological grounds, this seems most obviously true—until we make the quantum leap to metaphysics and ultimate reality.

If and only if a metaphysical view of the universe and our place in it could be confined to the *infinitesimal* sliver of reality that it pertains to, can we clearly or unambiguously use terms like *Being, Consciousness and Now*—terms that Tolle and other Perennialists use extensively—to denote something *felt to be ultimate* on the basis of the deepest intuition, to be *real, true and good*. The difficulty of this task lies in avoiding the landmines of language and tradition that are religious and psychological in origin; and Tolle, for one, is acutely aware of the inherent danger in using the language of absoluteness in almost any historical context, given the quagmires of controversy that await one. Clearly, the language of metaphysics, philosophical idealism and spirituality are sources of misunderstanding, confusion and illusion.

The alternative is to completely drop all reference to anything absolute, religious or spiritual, and never stray from the natural, personal and social world—as most skeptics, atheists and naturalists have done. But this would strip the heart, soul and head from the Perennialist message of *ultimate* meaning, purpose and certainty. Indeed, the collapse of organized religions in recent times and the replacement of them with a materialistic culture of consumerism, scientism and technology, is arguably, the primary source of personal alienation, de-humanization and nihilism in the contemporary world. And it is the same syndrome that prompted Friedrich Nietzsche to declare in the mythic character of Zarathustra that 'God is dead and man has killed Him'—which implies that once God was alive in the world!

For sure, the Perennial wisdom must confront the universal or ontological *uncertainty of existence* if it can pass the test of philosophical *realism* or the knowledge that is gained through human experience, reason and discovery. A dualistic or divided view of reality serves no one's interests or intelligence in a healthy way and certainly not the values, concepts and perspectives that can be used in the development of an integrative or holistic Perennial philosophy.

If a dualistic or divided way of thinking guides our ways of experiencing and knowing the world, it is first due to the negative emotions of fear, hatred, and greed. Second, such negative energy from the limbic brain is wired to more abstract cognitive processes of the higher brain, the cortex. Third, the activation of cognition is linked to the symbol or language centers of the brain where speech and writing become possible. What is not named or described in this abstract view of the brain is *consciousness* itself or the means by which awareness occurs.

Consciousness is connected through the cellular and neural structures of the body to the experienced or real world. Furthermore, consciousness—so far as we can know—is utterly dependent upon the structures and functions of a living organism. But if I believe—as mystics and metaphysicians tend to—in a transcendental dimension of the human organism, then a singular Force is introduced into ordinary experience that cannot be understood through nature and conventional science. It is this divided view of ourselves and human knowledge, that the Perennial view of things attempts to confront and resolve into a more integrative, holistic and humanistic perspective.

In the Perennial pursuit of wisdom, truth and beauty, there can be no resolution of the sense of lack and division within us as long as humans remain exclusively preoccupied with the animal, personal and social forms of consciousness. As Nietzsche wrote in the 19th century, humans are stuck between the ape and the Superman (*ubermensch*); and it is only the latter form that represents a true individual, one who becomes fully human, creative and self-realized.

Nietzsche's most admired philosopher, Arthur Schopenhauer of early 19th century, believed that it is only the 'saint, artist and genius' who can become truly self-realized persons. It was this elitist view of self-realization and enlightenment that has created the class-based obstacles for the democratization of education, knowledge and wisdom. Furthermore, many of the same established interests in economics and politics can be found by those who promote values of moral and religious education.

That said, There is much to be learned and understood about all religions or notions of spiritual Truth in the Perennial philosophy. In one fell swoop, one can put into perspective the entire spectrum of religious philosophies that billions of people now and in the past have claimed that they follow or identify with as their faith. And this fact alone is enormously important in understanding the human condition and its multiplicity of faith-based, life-worlds.

In the end, one is entirely alone in choosing and living on the Path that makes the most sense for a meaningful, purposeful and authentic life. The choice between truth and self-deception is a subtle, ambiguous and existential one since it concerns personal living, being and nonbeing. An authentic, meaningful and purposeful existence is the possible prize; and whether or not you find the whole project of living and being satisfying and worth the effort, can only be known in the depths of your own intuitive and psycho-physiological processes and not necessarily in the language and symbols of abstract ideas that too easily delude and bewitch us.

Finally, this book is written for a general audience rather than one academically trained in one discipline or another. I hope that it opens some new horizons of awareness for the reader. In the *Appendix,* there is a *Glossary of Terms* relating to Perennial Philosophy and the wisdom tradition. Some of these terms and phrases used to develop this text appear as chapter headings and subtopics. I have also added several memorable quotations at the beginning of each chapter which are biased towards the mystical themes of Perennialism. Last, there is a list of selected readings that support each of the twenty-five chapters of *The Perennial Wisdom.*

And finally from the vision of one of the great mystics of Western philosophy, the Egyptian Neo-Platonist of the 3rd century, Plotinus:

"In this state of absorbed contemplation there is no longer question of holding an object in view; the vision is continuous so that seeing and seen are one; object and act of vision have become identical; of all that until then filled the eye no memory remains. The first seeing is of Intellect knowing, the second that of Intellect in love.... The vision floods the eyes with light, but it is not a light showing some other things, the light is itself the vision. No longer is there object seen and light to show it, no longer Intellect and object of Intellection; this is the very Radiance that brought [everything] into being. (9)

This remarkable passage from the *Enneads* of Plotinus focuses upon the mystical One of eternity. Related to the One are the physical world (the first three *Enneads*), the Soul and Intelligence—the latter two *Enneads* which have an ethereal status like that of the One. Although Plotinus' *Enneads* clearly show how the mystical consciousness can be used to think inclusively about nature, the human self and the One, it has failed to persuade those who are cut from a different philosophical cloth—the atheists and skeptics especially although the pragmatists occupy a more tolerant, action-based view of *spirituality* in terms of the actual difference that belief can make for its value in experience.

PART I

AWAKENING TO NOW, PRESENCE AND

THE MYSTERY

Although words can be spoken and written, they are not the same thing as split oak and maple wood stacked in a pile under trees standing tall with green summer leaves. Although everyone knows that we will not live forever, the effort is always made to stay alive, well and happy for as long as we can. Although everyone experiences awareness in waking to a new day, we take for granted that we will always be aware of the here-and-now. Although everyone knows how to perceive, remember, imagine, and conceive, the passage of time is imperceptible and eternity is beyond comprehension. Although everyone knows that there is infinitely more than we will ever know—everyone knows the here-and-now and forgets the Mystery.

When we awaken, we are present to Now or the Great Mystery of Being. Ordinary consciousness or awareness is the inner sight, the silent witness, to Being or what-is. We experience everything always in the Now, the eternal moment that is forever changing. We desire what gives pleasure, joy and fulfillment; but mostly we long for love or the feeling of unity, oneness and discovery. We breathe, we eat, we sleep, in silence and stillness; and everything is fulfilled and completed in the stillness of silence.

We awake to a new day, a new self, and a new sense of Being every moment, in its Eternal Presence. What is past, what is ahead in the future, are unknown compared to the immediacy of Now and Presence. We perceive, we reflect, and we conclude that we exist. We use our senses, emotions, thoughts, words and they use us. Everything is interacting, interpenetrating and transforming everything else. We exist in a swirl of complementary oppositions, contradictions and paradoxes.

There is only the Mystery—the mystery of you and me and the universal and unmanifested Energy of Eternal Being, Now suddenly appearing, disappearing in the forms of change as you and me. The essence of existence can be named, but it exists without a name like you and me. Your essence is unique and like everyone else, different and the same—your name symbolizes an essence of Being or soul; it is who you are, hiding beneath the manifestations of ego, role, mind and body. If you awaken to the stillness, silence and perfection within, you can experience and know everything that is necessary for your *liberation from existence.*

Chapter 1

AWARENESS AND THE PRESENCE

OF ETERNAL BEING

What does Being mean in relation to the awareness of being-a-person? Can we experience and know *something* that is eternal, independently existing, yet absolutely continuous with the changing world of forms and material relations? And why is it impossible that eternal, universal Being cannot exist beyond all beginnings and endings, creation and destruction, things and viewpoints?

"Being is without beginning and indestructible; it is universal, existing alone, immovable and without end: nor ever was it nor will it be, since it now is, all together, one, and continuous." Parmenides

"Behold the One in all things; it is the second that leads you astray." Kabir

"Lay up your treasures in heaven where neither moth nor rust doth corrupt, and where thieves do not break through nor steal." Matthews

"Creatures are all striving after their primitive pure nature, after their supreme perfection." Meister Eckhart

"The stream of creation and dissolution never stops....All things come out of the One and the one out of all things." Heraclitus

Heraclitus, the ancient Greek philosopher, who believed that a universal Fire is burning within all forms, also believed that the four root elements of nature—earth, air, fire and water—are in a ceaseless flow of *change or flux.* The fragments that remain of his philosophy, suggest that he was one of the first in the West to see

5

the Perennial Truth of the *One and the many*, in the mystical and natural, spiritual and pragmatic moments of a divine Unity. The emphasis of Heraclitus on the four elements or the manyness of nature put him at odds with Parmenides' intuition about Being or the Eternity of what-is—beyond all change, forms and viewpoints. (1)

Perception, Consciousness and the Body

Perception occurs in two differing modes of experience, external and internal. *External perception* is the result of consciousness interpenetrating the five senses as seeing, hearing, smelling, tasting and touching in relation to physical objects in the environment; *internal perception or proprioception* is the result of consciousness in relation to emotions, memories, images and other sensations of the whole body. Both modes of perception produce impressions upon the brain which we can then reflect upon through awareness, creating more abstract impressions or forms which we call *ideas* or thoughts. *Meaning*, as such, arises through the interaction of the senses, emotions and thoughts, reflected upon, expressed and interpreted in symbolic forms.

Empiricists claim that experience is perceptual or sensory in origin and the primary basis for knowledge; *rationalists* claim that reason or our ideas are the basis for knowledge and our experience of reality. *Perennialists* claim that intuition, insight and even Revelation provide us with the most basic kinds of experience and knowledge. Realistically, no one can become fully human without the experiences that *perception, reason and intuition* can make possible in our daily functioning as real persons in the real world. (2)

We are aware of space, time, and the various life-forms and know that they are necessarily related through the four physical laws of the universe or gravity, electro-magnetism, weak and strong atomic forces; but we can only assume that an *infinitely perfect Being or God* has created space-time, the forms and laws of the physical universe and the whole shebang; while our subjective sense of time, experience and meaning are properties of our human world. Each of us embodies an energetic, precious connection with the infinite, impersonal Life-force that is the basis for our finite and personal existence.

We each possess an innate or inalienable freedom or power to decide what to do in our existing life-world. Although human beings can create and destroy particular life-forms, we are powerless to fundamentally alter or change the universal Life-force that sustains all life-forms. In reality, our individual and collective experience of Life in its formed states of being is only a temporary manifestation of an underlying, eternal and universal condition or Life, which is present to us in mystery, wonder and terror.

An important distinction that does make a difference in this book is between consciousness (un-capitalized) and Consciousness (capitalized). When consciousness is not capitalized, it denotes awareness in its ordinary, limited or worldly functioning; and when Consciousness is capitalized, it denotes an extraordinary and *unlimited potentially* in knowing and experiencing. The truth is that no one can know what the future actuality of human experience and knowledge may be, given the uncertainty of existence and the potentiality of an evolving consciousness.

Meanwhile, the evidence for a Supreme or Creator Being (God) existence is not merely an intellectual belief, but an experience that we can *subjectively* feel and intuitively know; but as Soren Kierkegaard, the Danish Existentialist has written, the 'existence of God is *objectively* uncertain'; and the difference between subjectivity and objectivity is a crucial one in thinking about such matters since it points to differences between religious and scientific ways of thinking and being.

In our actual experience of things, subjectivity and objectivity are interrelated or unified states of being within consciousness. Or more simply put, *consciousness is a unity* of the subjective or inner experience of reality and the objective, surrounding world of things, humans and events. That said, the differences between our inner experience of reality and things themselves in the outer world can be from superficial to profound.

7

When we begin to reflect upon our feelings pro and con for the existence of creative Being or the universal Force, it is where the 'rubber meets the road'. For better or for worse, Tolle assumes that there is a crucial difference between 'having a life' and 'being life'. Or 'I and Life are one'; and it is in the experience of the oneness or unity of ordinary existence, where we can get a clue to the Mystery of universal Life. (3)

Initially, we say that awareness is made possible by perception or the immediate functioning of the brain. What is called *consciousness* mysteriously arises from the material conditions of the brain and the entire nervous system of the body. Consciousness is mysterious since no one really understands how something non-material spontaneously arises from material states, become translucent and transcends bodily states through memory, imagination and speculation.

In thinking about whether or not we can ever lose our lives, Tolle asserts that we cannot since we cannot lose something that we do not have in the first place! 'I am Life' or universal 'Life has me' would be a more accurate and truthful statement of our situation. And since we possess nothing but illusions, so far as the ordinary world is concerned, all that we know for sure is what we can immediately or directly experience.

Last but no least is the body. We are an organism living in an environment and our functions, potentialities and skills as a person are housed within it. The body is perhaps the most noticed and least acknowledged truth about our real being. Consciousness does not arise independently of its life-form nor does perception, memory, imagination, or reflection. In fact, all of our many other potentialities for the experience and knowledge of the universe and what may ultimately be true are grounded in and through the sacred organism.

The Design of the Universe

When we gaze into the night sky that is full of stars and galaxies, we are looking upon the handiwork of an unknown Designer.

Astronomers tell us that this universe is about 14.7 billion years old and that there may even be an infinite number of such universes. But no matter how old or how many universes there are, we can only directly know something about this one universe and its incredible vastness. Our ordinary consciousness is sufficiently complex and spacious that it imparts feelings of awe before the universe; and our technology enables us to perceive and understand nature and the universe far beyond our unaided senses.

The consciousness that each of us possesses and is possessed by is like a single cell or atom of universal Being. We cannot know more about reality than what consciousness makes possible; but consciousness seems infinite like the universe and there appears to be no limit to what we can learn, know and appreciate. Through the structures and functions of the sensory organs and the entire nervous system, worlds within worlds of information, experience, and understanding are available to us, through the miracle of ordinary and universal Consciousness. Through our senses and their technological extensions into space and time, we are learning many new things about ourselves and the universe all the time.

It may very well be there are an infinite number of universes; and our potentials for imagining, speculating and theorizing enable to see, experience and know what the instruments of astronomy and space technology only tantalizingly suggests. For example, we know that there are many planets and probably innumerable inhabited worlds beyond our solar system that are more rich and strange than our most bold and daring imaginings. According to ancient seers, mystics and yogis in possession of astral, karmic and metaphysical powers, what we dimly perceive as the universe may only be the beginning of a dim horizon without a knowable ending.

Whether or not a supreme God or Designer really exists is a philosophical question that has many answers. However, the universe that we can actually observe, understand and experience is not a complete mystery since we are learning more about it every day. Yet the more that we learn about the universe the more questions that we have and the more we realize we do not know.

If the so-called *Big Bang* or the initial beginning of the known universe occurred 14.7 billion years ago, we are only Now witnessing the results of that terrific, super-atomic explosion into the rapidly accelerating and expanding universe of galaxies that may number hundreds of billions. But we may wonder: what caused the Big Bang and 'why is there something and not just nothing'?

One answer to the 'why' question came from Gottfried Leibniz of the sixteenth century: God created heaven and earth and all forms of the universe. In other words, Eternal Being is the initial *Uncaused Cause*—as Aristotle and Aquinas called God in one of their definitions—and the reason for existence as we find it. And the usual answer from skeptics, materialists and nihilists is that there is no answer to such questions since there is no *ultimate* meaning or purpose. (4)

More immediately, what is the meaning and place of the human species in the universe? Do we individually and collectively serve some 'grand purpose' or not? And finally, how could a universe that manifests so much lawful order, design and complexity simply happen by random accident or blind chance—as some evolutionists claim?

Nature as Living Presence

What is meaning of Presence? Nature or the totality of living and non-living material states is present to us, we make a statement of fact that can be verified or falsified by the senses. Our outer senses give us information about nature. But what gives us understanding? It is consciousness or the Presence of what is divine or sacred in us and nature. Without Presence, nature is dead, indifferent, and perhaps threatening to who we are as individuals and a species-being. But we could not be alive in this body, have consciousness, a free will and a soul without the elements and energy of Nature as a living, intelligent Presence. Nature is physically 'out-there' and it is present 'in-here' as our inner, subtle, energy body and the cellular basis for our potentialities.

Presence is the sheer fact of nature as our life-form or the unity of body, mind and soul, and our most intimate experience of nature. Most religions have created images, thoughts, and symbols about life, a soul, and God from the perceptions and experiences of Nature; and many of our sciences, arts and humanities are based upon the experience and knowledge of nature as living Presence. Thus, we can say that nature is *sacred*, owing to a universal Life-force that sustains all life-forms mysteriously within it.

On this basis, we can say that all human and non-human life-forms are sacred and possess a miraculous degree of consciousness, due to their natural structures and functions. In the same way, minerals grow structures in geometric design, plants lean towards the sunlight for photosynthesis; and non-human animals sleep, wake and eat in biological cycles, care and protect their offspring, in ways that are similar to humankind. In other words, there is a unity and sameness that can be perceived throughout the mineral, plant, animal and human realms of the natural world; and we have more in common with one another in the human world than there are real differences!

Everywhere, Nature is alive in potentiality if not actuality on the Earth. In fact, there is good reason to believe that nature is a Presence throughout the universe owing to its sacred and emanative origin in Eternal Being. Yet consciousness—as universal Presence within Nature—cannot just be reduced to natural structures, patterns, and functions.

For example, there is ample narrative, speculative and theoretical evidence that Consciousness (higher) exists independently of the body. And if this is so, is there an essence or potentiality within ordinary consciousness and the body that transcends or survives death? And is the answer to Life's 'most persistent questions' or the perennial ones, already present within the dynamics of nature and ordinary consciousness? I believe so.

Language, Being, and the Real World

Awareness is the presence of Being or what-is; and Being is sacred and mysterious. We are organic, complex, and finite beings from the same infinite, sacred, and eternal Source. Whatever has evolved on Earth and throughout the universe comes from the same Source. And all life-forms are embedded in the eternal, all-pervasive Mystery.

Eckhart Tolle has written: "All spiritual teachings originate from the same Source….Once they become verbalized or written down they are obviously no more than collections of words—and a word is nothing but a signpost…pointing the way back to the Source." (5)

Language, our most important means of communicating, is a great mountain of 'signposts', ciphers, and symbols inherited from generations of seekers, thinkers, and ordinary persons who have contributed to the ocean of meanings, essences, and symbols that make up every human language. No one can entirely do without language and be fully human and yet our distant ancestors survived and flourished for thousands of years without anything that we presently call a language.

The mystical view of language is that a word is (literally) the thing it represents. The symbolic view of language is that a word is a metaphor or symbol for the thing it represents. Much confusion and nonsense comes from taking literally what has only been spoken, written or meant metaphorically; and a prime example of the metaphorical use of language are the sacred Scriptures of the world religions. Yet many people who read the religious writings of the world believe that every word is literally true!

For all the wonder of language, a word is not the thing it symbolizes or points to; a word or symbol is a metaphor for what-is. Language is contained in the energy fields of the brain-mind, heart and soul of the body. Now—owing to the global internet—language envelopes the planet in a cocoon of sounds, images, and meanings. Yet there is an important difference between what-is and the language of human beings; and the difference creates gaps in our experience and understanding of things.

Written and spoken language is a byproduct of higher cognitive processing in the brain and nervous system that expresses experience and meaning, thought and belief, memory and imagination, and situates us in the here-and- now. Being, on the other hand, is the totality of what-is, infinitely exceeding what is known or can be experienced and our powers of language, understanding and reason. Being symbolizes the vastness of the known and unknown universe and beyond space, time and the relative world.

Owing to the structure, function, and complexity of human identity, we can do a number of things that other animals of the Earth cannot do. For example, we can speak and write with a language that creates meaning about experience—where there may be none. We know that all natural life-forms of the Earth—minerals, plants, animals, humans—are part of the same Life-force that is creative and sacred. And some persons believe that the religions of the world refer to the same creative Life-force that sustains each and every life-form of Earth.

We are not ordinarily aware of the infinite complexity of existence. Even though we can be conscious of who we are, our purposes in life, and the meaning, truth, and beauty in daily living, we continue to be completely ignorant of ultimate reality or what may exist beyond all changing forms, time, and space.

Parmenides in ancient Greece gave us the first known *glimpse* of Being in Western thought; he referred to Being as ultimate, eternal and infinite; and that all change and finitude is the stuff of illusion and lacking in ultimate truth or reality. Later philosophers like Martin Heidegger of the twentieth century would claim that Being is ambiguous, paradoxical, and the underlying condition for human experience, freedom and ultimate meaning in the world; and that unless we assume full responsibility for our own Being-in-the-world, we cannot live an authentic or moral existence.

Ancient philosophers in Greece, India and China struggled, in varying degrees, with the question of how anything that is Permanent or unchanging could at the same time, be the basis for everything that is constantly changing. First there were the Monists or those who said that there is only One Reality, Truth or Source of everything; second there were those who settled on two Principles of Creation like Spirit and Matter or the Dualists; and third, there were those who insisted that there were many elements in nature like earth, air, fire, water, wood, and metal, that caused everything to be; and they were called the Pluralists.

If you do not believe in anything like Being or something Permanent in the universe, it does not mean that you just genuflect to the god of materialism, money, and greed that pervades society. It means that we should take a critical, moral, and intelligent stand against mediocrity, superficiality, and dishonesty in living. The sense of responsibility for your own being or life-form begins with self-awareness, vigilance, and prudence.

Finally, personal being or existence is ultimately grounded in the uncertainty and Mystery of Being. If we embrace both the finite and infinite dimensions of Being and accept the contingent realities of our lives, as givens, then we can more realistically go forward from the present moment towards the original Goodness of nature, humanity and existence.

Perennial Philosophy: The One Ultimate Source

For centuries, philosophers, theologians, and mystics have had a term for the unitary Oneness of everything and it is *philosophia perennis* or the Perennial Philosophy, as thinkers from Gottfried Leibniz of the sixteenth century to Aldous Huxley of the twentieth century have called it. In religious history and mythology, the record is even longer and more esoteric since many stories, parables, and myths are cloaked in symbols, metaphors, and experiences from ancient and pre-historic mythologies. In the new sciences of the twenty-first century, mysticism and the Perennial outlook are stronger than ever, since scientific discoveries, explorations and experiments have uncovered many new life-forms and new connections between phenomena known and unknown, visible and invisible, secular and sacred. In fact, confirmation of the unitary outlook of the Perennial hypothesis is implied in the search for extraterrestrial life-forms in our solar system and beyond it in the SETI program (Search for Extraterrestrial Intelligence).

Everywhere that we can look in nature, culture, and evolution, there is a new appreciation and understanding of the rapidly expanding, changing, physical universe and how human beings, owing to the presence of Consciousness, are an integral part of reality. In this sense, Consciousness and matter appear to be the most essential conditions of the universe wherever life-forms evolve; somehow Consciousness manifests itself from inchoate matter when there is a sufficient degree of complexity in the structure and function of an organism. Whether Consciousness can appear or continue to exist independently of organic life-forms cannot be empirically confirmed; all we can say is that the Presence of Consciousness is an essential aspect of the Mystery.

Aldous Huxley wrote and compiled the discursive anthology, *The Perennial Philosophy,* in the middle of the twentieth century. It is a seminal source for understanding and appreciating the religious, theological, and mystical roots of the primordial philosophy. It awakened several generations of seekers and the students of spirituality to the unitive and integrative basis of the major world religions. And this philosophic tradition continues to live, clearly and insightfully, in the writings and thought of Eckhart Tolle.

Huxley wrote that there are four premises of *Perennialism:* 1, there is a Divine Ground that exists as the hidden basis or Source for all life-forms; 2, human beings have a dialectical nature or structure and function, i.e. a Higher, Transcendental Self and lower, empirical body, that is grounded in the Divine Unity of everything; 3, intuitive or intellectual insight is superior to discursive or logical reasoning in awakening to the transcendental Self of higher Consciousness; 4, the meaning and purpose of Life is to awaken to the inner essence of the divine Self that exists in union with the Divine Ground of everything. (6)

Many questions, problems and possibilities arise from the Perennial philosophy; and we will explore them throughout the text, in differing perspectives, contexts and disciplines. Certainly one of these questions involve the 'meaning and purpose' of human existence in view of all the noble values, traditional ideals and beliefs of the established religions and the philosophies of change, uncertainty and absurdity.

Meaning and Purpose in Life

The awareness of higher Consciousness is the seed of our awakening to Life and its universal Presence. Awakening to consciousness at any level of existence is one of the most intimate and intangible of experiences in Life; but it is also the most familiar, immediate and profound of experiences. Consciousness brings us from the uncertainty of mere belief to the certainty of perception and awakening to the invisible Spirit or Life-force that energetically flows through our own life-form and all others. The awakening to the Life-force of sentient existence is also the beginning of trust in the wisdom of nature, the sacredness of the body, and the incredible universe.

Discovering the essence of infinite Consciousness within the mind and body enables one to become fearless before death and not be afraid of anything that happens in life since the *soul* is the eternal essence of Being within every human being. Believing in something eternal or unchanging is the greatest challenge in existence; it is completely counter-intuitive to do so since universal change is the most obvious truth about the real world.

For sure, most people do not instinctively desire to die since death means the absolute end to this body, ego, and experience of the world. But if universal Life is eternal, in any and all of its manifested forms, what dies is personal being or the individual manifestation of universal Life. We live and we become attached to this or that and it is a natural response of needful desire and attractions of the world. Desires, needs and wants are the glue that binds us to things, persons and situations.

We naturally grieve and become deeply saddened from the death of a loved person, animal, or significant relationship of any kind, since it is entirely natural to become attached to what or whom we love. Only the Life-force is eternal and we, as persons, are merely conditional forms of Life yet we embody visible evidence of *something* deeply mysterious in existence, namely ordinary consciousness and the eternal *soul* that brought us into the world.

The soul or the essence of Being is uniquely individual while a Higher Self—called *Atman* by the ancient Hindu of India—is the basis for the universal equality or sameness of all souls before *Brahman* or the infinitely perfect Source of all creation. If there is any ultimate meaning and purpose in collective existence, then *Atman—Brahman,* the universal Self in relation to God, is the immanence or divine presence of each soul. If not, from an existential point of view like that of Soren Kierkegaard, we are condemned to a 'sickness of the soul' unto death and a perpetual unknowing or ignorance. And there is the view of the skeptic, atheist and fatalist like Bertrand Russell who wrote that it is only on the 'firm basis of an unyielding conviction in the total destruction of the universe that the soul's existence can be firmly established'!

In other words, it is only by confronting the grim realities of contingent existence, both of your tiny, vulnerable self and the vast, unknown universe that you can even begin to see the paradoxes and uncertainties that we continuously live in and through. Thus if you assert that there is an 'ultimate meaning and purpose' in Life—as the Perennialists do—then you commit yourself to the greater, mystical Truth; but if you merely play it safe and stick to the facts of existence, then you commit yourself to an entirely conditional, relative and impermanent existence where there are no 'ultimates', 'universals', or 'ends' that transcend the ever-changing here-and-now. And between these two extreme tendencies there are innumerable possible meanings and purposes.

Among the poisons in existence, none may be greater than the positivist's doubt since it often destroys the belief in any form of immortality or ultimate meaning. A life lived entirely on the basis of systematic doubt is a hopeless and cynical life, one 'full of sound and fury and signifying nothing'. I have never found any consolation in faithless reasoning and even less solace in a conviction that *this life-form* ends in total oblivion. Albeit, there is no absolute certainty that it does not; and even if there is no survival of death, you still have the obligation, owing to your innate free will, to choose authentically and live responsibly in the here-and-now.

Existential *doubt and uncertainty* make an enemy of nature, life-processes and the experience; and death becomes a constantly threatening presence to your life-form and existence. Existential uncertainty and insecurity can cast a long, dark shadow over everyday choices and events—if you let it; but on the sunny side of existence, this precious body, mind and life-form are the divine gifts—not curses—of a Creator Being whose handiwork is us. Of course, you can easily say that human beings have made a mess of, abused and misused the gift of Creation.

I do not recommend a life-time of doubt or disbelief since it leads to existential alienation in one form or another; but I do recommend the essential way of Consciousness, i.e. the soul and the higher Self of Being, since these truths can lead us out of misery, uncertainty, and a meaningless existence, and to a spiritual experience of truth, sanity, and eternal Being. I freely choose to believe that we are here to 'enable the universe to unfold' from the Unmanifested realm into the manifested realm or the everyday life-world of each of us. But we must do this with intelligence and reverence for all sentient beings and a commitment to make this a better world.

Chuangzi: On the Language of Beginnings

Chuangzi, the ancient Chinese Taoist, is among the most enigmatic of philosophers. In the passage below, he writes about his intuition of beginnings. Certainly his insight raises many questions about the limits and wisdom of expressing ideas in words or through logical thought processes. But it also raises large questions about reality, meaning, and experience at the most fundamental level of origin, change and destiny.

"There is a beginning. There is a not-yet beginning to be a beginning. There is a not-yet beginning to be a not-yet beginning of a beginning.

"There is something, There is nothing. There is a not-yet beginning to be nothing. There is a not-yet to be a not-yet beginning to be nothing. Suddenly there is nothing. But then I don't know whether nothing is or isn't." (7)

Chuangzi is quoted here not to confuse the reader but to assert that just because we may be able to express ourselves verbally does not mean that we really understand what we are saying. Chuangzi's deconstructions of language and thought serves as an antidote to human thought and action of many kinds and especially those beginnings that may only be 'nothing'.

Chuangzi is a master of the short story form, paradox and metaphor; and he is known to some in the *crazy wisdom* tradition of Chinese literature and philosophy. His philosophy is also a reminder that *wisdom* appears in many perspectives and it cannot be reduced to one formula, one philosophy or viewpoint.

Chapter 2

NOW, THE FUSION OF TIME AND ETERNITY

What is Now in relation to awareness, time and Eternity? How—if at all—can we experience or know Eternity while we are situated in time and changing existence? And why is it important to be aware of the present moment of experience—whatever we are doing?

'He who pursues learning will increase every day; / He who pursues Tao will decrease every day. / He will decrease and continue to decrease, / Till he comes at non-action; / By non-action everything can be done.' Tao Te Ching

"It is God Himself who is sporting in the form of man." Sri Ramakrishna

"All the inner forces and the hidden souls in man are distributed and differentiated in the bodies. It is, however, in the nature of all of them that when their knots are untied they return to their origin, which is one without any duality and which comprises the multiplicity." Abraham Abulafia

"The past cannot be changed, but you can change tomorrow by your actions today." David McNally

"Do not occupy your precious time except with the most precious of things, and the most precious of human things is the state of being occupied between the past and the future." Ahmad b. Isa al-Kharraz

The awareness of the shortness of any life-form compared to inexhaustible time and the infinity of Eternity is appreciated everywhere in philosophy. Here the Arab philosopher, Ahmad b. Isa al-Kharraz, reminds us that time should not be wasted. The wisdom of this view can be seen in the experiencing of the present moment of time, which may seem to be always *here* until we realize that Now is *Eternity* suddenly manifested between the past and the future as Awareness; and in the language of Alfred North Whitehead, Being is *the undifferentiated aesthetic continuum* of Now manifesting as You and Me (see quotation from Ramakrishna above). (1)

Now as the Presence of Being

'The loss of Now is the loss of Being'—Eckhart Tolle states in many ways. We live in and through the present moment of time. Even when we remember the past, imagine the future and project thoughts into the surrounding world, we always exist in the Now. The Now is the meeting point, infinitely structured, of eternity and temporality. Whatever we are doing, thinking about or feeling, we remain in the Now or the Presence of eternity.

The presence of Now, the ever-present moment or infinity of individual experience, is also the window into fundamental Being. Ordinarily we exist between the past and the future, in the illusions of history, ethics and worldly change. Every form that we create through the mind and its capacities of memory, reason, perception and imagination is real at the constructed level of experience and knowledge. However, everything is in flux or change and nothing remains the same for longer than it takes an electron to jump from one ring to another or a cell to divide in the body.

The social world, the so-called real world of society and culture, is an entirely contingent and conditional world where the karmic or causal processes of material being dominate and absolutely control birth, life, death, and re-birth. What is different about Now is the possibility that a real transcendence exists that can free an individual from causal pre-determination. In other words, we each possess the potentiality to transcend or rise above conditional space and time through the innate freedom of awareness.

Or in Tolle's words, we are here to enable the 'divine purpose' to unfold or disclose itself. The idea of human purpose and meaning as intimately related to the divine purpose and meaning is nothing new in the history of ideas; it is only that Tolle has placed this old idea in the new language of human potentiality, existential meaning and human purpose. Furthermore, Tolle does not assume that the universe and the Earth, in particular, is alien, indifferent or an enemy of our actions; rather the *Earth* is a potent symbol and material force where Being is unfolding and becoming through us—our intentions, actions, successes and failures. (2)

Presence is another way to express the concept *and* experience of Now. This means that neither Presence nor Now is merely a concept or form within the mind. Both of these phenomena must be intuitively understood through a depth of mind or insight that exceeds concepts or abstract ideas. And although this may seem to be very abstract and difficult to fathom, neither Presence nor Now is merely an intellectual concept. They exist in the momentary experiences of sensory and affective knowing through the neural pathways of the body's entire nervous system. Furthermore, the sensations, feelings and insights of momentary awareness are often the most subtle kind emanating from the energy of a soul that carries the karmic burden of existence.

It is also in the Now of momentary experience where 'education as liberation' takes place. Of course, this is not the usual conception of education which is burdened with a crazy mixture of conservative and liberal, worldly and scientific values. If education was focused upon the experience of liberation or awakening of the intellect through passionate interest and effort, then a wonderful result for all who are involved in the learning process would be realized. Instead far too much time, effort and money is lavished on 'top-down teaching' or the canned, pre-planned curriculum implemented through the established ends and means of the Corporatocracy.

Karma is the obstacle, the causal necessity of nature, society and existence that challenges our desire for salvation or liberation. When we realize or awake to the drama between the forces of slavery and freedom, being played out in the Now, we can seize the opportunity and opening to Being and see the Truth about our condition. The experience or Consciousness of Presence—the 'brain of God' as Einstein once remarked—exists in the Now or not at all in the universe. And this is the existential and metaphysical importance of Now since it embraces both temporality and eternity in the Oneness of reality. (3)

Two Forces: Material and Spiritual

Not all feelings, thoughts or perceptions experienced in the Now connect us with the core or center of Being. Many such phenomena are fragmentary, technical and academic mind-trips or attachments to memories of the past or speculations about the future. The meaning and purpose of Life lies in the experiences of Now where ordinary consciousness can bring us to the threshold of the soul. Contrary to the mythology of progress and global Capitalism, the purpose and meaning of Life is not to accumulate as much material and financial wealth as possible in this one life-time, but to become aware of your infinite connection with all life-forms and compassionately serve others.

As we grow in awareness from the unfolding or evolution of consciousness, as a body-in-nature, we transform ourselves from a mere sentient, limited life-form to the awareness of Life as universal consciousness. Life is eternal but 'we' as individual beings are finite, mortal, and destined-to-die. Universal Life transcends all life-forms, their karmic or causal destinies, and inevitable endings. This is self-evident in that 'dead men tell no tales' but it is for us, the living, to continue the narrative. But even for us, the living, Nature or the material force of existence, cannot be forsaken or else it will make a fool of us.

It is only the awakening to Spirit or the universal Life-force that can save humanity from itself and the overwhelming forces of physical and organic Nature. Spirit and Nature are the two universal forces in the on-going creation of total being. The spiritual force of the cosmos is the Life-force and the vital presence of creative intelligence in nature, society, and humanity. We are saved not by nature alone but only by Nature transformed, raised to its essential creativity through the presence of divine intelligence working through consciousness and the life-forms of nature. However, we cannot know the infinite intelligence, creativity, and freedom of the divine Spirit within nature except through the finite and mortal intuitions of self-existence.

Being itself appears in glimpses, profound insights, and moments of meditative stillness, vision, and tranquility. Those who are ready or primed in their individual development by 'God's grace' or good 'karma' can achieve or realize moments of awakened Being in the Now. It is not a question of waiting until we die, or looking for your guru or master to show you the way; the real guru is within you—the universal Mind or Consciousness that is deeply the same in all religions and metaphysical systems. All that teachers or gurus can do—if they are really honest or authentic—is to show you that 'enlightenment' or profound awakening is possible in the Here-and-Now, and give you the necessary confidence and feeling for your own awakening to the profound Unity of everything.

One must be vigilant about teachers of all kinds since some are only motivated by their egos and desire to control the unconscious and impressionable minds of others. Education—as it is presently structured—is too often a controlling rather than a freeing experience for the mind, body, and soul. The form of education that is most important in awakening a person to the reality of the soul or the essence of Now is the most transformative one. It is the experience of going beyond external conditions, expectations, and roles, and discovering who you really are, inwardly. It is most simply the experience of learning to live totally in the Now, without reservations or qualifications, inhibitions, fears, and negativity.

Mostly we are living through the unconscious mind or ego of personality and social conditioning. We desire to live in this body, mind, and ego, forever, but we instinctively know that it is not possible. Forever or eternity only exists in and through the Consciousness of Now and its essence as the soul. There is no place to go other than Here; and there is no other time than Now, in the essential, changing forms of experience. Here-and-Now is the eternal place and infinite time of Being. In this framing, Being is actually no-place and no-time even though we experience it as 'here—now'. It is a strangeness that is also quite familiar

The major pitfall or obstacle to being-here-now is the illusion that we are conscious when we are not. Mostly the body, the ego and internalized values of society are dominating our daily lives. We live largely out of animal habit, social conditioning, and mis-education through the roles that we play and the mental and emotional melodramas that we engage in. Our nervous system permeates all organic systems of the body and the interactions between these systems and organs, at cellular and neural levels, are more complex than anyone can presently know or understand. Furthermore, we remain largely unconscious of when, how and why our various bodily systems and their organs are functioning as nature intended, for us to remain healthy, sane and alive. (4)

Being, Now, and Consciousness

Thus we must stand in awe of our biological, psychological and social being since that is *what* we really are—natural or evolving beings. But Now also constitutes us at higher levels or dimensions of nature and Being, levels where the soul exists within as spirit, as pure consciousness and presence. The soul is the natural energy of Life, a divine essence that no scientist can analyze or know, but which everyone can experience through Consciousness or an awakened sense of being. And this is what Now most simply means: you are alive and you know that Life is the essence of your existence or the life-form in which you are able to live, as a person, in the here-and-now.

How can we access *The Power of Now*—the experience of Presence in our lives? This is a primary question that Tolle raises in his first important book. It is the most basic question for every-one in every situation since so much else in existence depends upon answering it. If we are not consciously or fully present in the Now, we cannot be fully present to ourselves or others. Furthermore, this has a direct relevance to authentically playing a role or not.

What is the answer that Tolle offers in the *Power of Now?* In essence it derives from your "natural state of oneness with Being....Being is the eternal, ever-present One Life beyond the myriad forms that are subject to life and death. Being can be felt, but it can never be understood mentally. To regain awareness of Being and to abide in that state of 'feeling-realization' is enlight-enment." (5)

Granted that Tolle makes it sound quite easy to become 'enlightened'—the spiritual buzzword of the New Age. But becoming enlightened is no easy matter since it means getting rid of years of conditioning, identifications, ego-centered roles, and attachments. This translates into layers of the self, armoring against change, and fear of the Unknown. Without the purifica-tion or therapeutic process that must take place for something like enlightenment to even begin to occur, the word is meaning-less and empty of any real human content or realism.

Being present in the Now means that you are conscious of your contingent *and* eternal Self or soul as embodied. It is being in touch with the living paradox of Being. It is knowing that you cannot escape from existence alive, in this body, but only trans-form yourself while alive, in the Now, and merge with eternal, formless Being. This is the awareness that saves you from re-birth, misery, and ignorance.

Persons, Existence and the Life-force

Persons or embodied souls do not exist independently of a universal Life-force. Human beings are only one among an unknown number of life-forms in the universe. However, the inner purpose of all sentient beings is to realize the Source that is within, to better meet the challenges of their present sense of Being-in-the-world. In this sense, the inner purpose and the outer actions of existence should not be in conflict with one another in order to realize what is most sacred: the Life-force.

When we realize that individual or existential consciousness is a subjective manifestation of what-is prior and ultimate in nature, i.e. the unmanifested realm, we begin to awaken to who we are and what our life-world can become. Before then, we mostly live at an unconscious or subconscious level of existence. We are conditioned by nature and society to develop an ego or personality that we show to the world as an everyday 'self' or personality; but this social self is mostly an unconscious condition that we have not freely chosen. Before realizing or awakening to universal Consciousness or the Presence of God, we move through the world like lost souls or beings that are asleep to the wonder and mystery of Creation.

We are a mystery to ourselves since we do not really know what, how, or why we are here. In reality, it is a wonder, mystery and terrifying fact that we exist at all. It is a wonder since Life is a miracle in its myriad manifestations and it is also terrifying since the body or any finite form of Life can be utterly destroyed at any moment from the least of causes or contingent conditions. Thus we intuitively realize, from a quite early age, that our birth and life-form mean that we will die; and at about the same time, socially, many are taught to believe that a soul, Self or consciousness that is housed in the body, does not die or is immortal. However, common sense, science and existence combine to question the belief in an immortal soul or eternal Self; and thus many, through the history of thought, have questioned whether any form of consciousness, self or soul survive the destructive power of death and dying.

If we awaken to our ignorance about the most basic of *Perennial or Existential* questions: Why are we here? Where did we come from? Where are we going? And what does it all mean?— and admit that we do not know, we can begin to see and appreciate that it is a wonder *that* we are here at all, in this particular life-form. And what before appeared merely as a belief, something 'fixed' by fear, rote memory, and religious indoctrination, now takes on a new significance and meaning, as a great insight into what is really true, since you may feel, see, and sense the potentiality of consciousness and its innate free will. (6)

When a mere belief becomes an experienced truth or insight into reality, you, as a whole person, undergo a psychological and ontological transformation—you feel like you have become a new being, from the inside out and in the way that you face the world. I personally have undergone such transformations several times in my life but perhaps none greater than when I read and awakened to the Perennial vision of Eckhart Tolle—truths that I once merely believed in, without fully sensing, feeling, or seeing in the Now.

Non-attachment and Letting-Go

Learning how to detach ourselves from the loving relationships that we form in Life when that person is no longer in the world is one of the most difficult things that we can go through, psychologically. Life is a very difficult process of learning, growth, and transformation when it is accompanied by the existential awareness of loss and gain, tragedy and comedy, madness and sanity. Nothing lasts forever in this world of finite forms, fickle dreams, and daily illusions; and it is our relations to persons closest to us where the truth of impermanence is most difficult to fully accept but where the challenges and opportunities are also the greatest.

Eckhart Tolle asserts that "You are here to enable the divine purpose of the universe to unfold. That is how important you are!" Tolle's vision draws upon many diverse sources and each is embedded in the matrix of the Now or the intersection of time and Eternity. Realizing the eternal Now in each moment of here-and-now, we gain access to a Power that is infinitely greater than anything else on Earth. This power is divine since it is the eternal Source of every form in the universe. (7)

In Platonic philosophy, the earthly Now is like the heavenly Idea of eternal Goodness or the creative and dominating Force of the universe. In a metaphysical *and* ethical sense, eternal Goodness is the ultimate origin of all our imperfectly conceived ideals and plans that are continually being tested by the contingencies of the real world. In the history of Western philosophy, the idea of Goodness, as a metaphysical Absolute, was the dominant idea from Plato of ancient Greece to George Hegel of eighteenth century Europe. Since then, Tolle's vision of divine purpose in the Now is but one vision of many that have morphed and segued into many similar forms of absoluteness.

In theory, living in an attitude of non-attachment should be quite easy. In practice, it is anything but easy since we form attachments to many kinds of phenomena through need, desire and pleasure. Habits multiply from the repetition of actions that bring satisfaction to us. And sense of security that comes from attachment, habit and repetition creates the illusion of permanence. In actuality, the organic body and environmental conditions of nature and the Earth are always changing and threatening personal existence, whether we perceive the changes and threats or not.

Thus letting-go of habits, relationships and roles is among the most difficult of acts in one's life-world. Letting-go means that we welcome change, initiate change, anticipate change. It means that we must be present with no expectations or designs upon the future and no regrets about the past. It is learning to live totally in the present moment. It is learning the hard lesson of dying before we know that we are dying and learning how to live in *existential or ontological uncertainty* without feeling anxious or worried about the future.

Chuangzi: a Sign of Natural Goodness

Chuangzi is a famous Taoist philosopher and Chinese writer of the 4th century BCE. His courtly friend, Huizi, is a character in several of his stories. In the following dialogue between the two men, the subject of 'essence' is taken up and then disposed of, in typical Taoist moment of 'crazy wisdom'. In my version of the dialogue, I have changed 'essence' to a soul, and it is based upon several English translations of Chuangzi's writings.

Huizi asked Chuangzi, "Can 'people' not have a soul?"

Chuangzi replied, "Yes they can."

Huizi then asked, "But if they have no soul how can they be human beings?" Chuangzi explained, "Heaven gave them a life-form and the Earth gave them a face. How can you not call them human beings?"

Huizi asked again, "But if you call them human beings, how can they not have a soul?"

Chuangzi explained again: "'right' and 'wrong' is the way of society. If people do not let 'good' and 'bad' corrupt them, they can follow the *Way of Nature (the Tao)* without difficulty. This way, they can never forget that they have a soul." (8)

Chapter 3

THE EXPERIENCE OF STILLNESS

What is the stillness within the self and how can it be experienced? How does the experience of stillness in meditation, concentration and contemplation enable us to know the truth about our lives? How does the concentrated or one-pointed mind penetrate the layers of conditioning and distraction to the Truth? And why is the stillness and silence of consciousness a key for unlocking the door to the Perennial Wisdom?

One momentary glimpse of Divine Wisdom, born of meditation, is more precious than any amount of knowledge derived from merely listening to and thinking about religious teachings." Gampopa

"The living come from the dead, just as the dead come from the living." Plato *(Phaedo)*

"The sagely man rests in what is his proper rest...the multitude of men rest in what is not their proper rest....(Thus) take no heed of time, nor of right and wrong. But passing into the realm of the Infinite, take your final rest therein." Chuangzi

Wise people, after they have listened to the laws, become serene like a deep, smooth and still lake." Dhammapada

"The more you meditate the more you will enjoy an intense inner spiritual life...." Swami Shivananda

Swami Shivananda, of the 20th century, was an Indian spiritual leader among Hindus. This brief statement from *Concentration and Meditation* expresses the view of most meditators that the short and fastest way to awakening the inner body or self is through meditation and concentration. Every tradition of spirituality teaches different techniques for meditative experience which, according to mystics of the perennial Way, all reach the same end or goal if the meditative and spiritual practice is sincere and disciplined. Consider Shivananda's statement with that of Gampopa, the Tibetan Buddhist, and the latter's belief in 'one momentary glimpse of Divine Wisdom' for the possibility of liberating awareness. (1)

Saint Augustine: 'Love and do what you will'

When St. Augustine wrote "Love and do what you will" human consciousness awakened to the innate, divine will as perhaps never before in history. At the same time, Tolle assumes that 'stillness is the language of God'. Everything else is meaningless by comparison. Why? The inner stillness and silence of consciousness is the divine unity or oneness of all beings. It is where we find love or the divine energy of creation otherwise called 'God' in many religions. (2)

When stillness is not present in awareness, there are only movements, vibrations, and agitations of some kind. It is not that the lack of stillness is bad or somehow wrong, it is only that in being constantly busy or 'never having enough time', we stand to loose touch with the Self or our highest potentialities for being— the stillness within higher consciousness. And this perfect stillness, equanimity, and peacefulness of the Self is embodied in the individual soul and expressed most completely through Love.

To a great extent, the whole of reality, from the smallest forms, cells and atoms, etc.—to the largest forms—the stars and galaxies of the universe, is a dance of subatomic particles, chemical interactions, and electromagnetic vibrations. In Hindu mythology, the myriad forms and movements of the universe are controlled by the Dancing God, *Shiva-Nataraga*. The soul, Consciousness, and Absolute Reality are believed to be among the many manifestations of this primal Energy of *Brahman*, the Supreme Being.

Upon death, awakened beings or life-forms are said to merge with the various perfections of *Shiva*—who gives birth, preserves, and transforms everything in personal existence. Awakening to universal Love and innate free will we can rise through the levels of awakened consciousness and know the Unity of being-in-love. There is no need to 'wait' for death since you can experience in the inner stillness of meditative Being, the divine Love of *Shiva* who is one of the three manifestations of *Brahman*, the other two being *Brahma* or the creative Life-force and *Vishnu*, the sustaining, loving Presence of *Brahman*. (3)

Stillness, Sleeping and Waking

The stillness that human beings can experience is not just physical, psychological, or intellectual; it is ontological, meaning profoundly formless and without a detectable disturbance. Such moments of conflict-free and stress-free experience may be rare in the life of the average person, but it is possible and highly desirable. In fact, the lack of any absorption in stillness during waking awareness, can lead to the most serious of emotional disturbances.

Sleep and the experiences of meditative awareness are natural anti-dotes to the madness, over-organization, and stress of modern life. In fact, sleep and to a certain extent dreaming, have evolved in sentient life-forms to compensate for the conflict, anxiety, and stresses of ordinary existence and civilization. Sleep-deprivation can result in serious cognitive dysfunctions and eventually total unconsciousness in animal and human life-forms.

The potential stillness of consciousness and sense of being that occurs in deep sleep is of tremendous benefit to humans. In dreamless sleep, we are usually in a deeper sense of self. This means that the physical body, the intellectual mind, and emotional parts of the brain are rested, quieted and renewed following deep sleep—even when it is only a short term sleep or cat-nap. And when we make the same connection during waking consciousness with the higher self or soul, we maximize the benefits of stillness and thus feel even more energetic and renewed.

All of this is of supreme value, i.e. feeling renewed for ordinary living; but what is of even greater value—in the lives of many saints and seekers—is the experience of sublimity or ecstasy that deep stillness can easily and naturally lead to. If we define stillness as the lack of disturbance of any detectable sort by ordinary consciousness, then the sense of peaceful inwardness, tranquility and equanimity of self, can lead us into the most sublime states of awareness that humans can experience. And all of this can occur naturally in states of attunement with the inner body, Nature and other sentient beings.

Restoring Health the Natural Way

The many mind-altering and body-depressing drugs that are available today mostly lead us away from the experience of attunement and stillness. Most drugs stimulate immunological, chemical, or nerve processes creating altered states of awareness—anything but stillness and peacefulness. There are exceptions, of course, but mostly the drug culture should be avoided if the stillness of consciousness and Being is your goal. You cannot get to stillness through means that are agitating, conflict-ridden, and stressful—however they are advertised or commercially available.

For sure, there are drugs that really help people with serious, systemic, and life-threatening diseases. I am not speaking about those drugs, nor am I speaking about aspirins or similar pain-relievers, or vitamin and mineral supplements for nutritious and healthy food. But there are so many claims and counter-claims made by the big drug companies today about the latest gee-whiz remedy for colds, erectile dysfunction, arthritis, high-blood pressure, depression, cancer, heart disease, etc. that later prove to be worthless or harmful (and always expensive) that one needs to have a good crap-detector always at the ready—to see through the advertising campaign.—Television and the Internet continue to be the biggest boon to Industrial Health Care and the Capitalist economic system.

If your present social sense of reality is agitated and stressed, the natural or original self needs time and a suitable place to recover from the electronic and environmental assaults upon your mind, body and soul. Modern life, with its complications and emphasis upon speed, efficiency and hyper-organization, is anything but still and peaceful; and most people do not need to be persuaded about the recuperative value of retreats and real vacations.— Time-out and away from the advertising on television, the ringing of telephones, and hype of the global Internet, in itself, is tremendously renewing!

What can we do to overcome the lack of stillness or stress in our ordinary lives? First, turn off the television, radio and internet; disconnect the telephone; and if practical, cut the electric power into your house or apartment. These simple, cost-saving and quieting measures can work wonders in your life and restore your mind, body and soul to their natural states of sanity, health and spirituality. In a short while, you will also feel less need of pain-relieving substances, including vitamin and mineral supplements since you will want to have only real food, healthy drinks, and stress-free relations with others.

Sleep, especially deep and dreamless sleep, is probably the most natural and health-giving medicine for the body, mind, and soul. In fact, sleep is Nature's medicine for all life-forms; and the best sleep takes us out of the higher cognitive functioning of the brain and into the limbic and stem brain functions of our mammalian or animal self. Not only is deep, dreamless sleep necessary for our waking alertness and healthy functioning, it puts us into the most natural and enriching contact with natural Being. Following good sleep, we can feel euphoric, renewed and happy since endorphin hormones are flowing to our cells.

During waking states of awareness, you can learn to do conscious breathing or meditating upon the life-giving breath that comes into and out of your body. If you practice following the breath with awareness, closely and consciously, you can awaken yourself to the perfect stillness that is naturally present in the soul or the deepest, intuitive sense of self. The simple practice of just breathing consciously and deeply, felt through the rising and falling movements of the abdomen and not the more shallow ones of the chest, are acts of breathing that restore confidence, balance and a grounding experience for the self of everyday life.

Breathing consciously is a traditional form of meditation or inwardness practiced for millennia in Asian religious philosophies, especially those influenced by *Yoga* and *pranayama* philosophy. In fact, whenever we focus our consciousness upon the body, mind or soul and just watch the conditions that are naturally present without judging or analyzing them, we engage meditative processes. Moreover, the deepest or most absorbed ways of meditating, take us beyond all forms in the world, i.e. thoughts, feelings, perceptions of things, to the formless or unmanifested realm of Being. (4)

Reality and the Freedom from *Karma*

Reality is 'infinite in all directions' of space-time and independently of our own existence; yet we are subjectively and intimately connected to it. Our experience of *reality*—a philosophical buzzword if there ever was one— is created by the body, mind, and soul or our total sense of being. The soul is essentially knowable through the conscience or one's sense of right and wrong, goodness and its lack, and desire and its absence. The mind is essentially known through thinking—especially good thinking or thinking that is based upon healthy values and rational states of awareness. And the body is essentially known through the sacred Life-force and the various structures, functions, and needs of a person's life-world.

A major source of stress and ill-health leading to the lack of stillness and peace is the over-use of language. For sure, language and the experience of communication is a wonderful human (and to a less extent animal) accomplishment. But when language and a flood of words dominate our daily lives, a new challenge to stillness appears. The neuro-linguistic brain is a miracle but it can easily be misused and become a source of stress to users. Stepping back from language and meaning-making, consciously and deliberately, is a way to discover and experience the deep stillness, wordlessness, and pre-cognition that is the soul's innate nature and gift to us.—Once you experience the pleasure and peacefulness of a day without the noise of language, you will not want to go back to the way it was!

The most important thing to consider is that both the mind and body bring conflict and stress to your consciousness, in ordinary waking states. The body's many biological systems require our constant attention, at some level of existence; and the mind creates tension and conflict through its vast cerebral network of neurons and synapses that internalize its many connections with a world that is constantly changing and challenging us. In fact, most people are increasingly stimulated, distracted and agitated at superficial levels of the self from an over-organized and artificial world; and 'sitting quietly and doing nothing' or meditating would be an ordeal of supreme restlessness!

At the deepest level of being, *a pure soul (jiva)* exists that is concealed from view—the Jains of India believe. The soul carries a karmic charge from previous life-times through its atomic structure and function in the body. The soul is utterly unique to each person, animal or sentient being, connecting us with all life-forms. If (and only if) we *see* the soul or realize our true essence or the purity, perfection and eternity of the soul, then we can become liberated from cyclic existence or reincarnation (*moksa*). Otherwise, it is back again and again and more rounds of pain, suffering and unsatisfactoriness (*samsara*)! (5)

Karma and Subjective Experience

In Indic lore, awakening involves remembering who you were in past life-times since there is a strong belief in re-incarnation or the *karmic* lawfulness of existence. This way of thinking implies that everything exists for a reason or is part of a causal pattern established in our mostly forgotten past. Since the evidence for past lives is essentially mythic or narrative, re-incarnation can only be taken on faith as being the truth about existence.

In *karmic* or causal time, the past or the future may be two seconds or two hundred years in length since its span stretches continuously from one eternity (pre-existential) to another (post-existential). Time in either direction as 'going backward' or 'going forward' is an abstraction from the present moment, where neither really exists since time is existentially experienced in the present or passing moment.

In other words, existence is the experience of living in the here-and-now of being a subjectivity that is always in-the-world. The causality of *karma* is essentially that of personal existence since we necessarily live the narrative that we have created for ourselves. If we want to live in a different way then we must change the narrative, the story-line that our choices, actions and thoughts are creating. For we first live the life that we desire or are driven to, by the will-to-meaning and purpose, then we create the narrative or essence of our identity.

'Going forward' or 'backward' in time is an illusion created by the mind of history, speculation, and emotion, which takes us metaphorically or virtually out the present moment. Existentially or karmicly, we are always in the present mode of time, and being a 'freedom towards death' only expresses the living paradox that existence implies. Rather than removing us from the paradox of existing as a free subjectivity, it merely reinforces it with the inevitability of death.

If we merely repeat our past, endlessly, as Nietzsche's doctrine of eternal return assumes, then an absolutely free will is an illusion, a fiction created to make us feel better about our lives. This view like that of the Greek myth of Sisyphus who is condemned by the gods to push a bolder up to a mountain top only to have it fall down again, for all eternity, is nothing that anyone should identify with. Yet awakening to existence means that each act of the will is a free opportunity to re-make ourselves, change our mind and take different actions. The path to enlightenment is never a straight one but it is strewn with obstacles, challenges, and opportunities, all along the way.

Finally, if *karma* or causality is merely a convenient fiction or interpretation of existence, we have placed a question mark before the doctrine of pre-determination. The quantum theory of reality assumes that we cannot know reality with absolute certainty; and what we experience as subjective or existential time, is the inward sense of reality as we immediately and humanly experience it. In this context, *karma* is only a theory of causal relationships outside the realm of subjectivity that slices and dices material reality in the same way that measured or clock time divides the subjective experience of time.

Least you become too confused or dismayed by the many theories for spiritual liberation, consider Eckhart Tolle's simple but deep wisdom: "All spiritual teachings originate from the same Source. In that sense, there is and always has been only one master, who manifests in many different forms, and I am that master, and so are you, once you are able to access the Source within. And the way to it is through the inner body." (6)

The inner body, the invisible, unmanifested body, beyond the thin veil of the physical body, is a very basic assumption in the *Yoga sutras* of Patanjali and other awakened yogis. For the inner body contains the experience of eternal Being, resident in the soul or energetic core the ordinary self. And its outline is clearly indicated by the *chakras* or neurological centers of ordinary and extraordinary functioning within the human self.—I will return to this theory in later Chapters.

Meditation: the Awareness of Stillness

Last but not least is meditation itself. Meditation is stillness, a natural quieting of the mind, a stilling of the body—outwardly— and a connecting with body, mind or soul, consciously and intentionally. Every normal human being of no special intelligence, education, or background, can meditate, and in fact, does so, on a daily basis but without awareness. The challenge is to increase your level of awareness about the moments of natural meditation and then make them habitual or integral to your daily existence.

To meditate—simply focus ordinary consciousness or awareness upon breathing, the most basic function of your body and follow your breath. Close your eyes and follow your breath as it flows in and out of your lungs. Feel and visualize the air flowing in through your nostrils and down the windpipe into your lungs. Watch for a still point where the flow of oxygen coming in, turns and goes out of the lungs. Follow the air back out of your windpipe and nostrils. Do this for a count of seven complete cycles of breathing, following the breath into and out of your body.

Then, in your mind, become aware of any form in your field of awareness, such as a memory, image, person, idea, thing, feeling, etc, and observe its presence without judging or analyzing. Then consciously let-go or detach your consciousness from the object in your awareness. Practice this at different times of the day, so that it becomes habitual for you. And if you are in the habit of dreaming about experiences that are disturbing your sleep, consciously bring the habit of letting-go or non-attachment to your sleeping states. With continual practice, you can deepen your sleep and not be disturbed by dreams that may even be horrible.

Finally, meditation is the awareness of stillness. Everything is in constant motion, changing from one form into another. When you are really aware of any changes in your body, mind and soul, you become absorbed in the consciousness of *experience.* For example, when you are really engaged in an activity like chopping wood, picking blueberries, or observing the stars at night, you are not thinking about self or anyone else either. Your mind and body are fully connected in just those acts of chopping, picking and observing. It is just *you acting with things.*

Meditative awareness may shift from one situation or context to another or between the self and the not-self or inwardly and outwardly. The most constant aspect of meditation is simply *awareness*—awareness of self and the not-self, the region inside the skin and outside the skin. If you are really aware or concentrated upon and absorbed by the object of your attention, that experience becomes liberating, purifying and satisfying; and you will feel better after the experience of meditation like Now you can start fresh with whatever you need or are interested in doing.

In sum, meditating begins most simply by engaging in breath-awareness, watching or witnessing any form or phenomenon in your field of awareness without judging or analyzing, and then letting-go or dis-identifying from these forms. But meditation is essentially awareness, in the present moment or the eternal Now, where stillness and change, the self and the not-self, play in perfect Oneness.

Huang Po: Meditating upon Absolute Mind

Death and dying are considered crucial events by most people of the world. In this passage, what a famous Chinese *Ch'an* (Zen Buddhist) master wrote about the dying experience is for one who obtains Enlightenment 'in a flash'. Huang Po' reference to Mind (an Absolute or universal phenomenon) is like pointing to something invisible, unmanifested and believed to be real.

"If an ordinary man, when he is about to die, could only see the five elements of consciousness as void; the four physical elements as not constituting an 'I': the real Mind as formless and neither coming nor going; his nature as something neither commencing at his birth nor perishing at this death, but as whole and motionless in its very depths; his Mind and environmental objects as one—if he could really accomplish this, he would receive Enlightenment in a flash....He would be without the slightest tendency towards rebirth....He would just be himself, oblivious of conceptual thought and one with the Absolute. He would have attained the state of unconditioned Being." (7)

This then is one ancient speculation about the experience of dying that illuminates Consciousness with the Way to final liberation and the end of cyclic existence. And the awareness of Absolute Mind is an attitude of heart, mind and soul that one can bring to the situations of ordinary living.

Chapter 4

THE EXPERIENCE OF SILENCE

What is the experience of perfect silence? Can it be likened to 'one hand clapping'? How can meditation and contemplation help us awaken to inner silence and the silence of ordinary objects? How does the silence of the inner body, mind and soul enable us to awaken to the truth of who we are or self-knowledge? And what is the value of this aspect of self-knowledge in our lives?

"The three essential—obedience to ethics, meditation and intelligence—are a great summary of the whole of the Buddha's ancient Way." Hakuin

"The cause of human happiness and misery is a false representation of the understanding. This world is a stage stretched out by the mind, its chief actor, and Atman sits silent as spectator of the scene." Yoga-Visishtha

"The function of the mind is thinking: when you think, you keep your mind, and when you don't think, you lose your mind. This is what heaven has given to us. One who cultivates the higher self will find that his lower self follows in accord. That is how a man becomes a great man." Mencius

"No matter what path you follow, yoga is impossible unless the mind becomes quiet. The mind of a yogi is under his control; he is not under the control of his mind." Meister Eckhart

"The mind from the beginning is of a pure nature but since there is the finite aspect of it which is sullied by finite views, there is the sullied aspect of it. Although there is defilement, yet the original pure nature

45

is eternally unchanged. This mystery the Enlightened One alone under-stands. " Asvaghosha

Asvaghosha is an ancient Buddhist philosopher of the *Mahayana* persuasion. He taught that we are born with an 'original pure nature' which becomes soiled or defiled by finite views and worldly existence. He claimed that only the historical Buddha, Shakyamuni, understood this mystery although there is no agreement among Buddhists about this and other claims about what the Buddha taught.

Manifested and Unmanifested Realms

Silence exists within and between the atomic vibrations of every mental and physical form. All atomic particles, waves of energy, and forms of matter, come from the original silence of nature, the soul and the universe. It is called the Unmanifested or Formless realm.

Silence and stillness are not separable except intellectually in our primal experience of self and world. If we experience the inner stillness of the body, mind, and soul, we simultaneously experience the outer silence of the world. In this context, 'world' is simply the simultaneous arising of nature, society, and the universe as a unity or synthesis within the mind. In most instances, the world of perception is not experienced as a silence or stillness at all. It is continuously moving, changing, vibrating with noises, sights, smells, tastes, and often charged with feelings and thoughts of all kinds.

There is really no conflict or dualism between 'appearance and reality'—a traditional 'problem' among many Western philosophers. What is 'real' appears in a particular system, frame or context of experience and knowledge. For example, the songs of birds, their colorful feathers, and their migratory paths all appear to us through our sensory system and knowledge of their habitats. More abstractly, certain ancient philosophers like Plato believed in a heavenly world of eternal Forms that were the source of every changing form on Earth; and the original or heavenly Forms were considered *real and true* while the latter forms were merely *appearances* or illusions of *Reality*.

The simultaneous occurrence of events, levels and dimensions of reality is obvious when we consider the mass media. There are thousands of stations, channels, and broadcasting signals around the Earth and they are all happening now due to the force of electro-magnetism and electronic technology. In turn, the organic systems of the body, particularly the brain and nervous system, can tune into or receive any of these microwaves of energy through the appropriate technology. In other words, human creativity has enabled us to bridge the difference between manifested and unmanifested realms or appearance and reality as if they never existed.

From a non-dualistic perspective, there is only one reality, one world and one Truth. Dividing appearance of the world from Reality as Plato and other dualist philosophers have done, represents a reifying, intellectual habit of mind. Although intellectual distinctions are commonplace in any language, philosophical or not, when they are confused with the way things really are, it can be quite confusing. Such use of language creates an illusion about knowledge and the real universe and not one that we just think is there.

Meanwhile, the five external senses, the emotions, and all our thoughts are constantly stirring up the great pot that is the life-world of the each individual self. Furthermore, the deeper, instinctual and unconscious aspects of the mind are intimately involved in our everyday experience of the world. Eckhart Tolle makes this point in a number of places. Here is one:

"The Unmanifested is not separate from the manifested. It pervades this world, but it is so well disguised that almost everybody misses it completely. If you know where to look, you'll find it everywhere. A portal opens up [to the unmanifested realm] every moment." (1)

Tolle goes on to explain that every passing and present experience, no matter how slight or insignificant, can be seen as a sign, a pointer, or a signpost, on the way to the realization of the

Unmanifested realm. It is without doubt one of the most exciting and promising insights of his entire philosophy since it bridges the gap between this world of illusions and sensations and the other, hidden world of, silence, stillness and oneness.

It is important to see that there is no dualism, no real gap (only an illusory one) between this world and the other—the Unmanifested realm. Rather, this world is like a window or 'portal' as Tolle expresses it, to the greater Universe beyond this house of illusions. Yet we become attached to the forms, things, and relations of the manifested realm and believe that there is nothing else beyond the forms of the mind, body and this life-world. And those who think this way—materialists and empiricists—never doubt that the external senses give us all the evidence that we need to make decisions and form judgments about various phenomena in the world.

If you hear sounds in the distance—and we almost always do in the waking state—Tolle advises us to 'pay more attention to the silence than to the sounds' or the gaps between the sounds. 'Running' the gap or going through the gap, we break into a new awareness of the silence from which all sounds appear and into which they disappear. The very moment that we become aware of the pervading and underlying silence of everything, whether it is outward or inward, the 'mind becomes still' and we can then open a window to the Unmanifested realm.

Form and Formlessness

Plato, the most important early writer of Western philosophy, wrote that the universe is pervaded by 'Absolute Goodness'. Furthermore, he believed that perfect Goodness is an objective Idea or Perfect Form existing in a timeless realm of Being. Goodness dominates and controls all other Ideas in the Heavenly and Earthly realms and it is responsible for all the particular forms of this or any other world in the universe. It was the single-most important assumption made by Plato and many other ancient Greek philosophers and it has powerfully influenced Western thought, belief, and action ever since. (2)

Tolle is certainly aware of the influence of Plato but differs from him in thinking that the Ultimate or Unmanifested realm—what Plato called the Heavenly Realm—is formless like a great luminous, energetic Presence that shines through various 'portals' into this world. Virtually every sensation, emotion, and thought of the ordinary self can become a window for seeing the Presence of supreme Goodness or the Unmanifested realm. Just as every cell of the body contains the DNA and RNA blueprint of the entire body, every experience in daily life can be the occasion for 'going through the gap' between this manifested world and what is Ultimate.

A related distinction that Tolle brings into his philosophy is that of 'Formlessness' which is considered one of the three realms of reality, i.e. desire, form, and formlessness. Among Buddhists, formlessness (*Sunyata* or profound Emptiness) is considered ultimate but it is also virtually unknowable apart from the forms of the world. It is one of the reasons why Buddhism and Jainism of India are considered atheistic religions since both philosophies hold that humans cannot know what is ultimate or beyond the limits of reason and perception. Thus even if 'God' or an absolutely perfect Being exists, such a Being is unknowable by ordinary, perspectival means. Coincidentally, you can find the same concept about the unknowability of God or *Allah* in the Moslem's Scriptures, the *Koran*.

This, of course, is not the end of the story since it is claimed by mystics and Perennialists that intuition and faith are capacities of an omniscient or purified soul which is superior to reason and intellect; and thus we have the capacity to experience and know what is ultimate, i.e. God, through personal faith, intuition and the experience of Enlightenment. It seems that no matter what limits are placed upon human reason, someone has found a way to circumvent them; hence theology and mysticism!

The more traditional way of establishing the existence of God is on the basis of our resemblance to 'Him' as a Superman or Hero. This way of thinking about God is entirely anthropomorphic and it has been discredited since ancient times for committing the fallacy of projection; and yet the anthropomorphic imaging of God in human form remains popular in the Christian religion owing to the belief in the divinity of Jesus Christ or God-in-a-human-form.

Traditionally, the silence of the universe has been interpreted as the Silence of God by many mystics. Others claim that the manifested universe is not different from the unmanifested universe since the latter is prior to the former in its unfolding through the manifestations of evolution. Ambiguity cannot be entirely removed from our experience and knowledge of Being or what-is real, true, and good; and in the postmodern world, reasoned interpretation or medieval *hermeneutics* has become a major approach to questions about Reality, Truth, and Goodness or the eternal Ideas of Platonic metaphysics.

Meditating upon Silence and Stillness

Meditating or learning how to be still and silence, is a technique for waking up to the Unmanifested. Sitting, standing, or even walking quietly and without mind-chatter, provide an opportunity for experiencing the stillness of nature. The silence that we can experience is more beautiful than the most beautiful music that humans have created. In fact, the creators of great music have all been deep listeners and have certainly heard the 'music' of the Unmanifested. And they have accomplished this by quieting their minds long enough to hear beyond sound and respond sensitively through their own soul or essence of Self, to the natural sounds that pervade this universe. (3)

The experience of perfect silence, as in a natural setting or the stars of any night sky, is one that leaves you breathless—its beauty can be so great. Indeed, the experience of breathlessness is a sign that thinking, mere thinking has stopped and you have begun to experience the world more deeply, as it really is. If you can become perfectly still, inwardly as in a moment of meditation and not-thinking, you can experience the natural, pervading silence in even the noisiest environment in the world.

Silence is just-always-there underneath and deeply within the noise and constant vibrations of everything. It is the center of the world that is unchanging and essentially unmanifested. Silence is the real presence of 'God' or what is ultimate in experience. In fact, Silence is the unmanifested condition of the natural world and it is the eternal Life-force that makes all finite life-forms possible. And it is all happening in the Now or present moment of experience.

Tolle relates how the experiences of silence and stillness within the body and mind can benefit us. He wrote:

"Having access to that formless realm is truly liberating. It frees you from bondage to form and identification with form. It is life in its undifferentiated state prior to its fragmentation into multiplicity. We may call it the Unmanifested, the invisible Source of all things, the Being within all beings. It is a realm of deep stillness and peace, but also of joy and intense aliveness." (4)

The stillness within and silence without are entirely complementary and overlapping in their influence upon one another— like Yin and Yang or the oppositions of all things within the Tao of this world. When you learn to ride the tiger of your life, your sense of aliveness will be boundless, creative, and free as the wind. In Chinese Taoist philosophy this is what is known as merging with the *chi* or essential energy of your life and world. And when you do so, you will experience yourself for the first time through the formless and translucent essence of Consciousness or the living Presence and Source of all things—the Unmanifested.

The Soul: the Liberation from Existence

All you need is a few moments in each day when you do nothing in a quiet room or out of doors, in a beautiful setting like the sea shore or beneath the trees of a forest to feel and sense the Life-force flowing everywhere. Just be present to the whole experience of the here-and-now, what is happening inside and outside your body. Become aware of the senses and their objects like the sight of the moving ocean water, the sound of the waves against the beach, the wind sighing in the sea grass, the smell of salty sea air, and the feeling of sand on your bare feet. Become absorbed in just these sensations and the awareness of breathing. Then focus your awareness upon the stillness, silence and empti-ness within the self; be in the Now of awareness where the energy of the soul fully exists.

If—after only a few minutes of deep meditation—you then focus your consciousness upon the crown of your head, you will see the radiance of the higher Self. The *Sahasrara-chakra* is the highest form for Kundalini yoga; concentration upon the divine energy of the *Sahasrara-chakra*—located at the crown of the head can result in the highest form of awakening—the experience of *Nirvakalpa Samadhi* or the deepest sense of absorption in the uni-versal Life-force. And the experience can be empowering, trans-formative and immeasurable.

The *soul* that is awakened within is not located in just one region of the body; its Life-force or vital energy is linked to every anatomical and physiological system through the atoms, chemi-cals, molecules and cells of every gland. To assert that the soul is pure, perfect and eternal is to express a doctrine of belief and experience. In the real world, nothing is 'pure, perfect and eter-nal' except what we can imagine, reason about and hope for. If the soul is merely a doctrine of belief then the immortality much less the eternity of the soul is merely a speculation, a necessary illusion about the *Life-force* or similar metaphysical expressions.

In ancient Indian religious philosophies, the belief in an eter-nal soul is a necessity to give hope to the believer. Without it, the lack, absence and emptiness of being that may be experienced leads to a profound alienation from existence and feeling of meaninglessness. An unshakeable conviction that the soul exists and is the dynamic and energetic means for the survival of death can lead to the experience of *moksa*—the spiritual payoff or experience of liberation from cyclic existence or re-incarnation.

Is *moksa*—the release from cyclic existence— an absolute certainty? In the real world, nothing is absolutely certain about the future. However, the existential experience of the here-and-now that leads to a feeling of freedom within self-being, and a release from pain, suffering and unsatisfactoriness, is really possible. The sense of reasonless joy or happiness in the moment, the feeling of sufficiency or the fullness of being, and a satisfaction that comes from good health of the body and sanity of mind—all this is the vital energy of *moksa*.

Finally, *moksa* is simply freedom—the freedom from cyclic existence, karma and the insanity of the world. When you become aware of the stillness, silence and perfection of the soul, deeply within the self, then you can experience what it means to be liberated from the violence of existence.

The Flower Sermon of Siddhartha: Truth is Wordless

Among the thousands of sermons or teachings that the historical Buddha (Siddhartha Gautama) gave during his forty-five years of teaching, perhaps none is more famous than the one in which he sat in silence. It is known as the "Flower Sermon" during which Siddhartha sat in meditative silence before hundreds of his faithful followers and did not speak a single word. Instead, at one point, he merely raised a single rose from an arrangement of flowers and held it up so that everyone could see its wordless Presence. (5)

In the somewhat puzzled assembly of monks, Siddhartha caught the eye and smile of one monk, Kashyapa, who intuitively understood what he was 'saying' in the single gesture. Furthermore, this realization resulted in the one of most important teachings of Buddhist philosophy, i.e. that the complete truth about reality cannot be expressed in words or concepts. It must be experienced through an intuitive, psycho-physiological movement of mind and body that takes us beyond simple 'right' or 'wrong', 'yes' or 'no', either / or answers to the immediate Presence of things in experience—which in this context means a perception guided by the intuitive understanding of reality.

Such truth-seeing is the fullest, most concrete and reliable truth since it directs our attention to the non-verbal, silent reality of things. 'Zen' in Zen Buddhism means 'sitting' as in a sitting meditation of silence and stillness. The experiences of meditation, whether sitting, standing, walking, or lying down, are those of a focused and quiet concentration of the mind. In Zen meditation, we empty our consciousness of all ideas or forms, in order to experience the perfection of Mind, in the universal sense. When we are focused on the immediate, passing moment and the energy of eternal Consciousness, we can know all there is to 'see' since we become intuitively present to experience.

Perhaps years of schooling have linked words and thoughts, words and things, words and feelings together so closely that we believe that unless we know a word for something, it does not exist! When, in fact, it is at least equally true that physical things, emotions, and thoughts are as real as words in our daily experience and relations with others. What we usually do not detect in our awareness of things are the neuro-physiological structures and processes that make ordinary consciousness possible in the first place.

To Tolle and Zen practitioners, it is this underlying, non-verbal experience that is the real basis of experience. The language that makes knowledge and meaning possible is really secondary or derivative to non-verbal or neuro-physiological experience. Sitting in silence and stillness gets us closer to the truth about everything and this is also why listening, seeing and feeling are so important in our communication with others.

Chapter 5

THE UNITY OF EXISTENCE AND ESSENCE

What is existence in terms of your embodied life-form and essence? How is existence related to your body, mind and soul or who are you, as a sentient being? Why is awakening to your total being important in discovering your purpose or goal in Life? Which is more important to you: having experience in living or finding meaning in Life?

"The secret to man's being is not only to live but to have something to live for." Dostoyevsky

"Heart is merely another name for the Supreme Spirit, because He is in all hearts." Sri Ramana Maharshi

"Since God is the universal cause of all Being, in whatever region Being can be found, there must be the Divine Presence." St Thomas Aquinas

"Find the truth of Buddha in your own heart...." Eisai

"You are a principal work, a fragment of God himself, you have in yourself a part of Him. Why then are you ignorant of your high birth?... You bear God about with you, poor wretch, and know it not." Epictetus

Epictetus was a Roman slave and Stoic philosopher of the 1st century. His theistic view of reality and the human self is not unusual among Stoics since most Stoics consider that human existence is bounded by organic nature, existential fate, and responsible freedom. Stoic ethics is based upon certain conventional virtues like health, wealth and honor; but no matter how powerful and well-born, wealthy and famous, wise and prudent, nothing can save the individual from the certainty of death and the mall of time. In this sense, the Stoics resemble the Existentialists of 20th century in their view of time and Eternity, the primacy of bodily existence, and *sacred reason* (*logos*). (1)

The Unity of Existence and Essence: the Existential Perspective

What does it mean to exist as a person? How is personal existence related to the body, mind, and soul? Are we all related to a universal or Higher Self as the Hindus claim or are we all uniquely different being, owing to a soul as the Jains and other religious groups claim? Or, are we 'nothing but' a body with special powers of mind that has undergone developmental and social conditioning? What is the whole truth about our identity as human beings?

In our relation to Life—the universal and eternal Energy within the body and living life-forms—all sentient beings are ontologically equal. In relation to existence—the physical, contingent, and conditional nature of a personal self—we are unique, individual, and different. Thus we can say, with the Perennialists, that we exist both personally and impersonally, uniquely and universally, empirically and transcendentally. We are discretely differing beings when considered horizontally or temporally and we are spiritually identical beings when considered along the vertical axis of eternity. We are 'One and the many', beings of 'essence' and 'existence' simultaneously, alive in the here-and-now of an existential situation that we term *Life*. (2)

Essence as Tolle uses the term points to the ineffable and transcendental nature of existence; and without the Life-force, we have no life-form or body, mind, and soul in existence. It is essence or the universal Life-force that makes each life-form existentially possible. But if you try to define or even describe what essence 'is' words will carry little meaning apart from real life situations of existence.

Jean-Paul Sartre, the atheistic existentialist, defined human essence in terms of the will or the freedom-to-choose. Contrary to Rene Descartes and other rationalists of modern philosophy,

Sartre claimed that we first exist as a totality and then we create or develop ourselves as unique beings through the choices that we make and actions that we take, in the real world. As Sartre wrote in *Existentialism is a Humanism, existence precedes essence.*

"What do we mean by saying that *existence precedes essence?* [Italics mine] We mean that man first of all exists, encounters himself, surges up in the world—defined himself afterwards. If man as the existentialist sees him, is not definable, it is because to begin with he is nothing. He will not be anything until later, and then he will be what he makes himself. Thus, there is no human nature, because there is no God to have a conception of it. Man simply is....*Man is nothing else but what he makes of himself.* This is the first principle of existentialism.... existence is prior to essence; man is responsible for what he is." (3)

Existential philosophy was given a big boost by Sartre's essay in 1947 and proponents launched a crusade in Europe and the United States to find the 'meaning of life'. Of course, this was only the public image of this rather pessimistic, anachronistic and agnostic philosophy from the academic halls of Germany and France. Prior to the twentieth century there were the intensely critical and unconventional philosophic styles of Soren Kierkegaard and Friedrich Nietzsche of Denmark and Germany, counted as the forerunners of this philosophy.

Kierkegaard was the unorthodox Christian philosopher and Nietzsche the irreverent anti-Christian, pro-Buddhist philosopher of inchoate existentialism; and these two branches of existentialism flourished in the first half of the twentieth century, developing its own method of thinking in phenomenology or a theory of consciousness, nature and existence on the ground of philosophical realism.

Sartre, of the twentieth century, wrote in a more technical, academic style, his *Being and Nothingness* which was inspired by his principle mentor, Professor Heidegger of Germany, author of *Being and Time,* and former card-carrying Nazi party member. I have discussed *Being and Nothingness* elsewhere but I will paraphrase what I said there, in what follows:

'I am condemned to be free or for-itself as long as I live as a human being. I was thrown into the world, and abandoned to freedom; I am immersed in a condition of incomprehensibility. The only thing clear to me is that I am alone and I am responsible ultimately for what happens to me. And although there is no God in my world, I strive to become God. That is the ultimate truth and impossibility for human beings. We desire to be, especially "being in-itself- and-for-itself" or the impossible synthesis of being. Thus our most basic desire on Earth is to be God but this is an absurd desire, a useless desire, since it ends in failure'. (4)

Evident here in Sartre's viewpoint is the skepticism and atheism that posits an impossible freedom in the place of God: absolute, pure, and cut-off from nature, others, society and authentic Being. It is a philosophy that clearly defines what *alienation* looks like, the *unhappy consciousness* of Hegel, the inescapable condition of ordinary man, woman and child. *Being in-itself-and-for-itself* is the imagined synthesis, the perfection of knowing that is never realized except in the momentariness of consciousness. It is the *cogito,* the inner thinking act of consciousness only, raised to the level of Being, which is the profound emptiness or nothingness of consciousness that is frustrated by its attempts to dominate nature, *being-in-itself,* forever.

By a rather stark contrast, Tolle assumes that 'essence' is eternal whereas Sartre asserts that it is not; and this is a primary difference between atheists, like Sartre, and theists (qualified) and mystics, like Tolle. Although both Tolle and Sartre see the need for the synthesis of consciousness and Being, in order for humans to realize states of genuine happiness and well-being, only Tolle is successful or even believes that it is possible. In Sartre, human existence is an unresolvable paradox since man can only dream of the infinite power and knowledge of God; whereas in Tolle, each individual is already God-like, a Buddha-in-potentiality, and the *essence* of Being as an embodied soul.

Although existence is *ambiguous*—especially in the context of Being—the 'I am' of human identity means that I exist as a totality or not all; or individual existence is physical, sexual, social, moral, intellectual, etc. In the real world of nature and society, there is a phenomenal *unity*—owing to consciousness— between existence and essence or existence and the embodied Life-force. Personal existence or the unity of subjectivity, consciousness and the real world is the primary basis for connecting with the Truth about existence and the experience of universal meaning and purpose.

Meaning only exists on the basis of the brain-mind and its regions of language, emotion and cognition; and the mysterious arising of consciousness creates the awareness of what most call the 'mind'. Consciousness is always a *consciousness of something* specific, mentally or physically, whereas the *mind* is a general capacity or potentiality without a focus or concentration of attention. The mystery (and wonder) of existence is compounded when we realize that through the innate freedom of consciousness, its no-thing-ness, we have the power to create *essence* or meaning from existing in the Now of experience.—Nietzsche referred to this as the *will-to-power*.

Dwelling in existence means that we are living in the here-and-now of a certain place, time and situation. In this context, nothing seems mysterious indeed it is all quite ordinary or mundane. When we consider our ordinary existence in the frame of choosing what, how and why to live, ordinariness is bracketed or set aside momentarily; we only do so for the purpose of problem-solving or concentration in one form or another. However, the *eternalist* perspective of the mystics, perennialists and theistic branch of existentialism, view ordinariness in the momentous light of Being or Now, which connects ordinary experience with something Extraordinary, always, everywhere.

The significance or *meaning of life* is then magnified or enlarged to include possibilities of all kinds. In philosophical eternalism, ordinary existence is unlimited and without boundaries. The uncertainty of ordinary existence is deepened and becomes a focal point or goal in the here-and-now—owing to a new openness to the future. To experience and know the essence of who you are, is to end the *delusion of time*, i.e. the rigid separations between past, present and future, since all time is present-time or what is ordinarily called Now.

When we really live in the present moment, space-time and relationships of all kinds, we experience the world perspectivally and subjectively or the way it ordinarily appears. The *warning* about Being or any eternalistic perspective is: do not forget the real world, where you are and what you and others are doing. Philosophical *realism* must be the watchword, the independently existing world that is not dependent upon my or anyone else's existence. The world of 'I am' is as much within consciousness as it is outside the body, in the real world of nature, society, and the universe. And the independently existing world and universe beyond my skin and body can only be known, as it-is, approximately through the unity of inner consciousness.

Whoever you are, how you exist and why you exist, can always be experienced in the unity of body-mind-soul or the sense of Being a person; and by necessity, you simultaneously experience yourself within a particular environment. From the viewpoint of phenomenology or the consciousness of living-experience, there is no escape from the first person point of view or the subjective perspective of experience. *Perspectivalism* is sixty-four dollar word that exists at the heart of existential phenomenology and the way that everyone ordinarily experiences and knows the world as it-is, through the unity of existence-and-essence. Enjoy and celebrate!

What does it mean to *Wake Up?*

What does it mean to wake up? To awaken is to become fully conscious of who you are and how you differ and are like every other life-form on Earth. Becoming conscious is rising to a higher level of experience than you may normally have; it is realizing a higher form of consciousness and the realization of universal being. Universal being is a familiar idea in Indian philosophies where spirit is similar in meaning with a soul, consciousness or Self in the Jain, Buddhist and Hindu philosophies respectively.

Waking up to Life or universal being is the essence of the existing self. When you realize that the essential or universal 'you' is eternal and it is your body and mind that are finite, then the difference between existence and transcendence disappears. It is ending the delusion of time as past or future and becoming fully present in the world. Birth and death are necessary boundary conditions of personal existence; only Life and its universality is not limited by our boundary or existential conditions. When we learn to live without boundaries in existence, we awaken most fully to who we are, as an essence that we have created through the freedom of the will and the possibilities that open to a life without fixed boundaries.

At the level of highest level of consciousness, i.e. the *sahasrara-chakra* at the crown of the head, it makes no difference whether you think of yourself as absolute or relative, essential or existential; you are an individual being, existing as a unique totality of Life, in the present moment. When you can watch or 'witness' what is happening, without attaching meaning, judgment and opinion to this or that, you become more free to really experience things as they happen and unfold without prejudice. And this is what 'waking up' means in a non-attached mode of consciousness, where events, thoughts and feelings often tumble together in the streams of consciousness.

Seven Factors of Awakening

According to Buddhists there are at least seven mental factors leading to profound awakening. They are: 1, present-moment awareness, 2, the desire to investigate phenomena, 3, the awareness of energy in consciousness and will, 4, the condition of enjoyment or mental and emotional delight, 5, the presence of tranquility or peacefulness in the mind, 6, the presence of concentration in awareness, 7, and the presence of equanimity or balance in the mind and body. (4)

If just one of these factors is present in a person, then awakening will begin in the present moment; if two or three of these factors are present then more awakening will occur; and if all of these factors are simultaneously present, then full awakening will occur and be sustained as long as a person remains diligent in mind, body, and soul and continues to seek full awakening throughout personal existence.

If none of these factors giving rise to awakening is present, then the person will remain dull, inactive, undisciplined, and superficial in understanding and living. If you become aware of the presence of any one of these factors which is conducive to awakening, all is not lost in this life-time. For each birth is the bare beginning of true consciousness and liberation in existence and the ending of *unconsciousness* which keeps a person enslaved, ignorant and beyond the reach of real *education* or learning that leads to personal liberation.

As Sigmund Freud and his numerous followers have thought and practiced, the purpose of psychotherapy is to enable the patient to discover the unconscious complexes or obstacles that block his or her path to greater consciousness or awareness of repressed feelings and experiences that may interfere with every-day functioning, the free will and happiness. Freud's model of the human self as threefold, i.e. the id of instinctual, unconscious processes, the ego of everyday functioning and behaving, and the super-ego of internalized values of society, have profoundly influenced many views of the human self, among them certain Existentialists, Buddhists and Tolle.

The Mystery of Being

All the religious philosophies agree that we are here to enable Being or what is Ultimate to become manifested in the world. But how can finite beings, such as human beings, empower an infinite, eternal Being? This may be the biggest mystery of all mysteries. And the second biggest mystery is how can mortal, finite creatures such as human beings who are born with the potentiality to fully awaken to their own divine, omniscient nature, die without doing so?

There are many models for understanding our own nature or being. Virtually all religions, psychologies, and philosophies have a theory about human nature; and the biggest difference between them is determined by the differing assumptions of science and religion, empirical evidence and speculative reason, perception and imagination, etc. Those views about human nature that assume we are entirely finite beings tend towards skepticism and materialism; and those which assume we have an unlimited, infinite potentiality for awakening to our essence or true nature tend towards mysticism and spiritualism.

Awakening to the truths of the body, mind and soul is really intimately linked with awakening to the Mystery of Being itself. Scientific theories tend to leave out of consideration any 'Big Picture' questions, i.e. whether God exists, the soul's existence, an afterlife, or the ultimate meaning and purpose of existence. Religious theories make these questions and others like them, central, but all of their answers are mythic and speculative although personal experiences are often crazily mixed in with beliefs.

Existentialists, who can be either theistic or atheistic, tend to agree that ordinary or social existence is absurd, superficial and tragic owing to a civilization that is based upon materialistic, quantitative and financial values. What this means is that the particular configuration that is 'you' is largely conditioned by the social and cultural contents of character or personality. For example, the language you speak and use, the cloths you wear, the gadgets that are in your life, what you do for a living, your earnings, your relations with others, etc.—all these and more figure into who you are, at social and psychological levels of your identity.—And what is left out is any discussion about your relation to a deeper sense of Being.

Tolle writes about awakening to who you are, in a great number of places. In a section called "The True Nature of Space and Time" he finds both the 'body' of God and your inner being. At the same time, Tolle gives us the Perennialist answer to the 'why' question, i.e. why are we here? He wrote:

"What you perceive externally as space and time are ultimately illusory, but they contain a core truth. They are the two essential attributes of God, infinity and eternity, perceived as if they had an external existence outside you. Within you, both space and time have an inner equivalent that reveals their true nature, as well as your own. Whereas space is the still, infinitely deep realm of no-mind, the inner equivalent of time is presence, awareness of the eternal Now. Remember that there is no distinction between them. When space and time are realized within as the Unmanifested—no-mind and presence—external space and time continue to exist for you, but they become much less important. The world, too, continues to exist for you, but it will not bind you anymore." (5)

The implication is clear that 'God'—as the infinity and eternity of Consciousness or universal Life—exists within the body- self. Although Consciousness does not exist like a physical object, it does exist as an atomic structure; and this can be approximately understood through the Jainist theory of the soul. Furthermore, inner and outer, higher and lower, are quite relative terms since they are only spatial dimensions, metaphors and tendencies within the existing self. Tolle continues, tying up a few loose ends:

"Hence, the ultimate purpose of the world lies not within the world but in transcendence of the world. Just as you would not be conscious of space if there were no objects in space, the world is needed for the Unmanifested to be realized. You may have heard the Buddhist saying: 'If there were no illusion, there would be no enlightenment'. It is through the world and ultimately through you that the Unmanifested knows itself. *You are here to enable the divine purpose of the universe to unfold. That is how important you are!*" (6) [Italics mine]

This is a pretty amazing claim, i.e. that you are here on Earth to enable the universe to unfold. It imparts a momentous significance to ordinary existence. And it is our awakening to Consciousness or our highest potentiality for being that we transcend the world.

All of the various scriptures of the world's religions usually answer the *why* question in a similar way. Their languages, rituals, and ideologies all differ, but the essential meaning and inner purpose of religion remains the same worldwide, i.e. surrendering or submitting to an unseen 'God' or Ultimate Source, for the promise of eternal being in a heavenly realm. In other words, the game of Life is not just about making money, raising kids, being a good citizen, etc., but it is about surrendering to the unseen and unknown 'God' of the Unmanifested realm.

The big question remains: can we know the truth about the 'divine purpose' as it vitally influences our daily life? Is surrendering the ego the key to releasing us from the illusions of separateness? And if there is not sufficient faith in the existence of a Supreme Being or God can we ever realize our 'divine purpose'? –

Tolle answers these and similar questions in the affirmative that we can transcend this world and realize the hidden or Unmanifested realm of existence where the greater Truth is found—even without a clear understanding or strong faith in one traditional idea or another of *God.*— It is one's vision of Presence or eternal Being that mostly matters and not one's attachment to or identification with one idea, form or tradition.

Aging, Dying and Death

We are aging from the first day of birth into the world, although from the ancient Chinese viewpoint, aging really begins from the first moment of conception or the initial karmic beginning of your existence as the fertilized egg in your mother's womb. So least you fret over aging and become older, remember that this process has been going on since the first moment of your biological presence; and aging is simply a natural result of your continuous development as a life-form through the various stages of existence and Life.

Meanwhile, we can add to the 'Mystery of Being' to get Tolle's more existential view of things, i.e. transcending the 'pain-body', getting rid of the mind-created ego, detaching or dis-identifying consciousness from thoughts, emotions, sensations, time, space, things, etc., and merging with the inner body of Consciousness in the Now. But if you missed all the many opportunities for awakening to your essence or soul, and you are dying, all is not lost!

As reported in the ancient *Tibetan Book of the Dead,* there is a 'luminous splendor' that appears in the pure light of Emptiness following the death of the body. According to this eschatological book, we know about the initial afterlife state from mystics and others who have had 'near-death experiences' and come back to tell us what they experienced. Of course, we must add that there is conflicting evidence about near-death experiences since there are many who report absolutely 'nothing' and nightmarish horrors in their near-death experiences as those who report upon extraordinary, out-of-body experiences. (7) (8)

The window for seeing the Light of Being opens but once following death, and if we are truly *present* to the experience and are not carrying a lot of baggage with us, i.e. fear, regret, bitterness, hatred, greed, delusion, etc. and identification with the lost worlds of our past, then you can more easily pass into the realm of the liberated or freed souls. But we all have much dis-identification or un-learning to do in the manifested world; and there is new learning to realize in the Unmanifested realm before we can die, without being re-incarnated, and enter the realm of the liberated. Otherwise, another life-time could be even worse than this one, with greater suffering, madness, and absurdity.

The absurdity of how we live shows up most clearly in the way that most people approach death and dying. We live thinking that everything we experience is real, i.e. perceptions and the things of perception, emotions and their feeling states, thoughts and their mental forms. All this and more are the stuff of illusion; and when we are moribund and preparing to die, we believe that death is something real or objective too, when, in reality, death only exists as we mentally and emotionally construct it.

The psychological stages of dying as discovered by Dr. Kubler-Ross are certainly valid for all those who have lived in the denial of death. The bargaining stage with death where we may consider what we have invested in the game of living may be real too for those who are attached to things and relations-in-the-world. And finally there is the stage of acceptance where you can no longer deny the inevitability of your own dying and death and you slip into a natural coma of unconsciousness that protects from the separation experience.

The awareness or immediate experience of Now is the essence of Being or 'what-is'. If we learn to see through everything, in the translucence of higher Consciousness, then we can experience the freedom from suffering long before we experience the dying process that leads to death. If you think about your ultimate purpose in Life when death is approaching, the experience of the present moment becomes everything during the dying process.

The real purposes of being alive are not just 'aging, dying and death'; and if it were, then why wait around for the end if your life-form has become a source of misery? From the karmic view of things, it is becoming liberated from the dissatisfaction of existence, and learning to experience the joy, tranquility and real happiness that comes from what is called *moksa* in ancient Indian philosophies.

In the Hindu philosophy of India, *moksa* is the final stage and goal of life or the union with God or ultimate reality. The other stages and goals in the life-process are *kama* (or youth, sensual desire and pleasure) *dharma* (or middle age, learning and responsibility) and *artha* (or adulthood, wealth and possessions).

By most estimates, there is nothing inherently wrong or evil about the stages of existence, provided one keeps one's *dharma* or place in the moral order of the universe in view. In fact, it is precisely one's moral and ethical development as a person that is the most critical element in the experience of *moksa* or final liberation from *samsara* (or the endless cycle of birth, life, death and rebirth) otherwise known as ordinary existence. (9)

The Eternal Now

Life is really not about death or even birth since they are merely the boundaries of existence. Life is about discovering who you really are, and awakening fully to your total being, Consciousness and the soul or what Paul Tillich calls the *Eternal Now*. Everyone wants to know the truth about death, but its mystery is no greater than your birth from eternity. Your essence or unique soul is all that you need to know to survive the process of dying in the manifested world. For everything that you have identified with in this life-time, may completely disappear from your Consciousness in any afterlife states, and all that will remain is your eternal essence or soul in the mystery of the Unmanifested.

Jesus, in the humanistic image of Divinity, is infinitely patient, forgiving, and compassionate. You will get as many opportunities to awaken to Life as you free yourself from the delusions of existence or identifications with the forms, meanings, and things of this world. You can start awakening to your essence, in the present, by simply withdrawing attention from the past or future and focusing upon this passing moment.

The Now of perception, feeling and thought is the always-present window for seeing and becoming conscious of birth, death, and rebirth. When we know who we are and have lived a life without craving attachments, death should be easier to accept and the passage to eternity a smoother one. When we die, we *may* then fully realize that our Life-consciousness is eternal and infinite or one with the wonder, mystery and divine grace of *God*.

Chuangzi: Respecting Difference

There is a famous story from the Taoist philosopher, Chuangzi, of the 4th century BCE. It highlights the importance of respecting human differences and not 'killing' others with attention or what may be considered kindness. Although the names of characters are fanciful and their actions even more bizarre, the consequences of unwanted actions—despite the motive—can be fatal to the subject.

"The emperor of the north sea was Whish. The emperor of the south sea was Whoosh. The emperor of the center was All-full. Whish and Whoosh sometimes lodged together at All-full's place and he treated them exceptionally well.

"Whish and Whoosh decided to return All-full's kindness. 'Everyone has seven holes to see, hear, eat and breathe, but he alone has none. Let's try drilling him some!'

"Each day they drilled another hole. In seven days, All-full died." (10)

What is the moral message of this story? How does it apply to your present human relationships? And when does *thinking* that you can help someone prove to be harmful or even fatal?

PART II

AWAKENING TO SELF, LANGUAGE, AND THE

REAL WORLD

What is the self? How does the psychological self differ from the spiritual or metaphysical Self? What is the function of language in the discovery of self-knowledge? And why is self-knowledge so important in ordinary existence, human relationships, and the roles that people play in the world?

Consciousness enables us to have self-knowledge. It gives us the ability to observe our actions, reflect upon our motivations, and really be present to ourselves and others. It is an innate potentiality for all life-forms. As we grow and develop as persons, so does ordinary consciousness or our awareness of the world. Experience is the result of the contact that the self makes with the world; and the unseen, perceiving neural network of consciousness. Experience is the life-activity of the brain and the human nervous system informing consciousness and making impressions from the senses, emotions, thoughts and their objects in the world, upon the total self.

The ego is just awareness of a separately existing sense of 'I'. Its possessive forms are *I, me, mine and yours*. It makes separations and divisions between persons and within the self. The ego is also the center of desire, pleasure-seeking and satisfaction. As the ego exists in relation to others, it develops defensive, offensive and protective measures. It develops ways to cooperate and compete with others. These ways of acting, speaking and thinking are fearful, territorial and aggressive. However, the social roles of the ego are also protective, self-enabling and gratifying when they are *successful* in the social world.

The self, language, and knowledge all arise from the unmanifested realm of potentiality or Being. We live consciously at the manifested realm of existence or the real world which is constantly changing and uncertain. We always, everywhere live in the Now where eternity and temporality intersect. And there is no escape from existence except through the *liberation from* attachment, identification and violence of all kinds.

Language and thought mutually arise in the creation of knowledge. Language can only symbolize or point to what may be Absolute; but there is no objective certainty about any metaphysical Absolute. There is only subjective certainty about belief, feeling and thought; and language enables us to express what we know and have experienced in the world. Language is infused with the divine energy of higher Consciousness and universal Goodness that is progressively and inevitably disclosing the eternal laws of the universe.

Chapter 6

CONSCIOUSNESS, SUBJECTIVITY AND PRESENCE

What is awareness or consciousness? How is consciousness created from the subjective or inner self and the objective conditions and phenomena of the real world? Is consciousness necessarily or lawfully unified? And what purpose does consciousness serve in everyday existence and the Presence of something sacred in the universe?

"An animal organism, which has its history in time, gradually becomes the vehicle of an eternally complete consciousness, which in itself can have no history, but a history of the process by which the animal organism becomes its vehicle." T. H. Green"

"The Sufi is he whom thought keeps pace with his foot, i.e. he is entirely Present: soul is where his body is, and his body where his soul is, and his soul is where he is....This is the sign of Presence without absence." Hujiwiri

"The foolish man conceives the ideal of 'self'; the wise man sees there is no ground on which to build the idea of 'self'." Asvaghosha

"There is a perfection in Christ that is above Adam and beyond falling...it is grace...." George Fox

"The One Mind alone is the Buddha, and there is no distinction between the Buddha and sentient beings, but that sentient beings are attached to forms and so seek externally for Buddhahood. By their very seeking they lose it...." Huang-po

Huang-po was a Chinese Ch'an or Zen master of the 9th century. His use of the One Mind in this translation places him in the Perennial and mystical tradition of Buddhism. The ignorance of sentient beings is due to their attachment to the forms of contingency and not realizing that they are already One Mind or the Buddha. Furthermore, in seeking for something as in the future mode of time, we lose awareness of Now.

It can be valuable to compare and contrast someone like Huang-po with the Sufi master, Hujiwiri, who (from the quotation above) claims to be entirely Present from his feet up, as an embodied soul. Can these different perspectives be reconciled on the basis of a body, mind or soul? How? (1)

Consciousness and the Sacred Presence

Consciousness is our waking state of Now in its infinitely varied and eternal Presence. If we begin to analyze consciousness with the great number of different vocabularies that are available from various disciplines of knowledge, our gain in understanding may be enriched but it is not necessarily deepened. That is, if we subject consciousness to scientific scrutiny, we will engage in analysis, explanation, and judgment about its nature and function, but without necessarily grasping it as a whole.

If we ask, what is the origin of consciousness? We must look to present experience if we expect any significant insight. How did consciousness arise from the brain and its bewildering network of cells, neurons and synapses? All we can say about such phenomena, i.e. the brain and the nervous system through which it arises, is that we possess the potentiality for consciousness as do all mammals, birds, and reptiles. But where does this potentiality for consciousness come from, and how did it begin from the inanimate, insensate elements and conditions of nature?

It is obvious at the outset that there are no blinking lights or arrows pointing the way to the ultimate origin, presence, and destiny of universal as well as individual Consciousness. It is one of the great mysteries of existence and yet the answer, in part, to this mystery may lie immediately before us. Let us see if this is true or not.

Consciousness: the Unity of Subjectivity and Objectivity

If 'Consciousness is God'—as Tolle asserts—then Consciousness-God is the manifestation in all our waking states of Being as well as what is Unmanifested. If we ask just how can anyone know God, i.e. an eternal and infinite Being that has been described with the highest superlatives of every language? It is like asking how can we know what is Ineffable, in its totality?

Tolle's answer appears to be that we can know God from the light of Being within us as Consciousness. Hence, the awareness of Consciousness is simultaneously the awareness of God, as subject and object, as means and end, as this and that. Our knowledge of God extends no farther than our own sense of Consciousness and what exists.

The philosophical theory of consciousness that goes by the name of 'phenomenology' is the consequence of the history of Western philosophy from Aristotle to present times. This theory assumes that subjectivity and objectivity are unified, purposeful, and meaningful. The original intent of the theory was realistic, naturalistic and even positivist although it has been used in more speculative and theological ways in the 20th century. Like any theory that endures for very long, its forms of interpretation have taken it in many directions—from positivism to idealism, from materialism to introspection. However, there is one point that all phenomenologists agree upon, i.e. that consciousness arises from a subjective or personal core of Being that is immediately situated in the world. Upon this existential basis, a wide spectrum of viewpoints has taken phenomenology and its theory of consciousness into their favorite sanctuary or view of things. (2)

If we wish to see and experience subjective consciousness connected with the objective world, we merely do this through present experience, present knowledge, and present time. We are conscious beings through ordinary perception and without the need for explanation or analysis. The world simply presents itself naturally and concretely through perception, continuously, in our waking states of Being as Consciousness. But the totality of the world is an ideal in knowing that we can never realize in any absolute, final, or complete way. Instead of total knowing or understanding, we find that subjectivity is inextricably connected with our objective sense of the world, and situated in the contexts of the first personal singular experience expressed by the term 'perspective' and the pronoun 'I'. All experience and knowledge is perspectival or conditioned by the first person viewpoint of existence.

A more familiar way of expressing this is that all knowledge is relative, conditional, and situationally related to subjectivity. The ideal of objectivity in knowing is a myth in so far as comprehending the total picture of things or understanding everything. All knowledge is biased and perspectival, conditioned by human values and subjectivity. We never really see or experience things as they 'are', but only through Consciousness, subjectivity, and through a 'glass darkly' or with 'data' that is perpetually incomplete and in need of interpretation. However there is a great difference between blatant, explicit prejudice in knowledge and the effort to be fair, balanced, and 'objective'.

Now, Consciousness and God

Tolle puts forth the bold and self-evident proposition that "Consciousness is God" or at least a personal manifestation of infinite and eternal Being. This tautology appears to answers the perennial questions about the origin and essence of consciousness through the presumptive existence of God. Indeed, in this provocative assertion our everyday, mundane awareness in the here-and-now is putative evidence of God's existence.

If, indeed, God exists in and through our personal consciousness, then we cannot expect anything more or less from God than we actually experience and know. Furthermore, we cannot realistically expect any more from God than we can from the actions of any other human being; and does the Presence of God in the world therefore depend upon the actions of all human beings? And if God exists in and through human consciousness, then why should not God exist in the entire spectrum of life-forms—as is claimed by animists, pantheists and mystics?

In particular, this new significance of human consciousness could inspire ecological renewal and protection of forests, waterways and the quality of the air from the destructive pollution and poisons from unregulated technological development. In terms of social change and human welfare, this new consciousness could mean an energized commitment to remove life-threatening poverty, bigotry in racial relationships, gender inequality and oppression from the Earth once and for all. And these few changes in human society would result in a breakthrough for human consciousness itself since whatever actions we take in the spatial, social and environmental world is necessarily reflected within consciousness at moral, aesthetic and intellectual levels.

If we assume that the soul is constitutive of consciousness, then it is this infinitesimal field of energy of a divine soul that is unique to each body or self. At least this is the ancient doctrine of the Jains of India, i.e. that a pure soul exists within the identity of each person that is continually undergoing the corrupting influences of the violence of speech, human beliefs, thoughts and actions. In other words, violence or *himsa* is the problem in existence that creates human suffering or the corruption of the soul.

In the Indic mind of Hindus, the question arises: can the soul be saved from dubious prospect of 'eternal return' or reincarnation since it is the karmic debt of the soul that causes birth and Life in the body in the first place. Tolle, from his more Perennial viewpoint, answers in the affirmative the question of salvation or the redemption of a violent and destructive life-time in the context of Now:

"There is nothing you can ever do or attain that will get you closer to salvation than it is at this moment. This may be hard to grasp for a mind accustomed to thinking that everything worthwhile is in the future." (3).

In other words, a divine Life or one lived through the energy of a pure soul is potentially Now or never. Furthermore, Tolle affirms that we are accustomed to think that we must first "find, sort out, do, achieve, acquire, become, or understand something before you can be free or complete. You see time as the means to salvation, whereas in truth it is the greatest obstacle to salvation…. You 'get' there by realizing that you are there already. You find God the moment you realize that you don't need to seek God. So there is no only way to salvation: Any condition can be used, but no particular condition is needed. However, there is only one point of access: the Now." (4)

For the Perennialist, this is perhaps the most crucial assumption in Tolle's philosophy; but to the more conservative or orthodox religionist, it may be the offensive since no particular religious ritual or belonging is necessary for the momentous awareness of Now.

In Tolle's public interviews with Oprah Winfrey, particularly her television seminar that featured him, Tolle stated that he is not offering a new religion or even endorsing an old one. Rather, he uses insights into the *Truth*, conceived of in an ahistorical or eternal perspective, about reality wherever he finds them. And Tolle's writings reflect a wide variety of religious and metaphysical perspectives that rather neutrally reflect the values of Buddhists, Christians, mystics and others.

It may seem strange to think about Consciousness as the basis for salvation and it is until you realize that it is the Essence of who you are or your divinity. Furthermore, from the Jain or a mystical perspective, the soul is like a sun within Consciousness shining through its orbits of energy wherever we are awake to the here-and-now. The rays of the soul are consciousness itself which are as strong and bright as the mind, body, and worldly conditions allow. Its light and energy informs our total being-in-the-world even when we are not paying our soul any attention.

A traditional religious belief is that there is a soul of divine origin existing within persons ensuring immortality or survival of death. However, in these times of rampant skepticism, scientism, and materialistic living, the belief in an immortal soul, an innate will or freedom, as well as the existence of God have been under constant assault from relentless questioning, doubting, and disbelief. But a glance at the history of philosophy, world-wide, discloses the fact that skepticism about religious Truth has existed from the earliest of times.

Philosophy, Ignorance and Joy

Philosophy is an intellectual game that is based upon differing ideas or assumptions about reality, knowledge, and human values. There exist the views of science and religion, reason and faith, within its long history. More traditional philosophies embrace mythology, religion, and science and the attempts to reconcile their differences. But even the reconciliation of spiritualism and materialism or religion and science is only one viewpoint among many others in the history of philosophy and religion.

In fact, philosophy is essentially a subject-matter of non-agreement between conflicting viewpoints or irreconcilable biases. Perhaps more than any other discipline of knowledge and experience, philosophy entertains multiple perspectives or a pluralism in thought and culture. Yet even this definition can be misleading since there are schools of thought within philosophy that are severely reductive and analytic compared to the more inclusive and holistic perspectives. For example, positivism, analytic philosophy, and empirically based ways of thinking figure among the more reductive and technical conceptions of philosophy.

Perhaps no one among students and scholars of philosophy would doubt the value of mind or thinking. Without the ability to think, solve problems, use concepts and language, etc., humans would be little better than our nearest relatives in the mammal kingdom. The power of symbolizing and creating meaning through the mind is beyond measuring. However, a certain tyranny—not just of language—but of meaning itself has beset humankind and especially those who have excessively studied philosophy! And meaning especially the 'meaning of meaning' can become an obstacle to consciousness and living in the Now.

Therefore it is best to practice philosophy with a certain lightness of heart and mind and not think that just because we are philosophizing, we are going to figure everything out! In fact, those who study philosophy or knowledge in any depth, quickly realize that no human being can 'figure everything out' or understand reality in its totality. Hence, becoming aware of how little we really understand about reality and universals like Life, God and Truth, is the real, humbling beginning of wisdom. And at the same time, realizing even our limited capacities before the complexity of nature and the vastness of the universe can open us to the greatest joys of ordinary awareness.

Salvation is the Joy of Being

Tolle's statements on salvation are unconventional in that he relates the experience more to a spiritual Presence than a religious one. Keep in mind that the rays of Consciousness—Now present—are coming from the soul, a property of the innermost essence of Being. The rays of Consciousness shine upon every phenomenon of nature, self, and the world. And each ray is like a portal or window through which you can realize who you are.

"True salvation is fulfillment, peace, life in all its fullness. It is to be who you are, to feel within you the good that has no opposite, the joy of Being that depends on nothing outside itself. It is felt not as a passing experience but as an abiding presence. In theistic language, it is to 'know God'—not as something outside you but as your own innermost essence. True salvation is to know yourself as an inseparable part of the timeless and formless One Life from which all that exists derives its being." (5)

There is no independently existing 'self' or individual. It is purely the stuff of fiction, theory, and illusion. "Life, liberty, and the pursuit of happiness" depend upon a myriad of supportive, interrelated and overlapping conditions of self and world. However, there is one 'thing' or phenomenon that is absolutely Unconditional, and that is *Being* or the joy of immediate Presence.

Tolle refers to Being as God or an infinite and eternal Presence; and by implication, an 'innermost essence' or soul. For sure, these are very elusive phenomena existing beyond conceptual understanding as affective, aesthetic and spiritual experiences.

When we begin to see and really experience the body as it exists for each of us, uniquely in relation to Consciousness and the world in which we are situated, we can glimpse the wholeness of Being. The particularities and contingencies that arise in these relationships—between Consciousness, body, and worldly Being—are real and form a seamless unity in the depths of experience. But the surface realities of sensory, emotional, and intellectual existence can also be the occasions for the 'joy of Being' without any questing for 'more', 'having', or even 'goals'.

It is the relationship between Consciousness, body, and total existence that is the basis for happiness or the liberation from pain and suffering. It is an end that has no beginning, and a consciousness that is seamlessly related to reality through immediate experience or the Eternal Now. Indeed, Eternity, in the Perennial perspective of Tolle and others, is Now and not before or after individual existence; and there is no more complete or fulfilling experience of Being than that which brings us closest to the simple and immediate joy of the Eternal Now.

Parable: the Way of Ducks and Swans

Tolle relates a story that illustrates my previous point about meaning and conflicts quite well. It is based upon his observation of ducks—although I have seen the same behavior in the beautiful swan. When ducks or swans get into a fight over a mate, a piece of food, or a watery territory with each other, they will go at it with a flurry of wing-beats on the water aimed at each other. I have only seen this happen on a few occasions although I have never seen ducks or swans being harmed by one another. But as Tolle reports from his experience, just as quickly as a fight or altercation develops between ducks, so does it end, with each swimming off in opposite directions and proudly flapping its wings again against the water, as if to say 'enough already, it's over'.

But this is usually not the case with human beings especially those who are obsessed with being 'right' and making the other 'wrong'. Typically when humans go at it, verbally speaking, the mind, its ego and emotions get entangled with being 'right' or having the better argument. And just as typically, human beings will not just swim off, flap their wings, and get over it; they will keep arguing and talking with no let up, and emotionally, they will remain in turmoil long after the other is out of sight or sound.

Instead of just being aware of the present moment—the rising and falling of emotions and thoughts of revenge, strategy-making, and future fighting—humans cling to past conflicts with others, turning them over and over in their minds, and then make up stories to justify their contentious positions! Tolle concludes: "This is how most humans live all the time. No situation or event is ever really finished. The mind and the mind-made 'me and my story' keep it going." (6)

Fighting and then keeping the fight alive by constantly returning to it, is a dreadful sickness of the soul, mind and heart of humans. Furthermore, whereas negative emotions, fighting, and conflict release toxic chemical substances into the body, the more positive emotions like love, joy, and kindness, release powerful healing chemicals into the body, strengthening the immune system and our sense of happiness.

Tolle implies that we, as a species, can find our way back to goodness, happiness, and joy, if we just learn to 'let go' of the emotions and thoughts of the ego and its aggressive tendencies, by 'flapping our wings' to release any tension and give up arguing. Conflict and tension may be natural consequences of living, but we can find more creative and tension-releasing means for dealing with it, starting in the present moment.

Chapter 7

EGO, UNCONSCIOUSNESS AND SOCIAL ROLES

What is the ego in relation to the self and society? How is the ego, mind and essence (soul) related to the roles that we play in society? How can one who is identified with the roles that they play become an authentic or integrated person? And why are the ego, mind and roles often obstacles to being an authentic human person?

"Who are these by whom you wish to be admired? Are not these the men whom you generally describe as mad? What do you want then? Do you want to be admired by madmen?" Epictetus

"Our soul will never rest in things that are beneath it." Julian of Norwich

"Philosophers have no honor in their cities." Plato

"Someone asked, 'What is Sufism?' The Shaykh said, 'To feel joy in the heart at the coming of sorrow." Rumi

"We must learn, in our pursuit of wisdom, to listen with equanimity to the reproaches of the foolish...." Seneca

"The whole human race is so miserable and above all so blind that it is not conscious of its own miseries." Comenius

Comenius, despite his mystical and pantheistic tendencies, was very influenced by the *new inductive* method of Francis Bacon and other Renaissance Pragmatists. This quotation from his *Great Didactic*, although giving us a glimpse of his critique of the human race, does not give us a view of his solution to the problem (their misery). Comenius' overall solution to the problem of human blindness and ignorance was (and still is) Education—but in a higher register than usually experienced or a system based upon nature and sensory experience, the inclusion of both sexes, learning rather than teaching centered, a comprehensive curriculum of all knowledge, administered by means of kindness and compassion and directed toward the Love of God. It was a *perennialist vision of educational philosophy* that was to importantly influence the 20th century Pragmatist, John Dewey. (1)

Ego, Mind and Society

The ego is a product of the thinking-mind. We are not born with an ego yet it is responsible for most of our pain and suffering. It enables the formation of what Tolle calls the 'pain-body' or a magnet for the various forms of negativity. Just as the pain-body is an energy field that becomes a ghostly entity within a person, the ego closely accompanies it as an incestuous companion.

In Chapters Two through Four of *A New Earth*, Tolle develops his theory of the ego which exists at the core of the illusory 'self'. Language, perception, and thinking establish the separation of facts and ideas, things and forms in ordinary experience. We acquire an understanding of the world that is superficial, partial, and illusory, at best, through the social conditioning process which begins at birth and continues until death. And the fact remains, often unsuspected at conscious levels, that "everything, a bird, a tree, even a simple stone, and certainly a human being, is ultimately unknowable. This is because it [Being] has unfathomable depth. All we can perceive, experience, think about, is the surface layer of reality, less than the tip of an iceberg." (2)

The ego, ordinary mind, and society are intimately related, neurological formations of the body. Mind or the thinking dimension of the self, is largely an unconscious, limbic brain phenomenon, that begins to grow an ego in the earliest childhood years and more rapidly increases with the onset of puberty, the teens and early adulthood. In middle and late adulthood, the ego reaches its greatest dominance, when it is strengthened by its social responsibilities. With the onset of old age, the ego naturally diminishes in its influences upon the self. The sense of peace that normally attends the later years of adulthood can be realized much earlier if there is a sufficient degree of awareness about the insidious influence of the ego.

During this entire process of ego development, the ordinary self becomes socialized or 'civilized' through a subtle and largely unconscious process of internalized values, roles, and habits. Essentially, however, ego states are boundary formations that the brain—and later the reflective mind— creates in relation to others and the threats, imaginary or real, that they may pose to a developing person. Fear is the most instinctive of emotions and it attaches to any object that presents itself in actuality or symbolically, that threatens the ego. *Fearlessness* is a yogic ideal among spiritual seekers and adventurers alike, and it raises consciousness to the highest states of Being once it is fully realized.

Sri Ramakrishna, a Hindu sage, has said that once you annihilate the mind the ego dies, and with it the sense of 'I' or something separate from Being. We go through this life in ignorance of our own ignorance, thinking that we know something or other when in actuality we only know fragments or small parts of the totality of what-is. Or we are like blind people who do not even know that they cannot see what is real. And when you wake up from your condition, you realize what an infinitesimal part that you play in the world and see the wholeness of Being or *Atman-Brahman* seemingly for the first time.

Consciousness and the Levels of Being

Consciousness is truly one of the wonders of Nature and Spirit. It is like a highly mobile telephone, television, and internet system in one software device called the body. The analogy breaks down of course since the body is not a 'device' or mechanism except in the crudest of senses; the body is the home or temple of the universal and sacred Life-force that daily sustains us. Within the body, lodged genetically throughout its neurological circuitry is awareness itself, which in more philosophical language is known as Consciousness.

The levels of consciousness can be matched or paired with the seven *chakras* or energetic centers of the inner body, the subtle body of the Life-force or Spirit. Consciousness is essentially a highly mobile system of awareness that intuitively creates a sense of space, time, and meaning simultaneously in experience. It is infinitely greater than the mind since it can function independently of language, reason, and meaning. The ego essentially exists at the social or societal level of consciousness which in Kundalini yoga theory is the third level of consciousness. This level is largely unconscious or autonomic; and its thought processes are insidiously undermined by irrational needs, interests and values which may have counter-intuitive value for survival and security.

For example, many young men and women from poor families often sign up for military service during a time of war—morally justified or not—just because the military offers them a job and a ready-made escape from the ghetto that they were born into, or a dysfunctional family, or the promise of money for college. However, few such desperate young men and women carefully consider the probable harm that they may suffer once they are in a military uniform and serve their country in a violence-torn theatre of war like Iraq or Afghanistan. And if the tragedy of mental or physical trauma comes to such recruits, as it does in nearly half of their numbers, there is an awful grieving process compounded by the realization that it did not have to be.

Tolle terms the structure of the unconscious mind and its ego-needs, the 'current state of humanity'. This phrase is not meant to be complementary but it is deeply critical of the present state of human civilization and its conspicuous lack of genuine awareness and the values of a higher, nonviolent ethics or way of life. However, once we realize the pain, negativity, and lack of Consciousness that we may suffer from, then the original depth of our essence returns to individual consciousness and we can become free from the sense of separation, alienation, and lack within the self. When we learn to disentangle our sense of Being from 'all the things that it has become mixed up or identified with', then we will take a giant step towards fearlessness, liberation, and higher consciousness. (3)

Personal Existence and Society

The ego is constructed by the mind from a false sense of self and our relation to society. It is based on the destructive assumption that 'I' or even 'we' are more important and somehow separate from nature and life-processes. The ego is a falsifying, superficial, and arrogant construction within the field of mind that we identify with and to our detriment. The ego that we develop in society separates us from the more important insights of Life or those deriving from personal existence.

In the normal process of development, we identify—and usually quite unconsciously—with the things, persons, and forms of our total environment. That is, we become them through a false sense of self. In fact, the act of identification with something or someone is the main way in which we develop as persons, role-playing and ego-building as we age and mature in society. If (and only if) this process of learning is truly conscious and we can maintain a sense of Being all the while, then a more authentic or genuine 'self' evolves and grows. But if there is only more unconscious than conscious identification with others, neurologically, the self becomes false, superficial, and irrational, by degree; and the authentic core of the total self becomes distorted, eclipsed, and hidden from everyday consciousness and functioning.

The most serious form of identification with another self can sometimes result in a "take-over" or psychic *possession* by the other. This process takes places through an internalization of the identity of the other. The self-delusion and identity-dislocation is most deep when the experience is reciprocal, i.e. when two or more selves participate in a psychic delusion. Any intimate relationship on the several levels of *Being* has this danger if persons are not sufficiently conscious of their existential separateness and uniqueness, as between narcissists. However, merely keeping one's psychic distance from others is not a real solution to the challenge of intimacy, since one only begins to experience others in superficial, inauthentic and role-playing modes of behavior.

Being is the realization of divine Presence. It requires no words, meanings, or reasons. It is synonymous with the full experience of Now. When a person speaks from the 'I' or soul of Being rather than a superficial, social identity, he or she speaks deeply, truly, and authentically. It is the language of the Heart—a universal experience known through the emotion of Love— rather than the ego; and this language of depth discloses the Presence of Being and the conditions sufficient for human fulfillment. It is the 'I' of love, joy, and peace since it is spoken from the higher, heart-center of the subtle body, the *Anahata-chakra* of Yoga. The 'I' of Being is the 'I am' of Now where the existing subject experiences Life as a concretely universal Truth.

Awareness of Essence and Society

Consciousness is the greatest healing agent available to us. No medicine is greater since consciousness is the eternal energy of Life, connecting us directly to God or Being. In fact, higher consciousness is our most immediate connection with what is Ultimate. We do not need cell phones or the internet for our connection with ultimate reality; in fact, they may only get in the way. The greatest sense of Being is the physical and energetic universe that surrounds the Earth and extends infinitely in all directions. Yet we are apt to forget this most basic of truths and allow the worldly ego—its goals, means, and values—to come between our awareness and the Supreme Essence.

The most ordinary state of awareness is sufficient for awakening to Being—the supreme essence of everything. One momentary glimpse of the supreme essence can dissolve the self-importance of the ego in an instant. The higher consciousness that we bring to everyday experience, from the supreme essence, is sufficient to this healing effect if the intention is present. However, any merely abstract reference or pointing to the oneness of the universe may not count as much as the focused attention or concentration of consciousness that you bring to your experiences of reality.

In relation to the supreme one, the mind and its ego-states are comparatively paltry but necessary states in our daily functioning. Realistically, the ego cannot be entirely gotten rid of since it represents, in part, the boundary conditions of real being or the body. However, our physical and intellectual being is only necessary to the wheels and gears of society and its institutions to the extent that it can be used or exploited by others, in a market-based, productive society.

The dominating influence of global Capitalism diminishes the role of the ego and even the individual at first glance. However, the reality on the ground is quite different owing to the significance of a profit-based, monetary system where the 'winner' takes all or most of the financial gains in a Corporation. Since we live in an economic and social system that is based upon greed, selfishness, and ego-centered living, individual being and personal initiative is greatly magnified in significance. In rampant Capitalism, each and every body, mind, and self assume an absolute rather than a relative or interrelated importance.

In the self-centered society that supports economic Capitalism, what is 'mine' is mine absolutely and what is 'yours' is yours absolutely. Albeit, it is a system constantly on the edge of dysfunction, unbalance, and distorting to individual lives. If we wish to change the oppressive, atomistic structure of society that enslaves the majority of persons—and especially those suffering from poverty, unemployment and ill-health—we must re-think what is done in the name of education, social welfare and individual well-being.

Indeed, the supreme essence of education is self-awareness. In a society where universal values have been reduced to financial and vocational goals, the experience of the self and the meaning of Life have become truncated. If formal education is to ever mean anything more than a means to an end—that end being employment in the Capitalistic system—it must restore in significant measure the humanistic values of learning and being.

We have presently gotten so far away from the humanistic values of education, that individual processes of learning, thinking and being have become eclipsed by teaching, manipulation and the canned curriculum. If we are to realize some of the Perennial values of humanity, i.e. justice, truth, beauty, peace and enlightenment, we must begin by challenging students to discover the means to their supreme essence in Life.

Consumerism: the Disease of Capitalism

About the mundane self of social existence, Tolle writes: "the people in the advertising industry know very well that in order to sell things that people don't really need, they must convince them that those things will add something to how they see themselves or are seen by others...their sense of self." All this is seductive and cunning to a high degree by associating a famous person, exotic or adventurous setting, etc. with young, sexy, and happy-looking people. (4)

What some people discover about the consumer-society of Capitalism—although often too late to change their minds about something they have impulsively bought—is that ego-satisfaction is extremely short-lived and over-rated. Sadly, most people just keep consuming one thing or another, in the hope that the next 'thing', movie, date, or car, will be better than the last one and bring the lasting satisfaction that they endlessly seek.

Most consumption in the market-place is unconsciously driven, blind, and irrational, spurred on by the illusion of an unlimited buying power from credit cards, and the even greater illusion that 'more is better' and that somehow, 'more' is equal to greater happiness. The result is a society of persons in enormous debt and having a life burdened with useless things— 'cargo' or stuff—and a growing sense of emptiness from insatiable greed.

In fact, it is the sense of lack or voidness in the self that drives the unquenchable desire for more of everything. At its core is the absence of real faith or meaning in life. If we really know who we are and are in touch with the roots of our own being, however that might be defined in words, then nothing can be more satisfying or fulfilling life.

All the stuff that people needlessly consume in a highly privileged society like the United States can be taken to the nearest landfill for recycling; better still, give all the things (including money) that you never use to the poor and needy people in this society and throughout the world. It is amazing how much better you can feel after you give away what you never really needed in the first place.

'Consume now and pay later or never' is the unspoken mantra of the capitalist economic system. The spoken mantra is 'just charge it' or words to that effect; add it to your personal debt level. Meanwhile the collective debt level, otherwise known as the federal debt, is in the trillions of dollars; and this is everyone's debt whether you charged anything or not. It is doubtful that this will be paid down (to the Chinese) in anyone's present life-time.

The poor or the vast majority of people cannot participate in the consuming societies of the world whether they live in Asia, the West, North or South. Of course, most can see what 'haves' own and may believe that they are missing something real; but all that materialism of the rich and wealthy classes of every country is a mirage of the senses, a hideous trap set by *Maya*, the Hindu goddess of illusions and an entry point into the hell of *samsara, the pit of endless pain and suffering.*

Or consider the following brief discussion of existence and freedom, from two different viewpoints, and consider whether there is any real escape from the sense of lack or emptiness that advertisers immorally try to satisfy for the sake of the 'bottom line'. Is consumerism a disease or a sign of the health of a capitalist society? Consider in your answer whether or not health has become just another consumable product in a capitalist economy—like disease, dying and death.

The Sense of Lack and Transcendence

Atheistic Existentialism and Buddhism offer complex and controversial perspectives on the experience of lack in subjectivity. For example, Jean-Paul Sartre conceives of the self in two modes of existence: *for-itself* and the *in-itself*. Here, *for-itself* is human freedom, the freedom of consciousness, while the *in-itself* represents nature or physical existence. The *for-itself* desires a union with the *in-itself* but it never close the gap or lack with *in-itself*; and *for-itself* remains forever alienated, unhappy and suffering from its sense of lack.—At least, this is the conclusion from the Sartrean perspective about human consciousness, freedom and the desiring self.

Siddhartha Shakyamuni, the founder of Buddhist philosophy, proposed a somewhat different perspective on the human self. First, the self is merely a concept of many layers or sheaths of tissue and living potentialities associated with the body, mind, perception, conception and consciousness. The gross and subtle, inner and outer, subjective and objective dimensions all collapse into the emptiness of all forms, in the living self; furthermore, consciousness, in its infinite potentiality of awareness, interpenetrates all experiences or actions of the self—essentially an emptiness.

In Shakyamuni's view there is no lack in the self since it is always, already whole and complete, in the present moment or Now of eternity. Sartre's view is a typical logical fallacy of an intellectual kind that makes categorical distinctions which become absolutes of a metaphysical kind. The Buddhist view of the self is like that of Tolle's concept of Presence or Consciousness at an existential level; but it is unlike Tolle since divinity is erased or left out of the experiencing self altogether. However, both perspectives agree that transcendence occurs naturally and lawfully owing to consciousness and the free will.

The transcendence of consciousness and its free will has been the ground for much speculation and belief. However, any thought or belief that removes us from the here-and-now of experience is a source of discontent, alienation and suffering. That said, alienation and dualism have never prevented people from believing in *the impossible possibility* of salvation or the survival of death through a soul. Indeed, this is the perennial view of religious philosophies, mystics and spiritualists around the world. Survival or salvation is the *sine qua non* of religion, in the perennial sense; and although the truth of the survival proposition is unverifiable, it is also not falsifiable. (5)

Voice in the Head: the Insanity of Thinking

At the ontological core of the false self is Tolle's 'Voice in the Head' which he defines as an entirely unconscious stream of talk and gibberish that masks an underlying unhappiness. 'Thinking without awareness' is a basic source of this confusion and mental noise, Tolle tells us. It comes mostly from the fact that we are conditioned to 'think' from day one in our homes and schools as if thinking were the only important potentiality of being human. Without feeling, perceiving, and experiencing ourselves deeply and wordlessly, as in meditative moments, thinking makes robots of us all, and reduces us to a machine-like, merely logical existence. (6)

A perceivable symptom of the unconscious 'voice in the head' is people who talk to themselves out-loud, even in public places. Mostly, compulsive talking is a symptom of how much 'thinking' unconsciously drives us, without any awareness of its purpose or meaning. Such tendencies are a form of madness and differ only in degree of seriousness.

Indeed, most of the so called 'problems' that people think about are not problems at all. Many 'problems' exist either in a past that is no longer with us or a hypothetical future that is not yet; or they exist so distantly in space and time that no pragmatic or existential relevance to the present moment exists. In other words, there are many mentally created 'problems' that are merely abstract and theoretical ones or they may exist only in purely imaginary or hypothetic contexts of speculation.

Another whole category of problems are moral, aesthetic, and metaphysical ones. These 'problems' are pseudo-problems in that we do not know how to readily 'solve' moral, aesthetic, and metaphysical problems, in a pragmatic sense. For example, moral or ethical problems are physical, psychological and social problems in that the body— its emotions and neuro-physiological systems—are invariably involved in issues of pain and suffering, enjoyment and happiness, and ends and means.

Aesthetic 'problems' are those that deal with feelings, techniques, and perceptions—conditions that are not readily susceptible to intellectual problem solving owing to their basis in personal experience, sensuality and human valuing. Metaphysical 'problems' are in the same category as moral and aesthetic ones in that religious or spiritual issues are matters of faith, belief, and value, and potentially connect us with the most significant sources of meaning and purpose in existence.

All three of these categories are not so much rational, logical and scientific problems of knowledge as they are psychological, existential and intuitive problems of experience. Indeed, it may be entirely misleading to think of these categories of knowledge in a pragmatic or scientific sense, since they are so deeply grounded in human feelings (ethics) and perceptions (aesthetics) and experiences (metaphysics) of the most subtle kind.

Constantly 'thinking' that there is an answer to every question or a real solution to every conflict or 'problem' in Life is a symptom of a psychological imbalance between intellectual and affective capacities that many educated people may suffer from. Learning how to give up constantly thinking about things is one quick and easy way to get relief from the stress and pain of an overly organized, fast-moving and technologically driven society.

The philosophy that has created the craziness of 'problem-solving' more than any other is American pragmatism although its merits greatly outweigh its obsessive, *scientific* tendencies. The only cure for pragmatism is to realize that 'there are more things in Heaven and on Earth than are dreamed of in your philosophy'!

Being, Alienation, and Non-attachment

The metaphysical assumption about the ego and the obstacle that it represents to enlightenment is clear. Tolle writes:

"Each thing has Beingness—is a temporary form that has its origin within the formless one Life, the source of all things, all bodies, all forms. In most ancient cultures, people believed that everything, even so-called inanimate objects, had an indwelling spirit, and in this respect they were closer to the truth than we are today. When you live in a world deadened by mental abstraction, you don't sense the aliveness of the universe anymore. Most people don't inhabit a living reality, but a conceptualized one." (7)

We merely think with our intellect through the ego. There is no feeling, passion, or sense of experience in the ego. The ego grows in disconnection from the body; and the body is the real source of health and wisdom since it is organically connected with Life. To the ego, the organic life-form of an individual has no real existence since the ego is intrinsically unable to experience the emotions, sensations, and feelings of existence. Furthermore, this existential alienation is due to the fact that the ego is a mental or intellectual formation within the mind; and in the experience of alienation, the body, as a vital organism, is cut off from rational thought processes and ceases to be the vital link with the universality and meaning of Life.

In Existential Philosophy, 'alienation' has become a slogan, a salient marker for what is wrong with postmodern society. It is shorthand for a long list of psychological, intellectual and social ailments affecting the body, mind and soul of stressed, unbalanced individuals. At its core is a felt lack of meaning, in the totality of existence or sheer being. It manifests itself in feelings of being cut off from the self, the body, reason, others, society and existence—in all their concretely lived immediacy. The cure for alienation is re-connection with everything and everyone, at an affective, participatory and active mode of real being—particularly through the senses, feelings and actions that lead to significant involvement and experience.

Existence is essentially impermanent, impersonal, and interdependently arising; and personal identity is a 'story' that we freely create as we live and make choices in the world. The sickness of alienation disempowers us and cripples our capacities for meaning, creativity and happiness. When we experience ourselves freely, we feel feelings more deeply and clearly and openly and fully experience the world around us through the senses. *Life* ceases to be an abstraction and we experience the present moment in its concrete, psycho-physiological immediacy.

In the acts of living freely we naturally develop attachments to others—persons, places and things. However, when 'others' become so important that you cannot live without them or would gladly die for, they become ego-trips and symptoms of 'ontological insecurity'. For example, if your worldly possessions—a major illusion of the 'me-mine' syndrome in personal existence—do not bring satisfaction to your life, then you will know that your possessions are merely fulfilling the ego-wants and desires of a hyper-materialistic society—fuel that feeds the suffering of the 'pain-body'.

The pain-body is an important concept in Tolle's vision postmodern humanity. I will deal with it more fully in Chapter Twelve, but for now it is enough to say that we freely create a 'pain-body' or a field of psychological energy that makes it very difficult to be happy, satisfied or positive about anything! And it is entirely paradoxical that we freely create something within the body and mind that cripples our capacity for the feelings of happiness and freedom; but the plus side is that you have the power to destroy the pain-body before it destroys you.

Oftentimes, breakthroughs in Consciousness and a personal sense of being occur after an emotional and psychological crisis. A psychological breakthrough to greater awareness can be triggered by many different factors. It all depends upon your readiness to change and your realization that things are not as they should and could be. The intrinsic and essential goodness of Life within each life-form is the perennial energy, ground, and inspiration for genuine breakthroughs to the transformation of higher consciousness.

Learning to detach yourself or dis-identify your thought from what is merely a passing phenomenon, is the most important step in getting over the habit of feeding an insatiable ego that thrives on false needs, wants, and values. Realizing 'all of human life is vanity, mere vanity' and a selfish desire to possess and make permanent what is essentially impermanent may be a triggering insight in personal existence. And the very moment that you cease to see or find yourself in the things and forms of worldly existence, you will experience the liberation and exhilaration that non-attachment, desirelessness, and transvaluation of higher consciousness.

Self-awareness is able to 'witness' what is left out of existence in the infinite unfolding of Now. We cannot ever say or reason fully or completely about what-is or the totality of Being. We live incompletely towards the ending of the life-form since we can only be fully present to ourselves in the wordless experience of what-is. It is a paradox that we ceaselessly try to know Being through our incomplete experiences of it; and vice-versa.

It is only in the attitude of 'Thou-ness' or spirituality that we can know the sacredness of the Other; and when we experience another person, place or thing as subjects of the Thou-world rather than objects of the It-world, we can experience their sacredness. In the attitude of surrender or giving up the desire to control the other, we begin to appreciate the depths and heights of real being and ecstatic freedom in the world.

Being, Having and Doing

A fundamental existential confusion exists in the ego between 'having' and Being. We are taught to believe in the values of a materialistic society where the more that you 'have' or possess the more you 'are'; when in reality just the opposite is essentially the case. Christ, the Liberator or Savior of Christians, implied in the Beatitudes that those who are 'poor in spirit' and matter are without the baggage of or identifications with the world. Such people are free to experience the 'kingdom of heaven' which is the 'simple but profound joy of Being' that is within your soul and energy of the universal Life-force.

Of course, believing that you have liberated yourself if you get rid of all your possessions may only be the occasion for another delusion owing to the cunning of the ego. You may begin to think that you are superior to everyone else because you are now materially and financially destitute! But you must first get rid of the neurological and emotional source of the disease of 'ownership' and attachment to things—the ego, its various roles and place in the pain-body, and the mind.

This is not easy for people of any age who have undergone intensive psychological conditioning in the materialistic societies of global Capitalism. The more socialistic countries of the world are more conducive to 'ontological existence' or the liberated sense of Being, presence to Life, and the joy of non-attachment. But whether you live in a Capitalistic or socialistic society makes no difference if an attitude of ontological freedom is not present. Even though the freedom-to- be exists absolutely due to the intrinsic goodness of human nature—ill-will, negative conditioning and a corrupted soul can create immeasurable suffering.

The "Illusion of Ownership" existentially means that we cannot really own anything. Yet the illusion of ownership feeds on wanting 'more' to fill the sense of lack within Being. 'Wanting' is typically a futile desire to fill the emptiness of Being with 'things', sensations and distractions that may have nothing to do with real, life-serving needs, interests and values. The wanting and desiring ego is an emotional, mental and social construction that no form, content, or thing can possibly satisfy or end the sense of existential 'lack'. And closely allied with the mind's ego is the pain-body, the ego's hand-maiden which deadens everything it touches or connects with, especially other persons who may have similar pain-bodies. (8)

What is Tolle's solution to this illusion of 'having' and the suffering that it inevitably brings? Tolle writes, summarizing much of the above:

"How do you let go of attachment to things? Don't even try. It's impossible. Attachment to things drop away by itself when you no longer seek to find yourself in them....If you are aware that you are identified with a thing, the identification is no longer total. 'I am the awareness that is aware that there is attachment'. That's the beginning of the transformation of consciousness." (9)

The transformation of consciousness is moving from the having or possessing mode of existence to one of Being, particularly being aware of attachment. Historically, the values of frugality, simplicity, and even poverty have served the experience of being rather than having, of non-attachment rather than attachment. This is not to say that living a life of material blessings and comforts cannot serve the joy of Presence and Way of Being. It is only that having 'more' rather than 'less' poses the threat of corrupting the free-will and innate goodness of the self.

Finally, doing; one can easily make a fetish, an object of worship of this too. What I mean is that all modes of being-a-person are potentialities that can be corrupted if brought to extremes. Balance, becoming centered and grounded are current metaphors in our language and they are good ones for the long and winding road to self-realization—whatever your field of endeavor may be.

Lighten up but do not give up since there is no reason to die before Nature decides it is our time. Action or doing that is *bhakti* or compassionate while being *karmic*, for the sake of its own joyful enthusiasm without attachment or expectation about outcomes, may be as valuable as action can be. It can be a grave error to load up a plan of action with heavy consequences, beforehand.

If the American Pragmatists have taught us anything, it is that 'truth happens to an idea' if it is a good one; and you cannot know, for sure, how a given course of action will turn out before taking it. Uncertainty, chance and luck all play into our most loved ideas or dreamed about plans; and reason, knowledge and imagination are ideals that are tested by the contingencies of experience and the real world, at every step of our Way.

Forgetting Being: the Disease of Thinking

When we forget Being we forget everything that is important in Life. '*I am*' is the most powerful expression in any language and one that denotes our deep connection with primordial being or the primal Source of all life-forms. 'I am that I am' merely reiterates the ancient assertion of divine origin and places us in the Formless realm of existence beyond this particular, finite, passing life-form. *Formlessness* or the *Unmanifested* can be found in all the mystical perspectives of the world's religions. It denotes a unitary perspective that transcends all religious ideologies through the sublime and ineffable experience of unitive Consciousness.

'I think therefore I am' is the symptom of the disease of modern philosophy and civilization. It was most famously uttered by Rene Descartes, in the 17th century, whose mathematical genius did not take him beyond mere thought and the thinking ego. Jean-Paul Sartre, the 20th century Existentialist, considered Descartes declaration and concluded that you cannot even be aware of thinking if we do not first exist—symbolized by 'I am'. Without the 'I am' of total being which is prior to thinking, acting, and feeling, we are like the dreamer who is totally identified with his or her dreams, and lives in a perpetual delusion without relief. (10)

The unconscious, driven, and dysfunctional mind of everyday life is totally identified with thoughts, feelings, and actions, and is unable to step back from it all, and live in the here-and-now without worry, attachment, or alienation. It may be true, sadly that most people sleep-walk through their lives, seemingly without any inner being or sense of Life and their souls are blackened over by their identifications of the mind, the ego, and a shadowing pain-body. When the translucent light of Being shines through consciousness, the soul cannot be seen or intuited due to the thick layers of social conditioning and robotic behavior of the pain-body, a profound unhappiness ensues.

A tragic loss, a shocking disclosure, or a threat to one's life and limb, can awaken most people to the radiance of inner Being and the preciousness of the Life-force in the body and mind. If you are really thinking, you are always thinking about Being or the Source of Life, and the prior basis of Now. Past and future, ego and mind, self and roles, are mere illusions and abstract players on the world stage of Life. There is only the Eternal Now, this moment of sacred Life and a 'Peace that surpasses all understanding' in the meditation upon the God—the Creator, Sustainer, and Transformer of the universe— knowable through the intuitive experiences of Consciousness.

In sum, ignorance or unconsciousness is the most problematic and stupefying condition of humanity. It denotes an absence of education, mindfulness, and awakening to who we are as individuals. The ego of social being is the most obvious manifestation of unconsciousness; and its drive towards fulfillment is a delusion of the pain-body. We can transform unconsciousness through Consciousness by dis-identifying with the social and external world and awaken to inner being or the radiance of the Life-force.

Chapter 8

LANGUAGE, WORDS AND MEANINGS

What is language? How do we learn to speak, read, write and communicate with others? How does our use of language function in learning, communication and interpersonal relationships? What is the function of language in acquiring knowledge and wisdom? Why is language important or not important to the experiences of meaning, purpose and Being?

"In this final world age which is the age of dissolutions....the wondrous law of the one mind is being discarded everywhere, and each individual is now thinking just as he individually wishes to think. Sometimes it seems as if the real desire to know the truth is there—almost as it were by chance, but it soon turns out to be nothing but a sort of philosophical discussion or an elegant fashion of talk." Hakuin

"When Ananda came into the presence of the Buddha, he bowed down to the ground in great humility, blaming himself that he had not yet fully developed the potentialities of Enlightenment because from the beginning of his previous lives, he had too much devoted himself to study and learning." Surangama Sutra

"It is only when we realize that life is taking us nowhere that it begins to have meaning." P.D. Ospensky

"Words derive their power from the original Word." Eckhart

"Philosophy is a struggle against the bewitchment of language." Wittgenstein

Ludwig Wittgenstein, British logician, empiricist and linguist of the 20th century, commented extensively and incisively about the insidious influence of language in our lives and thought.

Although he was certainly not a mystic or Perennialist, his sensitivity and acuteness of mind caused him to say in the *Tractatus*: "What can be said at all can be said clearly, and what we cannot talk about we must pass over in silence." And his linguistic definition of philosophy rightly warns us about the *bewitchment of language*. (1)

How do you compare the skeptical and critical view of Wittgenstein and by implication, philosophy, with the mystical and unitary view of Eckhart (see above) on the subject of language? Is one philosopher *wiser* than the other? Or do they merely represent different spectra or views about Truth through language? Do you believe that language derives its power in one original Word as Eckhart, the Christian mystic, does? Or does Wittgenstein have the more useful or pragmatic view of language?

Three Levels of Language Learning

There are many means, contexts and structures by which language exists. First, you can see and read words on a printed page or monitor, hear words spoken in real time, and read or hear words through an electronic device. Language is not just the most important means or medium for every writer, similar to what paint is to the painter, or the body is to the dancer or figure skater, but words are like a subtle, inaudible music that sound through the mind, heart, and soul of a reader and writer, when they appeal to our sense of meaning, truth and experience. Thus, words do not just exist in a physical or electronic way, but they have an immediate, intuitive, and unconscious appeal on many levels of experience, that we may not be immediately aware or conscious of; and this is mostly due to the fact that language learning is largely phonetic, neurological and behavioral.

The second sense or means by which language exists—beyond the neuro-physiological and behavioral levels—is the psychological one. This involves the mechanisms, glands, and systems of the body that function quite autonomously or apart from conscious awareness. Our auditory, visual, kin-aesthetic, gustatory, and tactile systems all play their subtle and elusive parts below the radar of Consciousness; by analogy, when we hear and speak words that convey meaning, the greater part is unconsciously internalized or learned. But as implied at the physical contexts of language, the psychological and developmental conditions of the person cannot be separated from the learning of language which begins at birth. Language soon becomes complexly related to communication beyond the learning processes of words, sounds, and symbols, to the extent that the entire self and its experience of the world are transformed.

The learning that takes place in language acquisition is largely unconscious and neurological even though it is manifested consciously and behaviorally. That is, the brain and the nervous system is our silent and invisible partner in everything that we do, think, and say. The brain is clearly the neurological basis for the mind but the mind must be distinguished from the higher levels of consciousness that morph into the Self, at the highest level of Consciousness—as Tolle's writings and insights clearly assume.

Since the mind is really something different from the brain and its myriad connections with the other systems and functions of the body, it is a useful simplification to refer to the mind "as if" it can exist independently of the brain. However, this practice is clearly misleading since we know that the mind is directly affected by the chemical, organic and emotional conditions of the body and its higher cognitive functioning depends upon neuro-linguistic, semantic, and intellectual learning.

The third level or sense of language is the social or cultural sphere of experience. We do not need advanced degrees in sociology or philosophy to know that we normally acquire a language just by growing up and living in a particular society. The learning of a particular language takes place largely below or beyond Consciousness in the neurological unconsciousness of an individual. This learning is autonomic, limbic brain dominant, to such a degree, that the typical pre-school age child is communicating through an oral language before he or she knows how to read or write.

Phonetic, emotional and kinesthetic impressions are commonly formed in the brain prior to any formal instruction or learning of a given language. The same Empirical principle of learning and experience occurs in others areas of cognitive growth in normal development, i.e. the sensory impressions from experience are the catalyst and basis for our ideas and understandings of abstract thought. The same sensory, psycho-physiological and behavioral complex of processes occurs beyond Conscious awareness in the neural networks of the cerebral cortex of the brain in all language learning and morphemic development. (2)

Neuro-linguistic Processing and the Irrational Mind

To say that autonomic or unconscious language acquisition is 'irrational' is to say that language learning often takes place beyond the reason and rationality of higher Consciousness. However, once we have learned a language and the semantic, syntactic, and grammatical system to which it belongs, we are more able to better control the energy of language in articulate forms. However, even in the mature use of a language, there continues to be a subconscious and somewhat creative process that inspires higher cognition in its articulate forms. Hence, the sub-conscious, neuro-linguistic formations within the mind that often determine what we say and think and how we behave and justify our actions, are largely irrational or without any ultimate basis in experience. Even our deepest affective states of Being, i.e. ethical, relational and spiritual beliefs or emotive states of mind, cannot be entirely separated from neuro-linguistic processing within the greater unconsciousness of the brain.

To assert that the human mind is more irrational than it is rational is to express a prejudice formed largely by our cultural impressions of experience. Such opinions beg the question about reason and the nature of humans, to begin with; and if we knew enough about either issue we would be in a better position to judge opinions on both sides about human rationality. That said, there is good reason to believe that human actions in general and language behavior in particular are largely influenced by situational demands and contingencies rather than global beliefs and ideologies; at the same time, instinctual, psychological and social drives within the reptilian and mammalian brain centers pulls the stronger cords upon our rational thought processes.

On the other hand, it is not unreasonable to assume that language and its cargo of intellectual, emotional, and aesthetic meanings that its words and structures convey, is an essentially logical and psychological process that involves varying degrees of genuine awareness. The learning or growth that may take place in language usage and functioning is usually a subtle, psychological, and aesthetic experience of the total being of a person that is impossible to meaningfully measure. Oftentimes, language usage is repetitive, formal, and empty of significant existential disclosure or self-awareness. Language often functions within specific environmental influences and demands; and it is simultaneously influenced by internalized roles, rituals and expectations. However, the neurotic and irrational 'Voice in the Head' that Tolle speaks about, seems to be an exception to the rule of behavioral influences upon language, and it is a neuro-linguistic habit that nearly everyone suffers from to some degree.

There may, in fact, be more instances of insane speech and writing than we are aware of, both in ourselves and others. Semantic insanity occurs whenever a person is driven, controlled, or dominated by words and concepts rather than the perceived reality or situation that they merely represent. The insanity of language usage can come from many sources, but the main one is due to our lack of situational awareness of the purely symbolic and neuro-linguistic nature of meaning and thought, in relation to wordless reality. This can be understood by the logical and semantic distinction between 'words', 'things' and 'persons'. For example, this unconscious neuro-linguistic habit can lead us to not confuse the word 'moon' with the language user and the great physical sphere in the sky; whereas a dog will typically not know what the word 'moon' means and only look at his master in puzzlement and the sound that he makes rather than the distant moon even if the word is accompanied by the pointing of a finger.

As every story teller knows, you can say or write anything that you please, in creating a narrative, as long as the illusion of reality is plausible, logical, and congruent with experience. Politicians, teachers, lawyers, salespersons, public relations experts, writers, journalists, etc. whose roles depend heavily upon language usage and effectiveness in communicating are usually more conscious than other professional or uneducated persons in performing their language-driven roles. But the truth is that everyone who participates in society, to any extent at all—save perhaps hermits, reclusive yogis, monks and nuns in silence—must become aware of their own language skills, habits and behaviors, if they are to become 'successful' or effective in community life.

Language is arguably the most important yet unconsciously acquired learning process that we undergo in our journey through society, higher culture, and life. However, what is learned unconsciously often becomes a source of un-freedom in the functioning self of everyday experience. If, for example, a person wishes to change his or her behavior, the difficulty greatly increases with every degree of unconsciousness in the self. A symptom and sign of the unconscious learning that is language acquisition is the automatic way in which an individual speaks or writes a native language. It is a phenomenon that decreases the quality of reason and understanding in the world rather than serving the higher ends of education, philosophy, and humanity. (3)

The Language of Higher Consciousness

The higher self or soul of Consciousness is inspired by the energy of universal Life in the Now. For sure, the experience of our spiritual nature or soul is a complex phenomenon in the language of metaphysics. However, when language, attitude, and prejudice block the Energy of the total self, the biological, psychological and social levels of language acquisition become irrational and unconscious.

Normally, the flow of energy from the inner Being of the self, i.e. the soul, circulates at all levels of the spinal cord and nervous system, in a structural and functional pattern; and it makes little or no difference which language is spoken or used in a given culture, to the experience of the higher sense of self or the soul. However, when the symbols, knowledge and wisdom of previous generations are ignored, distorted or even lost to a person, there is an experienced lack of meaning in Life that occurs.

Historically, this experience first occurred on a widespread basis in 19th century Europe, which underwent a great wave of pessimism about the meaning of Life and existence of God—which the atheistic philosopher, Friedrich Nietzsche, importantly observed. Arguably, when the energy of higher Consciousness ceases or is cut off for one reason or another, there are severe symptoms of anomie or alienation within the psyche of a person. Life begins to look entirely pointless, absurd and without any justification whatsoever. At which point, in the seriously affected, suicide is contemplated and in some cases, actualized. (4)

Extreme states of mind and emotion often lead to extreme actions that test the limits of rationality and the influence of higher awareness. The balancing or normalizing influence of language and communication can often bring a person back to his 'better angels' and senses in such states; but it is not always the case when neural processes lose their plasticity and harden in their connections. If we really understood how and why the brain works as it miraculously does, in normal or balanced times, we would much more about human illness, suffering and unhappiness and how to prevent it. But prevention and cure continue to be the hope of the brain sciences—in mental, emotional and medical disorders of the brain and higher cognitive processes; importantly among them is the learning acquired in language usage and habits.

The Language of Prejudice and Bigotry

'Resistance' of a psychological and ontological kind is the result of a self that is indoctrinated by unconsciously acquired meanings and language. 'Bigotry' is the manifestation of this same phenomenon when it is directed at a certain group of persons or issues. And 'prejudice' is the same psychological phenomenon that sinks to a more extreme degree of unconsciousness than bigotry and functions at emotional levels below the level of conscious control, reasoning, and change. The most destructive form of linguistic or semantic insanity occurs when persons or groups (who are typically unknown) are demonized by emotionally loaded words like 'enemy' or 'terrorist' or 'gorilla' motivating entire armies of soldiers to kill others—as in war and genocide.

The same destructive and falsifying effect from language occurs in relation to social groups that have been historically discriminated against. Words that have become like branding irons and vicious labels have been used to put down many groups of minorities or weaker populations by a dominant group in society. There is virtually no society that is entirely free from the tendency to misuse language, i.e. use it immorally or harmfully to deny the rights and freedoms of others. People of 'color', i.e. black skinned, red skinned, white skinned, olive skinned people, may have one group or another enslaved through the brutal practices of historic slavery and the consistently immoral misuse of language that perpetuated racial lies about the inferiority of people of 'color'.

The same practices and habits of speech, thought, and behavior can be seen among the same group of 'white' men (usually) towards women—virtually any woman of color, nationality, religion, etc. The lack of Consciousness about the inherent equality of all sentient beings is responsible for the historic discrimination and abuse of women, people of color, and poor people. These three groups especially—although there are innumerable others—have been the victims of semantic insanity, ignorance, and bigotry since the beginning of history. This evil, of course, is still with us, in the Now, due to the systemic conditions of slavery and the negative, irrational, and ignorant habits of mind that have been established by symbolic and linguistic means. Formal education could make a difference in reducing the levels of prejudice among white people toward black or brown skinned people; but the biggest reductions in racial ignorance, intolerance and segregation have occurred through political legislation, moral leadership and informal, social means.

Of course, the language that we use in everyday situations is both the cause and the effect of negative and positive kinds of experience and particularly experiences of pain and pleasure. In this sense, language or the words that we use and are used by, are merely the signs and symptoms of unconscious social conditioning, whether it is painful or pleasurable. Here, the concept of the 'pain-body' that Tolle uses has it counterpoint in the 'pleasure-body' or that body which we have shaped and shapes us, in personal experience. Our common language reflects like a mirror that is turned inward upon the self and the two 'bodies' or neural centers of emotional energy, i.e. the pain-body and the pleasure-body, which share the space and time of Now.

The language that we use also reflects our personal *Weltanschauung* or world-view and the collective Zeitgeist or Spirit of the times. Like the growing human self that internalizes and absorbs whatever it encounters, in the natural and cultural environments, through the cells, organs, and systems of the body— language learning is an innate human potentiality of all human beings as the work of Noam Chomsky and his associates have shown. In this sense, language learning and actualization transcends specific cultures or societies and binds all members of the human species together in a symbolic universe of experience and knowledge.

Hence, an essence of our nature is clearly symbolic or linguistic; language learning is as natural to our species as being able to walk upright or bipedalism. It is the result of a profound transformation of consciousness from the 'darkness' of unconsciousness to the 'illumination' of Consciousness which enabled our ancestors to gain greater control over their environment, total self, and sense of Life. And it remains a continuing challenge to our Consciousness in the Now as we 'go forward' towards the perennial uncertainty, wonder and terror, of the future.

Historically, our inherited genetic capacity for language usage and understanding has been turned against our instinct for survival, as a species, by those in positions of leadership, authority, and wealth, and who have strong pain-bodies. Politicians, police officers, soldiers, teachers, human service workers, nurses, doctors, etc.—literally everyone whose roles bring them into direct contact with others, are particularly susceptible to the influence of their pain-and-pleasure bodies through the language that they use and are used by.

The dark side of the miracle that language and communication symbolizes is that words and their morphemes or meanings in the brain can have a determining and controlling influence upon persons with a weakly developed intelligence or critical, questioning sense of everything. Critical thinking and the habit of questioning authority, experts, and established opinion, can go a long way in one's self-education and moral development; and the words that people use sometimes tell us all we need to know about where they stand, on a particular issue of consequence; otherwise, we must consider their non-verbal actions.

Whether we are considering the dark or sunny-side of our language powers, i.e. its moral and immoral, educative and manipulative, creative and destructive uses, the basis of language is its neuro-linguistic wiring in the brain and the entire nervous system of the body. Language development is so pervasive and dominant in the self of most people, that it has created great virtual networks of energy, meaning, and action, inside and outside the body.

Indeed, the worldwide network of communication—the Web that has a weaver and it is us—has created a virtual brain outside of the actual brain and it is of global proportions. And although we have only begun to fathom the neural effects upon human perception, cognition and communication processes, the potentiality for social and human change appears to be unlimited.

Consciousness or the energy of the Higher Self that is the Life-force within each individual is the real 'Savior' of each of us. The whole cultural phenomenology of organized religion is nothing more than an unconscious projection of an innate and divine energy upon an idealized 'Other' or any Being who radiates the same quality and frequency of Energy of an awakened Self. The astonishing popularity of single individuals in politics, sports, entertainment, art, science, business, and other fields of human endeavor, can be better understood from the standpoint of human projection of what exists unconsciously in the Self as the desire to be saved from death or nonbeing. We can learn to control our tendency to both divinize and demonize the 'other' through a Consciousness of language that is not emotionally loaded with prejudices or unconscious biases. (5)

The Language of Yoga: the Chakras

Philosophically, we exist at many levels of reality— seven in Kundalini Yoga. Counting from the base of the spine to the crown of the head, there are biological, psychological, sociological, ethical, aesthetic, epistemological, and ontological levels of the existing lower self / Higher Self. Together, the chakras symbolize the multidimensional structures and functions of a normally endowed individual with the innate potentialities for survival, pleasure, success, compassion, creativity, reason and enlightenment; and these correspond to each of the seven chakra centers of physical and spiritual energy.

All these levels can be plotted, described, and explained quite explicitly in intellectual and even scientific terms until we reach the 'ontological' level—which is strictly speaking no-level since it permeates the whole lower self as the Life-force. Without the energy or Life-force of the crown 'chakra' and its presence at the other chakras levels of the body, we will die.

Chakra means wheel or circle of energy. It is one site or 'nexus of nerves' on a model of the total self. Chakras do not literally or empirically exist like feet, arms, the heart, brain, stomach, etc. that make up the body. Chakras represent or symbolize vital centers of energy, sites where the body's systems have a controlling presence and means for awaking us to the interdependence of the physiological and anatomical systems.

Many scholars and yogic practitioners have thought that the chakra system represents the most inclusive model for understanding human nature, in the history of knowledge. This is quite a claim and the basis for it lies in the assumption that we are multi-dimensional creatures who possess many potentialities for awakening, i.e. the entire spectrum from physical to spiritual factors.

Kundalini Yoga theory is in part metaphoric and in part real in that its chakras refer us to actual biological phenomena, i.e. systems, organs, and functions, and to mythic characters like Shakti and Shiva. However, unknown numbers of yogis, scholars, and seekers have found support for their beliefs and experiences of extraordinary states of consciousness, through Kundalini yoga. One such person is Gopi Krishna, an Indian seeker of the 20th century who apparently completely awakened to Higher Consciousness through his meditations upon the 'evolutionary energy' of Kundalini. (6)

The articulations of language in the foregoing can enable us to better understand and be more conscious of religious and spiritual language. The words, tags, labels, 'isms', 'ologies' and concepts with which we festoon reality are only so many intellectual or cognitive projections of the ego; we inflate and congratulate ourselves with a parade of banners and slogans that supposedly represents understanding, insight and wisdom. The sad reality is that academics know little more the rest of humankind and a lot less than most if you consider the shallowness and sameness of their life-experience.

The higher levels of experience referred to in Yoga philosophy provide us with a rich clue about the deeper mystery of human unconsciousness, creativity, and freedom. These spiritual experiences create the illusion that we totally understand the ontological Source of everything, when in fact we may only know the language of Kundalini Yoga or similar mystical perspectives. For example, the Chakra-centers of mystical Yoga are an intellectual model or map of the inner, subtle body which must be disposed of, for the sake of awakening to the immediate experience.

The logical fallacies within the yogic tradition are no different from elsewhere in human knowledge when we confuse the word with the thing it merely represents. Originally, yoga theories originally developed from the yogic practices of unknown ascetics and monks who had little if no interest in formal philosophy. In ancient times, many differing ways of thinking developed on the basis of differing practices, beliefs, and needs, expressed by differing languages. The Kundalini theory that Patanjali developed in the Yoga Sutras was actually a highly abstract synthesis of many centuries of yogic experience and practice. Yet his writings remain of as a testimony to a tradition that puts experience or pre-cognitive action before thought and knowledge.

At the heart of Kundalini Yoga is the metaphysical belief that Eternal Being is prior to creation or the living universe. Its theory of the chakras is no more real or unreal than any other theory of the total self. That is to say, one must be willing to suspend judgment about its truth or falsity in order to derive any benefit or value from the chakra system; and one must be willing to use imagination and concentration when engaging each chakra with the mind and body. And although immense effort and discipline is required of the yogi in this system of practice, which involves ascetic austerities or extreme denial of the normal functioning self, involving fasting, meditation, and withdrawal from everyday life; the dominating or focusing object for meditation is the energy of the eternal soul located in the inner body.

The chakras are situated along the spine with nerve figures of electric energy extending invisibly to the eye in all directions. The chakras resemble not so much the 'wheels' of tradition as they do webs or ganglia in the tissues and cells of the body. They have been described as three to seven in number with the three most prominent of them situated in the solar plexus region, representing the energy of the body, the center of the forehead representing the energy of the mind, and just above the crown of the head representing the energy of the soul.

Otherwise, the full system of charkas is ladder-like with the bottom rung located at the coccyx area or lower tip of the spine and the legs of the ladder connect the yogi to the Earth. The *Muladhar-chakra* or so it is named in Sanskrit, is meant to represent the instinct of survival or the will-to-live. The second and higher chakra is the *Svadhisthana-chakra* and its meaning is derived from the instinct of desire and the will-to-possess. This energy center is not unsurprisingly centered upon the genitalia of men and women where sexual energy is initially felt in the arousal state of being. The third and higher chakra along the spine is the *Manipura-chakra* which represents the security and greed of our social being or the will-to-power.

The implication from these three lower chakras is that the majority of people spend most of their lives on the energies of these three chakras. Minding survival needs and adapting to a constantly changing world have dominated and shaped the evolution of the human species. However, higher needs, interests and goals have played an even greater role in the development of human consciousness.

For example, the heart-chakra called the *Anahata-chakra* represents the will-to-love and the ethics of caring and compassion. It is located in the cardiac plexus or region of heart and lungs. The fifth chakra, called the *Vishuddha-chakra*, is located in the laryngeus plexus of the throat and it represents the will-to-creativity. This center of our being exerts a strong attraction for persons who need to express themselves to others and perhaps gain a measure of recognition. The sixth chakra center, called the *Ajna-chakra*, refers to the will-to-know as in the truth of the self, world and universe. This chakra is located in the brain cavity and its energy controls reason, language and emotion, among other capacities of the mind and body.

The supposition is that these three higher chakras represent the needs, interests and values of higher Consciousness among *Homo sapiens.* On Earth, many other species or sentient beings possess similar needs and interests, in their care for offspring, welfare of the community, and constructive intelligence. However, the complexity and plasticity of the brain and nervous system, particularly in its symbolic and linguistic functioning, appears to set human beings apart from other mammals of the Earth.

This yogic perspective of the organism is a creature of language, reason, and experience. The various chakra centers are intended to lead us from the lower end of the spine in ascending levels to the crown of the head where the energy of the Higher Self is essentially resident, termed the *Sahasrara-chakra* in the Sanskrit language. The 'chakras' –energy currents shaped in circular forms or wheels—are centers of neural networks in the invisible or gross body. The entire epistemology of the chakras is an imaginative and metaphorical mapping of the spiritual Life-force that creates, sustains and transforms the body, mind, and soul, in the Eternal Now. In this sense, the chakras enable us to experience a union with eternal Presence through the various levels of language, reason and experience.

The consciousness and knowledge that we bring to the experience of the chakras determines the quality and depth of everyday experience. Thus awakening to the Life-force is a highly subjective response of the innate capacity for higher consciousness that each person possesses regardless of accidental or external circumstances. Language skills, in this respect, are only be an acquired or developed capacity subsequent to the yogic experience of the chakras which entail connecting with the full functioning of the body, mind and soul. (7)

If the language systems of the various religions and spiritual traditions were 'deleted' from human consciousness, libraries and data-banks of the world, little would change, arguably, concerning the existential conditions and experiences of Life. Yet the religions appear to answer questions that either philosophy or science can answer without violating their boundaries of knowledge. On the other hand, many persons searching for experiences and objects of ultimate concern have turned to the arts and the humanities or human creativity in general in its technological inventiveness. And still others have found ultimate meaning and purpose in the most mundane pursuits and activities.

Human beings have an innate capacity, wherever they are found, of enlarging and deepening the meaning of their lives with objects, relations and actions that are greater than their ego-centered lives. Human existence is, in this most important aspect, a story of metaphoric and symbolic intelligence, signifying the desire for transcendence and union (or yoga) with what-is.

In sum, there are no boundaries between spirit and matter, God and nature, Being and nothingness. Yet human civilization is complex record of national borders, international conflict and internecine warfare. At the same time, human beings have created a symbolic form of consciousness and culture that has enabled them to evolve more fully in the Earth. Whether or not more evolved, less violent beings exist elsewhere in the universe is a matter of speculation, at this time, although the possibility exists.

The human capacity for religious or spiritual language seems synonymous with the deepest and most primordial experience of Consciousness. The mystery, wonder and terror before the universe, is the symbolic ground for Perennial Philosophy or the mystical unity of the world religions. Thus, since the linguistic tendencies and habits for spiritual or yogic experience seem to be a pre-wired potentiality within humans, something resembling the present day religions will probably persist as long as the human species does and particularly the present capacity for higher Consciousness.

The Language of Love and Compassion

As seen above, through the miracle of linguistic-Consciousness, we have the capacity to awaken the higher chakra centers of consciousness, the culmination of which is the crown center or the Higher Self. The highest reaches of Consciousness are well-understood by Tolle, through his visionary use of language, the clarity of his thought and creative intelligence. At the same time, we should not ignore the chakra centers—conditioned by language, mind, and ego though they are—in actualizing our potentiality for awakening to our ultimate purpose in Life.

In discussing 'The Core of the Ego', Tolle wrote: "The very Being that you are is Truth. Jesus tried to convey that when he said, 'I am the way and the truth and the life'. These words uttered by Jesus are ones of the most powerful and direct pointers to the Truth, if understood correctly. If misinterpreted, however, they become a great obstacle. Jesus speaks of the innermost 'I Am', the essential identity of every man and woman, every life-form, in fact." (8)

This realization can lead us directly to the philosophy of Perennialism or the assumption that a core identity, experience and meaning exists for all world religions since they are grounded in who we are in relation to every other life-form. This universal Truth is symbolized by the identity of Christ, whose essence is within each self as the soul or creative energy of God. In this respect, Tolle wrote about the natural, inner connections between certain major religions:

"He [Jesus] speaks of the life that you are. Some Christian mystics have called it the Christ within; Buddhists call it your Buddha nature; for Hindus, it is Atman, the indwelling God. When you are in touch with that dimension within yourself—and being in touch with it is your natural state, not some miraculous achievement—all your actions and relationships will reflect the oneness with all life that you sense within. This is love." (9)

When we awaken to the spirit or Life-force that naturally dwells within the self, in all forms of life, we know the love of all ages, times and places. The 'sacred' or the 'divine' are not just words indicating a natural state of love within the self. What is referred to in the many religious traditions of the world as 'divinity' or the 'sacred' comes from the inner experience of love that we can naturally feel towards others in their myriad forms of life. And if we do not always feel this love or compassion towards all sentient beings is a challenge to our potential for fully awakening to whom we are and what Life is—a sacred trust and experience of the universal and creative Love.

It is difficult to identify the cause for the feeling of 'lack' or existential incompleteness that so many feel in everyday living, to just one factor or condition, but a measure of alienation can be attributed to the way we use and are used by our language or symbol system. Tolle makes the strong case that the pain-body and its negative energy field limit our present moment of experience, our openness to Life, and the total sense of self; and for sure, much of this is absolutely true. But conventional society and its promoters have devised all kinds of punitive means based upon fear and punishment for those who are 'cut off from the Truth that is within'. As Tolle wrote:

"Law, commandments, rules, and regulations are necessary for those who are cut off from who they are, the Truth within. They prevent the worst excesses of the ego, and often they don't even do that. 'Love and do what you will', said St. Augustine. Words cannot get much closer to the Truth than that." Indeed, they cannot; which is a good place to stop, meditate and experience the Love. (10)

Chuangzi: On Metaphorical Language

The following words were written 2400 years ago by the Chinese Taoist philosopher Chuangzi and they speak to a Perennial truth about language. Only a few names have been changed to protect the innocent.

"Of my sentences nine in ten are metaphorical; of my illustrations seven in ten are from valued writers. The rest of my words are like the water that daily fills the cup, tempered and harmonized by the Heavenly element in our nature.

"The nine sentences in ten which are metaphorical are borrowed from extraneous things to assist (the comprehension of) my argument. (When it is said, for instance), 'A father does not act the part of matchmaker for his own son,' (the meaning is that) 'it is better for another man to praise the son than for his father to do so.' The use of such metaphorical language is not my fault, but the fault of men (who would not otherwise readily understand me).

"Men assent to views which agree with their own, and oppose those which do not so agree. Those which agree with their own they hold to be right, and those which do not so agree they hold to be wrong. The seven out of ten illustrations taken from valued writers are designed to put an end to disputations. Those writers are the men of hoary elders, my predecessors in time. But such as are unversed. (11)

Language is metaphorical or a word is not the thing it points to. Chuangzi, Tolle, and writers and philosophers understand this fact about language all too well. At this level of awareness, everyone is aware of the difference between words and outer things; the question remains whether common awareness is connected inwardly, where yogic, neurological and psychological experiences occur. Once we learn to connect our words with what we say, experience and feel, then our more abstract and symbolic thought processes will become more spiritually meaningful. At that point only, we may begin to speak about the meaning of philosophy and life.

In sum, when our language dove-tails with our sense of Being, it becomes most truthful. Being present in the Now means becoming a symbol-using animal, at all levels of experience. When we learn to connect our sense of contingent, conditional, and relative being with absolute Being, then we are able to articulate that awareness coherently and vitally. When we awaken to the Perennial Wisdom we experience the Unity within all forms of Life, beginning and ending with the journey of the soul. And when we suffuse our awareness with the aesthetic immediacy of all that-is, we begin to experience the truth of the mystical Way in nature and life.

Chapter 9

SELF–KNOWLEDGE, ROLE–PLAYING AND

THE REAL WORLD

What are roles and how do we learn them? How can you transcend the role-playing that creates pain, suffering and dissatisfaction for yourself and others? What is your definition of the *real world* and how do you relate to it? And why is it important to play a role with love in your heart, compassion in your soul, and the certainty of self-knowledge?

"He who knows others is wise; / He who knows himself is enlightened." Tao Te Ching

"Origen says the soul's quest of God comes by self-observation. If she knew herself she would know God also." Meister Eckhart

"He who has exhausted all his mental constitution knows his nature. Knowing his nature, he knows heaven." Mencius

"You see reality in the transitory body because of ignorance. Remove this ignorance that veils true knowledge and know the Higher Self as pure, free, divine, and absolute." Sri Ramana Maharshi

"Jesus said: Whoever knows the All but fails to know himself lacks everything." The Gospel according to Thomas, log. 67

St. Thomas, one of the legendary disciples of Jesus, compiled his own Gospel of sayings from the living Jesus and before he moved to India. This saying about the central importance of the human self and the divine soul or essence within it, is typical of other *Gnostic Gospels*—none of which was selected by the early Church authorities for inclusion into the *New Testament*.

125

Of course, the Church did not want the Gnostic viewpoint to be known since it encouraged the followers of Christ to look within their own soul or self for divine guidance and not to a priest of the Church.

Among the sayings that St. Thomas allegedly wrote down from the living Jesus are the following: On death, Jesus was heard to say: "Have you discovered the beginning, that you look for the end? For where the beginning is, there will the end be. Blessed is he who will take his place in the beginning; he will know the end and will not experience death." #18

On knowing our origin and identity: "Jesus said. 'If they say to you, Where did you come from? Say to them, 'We came from the light, the place where the light came into being on its own accord and established itself and become manifest through their image. If they say to you, 'Is it you? Say to them, 'We are its children and we are the elect of the living. If they ask you, 'What is the sign of the living father in you? Say to them 'It is movement and repose.'" #50

Otherwise, the image of the ideal gnostic or mystic is a "solitary one" in the Thomas Gospel and the other Gnostic Gospels. To achieve salvation one must leave everything that binds one to this world. This is done by stripping away your roles and attachments to the world and passing by everything that is corrupted. (1)

Our Ancestral Past

The ego began to emerge from the mists of the distant past when our ancestors first developed a consciousness of their separateness from the physical environment and each other. The somewhat mythic 'undifferentiated unconsciousness' of primitive man began to differentiate itself, neurologically, from the surrounding universe through the growth of mind and the brain. Paralleling this interface between mind and nature, individual and cosmos, was the development of articulate speech and a communicable language. Then the dialectic of 'self and other', 'us and them', etc.—the existential hallmark of individual identity—became established in the agricultural, nomadic and tribal cultures of the world.

Today we are a long way in time—some 55,000 years—and technological development from the cultures of our initial beginnings as a small, nomadic band of adventurous individuals, out of Africa. However, similar genetic structures, physiological functions, and psychological tendencies have persisted for hundreds of thousands of years among human beings. Our neurological development— based upon unearthed skull sizes—was completed about 100, 000 years ago. Psychologically, there is similar evidence that our present instinctive, emotional and existential tendencies existed that long ago as well; and intellectually, the development of articulate speech probably paralleled the development of the present brain in its complexity and plasticity. (2)

Our evolutionary journey seems to be a remarkable species-specific story—especially if we knew all its chapters and verses; but our superior symbolic, abstractive and intellectual mind has come at an awful price to our moral or ethical potential. For one thing, the prior peace and harmony that our distant ancestors may have known in nature and with each other, in pre-historical communities, symbolized in the mythic Garden of Eden—has become a nightmare for the majority of the world's over seven billion people. In fact, owing to the alarming population growth rate, the global society and its many cultures are anything but a Garden of Eden for the majority of persons.

The Global Society: the Haves and Have-Nots

We are a global society of 'haves and have-nots', rich and poor, the few and the many, with a privileged middle class of wealthy individuals located between the extremes in the economic pyramid. About one-half of the world's population is extremely poor, earning about 1 to 2 dollars a day. And the rich and very rich (or those whose wealth and/or yearly income is measured in the hundreds of millions and even billions of US dollars) are inconceivably well-off and privileged, owning to the fact that over half of the world' s wealth is hoarded by less than 1% of the total population.

So where does this leave the rest of us—the great middle class of professional, educated, tax-paying, wage-earners? 'We' (the middle class) are a sizable group—perhaps two billion in all, and distributed like swarms of drone bees in many hives and in virtually every country of the world. Our numbers are more comfortable, secure and worry-free than the poor who do not usually have our rather oppressive expectations for financial or professional success. We do not have the option not to work for a living, as the rich do; but we are rarely in a given life-time, without adequate water, food, medicine, housing, and education; and we have the means to travel anywhere in the world and own a huge range of superfluous, unnecessary commodities –unlike the poor—that do not necessarily add anything to the quality and satisfaction of living.

Yes, we—from the lower middle class to upper middle class persons—are the 'wealthy' of the world, a highly privileged group of individuals who flourish in spite of, or sometimes because of, racial divisions, gender inequality, and social class warfare. Yes, we the comfortable, contented and secure who are often bored, stressed and over-worked in our so-called careers— are the worker bees, the drones for the Queens and Kings of the Capitalistic world who own, rent-out and manipulate politicians in all governments—no matter what they are called. Yes, we may even live in a voting democracy where we have the illusion of freedom, which means choosing from a list of candidates whom we neither know nor care to know, to make decisions about life and death in war-fare, health-care, education and the phony regulations of Banks, Corporations, the food system, transportation, education, etc.

And what is wealth? Can the wealth of mind, character, and wisdom ever be measured? Can we ever have 'enough' wealth in an economic system based upon debt, injustice and the scarcity of resources? And what hope is there to ever place limits upon income and wealth when selfishness, greed and indifference to the fate of others, are counted as necessary and admirable moral qualities? Indeed, how is anything resembling ethics or morality possible in a society where financial profit and money are more important than human life? (3)

In our Global Capitalism, Life as a universal reality does not really exist and is reduced to quantitative values and pragmatic goals. Social being or belonging is more important than an individual's inner subjectivity, meaning and purpose in Life.

In a collectivistic society, inner being ceases to exist as an experienced reality. Indeed, the value and meaning of existence is determined by an individual's ego-development, roles and success in society. One's background, experience, degrees earned at a university, profession, salary, possessions, and status in a meaningless pecking order, are among the extrinsic measures or 'biography' of a person's worth in a materialistic and competitive society such as our own.

Is it any wonder that existentially oriented philosophers have universally seen organized social life as a threat, humiliation, and degradation of individual life? Furthermore, the 'tragedy' of individual existence lies in the fact that no matter how heroic the journey, each individual remains alone and solitary within subjectivity, and experiences nature and the universe as contingent, conditional, and indifferent to his or her Presence. Yet in awakening to our inalienable free will, we realize our power to love, care, and cherish what is noblest, eternal, and sacred within the Self of all beings, regardless of circumstances and the accidents of Fate.

The Real World, Violence and Suffering

The psychological, social, and spiritual suffering that the hierarchical stratifications of humanity, i.e. the economic and social classes have caused are immeasurable; and whatever stress, conflict, and violence pre-historic humans endured, due to environmental threats, we cannot know for sure. Mythology and legend tells us that many of the most ancient stories in the oral and written traditions of history depict race, class, gender, religion, natural resources, and geography as reasons for slaughtering others by naming them the 'enemy'. So what, if anything, has significantly changed in over 100, 000 or even 10, 000 years of recorded history?

Are postmodern, 21st century humans merely putting on different masks and learning new roles to play the deadly game of civilization? Has anything significantly changed, within consciousness and the inner body where psychological, moral and intellectual transformations occur? Can we say that postmodern humans are closer to or farther from the experience of universal Consciousness? What are the answers?

First, our knowledge of the past or future is either in narrative or speculative form. The past is cloaked in the mists of memory and the future is shrouded in uncertainty, probability and possibility. We can only know the fullness of temporal reality—present past, the present moment, and the present future time—all from the viewpoint of evanescent Eternal Now. Speculative and the narrative imagination may be the basis for science fiction, ghost stories, and dystopias, but they cannot be the basis for awareness fully in the Now.

On the other hand, Presence or the full awareness of universal being is no guarantee that we will not exterminate ourselves as a species through the technological means readily at-hand. In former times, before the advent of modern warfare and gunpowder, men fought each other in hand-to-hand conflict and with physical strength. Now, modern warfare is fought with advanced technological means and an 'intelligence' of weaponry that is separated from morality. Thus, due to the presence of Weapons of Mass Destruction, i.e. thermonuclear, biological, and chemical, humankind is precariously suspended over an abyss of total annihilation.

Many if not most wars begin by accident, deranged leaders, and a sick population of people ready to fight to the death; yet it is almost impossible to say with certainty how the next war will begin. What seems absolutely certain is that another World War will end in total catastrophe if not annihilation for all sentient beings on the Earth. So if you care about the life-forms of the Earth, you will do everything in your power to prevent war of any kind and promote world peace and friendship between all people of the world.

Albeit, the end of civilization as we know it, as dramatized in many current images of the future, portray either a step backward to survivalist or Neolithic conditions or a leap forward through great technological, moral, and political changes to another Garden of Eden on Earth. Perhaps the only thing that we can know for sure about the future is its uncertainty. Otherwise, there will be war and peace, hope and despair, conflict and compromise, disaster and breakthrough, etc. And most humans will continue play unconsciously acquired roles which limit their freedom of thought, feeling and action.

Whether present nations will be drawn into a thermonuclear war that could destroy human life and other species altogether, on Earth, is unknowable but it is a distinct and ready-at-hand possibility. The technological means, the moral incapacities, and the political follies are real enough for Armageddon to occur, at any time. The complexly interrelated problems of post-modern civilization have been fairly short in the making, compared with the age of the species and the age of life on Earth, but they may be longer in the re-solving.

What has been left out of the story of civilization is the power of *The People*. The lack of informed decisions on the part of the majority in many areas of social and civic existence is not the fault of native intelligence or natural endowment; rather it is due to the lack of adequate information and education. Totalitarian governments remain tyrannical by denying the rights of its citizens like the right to know the truth, the right to assemble for whatever reason, and the right to criticize leaders and protest official policies.

The People are the Perennial threat to all oppressive and tyrannical regimes. Their Presence in society embodies universal Goodness and a constant threat to the prevailing political and social power; and this why all totalitarian governments must maintain large military and policing forces. Increasingly, in the electronically ordered world, every organization, institution and government, also maintains a large surveillance net to gather information about its members, to maintain control and power.

The People, Yes!—the unknown, nameless masses of people who are born, live and die in obscurity and never become famous, rich, or wise, are the real basis for a better future and even the best possible, most ideal one. It is so obviously true that the so-called leaders and governments of the world have mostly failed *The People,* their promises and possibilities, their potentialities and proven capacities. But just consider what The People have had to endure at the hands of their homicidal and morally corrupt leaders in the last century.

One of the most American of American poets is Carl Sandburg. His long, epic poem, The People, Yes, ends in section 107: "The people will live on. The learning and blundering *people* will live on. They will be tricked and sold and again sold and go back to the nourishing earth for rootholds, the people so peculiar for renewal and comeback. You can't laugh off their capacity to take it....I earn my living I make enough to get by and it takes all my time I could do more for myself and maybe for others. I could read and study and talk things over and find out about things. It takes time I wish I had the time....Beyond the finite limitations of the five senses and the endless yearnings of man for the beyond the people hold to the humdrum bidding of work and food while reaching out when it comes their way for lights beyond the prism of the five senses, for keepsakes lasting beyond any hunger or death...." (4)

It is a great celebration of humanity, the working class people, yet the poem towers above any class, racial or gender distinctions: "The people is Everyman, everybody. Everybody is you and me and all others. What everybody says is what we all say. And what it is we all say? In the darkness with a great bundle of grief the people march. In the night and overhead a shovel of stars for keeps, the people march: Where to? What next?" The poem connects with the essence of humankind, the soul of Being, everyday life, time and change. (5)

Just one hundred years ago, human civilization topped two billion people and seemed full of promise, energy, and optimism. And then in 1914, and again in 1941, a World War began that caused the deaths of over one hundred million men, women, and children, and there have been a long list of other lesser wars and genocides ever since 1945. Just how many people in history have been killed, injured, and suffered from the loss of physical, mental, and psychological functions due to human warfare, is unknown and perhaps unknowable. Thus, there are innumerable popular songs, poems, and stories that lament the waste, futility, and insanity of war and war-making and ask plaintively "when will they ever learn?"

Preventing violence by nurturing love, peace, and justice in the world should be a moral, political, and educational priority—Now. We cannot wait until the next war or group of war criminals take control of the seats of political power or merely report on the grisly statistics of past wars and genocides. A 'possible future' must begin in the present moment of time or it will not begin at all. If we have a vision about what is best, what will bring a maximum degree of happiness, liberty, and Life, to all sentient beings, then the vision must begin Now.

Only then do we, *The People*, have the chance to bring the eternal Light of Goodness and Nonviolence fully to the Earth.

Roles People Play: Strategies and Tactics of the Ego

Tolle is quite clear about the lack of awareness among people who are merely role-playing. He states, early on in his major chapter on the subject, "Usually people are completely unaware of the roles they play. They are those roles. Some roles are subtle; others are blatantly obvious, except to the person playing it." (6)

Unfortunately, the typical role-player is not aware of the difference between learning to play a role and the higher, deeper, inner Self. The awareness that is possible about all

133

relationships begins when a person decides to cease role-playing, ego-posturing, and mind-games, and decides upon a different approach to living, i.e. one grounded in the awareness of Life. When role-playing is genuinely playful, freeing, and creative, it is not destructive of our potentiality for Being or the experience of Life. However, when role-playing becomes the person and identifying with a social role eclipses one's feelings, spontaneity, and joy in just being, then 'role-playing' is merely a source of pain and suffering, sickness and dread—without relief.

At the root of Tolle's insight about the 'faces of the ego' is a "conceptual sense of self—seeing myself as this or that—the ego, whether predominately positive (I am the greatest) or negative (I am no good). Behind every positive self-concept is the hidden fear of not being good enough. Behind every negative self-concept is the hidden desire of being the greatest or better than others....All you need to know and observe in yourself is this: Whenever you feel superior or inferior to anyone, that's the ego in you." (7)

Nothing really good has come from the experience of the ego in human beings—only pain, suffering, and violence. It is easily the most destructive, distorting, and violent neuro-psychological development in the species at an individual level of being. This may occur early on in the typical individual who begins to play the roles of 'villain, victim, or lover'. And the boundary between a core sense of self and role more often than not gets completely blurred over from identifying with the role over time and through the constant struggle and suffering to, paradoxically, maintain the role.

Children instinctively strive for attention from others, to be assured that they matter, and if they cannot get praise or admiration, then they will seek to elicit blame or condemnation, thus confirming the existence of their separate ego or the energy of the pain-body that is the neurological residue of previous negativity, pain, and suffering. And there appears to be no level of ordinary existence that is entirely free of ego-development and the pain-body—except one, that of spontaneous and joyful being-in the here-and-now of sensory experience.

Humanism, Consumption and Emptiness

If one is to find fulfillment through a societal role, it can only be done with an attitude of humanity, compassion, and love. Humanism is one of the least known philosophies of culture because it does not serve the technocratic, bureaucratic, and alienating relationships of society. Whereas humanism promotes closeness, friendship, and intimacy in relationships, the prevailing ideology of Capitalism, i.e. its crass, materialist and technocratic pragmatism, promote and sustain relationships of distance, role-playing *personas*, and a lack of genuine trust and openness in its relationships.

There is, in fact, a systemic, prevailing fear of the *unknown* in contemporary society. The life-insurance companies, home-security companies, and other enterprises that specialize in security and surveillance devices are playing upon the nameless fear and anxiety that feeds the pain-body and sickens society. At the base of society is the illusion of ownership that Capitalism has essentially fostered; and at the base of this illusion is the fear of death and non-being or the Emptiness of life forms and the desire to fill the formless realm of Being with more of anything that has a form!— In the literature of existentialism, it is called ontological insecurity.

The emptiness of forms is not a problem to be solved and even if it is perceived as a problem and it is certainly not one that we can solve. Life is a divine Presence and it should be enjoyed as a human being is here to be experienced, enjoyed, and sustained—if desirable, pleasurable, and happy. To a person who is enjoying Life or at least struggling with a measure of satisfaction, suicide is never a serious or desirable option. In fact, the so-called emptiness or formlessness of existence need not be an occasion for depressing or despairing thoughts at all, since ordinary existence embodies Presence or the invisible individual soul and the hidden ground of universal Being.

Capitalism promotes and thrives on the consumption of 'things' of all kinds; but consumerism is a futile philosophy of life since we can never 'fill' the Emptiness of existence. The best we can ever do with the consumption of the things, artifacts, and forms of society is to meet our most basic needs. Desire and 'wanting' are virtually infinite; and living a life of desiring and wanting merely grows a 'pain-body' or one that can never find lasting satisfaction, peace, and the meeting of real needs.

There are more healthy, Life-giving, and harmonious ways of dealing with the emptiness of Being and its essential formlessness than through ownership, greed, and the quest for 'more'. For starters, we could recognize and realize the Life-sustaining energy of our own sense of Being that is essentially formless and eternal. Our relationship to essential Being—or the Being of universal Life—is infinitely more permanent and sustaining than anything that we can find in contingent, conditional, and relative existence.

Humanism, as it has been historically articulated, is not an entirely viable philosophy of Life—unless it embraces non-human beings, *Nature* or the physical, biological, and ecological environment, of universal Being. 'Eco-sophism' is another, deeper approach to the natural world which combines ancient spiritual Wisdom (*Sophia*), as found in the world religions, with modern scientific Ecology. Whatever configuration of humanism may be found and there are many—even its 'unenlightened', technocratic or one-sided forms—is clearly a better alternative to the present nature-destroying, anti-humanistic, 'bottom-line' mentality of Global Capitalism.

If philosophical humanism embraces the fundamental conditions of nature, society and Being as well as the existential fact of Emptiness and Formlessness at the heart of Being, then its usefulness in the Now can be realized. Such a form of humanism could be called an 'Enlightened Humanism'. If humanism fails to find its place in universal being and sacred Nature, then the one-sided, subjective, and idealist concepts will only be one more occasion for philosophical illusion-making. And the historical landscape of philosophy is strewn with the carcasses of idealism.

Illusions of Love and War

The common, romantic experience of 'falling-in-love' is a special insanity of the ego, its selfish wants and needs. The person who falls in love with another typically loses all consciousness of self as separate from the other, and narcissistically and erotically merges with the other—whether male or female. The typical thoughts are that 'I cannot live with the other' or 'he or she fulfills my needs completely' or 'I could never be happy with anyone else' and so forth. In romantic love, roles appear to collapse and lovers appear to go beyond the normal rules or even taboos of society, but it is only an illusion that deceives lovers who are blinded by their lustful passions.

Romantic love is a false and spurious form of love between persons. Genuine or authentic love comes from self-knowledge on both sides of a relationship, knowledge that has tested by time, experience and the real world. Young people who 'fall-in-love' really fall into a form of insanity, a loss of reason in exchange for lust and erotic passion, and from a lack of self-awareness and maturity—which is to say experience. Falling in love in the greenness of youth may make for a good Hollywood script but it does not usually work in the real world. And it is not unlike the romantic haze of patriotism that young men and women feel upon entering military service for the first time.

Rather than finding genuine love or the inclusive experience of Life, romantic lovers only find exclusion and the separation from a greater sense of humanity. Lovers typically drown in the illusory and exclusive attention of the other and lose all sense of inclusive being. Such intoxicating, lust-driven experiences are formed from extremes states of attachment and possessiveness—a tragedy that has been played out in many versions of Romeo and Juliet. Most often romantic love—besides ending in heartbreak and bitter sadness—narcissistically confuses self with the other and projects the deepest feelings of fear, uncertainty, and anxiety upon the idealized 'other'.

'You' or your very consciousness as a separate self becomes the role of being a marine, soldier, flier, or naval personnel. Similarly, the difference between male and female, black or white, rich or poor, etc. is erased by the brain-washing of Basic Training techniques in the military; and so is your sense of being an individual person. Furthermore, 'you' become the fighting unit of a group force since everyone is utterly dependent on the other for safety in battle situations. (8)

The lust, aggression, and hormonal energy that go into romantic love and passion are similar for those who enter and commit to military life. Such persons 'become' their roles or else they cannot really make it as full-time soldiers. The same hormonal excitement, lust, and intensity of passion experienced between lovers in love-making is often experienced among soldiers, embedded reporters in battle-field situations, and others even less directly connected with war and war-making.

In fact, there is a gigantic cultural apparatus which President Eisenhower named the "Industrial Military Complex" and warned against (to no avail) that has driven the military spending up to approximately 60% of the entire federal budget since his time in office. Supporting this lavish military budget and feeding off its gigantic war-making machine that the federal government and the tax payers unwittingly make possible are the mass media and its war reporters, the writers of war books, producers of war movies and documentaries and the whole sick ethos of super-Patriotism.

The lust of fighting and the desire to win and defeat the unknown enemy, i.e. death and nonbeing, are not just collateral to war-making, but it a direct motivation and unconscious instinct that drives nearly every soldier in the heat of battle. The complexity of the external causes and conditions are, of course, unique to every war, but it is no exaggeration that war represents the tragic collapse of civilization into chaos, violence and the collective pain-body. And as it has been said by many, 'if you love war then you love slaughter' since this is what war descends to after all the war-hype by the mass media and politicians who send the youth of every generation to their destruction.

Being realistic rather than 'romantic' about war and war-making does not really help the general cause of humanity—at least very much. The only 'solution' is to get ride of the pain-body that wants to fight, kill, and destroy. Each and every individual being must be cleansed or purified of the toxic energy, the sickness of the pain-body. If this could be completely or collectively accomplished, then there would be no more wars, and a great Peace would descend upon the Earth. At least this is the perennial hope of pacifists, idealists and anti-war activists of every generation, who may be a growing minority.

A world without war would be the truest and best possible basis for a more perfect and ideal world. This possibility would represent a true breakthrough or quantum jump in the transformation of human consciousness. Suffice it to say, every transformation in the evolution of consciousness begins with one person at a time.

Finally, the energy field of universal being that is radiating Goodness, Peace, and Love exists within each of us. We each have the power to begin the world all over again and bring it to its most supreme perfection.

Toxic Roles and Healing Goodness

Roles are the masks of the ego since they cover up the inner, deep reality of pain that is the basis for the ego. To desire admiration or condemnation are equally neurotic and sick motives in individuals since they are both based upon feelings of inadequacy and contempt for the other. Dis-identifying or giving up attachment to a role is a way to free Consciousness and self from the ego, its anxiety, pain, and fear.

Since we are talking about toxic roles or those that feed the pain-body, there are also healthy and even healing roles and situations that can help you get over negative patterns of the ego and mind. For example, any situation or activity that gives you genuine joy or where you feel as if you are really helping and serving others, are ones that can help you get rid of a role that brings you pain and suffering.

Ego-striving is the effort required to maintain the pain-body that is already established—from birth on—and to feed it with more attention from others. It is a vicious circle that we can never recover from unless and until we realize what we are doing and dis-identify from the ego, its roles and strivings for attention or recognition. It is entirely possible to 'rise above' ego-striving but we must not be deceived about the task or difficulty the energy of the pain-body has deeply and complexly established in the pathways of the emotional, social, and intellectual synapses of the brain and the entire nervous system.

There are many people in the developed countries of the world who have experienced the painful collapse of a marriage and the loss of a family unit. Most people get over such a loss but only after desperate efforts to heal the wounds through inadequate relationships and involvements. It sounds trite but it is true that time is a great healer of many kinds of losses but none can be so great as children who are lost in a divorce, whether you are the father or mother. Such loses or failures are sources of pain and suffering that keep the pain-body alive in us and prevent full, healthy functioning in the Now. But witnessing the pain-body through higher Consciousness and the loving Self of forgiveness is supremely healing.

The challenge of overcoming the ego is more like a deconstruction of unwanted growth and digging its cancerous roots out of the body. Of course we are speaking metaphorically, but the experiences of shame or pride, fear or hate, resentment or jealousy, etc. are neurologically and psychologically real due to the accumulation of negative energy within an individual. Tolle observes, that it is 'only rare beings' like Socrates, Buddha, Jesus, or Confucius, who saw the destructive influence of social differences based upon class, race, or gender, and became aware of the innate Goodness within each human being which can heal the wounds from an alienating and violent society where such discriminations are rampant. (9)

Self-Knowledge: Authentic Being

One sage after another has warned against doing anything without self-knowledge. In the real world, people are generally in such a hurry to do things, complete their education, start a career, and even relate to one another, that they leave no time for themselves. In individual existence, all we ever have is time and there is nothing more precious, in permanent scarcity and wasted, as time. Once we begin to do something, there is never any turning back or changing our mind; there are only twists, turns and detours in our way of life, much like the city roadways that we travel.

Self-knowledge is the knowledge of your total Being—your body, soul and mind; and in seeing how you are, through self-observation, reflection and feeling, in relation to the real world—the worlds of other people, their worlds and the wider society become ever more clear, understandable and real. From a spiritual viewpoint, when you know who you are, you know God, the God or Being who is here-and-now, in the Eternal Now. Such knowledge puts you on a higher, more pure and ineffable plane of existence that is within the deepest part of the self. And everyone possesses this potentiality, this innate treasure of awareness as a human being.

Self-knowledge is really the only sure basis for your life since everything in the real world is constantly changing, uncertain and beyond your control. When you know yourself you are aware of how you are responding to the world at this moment, without illusions, expectations and worries since there is absolutely nothing you can do to *really change* the way things are. At least two facts of existence are well-known: we have a free will but we will also die someday and there is nothing we can do to prevent it from happening. And no matter how rich, famous or intelligent you are, nothing can be done.

If individual existence has an ultimate meaning and ending, then we can be saved from the certainty of catastrophe—the catastrophe of death. An immortal life-form, even an eternal life-form is a distinct possibility to those with an open mind and heart. The belief in an individuated, perfect and eternal *soul* of divine origin is the existential basis for all world religions and the soul is the basis for ultimate meaning, purpose and Truth. At the same time, the soul and the free-will to which it is intimately linked is the key to authentic choosing, living and being-in-the-real-world. The soul is simply the missing link to a spiritual Life, a life-form that is ultimate and liberating.

PART III

AWAKENING TO EDUCATION, THE LIFE-FORCE

AND THE PAIN-BODY

Being refers to everything in the manifested and unmanifested realms of Consciousness; and Consciousness is the nebulous Presence of God or the image that we have of an 'infinitely perfect Being'. That said, ordinary human awareness is profoundly ignorant of infinity, eternity and Being and cannot see beyond the senses, emotions and thoughts of the mind, ego and self. Only the pure soul of the inner body is eternal and has the power to see the Truth about existence as essence, the Life-force of Being.

Meanwhile, education is the growth and development, the evolution of each person, learning the truth about existence, self and the Life-force; and it is awakening to the existential conditions of negativity, moral corruption and violence, as the pain-body that blocks the evolution of Love and the unfolding of Truth in the eternal Now.

The pain-body is the consequence of karma (causality) or the essential remains of the past— the violence, corruption and negativity of this and any other life-time; and the pain-body is the product of karma in the present moment blocking the creative, life-affirming potentiality of a person or the unity of body, mind and soul. The pain-body exists inwardly as an oppressive weight, a darkness and fatalistic attitude about what is possible or the potential of liberated human beings to discover the many truths about universe.

145

Once we awaken to the Truth, the One Absolute Truth about existence, then the many lesser truths about nature, the human self, society and the vast universe can be more easily experienced and known. Once we awaken to just the Truth about our own self, then we can begin to know the truths about everything else. And once we awaken to what we think we know, we will then discover how little we really know or understand and how much more there is to experience and know.

Chapter 10
LIFE, EDUCATION AND LOVE

What is universal Life in relation to life-forms? Are essence and existence unified through the energy fields of the life-forms? Is universal energy (*chi* in Chinese, *prana* in Sanskrit and *pneuma* in Latin) the same as the power of universal Love or something different? And what kind of education is important to the process of awakening to self-knowledge, altruism, universal Love and Compassion?

"Certain professors of education must be wrong when they say that they can put a knowledge into the soul which was not there before, like sight into blind eyes.... Whereas, our argument shows that the power and capacity of learning exists in the soul already." Plato (*Republic,* book VII)

"Music expresses the harmony of te universe, while rituals express the order of the universe. Through harmony all things are influenced, and through order all things have a proper place. Music rises from heaven while rituals are patterned on the earth. To go beyond these patterns would result in violence and disorder. In order to have the proper rituals and music, we must understand the principles of Heaven and Earth." Confucius

"Stop talking, stop thinking, and there is nothing you will not understand. / Return to the Root and you will find the Meaning; / Pursue the Light, and you will lose its source.... / There is no need to seek Truth; only stop having views." Seng-ts'an

"Equality is by nature prior to inequality.... It is also naturally prior to diversity; Equality, it must be concluded is eternal." Nicolas of Cusa

"Cherish that which is within you, and shut off that which is without; for too much learning is a curse." Chuang-tzu

What all of the above quotations are saying, from somewhat different perspectives, is that real knowledge, Truth and equality of things, is prior to what we are taught, acquire, speak or even think about. For example, Plato's view of the soul is that it possesses knowledge of the Truth prior to coming into the body from its journey through the heavenly realm; Confucius makes reference to the Taoist Heaven in talking about harmony; Nicolas of Cusa speaks about equality as eternal and not the inequality of diversity; and Chuang-tzu and Seng-ts'an speak about the curse or illusion of learned viewpoints. The implication for Socrates and Plato (at least) is an educational process that begins within the self of the learner and causes or inspires him or her to remember what was learned prior to the earthly embodiment of the divine soul. (1)

The Unity of Essence and Existence

How does essence differ from existence? Is essence prior to existence or vice versa? Essence is neither prior to existence nor is existence prior to essence since they both arise simultaneously within the Being or totality of each person.

The human actualization of Life is a dynamic given in the Now which has continually evolved since its initial conception in the womb. Although existence and essence are inextricably linked, like yin and yang, existence is finite while essence is infinite; existence and essence are necessarily related since they embody the finite and infinite, subjective and objective, and the material and spiritual qualities of universal Life.

Being is not a category, concept, or idea since it exists as an infinite totality whereas our concepts and ideas are all finite or limited. No one can really say what Being is or is not since it symbolizes everything that eternally and infinitely exists in manifested and unmanifested realms that we can only understand in finite and rational ways. Life is like the idea of 'God' but unlike most historical images of God, universal Life is more than the totality of known forms of reality.

The visible and the invisible, the known and unknown, the finite and the infinite, the personal and the impersonal—all these categorical distinctions have been traditionally used to refer to 'God'; but Being, Life and Compassion exceed everything categorical as the eternal Mystery. The really fascinating realization is that every human being—no matter how rich or poor, famous or infamous, wise or ignorant—embodies an infinitesimal portion of the Mystery. At the same time, 'existence' is the known or experienced totality of Being while 'essence' is the potentiality of who you are, that is continuously in self-creation.

The Only Dance There Is—the title of a classic mystical text by the American guru Ram Dass—symbolizes the dynamic and creative 'dance' of the Indian Goddess *Lila* or Being itself. It is the entire known and unknown universe doing its thing and asking us to join in as best we can, for this one life-form and life-time, and for the sake of any others preceding and succeeding this one. No one can know what the absolute truth 'is' except to say that it exists as the Mystery of everything, eternally symbolizes by Being or the creative energy of cosmic transformation in every life-form, in the here-and-now. (2)

Essence is usually thought to be your innermost Self or higher Consciousness; and this is certainly true as far it goes. But it can also be found outwardly in nature, other people, and the world. The whole subject of inner and outer being can only be adequately clarified through the structure and function of the body and the spectrum of consciousness. We exist as unique beings or persons existing both inwardly and outwardly simultaneously. It is never a question of the dualistic either/or when it comes to understanding and appreciating our real essential being. In other words, outer being or the body and the contingent, thingy world imply the Presence of inner being, i.e. mind, Consciousness, and the Self. And connecting both dimensions of being is the eternal soul or most sacred essence of the Life-force— the eternal, creative energy of each living organism.

The most momentous reality about universal Life—following its Presence in the moment of Now—are its manifested connections at subatomic, molecular, animal, human, and cosmic levels. Each of us is caught in a gigantic web of connections, influences, and radiances from and through unitary Being—just as we exist in the present moment. We really do not have to do, know, feel, imagine, remember, or believe anything—but only learn to give up egoic striving and surrender to sacred Presence, in the Here-and-Now, to see, feel, and experience the cosmic Radiance of Being or all that exists in the forms of the creative Life-force.

Thinking, Feeling and Living in Society

Academic intellectuals are typically obsessed with making an intellectual problem or argument out of everything. They love their ideas, concepts, and words, especially the words of the cloistered intellect and not those of main-street or the market place. They are also strongly identified with the academic discipline for which they have been 'trained' and hired to teach. The strong identification with the role of teaching and the necessary intellectual content that goes with teaching are all the ingredients needed for strong ego-development, intellectual obsessiveness and massively supported by the local bureaucracy.

Thinking without feeling or passion is a disease of the mind fostered by formal education. If your education does not liberate you from the tyranny of the mind—after you see its many intellectual games—it is not doing anything very worthwhile for you. In fact, higher education—even in the name of 'liberal education'—can have a destructive and poisoning influence in a young person's life if it is wrongly or inhumanely delivered by teachers. The same thing can also happen in any of the professional 'training' programs too, like law, business, education, medicine, the sciences, the humanities, etc. We have all been conditioned to take ourselves too seriously in the 'business' of education, and made to think that only we are doing something of supreme importance in society. The truth is that there are many other institutions in society that are at least as important—if not more important—to the multifarious structure and functioning of society.

For example, how could we have enough food to eat if there were not a vast network and unseen chain of workers, immigrants, growers, suppliers, distributors, and marketers who make up our food supply system? Or how could any of us use all the electrical gadgets and systems in our homes, i.e. computers, televisions, radios, refrigerators, toasters, dishwashers, stoves, lighting, heating, plumbing, etc. without those who work in the energy supply system of the country? Or for that matter, the vast fossil fuel energy system that supplies our cars, trains, planes, factories, and homes with the fuel and energy that we require. In other words, we take for granted the many natural, mechanical, structural, and bureaucratic systems of society that we continuously use in daily life; and they are all a vital and necessary part of the same sacred Universe that is linked to the mystery and wonder of daily living.

However, abstract thinking separated from feeling, perception, and action often leaves personal existence and Being out of consideration. It is an old story or one that gets repeated generation after generation by those who are obsessed with egoic needs, career roles, and consumption. Living fully in the material world requires an attitude of non-attachment if one is to live authentically or in attunement with the free will and essential Goodness of the self. The wisdom of Yoga philosophy rooted in thousands of meditative practice is aimed at the controlling the body, ego and everyday desires so that the nonviolent Consciousness of the inwardly existing, Higher Self can be known and experienced.

Since I have been employed in the higher educational system for most of my adult life, I have had to adapt to the role of teaching, for the purpose of teaching undergraduate philosophy. The humanistic reality of my role involves college age persons whom I have committed to serve or help. And if I ceased to believe in the value of formal philosophy, or I felt that I could no longer adequately serve students, for whatever reason, and then I owed it to myself and them to move on, turn the page, and retire.

In about 2013, this is what I decided to do in the following year, after a sabbatical leave. My intention during the sabbatical was to publish, by more public means, several books that were in rough, unedited form. It was a modest goal but one that I am grateful to the University for granting the time to actualize. That said, I also spent my time, with another part of my mind, reflecting on what I would do about teaching those last two semesters that were required of me when I returned. But what I did not expect was a surprise offer from the university system of Massachusetts to persons on sabbatical leave to retire with no obligation to teach! I went for it almost at once but did not anticipate how deeply I had become emotionally attached to my institutional role!

Teaching for over four decades has given me plenty of time to see human differences and societal change. I have had few if any illusions about my power to help or serve others in my role as a philosophy teacher. Moving ever closer to retirement has given me the motivation to reflect on the rather de-humanized bureaucracy of higher education. Whether the wisdom that can follow greater experience and knowledge is an adequate substitute for the enthusiasm and energy of youth in teaching or any other occupation is not a question I can easily answer, at the present moment. Perhaps later, post-retirement, if I am lucky, I will see and understand more about the role that I have been playing all these years.

However, I do know now with more clarity than ever what seems to be most worthwhile in Life, independently of time, place, and self. In the naive clarity of my youth, I believed that I had seen eternal truths of a Platonic kind in a heavenly realm, and that they only needed a little effort for their further development and actualization. Perhaps nothing is as vulnerable to external influence, suggestion and self-delusion as an uninformed mind—at any age.

Being in possession of a good crap-detector is the basis for all critical thinking and philosophy. But learning how to question, seeing through words to their concrete referents, and using concepts or ideas clearly is only the technical beginning of philosophy and real thinking. If we are really thinking, we are always thinking about universal Being or what-is. This was the view of Martin Heidegger, the 20th century Existentialist, who traced this idea back to Parmenides of ancient Greece; and Heidegger wrote extensively about it in criticism of modern philosophers who had 'forgotten' Being or what is universal in our lives.

If Being, God or similar metaphysical terms are imagined to be separated from the real world, then the world of action, things and persons become alienating and meaningless. At the same time, I have never shied away from using such terms; in fact I have been rather drawn to them, owing to my later mysticism and early Catholic faith. However, the more dominant side of my brain is definitely more pragmatic and existential in that I like to be active and involved in the real world and not just spend my time reading books or even writing them.

In my youth or teens, nothing seemed more real to me than my sexual passions. But I now realize, decades later, that it was only the trickery of Nature that made it so. The birds and the bees, the livestock of the barnyard, and every beast of the field and valley, differ little from human beings in this respect. But it was a wonderful, exciting, but often traumatic period in my own life that was dominated by the sexual drive (all for the sake of procreation) and that society romanticizes in song, story and film. And there is no need to wonder much what would become of *Homo sapiens* if this drive suddenly disappeared, as it naturally does in older people.

Nature, in her infinite wisdom and control, draws the outlines of our lives, from beginning to ending while we merely fill in the smaller details, choosing and acting from various inner promptings. Most of us may hardly know why or how or what we do once we have chosen a certain career path, a special companion, and a place to live. Even our individual choices are greatly conditioned by outside forces contingent upon our place, time and direction in existence and over which we always have much less than complete control; yet it is the intangible, vital center of subjective being, surrounding our essence or soul, that give us the feeling of really being alive and in control of our destiny.

The clear advantages of youth are too quickly over-ruled by the conditions, rules, and expectations of the adult world. Most young people live closer to the visceral, affective and primal sources of their original self than older persons. However, their feelings, instincts, urges, desires, and wishes often create an ocean of inner turmoil that drowns out the caution and prudence of older persons. But neither maturity nor age guarantees wisdom or a clear understanding of worldly truth since maturity or growing up is often interpreted in terms of a sick, unjust and corrupted society.

Some year ago, one of my colleagues in the Philosophy department confessed to me—after some 40 years of teaching—that he no longer believed in the worthwhileness of the entire intellectual approach in education and especially in philosophy. But it took an entire book to explain what he meant which is why he published his study on the Catholic Theology of Gabriel Marcel before he retired. He had longed throughout his career to find students who were committed to the Catholic faith at the depth he experienced, intellectually understood and genuinely identified with; but his dream was never realized at a secular, State University where the vast majority of students were variously indifferent, non-religious and even hostile to religion of any kind. However, in the defense of students, most undergraduates will admit to *spirituality* even though it is ill-defined.

Individual engagement, human dialogue, and real community life is too rarely found on a college or university campus although there is more chance of finding it at the smaller colleges. Abstract thinking of an intellectual kind is wonderful when it happens in a classroom or elsewhere on campus; but far too much time and effort is given to verbal or intellectual teaching by teachers and not enough time is given to the learning process, from the viewpoints of students.

Time out is needed for feeling, insight and passion to arise for any significant learning to occur. Feeling is more real in experience since it ignites a greater area of the brain and becomes the basis for our ethics or judgments about right and wrong, good and evil, desirable and undesirable action. And for these and other reasons, I have been deeply drawn to existential philosophy and psychology.

The complexity of existence, the limits of human reason and language, and the shortness of Life in our present form, make the activities of reading, writing, and thinking about big ideas and questions a satisfying but incomplete existence. I have known several monks and mystics in my life-time and their solution to the melodrama of living in society is to drop-out; and this is certainly one option in living. But another one is to stay in the game and accept the challenge for as long as you can, and try your best to make a difference and even better than as you found them.

Meditating: Awakening to Inner Being

Most of my life has been a struggle between these two paths in Life, the mystical and the pragmatic, and the challenge is to find the balance between these conflicting tendencies or that still point of meditative tranquility and equanimity known to meditators around the world. Sitting for hours, days and weeks in continuous meditation can often bring a tremendous renewal to meditators; but it is the transition to the real, social world and the roles that people choose and which choose them, paradoxically, that can undue months of meditative practice.

A really disciplined, integrated and grounded person however does not fall back on old, corrupting habits of mind, body and soul after a period of renewal. Therefore, it is mistake to think that you cannot survive as a creative person in the so-called real world. The effect or result of any period of inner experiencing of the self is always determined by the readiness of the meditator or learner to internalize the experience and make it an integral part of his or her identity.

Internalizing what exists in the outer world or newly present to you is another way of talking about learning, growth and education. Internalization is not the same thing as identification with or mistaking what or who you are not—in your innermost self. Identification is a dangerous and even life-threatening pattern in society that worships, romanticizes and makes heroes and demi-gods out of every kind of celebrity, entertainer or authority figure.

Education, as presently conducted, is unbalanced in the teacher-student relationship. It is all teacher-centered and teacher controlled with the bureaucracy supporting this relationship completely. If education is to become learning based, it will have to give greater control to the student. Most importantly for the meditative experience which requires self-discipline and self-responsibility, the emphasis must be upon the inward concentration of attention; and this attitude or orientation is foreign to most students who are taught to obey the authority figure or the teacher from the first day at school.

The experience of living in the here-and-now or the timeless and formless center of everything is a passionate involvement. Perhaps insight or seeing within the self comes closest to expressing the experience of really being present in a state of silence and stillness—the signs that meditation has begun. *Seeing* is most obviously an ineffable or aesthetic state since the body seems to defy the law of gravity at times. When you experience the stillness, silence, and peacefulness of that naturally exists, you may then realize something absolute within the self— like the moon that suddenly breaks free of passing, dark clouds.

Whether you have the experience of meditative seeing in an educational setting, a yoga retreat or the familiar surroundings of your home— there is no difference since meditative education is learning to live in the real world. If there is one tried and true way to get rid of toxic roles, thoughts, and feelings—no matter how or when they were acquired, it is this: find a place where you can experience yourself in solitude since you need time to be apart from others and make a connection with your original or primordial self.

Sit in a chair or on a firm cushion for the floor. Close your eyes gently and follow your breath that is moving in and out of your body. If any form, memory, sensation or image appears in your field of awareness, notice it and then let it disappear from your consciousness. Just watch your breathing without any analysis or judgment about it. And whatever form or sensation that may arise in the stillness of your body and the quiet of your mind, learn to let it go from awareness by watching it dissolve and disappear from consciousness.

When you can sit quietly with the minimum of movement, with a steady, concentrated and empty mind, and watch your thoughts and feelings without judging or analyzing them until they slowly dissolve in the light of Consciousness and the soul, you are beginning to purify your total being. In the non-action of meditating, you can dissolve and disappear toxic, poisonous, and negative states of Being that have infiltrated the self over time. And eventually, imperceptibly, higher, healthy and creative Consciousness replaces unconsciousness, negativity and ego-states.

No matter what your age or situation in life, you have an infinite potentiality for healing yourself of unwanted memories, attachments, and negativity that is the basis of the *pain-body*. As we shall see in Chapter 12, "The Pain-Body" everyone drags around with them a corpse-like entity that can suddenly spring to life when conditions favor its appearance—the remnants of a past-time or life that refuses to die a natural death. And if any of your life-experiences have been negative, painful and toxic— and whose have not?—there is this easy way to get rid of the corruption: go within the self through the gentle, nonviolent and purifying activity of *meditative seeing*.

The Buddhist View of Death and Re-birth

It seems that nearly everyone wants to believe that death is not the absolute end of a life-form and that there really is a universal Life-force that ensures some kind of immortality. The Buddhist monk, Thich Nhat Hann, wrote a book, "No death, No fear" in which he quotes from one of the most well-known *Sutras* of the historical Buddha: "There is no birth, there is no death; there is no coming, there is no going; there is no same, there is no difference; there is no permanent self, there is no annihilation. We only think there is." (3)

If you understand that Thich Nhat Hann is arguing from an absolutely *monistic* ('reality' is conceived as an undifferentiated oneness) tradition within Buddhist philosophy, linked with the assumption that 'thinking' distorts our view of reality, then you may be able to understand the statement a little better. But no matter how you approach the Buddhist view of Being or reality in general, you will end up with paradox, ambiguity and absurdity—on a rational level; the point being that we cannot really understand what is ultimately true, real or even good in ordinary existence since it is subject to one's perspective and interpretation, all of which is constantly changing!

"When we understand that we cannot be destroyed, we are liberated from fear. It is a great relief. We can enjoy life and appreciate it in a new way." Thich Nhat Hann has the view that consciousness or a soul is the real or essential basis for your life-form and the physical body is just an external shell or covering of the soul; thus the real 'you' or consciousness cannot be destroyed. Furthermore, it is the karmic soul or consciousness that causes re-birth and grows new layers of sheaths that Buddhists call the body-mind-self.

Re-birth, resurrection, re-incarnation, transmigration, etc. all require a willing suspension of disbelief and an active will-to-believe in the possibility of Life as a universal or eternal condition of all life-forms. If you decide that the present or perceived life-forms of existence are all that we can know for sure, then you must resign yourself to a form of agnostic materialism, at least. But if you are willing to believe and remain open to *possibility*—which quantum theory favors— then the many worlds and lives theory of Life may appeal to you.

Otherwise, the Buddhist view of *ultimate reality*—if they even entertain the concept—is divided at least between believers and non-believers, like practically every other philosophy known to humanity. The major difference between most Buddhist traditions and other philosophies of Asia and the West is its intellectually rigorous and critical approach to ordinary experience and knowledge that strives to eliminate illusion, negativity and suffering.— In this respect, it also resembles many noteworthy ontological, epistemological and ethical viewpoints, i.e. Hindu, Jainist, Taoist and Confucian in Asia and Pragmatic, Existential, Marxist and Humanist in the West.

Being, Learning and Questioning

Being is awareness of spiritual presence. Being is the great unifying force of creation, existentially manifested but essentially unmanifested. Being does not just unify differences in thought and practice, ideas and facts; being is the unity of polarities that thought and language create through their artificiality. Whatever the mind seizes upon and projects in the world—being or the unity of nature and the cosmos remains indifferent and undisturbed. In other words, there is a Power in creation that is infinitely greater than anything of human origin and that power can be experienced in the subtle presence of Now.

We are no match for the depth, gravitas, and complexity of primordial being. All of our concepts, maps, and models of being are perspectival and interpreted approximations of what-is. This is partly due to the fact that being is not an object, form, or thing in the world. Being is intimately aligned with time and eternity and their nexus in the Now. For this reason, being is most difficult to just 'think about' unless it is seen with a clear and deep sense of intuition or felt understanding.

Many may want to know: what would educating for Being really look like in the real world? Would this be a form of spirituality without religion? Does spiritual Being imply an ethics that must question the established conventions of society? Are schools, colleges and universities institutions that deny, cover up and obfuscate the truth about being, non-being and becoming?

How long can humankind continue to live the lie of non-being and deny the Truth about Being?

The Truth is that we are beings endowed with a paradoxical will and a soul that struggles to be free, free of a material world that it is attached to and dependent upon. And how long can we continue to cover over the fact that we are beings who are *freely oriented towards old age, dying and death*? What implications does existential truth-telling have for teaching and learning, the form and content of the curriculum, and the relationship of schooling to life in society? –Indeed, it may be absurd to ask such questions given how mechanistic, instrumental and bureaucratic schools, colleges and universities have become.

Consider how much better, more hopeful and helpful to the world the learning process could be if young people awaken to the Truth about Being. If parents want to do something really useful for their children, they should think of ways to save their souls in an inauthentic and dehumanizing system. In the process of preparing students for the so-called real world, the educational system is fast-tracking the majority for the oblivion of material and financial success.

What is the unknown Truth about Being among the unprepared for existence? We each exist as a unique soul at the core of the ordinary self; the soul is the essence of the Life-force sustaining your body and its functions as an infinite potentiality for experiencing and knowing reality, as it really is. Is there anything more urgent to the future of humanity than to realize the truth about the soul, the essence of personal being?

Who are the educated persons in our technological age of cyborgs and robots? Must we all become technocrats to be attuned with the times? Have we already moved beyond the age of dehumanization to the age of de-privatization where everything is known about everybody? Have we begun to lose the sense of an inner self or being and all notions of a soul and immortality? Does anyone really believe in anything, anymore—beyond their own separate, selfish sense of self?—These are the kinds of questions that the so-called educated class of persons must begin to ask, to save humanity from itself.

Schools of Tomorrow, Today

Prisons or concentration camps are constructed to destroy the heart and soul of an individual; and many do, quite beyond the will or free choosing of individuals. But there are a few individuals who have survived such horrible experiences and emerged stronger and wiser about living. Victor Frankel, a famous survivor of the Nazi Holocaust, was one such person, and he wrote about his experience in *Man's Search for Meaning*. Frankel, Anne Frank, the young Jewish diarist who hid in an attic with her family for most the War, and many others—were all caught in life's most extreme circumstances and they or their writing survived to teach us what they learned. The sad truth is that many millions have died in such places and not just physically, but psychologically, morally and spiritually.

I do not mean to suggest that today's schools are anything like concentration camps although there may be few that simulate their conditions psychologically. But there is often so much left out of the formal learning process that is good, beautiful and true in human knowledge that it is a wonder why generation after generation perpetuate a system that is outdated, underfunded and a source of more pain and suffering than it is of joy and freedom.

If there is anything absolute in the world, it is the free will of the soul and the more subtle, higher consciousness of each person. Human freedom is already, always connected with Being and the mystery of the consciousness that renders translucent our inner and outer sense of reality. We may have only the smallest fraction of Universal Consciousness within us, but it is as perfect as anything can be, manifested in the structures and functions of the body's neuro-physiological systems and the powers of the mind.

Consciousness itself is an irreducible totality existing apart from the mysterious complexity of the body and mind; similarly, there is an ever increasingly complexity and progress in human technology that parallels our understanding of nature, culture and the cosmos. However, the Perennial question remains: Will the human species grow and develop morally and politically to sufficiently support the technical advances of its global culture that continue to threaten its future?

Concerning philosophy, it has often been said that wonder and humility before nature, Life and the universe are needed to appreciate the full scope of its subject-matter. For sure, the survival and thriving of humanity depends upon the level of education realized by its participating majority; and we would be making a lot more progress in the reform of education, at all levels, if we trained and recruited teachers for their innate capacities of wonder, sensitivity, and the love of learning and persons.

In the schools of tomorrow, what *should* we find? Only this: *persons* who love to learn, explore and discover, for its own sake, and not just for a career or a higher paying job. In so doing, the gaps between thinking and feeling, knowledge and experience, theory and practice, could be more easily bridged in the learning and teaching process. Schools of tomorrow should be no schools at all but only life-as-lived, in the here-and-now of human existence and the cosmos. (4)

The most important experience in education is the experience of Life—its universality, sacredness and mystery. If we could break down the boundaries and walls of education, then the world becomes the classroom. For sure, with the advent of the world-wide web, computer technology, and the global curriculum, new dimensions of teaching and learning have evolved in the postmodern world, fundamentally changing the way teachers teach and students learn.

Now, more than ever, education need not be confined to conventional classrooms, bureaucratic scheduling, and quantified evaluations. The space of the new educational world is more naturally the universe; and the Life-force within the body, mind and soul of each individual is the most truthful basis for a new education whose aims must be the cultivation of healthy and nonviolent living, intellectual and aesthetic development of the mind, spiritual liberation, and compassion for all sentient beings

Education can become a liberating experience in teaching and learning if we are willing, as a society, to provide the necessary material, financial, and intellectual resources for its development. Thus far, most human societies—especially in the United States of America—have valued war and war-making far more than peace and peace-making. Extremes in experience often generate their opposite tendencies and perhaps human governments will learn how to govern in a moral, humane and democratic way to maximize human potentiality, justice and peace.

If we ever get serious about educating for a democracy, we must provide the necessary information to The People to awaken them to the political, ethical, and economic truths of vulture Capitalism and the oligarchical system that rules them. As things stand, formal education is a long and tedious process for indoctrinating young and vulnerable people with the myths, illusions and half-truths of a violent social system.

Dramatic, revolutionary change in the social system will require genuine leadership, a leadership of moral, intellectual and spiritual excellence, and not just leadership based upon mass, uninformed popularity. The future will appear to be far more possible if we awaken fully to the present moment and go forward with the wisdom of countless, unknown generations— the Perennial Wisdom.

Education, Love and Spirituality

Spirituality is a perennial theme in religious studies that can be oriented towards the challenges of teaching and learning. How can we teach about the religions of humankind without imposing a particular viewpoint upon others? Everyone has a view or belief about religion and its place in ordinary life; but too few have thought through the real connections between religion, education and living.

Many have never thought much about religion and formal education together since the former subject is left out of the public school curriculum, from fear of violating the separation of Church and State. But this is largely a bogus issue that symbolizes an irrational fear and timidity of school officials to confront the serious issues and questions of Life in society and everyday existence. The widespread lack of religious education and spiritual teachings in the schools and universities represents a lost opportunity and serious intellectual and moral lack of most curriculum planners.

Tolle does not directly or explicitly address the challenges of spiritual or religious education in his major writings although he does so indirectly or by implication. For example, in *The Power of Now*, he asks:

"What is God? The eternal One Life underneath all the forms of life." And later: "What is love? To feel the presence of that One Life deep within yourself and within all creatures. To be it. Therefore, all love is the love of God." (5)

Making a connection between God and love is a quite familiar one in the Jewish, Christian and Islamic religions. Tolle makes a further distinction between the love that is universal or Life-grounded and the 'love' of ego. The latter form of love is merely exclusive and divisive, leading to attachment, suffering, and fodder for the pain-body. This is what Tolle wrote on this all-important subject:

"Love is not selective, just as the light of the sun is not selective….It is not exclusive. The love of God…may be one person who reflects your love back to you more clearly and more intensely than others [or] that person sitting next to you on a bus, or with a bird, a tree, a flower. Only the degree of intensity with which it is felt differs." (6)

Education becomes spiritual when it awakens a person to his or her potentiality to love and to receive love. Everyone is born with this potentiality and most people probably experience unqualified love to some extent from others as a young child. Mostly, though, young people experience love in very qualified ways around adults whose primary function is too often experienced as oppressive and controlling. Children may only experience love as if there were never enough of it to go around.

Actually, Love, in a universal sense, is a deeply mystical and psychological experience, and there is no discernible difference between the universality of Love, Life and Being except semantic ones. In the spiritual or energetic sense, Love is infinite and sacred. In our own life-world and the common social world, it may seem that there is never enough love, compassion and real caring; and if we reduce everything to conventional time and space, there is not. But in the frame or matrix of universal Being which exists without boundaries, limits or distinctions, intellectual reductions and ego-inflations disappear into the Void.

Humanism, Education and Wholeness

The humanistic truth is that the vast majority of social institutions, i.e. schools, businesses, hospitals, prisons, armies, etc. are only concerned about the 'bottom line' or efficiency, productivity and profit. In the Capitalistic social system which has been spreading and metastasizing globally since its ideological inception, especially since Adam Smith's *Welfare of Nations*, in the 18th century, human beings are no more than 'digits on a balance sheet, lifeless objects to be used, and then discarded' by an inhumane social system.

'Humanism'—the philosophy of a more humane social existence—is a continuing challenge in all societies since most social institutions are organized on a bureaucratic, hierarchical and impersonal model. In fact, social institutions tend to diminish, fragment, and threaten the individuality and authenticity of persons nearly everywhere. The perennial, existential challenge in personal existence is to live a life in society that is authentic, integrated and ethical. There is no substitute for an awakened

individual to the potentialities for a meaningful and compassionate life or one whose moral purpose serves the Good of humanity.

The most serious problems of society are inevitably ethical,
political, and humanistic ones, since they point to the wholeness
our nature, i.e. the angelic and demonic sides, and the complex
issues of personal, social and existential being that need to be
addressed for a more perfect society. The challenge is to balance the psychological and social, ethical and political, the economic and existential regions of authentic *Being* where one lives
and dwells as a whole or individual being. The wholeness of our
humanity is inevitably the greatest challenge in authentic living,
owing to robotic role-playing, ego-centered thinking, and con-
forming to a hierarchical, impersonal and a-moral social system.

The most serious problems arise in individual or social existence when we cease thinking about Being or wholeness. For
example, the educational system has not prepared us to relate to
the transformations of consciousness that result from significant
engagements with the depths of Being. Education, from kinder-
garten through graduate school, needs to be oriented towards
authentic Being in its preparations for social, professional and
civic life, in order to educate persons who live freely, purposefully and responsibly, with self-knowledge in human relationships. Furthermore, we must educate persons to the new threats
to humanity from global climate change, the depletion of car-
bon-based energy sources and out-of-control population growth.

Rather than merely identifying the externalities of existence—whether they are the physical body, social roles, material
things, or the language we use—we must awaken to the inner
body where authentic existence or real being can be experienced. Many of the so-called problems of education and society
would cease overnight if we were awakened to the Life-force that
is naturally present in all modes of consciousness and forms of
existence. In ancient Yoga philosophy, the 'inner body' is one of
the most important insights about Life in its individual and universal meanings. The inner body is the 'home' of the soul, the
free will, and the Life-energy that brings us the sheer joy of Being.

Tolle speaks about the inner body in the context of meditation: "feeling the subtle flow of air in and out of the body as well as the rise and fall of your chest and abdomen, you are… becoming aware of the inner body. Your attention may then shift from the breath to that felt aliveness within you." (7)

Tolle opines that many people are so pre-occupied with their thoughts, roles, and problems that they cannot feel the natural aliveness within and that this is the 'greatest deprivation' of life. Engaging in the simplest of activities like walking, physical exercise and yoga can help you overcome this greatest of deprivations—an unconsciousness of the inner body or the subtle energy field connecting you to Consciousness and the Life-force sustaining all life-forms. And this shift in awareness from the outer world of physical being to the inner world of spiritual or energetic existence is a profoundly transformative consciousness.

Without the *energy or spirit* of conscious Life, physical, psychological and social existence becomes alienating, robotic and deadening. Therefore, the humanistic challenge for authentic existence is to become conscious of Life or our living connection with the present moment. *Humanism* and whatever is most ideal in the relations between persons, institutions, and nations, is the expression of a perennial Goodness, Justice, Truth and Peace of the spiritual Self that transcends place and time in the eternal Now of Consciousness. And it should be the hope of all educators, humanists, and mystics that a genuine moral change can be actualized in the global society that awakens humankind to authentic Being and the Consciousness of humanity's fragile place in the universe.

Wholeness is one of those words that sounds beautiful but is virtually impossible to capture in meaning. Perhaps the ineffable quality of wholeness is the point: we can conceive or imagine or feel and perceive something as whole and complete but describing it in words is beyond human power. The concreteness of experience as known through the senses of perception gives us discrete wholes or phenomena of all kinds, but in trying to reproduce them we discover our limits!

Jain Story: the Fasting Monk and Nun

There are many young, middle-aged, and old people whose souls appear to be dead or non-existent; and it is a sad sight. But the Jains believe that a soul is not beyond redemption or 'saving' if the body is still vital with Life; and if a person is visibly dying or the body is not vital or vibrant in health, the energy or Life-force of the soul is still present in the body, as a potentiality for spiritual liberation.

While living in India on a sabbatical leave from the University, in Winter- Spring months of 1998, I met an older Jain monk who was preparing to die. It seems that he had an inoperable brain cancer and he had only a few months to live. Although I did not know him very well, he was following a not uncommon Jain practice of 'fasting unto death'. Since it is unnatural for a person to want to die, it takes a great concentration and effort to overcome the urge to eat food for the nourishment of the body. When I first met him, he looked very weak and he could hardly walk on his own.

Years later I heard that he had an easy death, passing in his sleep onto his next life-form. Being a Jain monk—with the belief in reincarnation—he had doubtlessly worked to purify his soul of all *karma* or traces of past deeds, desires, and thoughts. According to the widespread Indian belief in reincarnation, if you do nothing to purify your soul before death, re-birth is inevitable. And if there is anything that the typical Hindu, Jain, or Buddhist believer does not desire, it is to be re-born into this world of violence, pain and suffering.

Attachment or clinging to anything in this world is sufficient to ensure misery and re-birth—unless special yogic and ascetic practices are followed. While in India I also heard about a Jain nun who had been living for several hundred days only on water and without any food. No one could believe it, least of all the doctors and nurses who cared for her. It seems that she had taken the vow of *Anasana* or fasting only on water and *whey* for the rest of her life, which it is believed will burn up most *karma*. (8)

Usually if a dying Jain takes the vow to 'fast unto death', it may be done with or without water. This can only be done with the permission and blessing of elder monks, in the ascetic orders, although lay persons may also commit suicide by starvation if and only they are in moribund conditions. Actually, this practice is more widespread than commonly thought; and other versions of fasting unto death are not unknown in the West and elsewhere.

Anyway I became very curious about this particular Jain nun and decided to see her for myself. The ashram where she lived became a pilgrimage site for the Jains and others who journeyed there to see this 'miracle'. Sure enough, there was this older woman in nun's simple cotton clothing living with other nuns who attended to her. When I saw her, she was lying down on a cot and she looked very weak from the lack of food for so many days.

According to one Jain monk whom I spoke with there, her living as long as she did was not necessarily a sign of great spiritual merit or powers. In fact, it could be a sign that she had a stronger attachment to her bodily form than most people. The other possibility was that—because of a greater accumulation of karma from past lives—her soul or *jiva* had more corruption or 'black karma' than normal, to get rid of before leaving the body.

Whatever the truth about the Jain nun's *karmic* situation was—the faithful Jains, Hindus and others were going to her in droves. The Jain nun and her simple village home had now become a major pilgrimage site since many believed that she possessed a divine or supernatural power. They wanted to touch her hands and make a connection with the sacred energy that they believed she possessed.

But I only watched from a distance since I did not want to wait in the long line to see or touch her sleeping body. Several days later, the nun died, but not from the lack of nourishment it was said, but simply from a fall that broke some bones and a deadly infection that set in from her weakened immune system.

It is very easy to be skeptical about any belief in an afterlife. Scientifically, there is no 'hard' or empirical or objective evidence to support such beliefs—only 'soft' evidence involving faith, official doctrines, and anecdotal evidence. Yet beliefs in re-incarnation, rebirth and resurrection exist quite widely around the world, in virtually all major religions, even though many questions persist and are unanswerable to skeptics.

Choosing to believe in an immortal or even eternal soul, consciousness or Self that links one life-form with another—as perhaps billions of people do, East and West— does not make you stupid of gullible as the critics claim. It only gives you a faith in the continuity of natural processes and universal Being. The belief in an after-life or before-life existence links us with the wider conditions of Life, beyond this finite life-form and with the infinite reaches of the universe. Such beliefs provide openness for speculation and meaning beyond the here-and-now of mundane existence.

To me, it is intuitively obvious that a Life-force exists that is eternal and which is not limited to our infinitesimal life-form. Also, it is supremely important that we appreciate and embrace the Mystery of ordinary life and never think that we have it 'all figured out'.

Chapter 11

THE INNER BODY, NATURE AND

THE LIFE-FORCE

What is the relationship between the inner and outer, subtle and gross, spiritual and material body? How can a person awaken the energy of the inner body and realize *perfect faith, thought and action* of the universal Life-force? What is the significance of Nature in the whole self-actualization experience? Why is the inner body important to actualizing the Higher Consciousness of Wisdom?

"When the Ten Thousand things are viewed in their oneness, we return to the Origin and remain where we have always been." Sen T'sen

"Wisdom is better than the weapons of war." Ecclesiastes, xi.18

"Whoever worships another divinity than his self, thinking, 'He is one, I am another,' knows not." Brihadaranyaka Upanishad

"He only is able to declare with spirit and power any truths or bear a faithful testimony of the reality of them who preaches nothing but what he has first seen and felt and found to be true by a living sensibility and true experience of their reality and power in his own soul. All other preaching (or teaching) whether from art, hearsay, books or education, is at best but playing with words and mere trifling with sacred things." William Law

"People say that what we're all seeking is a meaning for life, I don't think that's what we're really seeking. I think that what we're seeking is an experience of being alive, so that our life experience on the purely physical plane will have resonances within our innermost being and reality, so that we actually feel the rapture of being alive. That's what it's all finally about...." Joseph Campbell

171

Perhaps because of his deep knowledge about mythology, ancient cultures and mystical matters, Joseph Campbell is a real romantic at the heart level of the *chakras. Meaning* is too often a philosophical and intellectual obsession due to thinking without feeling or passion; and to Campbell, it is *experience* especially the kind that is *rapturous, passionate and heartfelt* that is most important in living. It is Campbell who famously said in an interview with Bill Moyers that you must "follow your passion" in life or suffer the sorrowful consequence of unhappiness. (1)

The Presence of the Body

The body exists non-verbally and non-conceptually. The body is immediately present to us as energy ('chi' in Chinese and 'prana' in Sanskrit) and the organic systems that constitute it; and the human body has been dissected, described, and explained by biologists, medical scientists, yogis, and many other researchers and experimenters of the human sciences. Yet the myriad structures and functions of the body's anatomical and physiological systems are as mysterious and unknown in their deep connections with the universal Life-force as they have ever been.

There is no field of knowledge that has been able to completely ignore the body's Life-giving Presence. Yoga philosophy views the body on at least seven chakra or energy levels, i.e. physical, sexual, psychological, sociological, aesthetic, intellectual, and spiritual. In this ancient natural philosophy, the physical body is seen as containing the essential knowledge of the universe since the natural or organic dimension of existence is not seen separately existing from the metaphysical or spiritual dimension. In this sense, yoga is a philosophy of non-duality since the natural and spiritual, physical and the metaphysical realms of experience are necessarily related through the unifying energy of Life, manifested in an individual life-form.

A conventional distinction exists between the biological and outer body and spiritual and inner body in Yoga philosophy.

However, this is only an intellectual difference and not one in the experience of real unitary being. The usefulness of this difference in practice lies in directing one's attention to the hidden and unmanifested potentialities that are within the inner body of the ordinary self.

When *Presence* is used to refer to the body, it means a *sacredness* that carries the immeasurable and unmistakable Life-force. The *divinity* of the body is no imaginary thing but an affirmation of the precious embodiment of a living soul, mind and *Purusha* or the spiritual person. It is this extremely subtle, invisible reality that separates the living body from the corpse or a body without a Life-force, soul or consciousness of any kind.

Yoga Philosophy

Yoga means 'union', a union or yoking together of separate realities or forms in existence. In yoga philosophy, reality is conceived of as existing in a sublime or ineffable Unity. Human thinking and language have artificially separated the different levels and forms of existence. Thus, the challenge in yoga philosophy, as a physical, psychological, and energetic practice, is to awaken the Higher Self of Consciousness to the natural states of the body, inwardly and outwardly. And the Higher Self of Consciousness exists as the Life-force that permeates the body through the chakra centers of the nervous system.

One of the most ancient of yogic philosophies is called Kundalini Yoga. This philosophy has its Asian roots in the Indian religion of Jainism although there is some evidence that this form of yoga had its earliest beginning in southern Africa. The Jain religious philosophy is based upon 'ahimsa' or the ethics of non-violence. 'Himsa' means violence in the Sanskrit language; therefore nature and the material world is seen by the Jains as inherently violent.

The ethical challenge to human beings is to rise above nature, as it-is, in their choices and habits of living, in order to realize a union with the soul (*jiva*), i.e. the human essence of Being, that exists uniquely within each individual's natural being. Thus, the soul, having to undergo another incarnation and corruption in a material form, the body (*a-jiva*) must be purified during this life-time to realize final liberation from *karma* and cyclic existence.

The Indian philosophy of *Samkhya,* one of the six schools of Hinduism, is based on the distinction between *Prakriti* (matter or Nature) and *Purusha* (spirit or Person), the two necessary forces of the universe that form sentient life-forms. The body, in this context, is present through nature but it cannot exist as a Person apart from Purusha or Spirit. In the Hindu religious philosophy, Purusha is known as the Higher Self, the energy field that is eternal and exists without boundaries. It is the Self (capitalized to denote the presence of Spirit) that is the divine energy or the 'inner body' in Yogic philosophy. Tolle refers to the 'energy field of the inner body'—or words to that effect—quite often in his philosophy.

In Kundalini Yoga—Kundalini means 'serpent power' or a mythic snake that lies asleep and coiled at the base of the spine—the aim is to awaken all the 'chakras' or centers of spiritual energy that exist along the spine so as to fully realize one's Self existing at the crown of the head, *the Sahasrara-chakra.* The practice of Kundalini Yoga involves a physically rigorous, psychologically and intellectually demanding cultivation of yogic habits leading to a full awakening of each of the seven chakra centers of energy that are the inner body or Life-force of each individual.

If we can open, circulate, and raise the energy of the *inner body,* i.e. the subtle body constituted by the chakras, we can become Self-realized in this lifetime, freeing the individual soul from 'karma' or the causal suffering that comes from unconscious, violent, and destructive actions. Once the soul is freed from the karmic conditioning of nature, it realizes the truth of its own essence while remaining in ordinary existence. The challenge is to live in a way that purifies and rids the soul of its corruption or violent desires and habits acquired from natural and social existence.

This is easier said than done and most yogis may spend an entire life-time to no avail maintaining the 'pure soul' only to go through cyclic existence once again! All this assumes a 'perfect faith, perfect thought and perfect action' that protects the soul against the violence of existence is a sufficient barrier to the corrupting effects of ordinary existence. Perhaps most obviously, a *perfect, absolute faith without even the slightest trace of doubt* (that a pure soul exists, etc.) is the first requirement of the practicing and meditating yogi; and without this perfection of faith everything else done in the name of enlightenment or liberation are just so many illusions and acts of futility.

And even if the first requirement is met, in Kundalini yoga, the second is no less formidable since one must not engage in any thought leading to absoluteness or the illusion that you can now know the Truth—the 'whole truth and nothing but the eternal, complete truth'! In other words, just as you must not maintain any doubt about the possibility of spiritual liberation in this life-time, to realize 'perfect faith', so you must not think that you know or have realized the absolute Truth about existence or the 'perfect thought'—the second requirement of the yogi. In philosophy, this can be expressed as seeing or realizing the truth of 'non-absoluteness' or the relativity of everything.

Then there is the third requirement: 'perfect action'. This means the yogi must never think that he or she can exist in this form—*jiva-ajiva* or as an embodied soul—completely or absolutely free from any act, process or trace of violence! Simple reflection upon this proposition would expose the profound self-delusion that would have to take place for this to be thought possible. Therefore, the very best that the faithful, mindful yogi can hope for, in ordinary existence, is to *minimize violence and maximize nonviolence*—the leading ethical principle or rule of conduct.

In conclusion, provided these three principles of the soul (perfect faith), mind (perfect thought) and body (perfect action) are practiced, in a universe that is relativistic, violent and uncertain, then and only then is the yogi able to go forward with the hope that a final spiritual liberation is a possibility. But if the yogi should shelter the thought that 'spiritual liberation' is an absolute certainty, then the practice is corrupted from the outset.

Mind, Being and *Shunyata*

The experiences of the body are more real, conscious, and sane than the mind. These are basic assumptions in Tolle's philosophy. Chapter One in *The Power of Now* is titled "You are Not Your Mind" and Chapter Six, "The Inner Body." These Chapters actually belong together—for the sake of better understanding the body and mind and their relationships to Consciousness or the transcendence of unconsciousness.

It may come as a big shock to some philosophers, psychologists, and educators, but Tolle sees the mind as the major obstacle to becoming enlightened. Whereas the body can be a 'point of access' or doorway into the realm of Being, the mind and its incessant stream of unconscious thinking, cannot. The resolution for this dilemma is clearly on the side of Consciousness or a higher awareness of our mind-body nature: if we are aware that we are consciously thinking rather than just unconsciously processing thoughts, beliefs, dreams, memories, images, etc. then thinking can do no harm to ourselves or others. But if we are not aware of the incessant 'voice in the head' then such 'thinking' is harmful to ourselves and others.

Meanwhile, the relationship of the mind and the body to Being is a fundamental or 'radical' one since it goes to the root of who we are. Although Being is essentially ambiguous and ineffable, our relationship to its totality has been a basic philosophical theme from Parmenides to Heidegger to Tolle, in the West. Tolle's view of Being is similar to the existential philosophy of Being, beginning with George Hegel in the romantic and idealist tradition of the 18th century, which privileged feeling, mood and sensation over abstract reason, thought and logic.

Tolle asserts that "Being is the eternal, ever-present One Life beyond the myriad forms of life that are subject to birth and death. However, Being is not beyond but also deep within every form as its innermost invisible and indestructible essence…. When you are present, your attention is fully and intensely in the Now, Being can be felt, but it can never be understood mentally. To regain awareness of Being and to abide in that state of 'feeling-realization' is enlightenment." (2)

The idea that 'Being can be felt but not understood' is at the core of Tolle's philosophy since Being is seen as the all-embracing metaphysical framework of everything; and in the philosophy of George Hegel, Being or the Absolute is more like feeling than a thought. Although we may be able to form concepts and use words that point to 'Being', these phenomena of reason or abstract thought are conditioned by the relativity of existence and the limits of consciousness. The analogy from ordinary language-usage is that the 'word is not the thing' or language is metaphorical and is not the thing it represents or points to in experience.

In the early 19th century, George Hegel's notion that the philosophical Absolute is a subjective feeling and not a concept became the basis for Soren Kierkegaard's radical Existential Philosophy and many other existentialists of postmodern philosophy. 'Subjectivity is Truth' Kierkegaard declared in his *Philosophical Postscript* and in the interest of ending Western, absolute rationalism. Soon after, the atheistic Friedrich Nietzsche would unknowingly join Kierkegaard's radical cause for subjectivity in the experience of truth and end the illusion that reason is the sole basis for philosophy, education, and culture.

As remarked before, similar conceptions of Being or something Absolute 'innermost' and 'indestructible' abound in Western philosophy—from Parmenides to Leibniz, Hegel, Heidegger and Eckhart. Tolle's namesake, Meister Eckhart of the 13th century, gives us the mystical perspective of the soul, embedded in the Christian faith of *God*—a word in Tolle's view that carries an anthropomorphic prejudice and is insufficiently inclusive. At the same time, Meister Eckhart's mysticism which is also similar in many respects to the formless emptiness or *Shunyata* of Buddhism.

Although many differing interpretations of *Shunyata* are present in the history of Buddhism, there appear to be agreement on three key doctrines: 1, the lack of permanence in all existing things or forms (*anitya*); 2, the lack of an independently existing self or essence (*anatman*); and 3, all existence (birth, life, death, re-birth) is characterized by suffering or unsatisfactoriness (*duhkha*). And although many persons especially theists, optimists and pessimists, have thought of Buddhism as nihilistic or based in fatalism and determinism, the central meaning of its many doctrines like the four Noble Truths and the Eightfold Path, are quite life-affirming, humanistic and pragmatic in its consideration of the human will, consciousness and the unlimited possibilities of human existence. (3)

The Body and the Inner Journey

In recent years, the body has become the subject of intense psychological focus since it is seen as embodying the emotions, thoughts, dreams, and complexes of human personality. Sigmund Freud, Carl Jung, and their innumerable followers in psychoanalytic, 'depth', humanistic and transpersonal psychologies have all made their genuflections before the altar of the body. Indeed, who can deny the body's salient role in the fabric and content, 'warp and woof' of our lives? Thus much psychological work has been done on the way we 'image' or conceive of ourselves, bodily, and the influence that such images, thoughts, and feelings have upon our relationships with others.

In this context, C. G. Jung wrote in his Foreword to D.T. Suzuki's *Introduction to Zen Buddhism*, "It is a well-known fact that the problem of spiritual 'healing' has been seriously occupying the most venturesome minds of the East for more than two thousand years, and that in this respect [their] methods and philosophical doctrines have been developed which simply put all Western attempts in the same line into the shade." (4)

Doubtlessly, those who are considered very 'beautiful' or 'ugly' by conventional cultural values and standards, may carry a larger emotional burden due to their body's appearance than people who are considered 'normal' or average in body appearance. Although one should not put undue emphasis upon mere physical appearances such as 'figures', sizes of body parts, facial features or 'secondary sexual features' as anatomists term them, they invariably become exaggerated in their importance due to cultural norms that value sensualism, sexuality, and physicalism. Norms of sexuality vary considerably from culture to culture and era to era, although there is no need to deny their underlying biological determinism.

Becoming Conscious of the body is the beginning of becoming Conscious of the unconsciousness and vice-versa. In psychoanalytic or Freudian theory, the body is the unconsciousness or unmanifested mind, and this correlates nicely with the autonomic nervous system which functions inter-dependently with the will and ordinary consciousness. Yoga philosophy, for that matter, is also completely grounded in body awareness; but unlike Western psychoanalysis, the yoga philosophy of the body includes an intuitive and affective experiencing of mental and energetic (spiritual) processes.

Typically, those who begin doing yoga postures and movements for the first time, undergo, at the same time, dramatic emotional and life-changing experiences that are buried deeply in the fascia, muscles, and bones of the body. Meanwhile, the silent partner in any physical movement is the human nervous system which is present everywhere in the body. These 'experiences' may include repressed memories from childhood, repressed conflicts from present-day relationships with significant others, and unfulfilled desires or goals interfering with present functioning and the full experience of Now.

We are only beginning to understand the role that the body plays in our mental, emotional, and spiritual health. The new neuro-sciences may reveal the myriad connections between our genetic self and the thoughts, feelings, and actions of everyday life in ways that are presently unknown. It has been perfectly obvious for thousands of years that a deeper and higher and innermost Self, essence or soul exists in the body and beyond the mind and its incessant thought processes. And for as long, mystics and other spiritual journeyers have experienced the stillness, silence, and peace that arise from an untroubled awareness of our innermost essence.

The religions of the world all agree that there is a deeper Truth than the truths of the physical body, the thinking mind, and ordinary social life (*the Perennial Wisdom*). This Truth is seen as eternal or a-historical and yet it can guide individuals and whole cultures inspirationally and morally in existence. No one can pretend to understand Truth rationally, much less speak its language, yet the intuitive, felt, and acted upon difference that it can make in a person's life-time, can be profound. Indeed, the history of morality, philosophy, the sciences and the arts, would be far less compelling than they are, without the experience of universal Truth.

In sum, being-in-touch with the physical body and its needs, desires, and appearances to others, is an essential experience of Being-in-the-world. The body is constantly changing, aging, and moving us closer to death, in the Now. It is our physical connection with eternity, time, and space, expressed by 'Now'. When we go beyond mere appearances, images, and thoughts, we experience the essence of Being or who we are.

The Perennial Truth of world religions is the deepest truth within subjective existence and essentially connects us with the intuitive and affective awareness of real being. In the next section, I will discuss how the Perennial Wisdom is at once universal and particular, absolute and relative, extraordinary and conventional.

Now as the Truth of Being

The quest for understanding, especially historical understanding, may seem to remove us from the Now, yet it really serves to deepen and enlarge our sense of Truth, by indicating our present connection with other persons and cultures and the times in which they appear. In fact, the perennial Truth implies that we cannot really separate the past from the present moment — in experience or action; and we cannot separate the future time from Now.

As Tolle sees the truth about being, the Nowness of inner experience implies that subjectivity pervades every conception of truth—whether it is conceived of relatively or absolutely; and since the forms of Truth are many, they are also conflicting, contradictory, and complementary. Indeed, ambiguity is one of the most obvious features of language; and whatever we say about Being or what-is true about reality, our words must be viewed metaphorically since they are merely intellectual and symbolic.

Seeing the truth about language and Being is really a matter of going beyond appearances of all kinds. It is learning how to see as deeply and extensively as possible. This takes time, effort, and dedication to the goal of self-realization in the Now. In fact, mere *learning for its own sake* can be an obstacle to self-realization or the experience of enlightenment if it means only a mindless accumulation of information, facts, and figures. However, when learning is goal-directed its energy is paradoxically more Now-centered and therefore more purposeful and meaningful.

It is far more important that people understand real differences in reality than merely memorize or learn for its own sake. In this way, education can become an adventure in learning about the real world, self-existence and the noble path to truth and being. It is through differences and the connections formed in Consciousness about the real world that we can intuitively understand Being and who we really are. And once we realize who we are, then we can much better realize what we must do and vice-versa; for the process of self-knowledge is an ever changing, progressive adventure of discovery and mystery.

When we see Being in moments of meditative or concentrated awareness, its light appears as the existential or subjective truth of the present moment. In this sense, the totality of Being is immanent, situational and transcendental in the ineffable Nowness of Consciousness. We can never really *know* the totality of What-is except in the fleeting moments of awareness; yet the Radiance of Being is present at the core of Consciousness and its rays extend infinitely in all directions.

Being and the 10, 000 Forms of the World

Tolle clearly prefers the term Being to God since the latter term carries with it "absurd beliefs, assertions, and egoic delusions." *God* has become a closed concept, personified, and invariably male, in the major religions and scriptures of the world. Being, on the other hand, is your essence, a Presence that is an ineffable Reality and appears as 'I Am' that is prior to any ego-role, thought, or even feeling. It is a small step, Tolle assures us, from the word *Being* to the experience of Being—if we are truly open to the experiences of the inner-body, Life-force and Spirit dwelling within its Radiance. (5)

If we rise above the tyranny of the mind and the 'disease of thinking' we can begin the process of awakening to the inner body or the sense of Being that is deepest in us. If we can get over the foolish habit of thinking that we have to understand everything or even that we can, a big hurdle can be realized in freeing ourselves from negativity, worry, and incessant thought that unconsciously controls our lives. In fact, real understanding comes from Being itself and the total sense of reality that we can experience from its Presence.

It is one thing to abstractly or conceptually know Being, but another to really experience and feel its Presence. The language of Being can only orient and point us in the direction of Being but it cannot show where It is. Language awakes us to the Presence of Being but we must make an intuitive leap to experience its Radiance. When we awaken to universal, omnipresent, and radiant Being we experience it at different levels, in differing dimensions and regions of higher Consciousness. The different regions of Being can be found, approximately, in the brain, spine and human nervous system of the whole body; the different levels can be experienced in the Kundalini yoga model of the total self; and the different dimensions of Being can be found through a multi-disciplinary approach to human experience.

Language can awaken us through the nervous system and higher cognitive processes, but its limitations are those of philosophy, theology, and formal education. When we learn to give up 'thinking' about Being, we must also give up its language, for the depths, heights, and horizons of experience where Being most truly exists. Once we know where and how Being exists in the uniqueness of the existing self, then language ceases to be merely rational or theoretical, and functions more pragmatically, existentially, and situationally.

The '10, 000 things or forms of the world' are really infinite in number and are interdependently related to the primal Source of everything. In Chinese Taoism, the *Tao* is the metaphysical Source and Unity of *Yin and Yang*. This means that all phenomena, mental and physical, are paired, complementary and dialectical. Furthermore, the empirical or real world is infinitely divisible, as differing 'truths', that are constantly changing or in flux. This universe and all others arose simultaneously in the beginningless- beginning of Being and its Presence is the same as its endless-ending. (6)

The path to Enlightenment or the subjective-objective experience of Being is most often blocked by unconsciously acquired language and the irrational habits of mind and emotion that result from mere thinking. These habits are typically established by neurological pathways in the brain—from our earliest years of experience through adulthood—that identifies words with abstract and physical things; when, in fact, words are only abstract symbols, tools and ciphers of cognitive processes and not the thoughts, feelings, and insights of Consciousness.

In other words, meanings arise from the symbolic experience of the mind through the medium of language. If we did not have the power of language, the universe and our ordinary experience of the world would not be as pregnant with meaning as it is. In this sense, language is the 'house of Being', the spaces, views and rooms where we experience the passing of our lives as subjective beings—beings of sensation, feeling, *and* meaning. In other words, we must learn to experience things without words, concepts and meanings, if we are to become fully human beings.

In sum, the experience of Consciousness is formless, translucent, and connected with Being through intuitive and affective processes of the inner, subtle body. Phenomenal or real being is mediated through ordinary cognition and experiences of the body. The multiplicity and complexity of the world is discovered in real thinking, feeling and understanding. Here, reality represents what we can know through the senses, feelings, and thoughts of everyday experience; and our experience of Being arises in the midst of such momentary, phenomenal experiences of silence and stillness—before a word is spoken or heard.

Mysticism and the Illusion of Progress

The *mystical experience* of Life awakens us to the sublime and ineffable Unity of creation. Education—in its moral, aesthetic, intellectual, and spiritual forms—is the elevation of ordinary consciousness to the knowledge of the mystical Truth of existence. In turn, this Perennial perspective of education as grounded in life-processes and experiences, assumes that we have given the biological, psychological, and social dimensions of life their due, in the curriculum that prepares one for living in the so-called real world. Yet from a mystical perspective, there is nothing real at all about ordinary life since all forms of existence are merely passing illusions, distractions and attractions that cause attachments, disappointments, and suffering.

The philosophical perspective of education is not one commonly found in brochures for schools and colleges or the official guidelines for teaching, learning and the curriculum. Here and there, however, we can find solitary and inspired teachers and administrators who articulate a vision of education that is grounded in the mystical experience of learning as living in nature, society and the cosmos.

Philosophy means the 'love of wisdom'; but it can only be legislated or codified into a rule of conduct that equally embraces all; that is, you cannot demand that everyone spends their time in the pursuit of wisdom although this would be quite desirable. In the educational process, one should be sensitive to the needs, interests and goals of the learner or their readiness to learn in formal situations; and that means understanding where they are and not imposing a 'canned' curriculum or course of study upon unwilling or disinterested and uncaring students!

If we wish to effect change in the schools, colleges and universities, for tomorrow and a better world, we must be realistic about the present consciousness and character of students, today. This requires patience, flexibility, and forbearance or the courage to take chances and experiment in the prevailing conditions of educational institutions—as undesirable as they may be.

Integrating our vision of learning, knowledge and experience with everyday life is a continuous challenge for everyone involved in formal education; and you will only be successful or feel effective if you act with humility, love and compassion for those who may sometimes look to you for inspiration, knowledge and understanding; and if they do not, not to take it personally or worse still, 'blame the victim' of a system that has stifled their desire to learn.

'Progress' or the Perennial belief that things can be better in human affairs than we presently find them, is grounded in the Power of Consciousness to effect desirable change. Nearly everyone who has lived for very long has ideals or values long languishing in inactivity. Schools and colleges—and their alternative forms for learning and awakening—present a 'golden opportunity' for the moral, educational, and spiritual growth of everyone, at whatever age or stage of Life. For contrary to popular beliefs, we are never too old or young to learn, change and grow for the sake of Goodness; and to discover the many, fascinating truths about ordinary existence and sublime Being.

If we ever want to create a 'Heaven on Earth' or experience *Nirvana*-in-*Samsara* (the Perfection of Creation in mundane existence) — it is with the engagement of a mystical, universal, and inclusive Love that we must begin. And when we 'see' perfection in the small forms of nature or human works, we begin to realize the universality of *Nirvana-in-Samsara* or the perfection of ordinary existence.

'Progress'—a really bogus term promoted by Capitalists and their cynical advertisers—was originally linked to the pre-existing, Creator God who infused every form with ultimate meaning and purpose (Aristotle). Corporate materialism, rampant Consumerism, and professional careerism—among a myriad of other related ills—have taken the global world light years away from the original metaphysical and mystical view of Progress as ethical, intellectual and spiritual. Indeed, it may seem quite ludicrous and pathetic to speak about the ancient values and perennial perspectives of philosophy, religion, science and art when one considers what most people value and live for in the real social world, today.

Love, in the universal sense, may not be *the answer* to every question in human existence, but it is the answer to every essential or important one. And the same could be said for a spiritual education whether it is based upon an organized religion or not. In its most enlarged or inclusive sense, education is the Consciousness formed by the unmanifested and manifested realms of Being-in-the world; and its most vital way forward is grounded in the human, all-too-human experience of Now.

The *Shakti-Shiva* Myth: Sexual Energy

Human sexuality has been the basis for many Indian myths and stories. In this Hindu myth, *Shakti* is the goddess of earthly, erotic energy while *Shiva* is the god of heavenly, phallic energy. Both of these energy forms are necessary to the creation of a human life-form, and the external characteristics and forms of *Shakti* and *Shiva* are meant to awaken the inner yogic body. (7)

We are not just the gross physical structure that we commonly call the body. Instead, the real 'you' exists inwardly and invisibly and beyond the stages of birth, life, death, and re-birth. The inner body is the concealed splendor of the eternal higher Self—like the god, *Shiva* of Hindu religious philosophy, at the crown of the head, and the goddess, *Shakti*, at the base of the spine.

In this seminal myth of Hinduism, *Shiva* waits patiently for the arrival of *Shakti*, who awakens at the base of the spine and rises imperceptibly through the *chakra* centers of the inner body, gathering energy and the intensity of consciousness; all the while, *Shiva* ecstatically anticipates his own fulfillment of Being when he unites in sexual union with his cosmic partner, *Shakti*. The elaborate, often erotic imagery of this myth symbolizes the sexual desire for copulation and fulfillment through the other; while at a biological level, the myth represents the irrational, blind, and unconscious drive for procreation in nature.

The energy released through the ecstatic union of *Shakti-Shiva* is radiant and explosive, sending electro-magnetic waves of light, warmth, and fire in every direction of the cosmos. Although merely mythic at the narrative level of Being, the symbolic importance the *Shakti-Shiva* myth in ordinary human experience is something that nearly anyone can identify with through their own sexual experience with a loving partner. Furthermore, in the myth, sexual energy is vital, cosmic energy connecting male and female life-forms with powers of emotion, thought, and perception that are extraordinary.

For centuries, the Hindus have worshiped *Shakti and Shiva* as the major goddess and god of human fulfillment. *Shiva*-temples with a large black phallus stone in the center altar area can be found all over India and often in small village squares. At festival days, villagers drape flowers over the phallus, sprinkle it with holy water, repeat prayers, and leave food and gifts for the divine couple. All this is believed to bring blessings to their lives and especially the natural, unitary Life-force within that is emotional, sexual, and spiritual in nature.

In Indian philosophy, Yoga means 'union' of the dialectical forces of Creation; in this case, the sexual and erotic union of *Shakti and Shiva,* the twin forces of creative Love within the subtle energy body of every person. When sexual energy is awakened, the most basic, dualistic energies of the universe are released and inspired to find fulfillment through the otherness of the 'Other'. No matter how briefly or long awakened erotic energy lasts, a profound psychological transformation often occurs from the experience of sexual love.

Externally, the experience of sexuality is focused upon the physical or gross body; and the experience results in a shifting of consciousness towards the inner or subtle body of energy. Typically, couples experience a healing effect from sexual union which is the unification of subjectivity with the object world through the 'ecstatic other'. Once the 'gate' to the inner Self is opened and the inner world is experienced— the knowledge and wisdom of mystical Consciousness is revealed; but this can also lead to delusions of the first degree since lust and sexual energy is often confused with genuine Love and Compassion.

The transformations of the ordinary self through the awakening of sexual energy opens male and female energies in the body, circulating sensations and emotions along the spine through the whole nervous system. Secondary sexual organs and their functions direct the energies of a man and a woman to the goal of procreation. Awakened sexuality provides the sacred and miraculous energy for procreation, i.e. arousal, copulation, orgasm and conception, bring a new soul into the mother's womb and later the infant's life-form fully into the world at birth.

Physiologically, the autonomic system overwhelms ordinary consciousness through the karmic Will, and the limbic brain is flooded with emotions and sensations of a supremely pleasurable kind. Lovers are typically drowned in an ocean of released, libidinal energy when the rising spiritual energy of *Shakti* along the chakras of the spine joins with the descending spiritual energy of *Shiva,* and they ecstatically fuse at the Heart center of the cardiac cavity.

Due to the energy of the inner or yogic body, we are all life-forms of the unmanifested eternal Life-force—birthless, deathless, and eternally present. The Truth that is revealed in the ecstasy of sexual fulfillment is the experience of Consciousness shining like a super-nova star for one ineffable moment. Yet the instinctual drive for sexual fulfillment and its memory become a catalyst for desire and an ideal for human happiness.

When you enter the doorway to the inner body, the higher Self, you enter the reality of divine Energy, Consciousness and Bliss; and you may feel the urge to completely surrender yourself to the Life-force within, and experience the full radiance of Being. In and through this experience you may feel with absolute certainty that "you are forever one with God" or the Being of everything. And this ultimate experience of Life can make the most profound of difference in one's ordinary life-world, leading either to genuine happiness or tragic illusions.

Chapter 12

THE PAIN-BODY AND NATURAL GOODNESS

What is the pain-body? How does real world conditioning create it? How can we overcome the negative energy of the pain-body that prevents us from actualizing our deepest potentialities for natural Goodness? Why is it so difficult to realize or see the truth of natural Goodness? And what are the psychological, social and existential conditions that create the obstacles in our experience of natural Goodness?

"I am the All, the All came forth from me and the All attained to me. Cleave a piece of wood, I am there, lift up a stone and you will find me there.... Whoever drinks from my mouth shall become as I am and I myself will become he." Gnostic Thomas Gospel

"In spite of warnings, nothing much happens until the status quo becomes more painful than change." L.J. Peter

"When the heart weeps for what it has lost, the spirit laughs for what it has found." Sufi Aphorism

"The world is so constructed that if you wish to enjoy its pleasures, you must also endure its pains. Whether you like it or not, you cannot have one without the other." Swami Brahmananda

"We are a species that has lost its way. Everything natural, every flower or tree, and every animal have important lessons to teach us if we would only stop, look, and listen." Eckhart Tolle

Tolle wrote these words in his Chapter on "The Pain-Body" in *A New Earth,* not out of despair but as a challenge to each of us, to change our way of Being-in-the-world. To change our experience or relation to the Earth, each of us must realize the unity of

191

mind, body, and soul and be who we are, in the Now or present moment of Life. And the first step in our transformation of ourselves is to really become aware of sense experience in relation to natural forms and leave off the role-playing, etc. (1)

A Zen Story

Tolle relates a story of two Zen monks, Tanzan and Ekido, who were walking along a muddy country road when they saw a young woman wearing a silk kimono and attempting to cross the road without ruining her kimono. Without thinking, "Tanzan at once picked her up and carried her to the other side."

For five long hours, the two monks walked in silence together without saying a word to each other. Nearing the temple, Ekido could not contain himself any longer, and asked in a somewhat accusing tone, "Why did you carry that girl across the road? You know that we monks are not supposed to even touch a woman."

Tanzan answered with the clearest of minds at once: "I put the girl down hours ago. Are you still carrying her?" (2)

Tolle then comments upon the story in terms of the burden from the past that the majority of people on the planet carry around with them in their minds. We carry the past or keep it alive through our memories, which in is not a 'problem' until memories begin to interfere with our present moment of decision-making, problem-solving and ordinary functioning. When this happens, "your personality, which is conditioned by the past, then becomes your prison." (3)

The way that we learn to escape from the 'prison' of the past is to 'let it go' and simply be fully in the present moment, through the wonders of the external senses, positive feelings and emotions, the simple joys of ordinary existence. And the Zen story underlines the assumption that natural impulses and instincts like that of wanting to help someone in need is more important than pre-established rules of conduct that may serve nothing but to maintain ancient traditions.

Finite and Infinite Potentialities

Your potentiality for being present in the moment, with full awareness, is greatly compromised by a personality and mind that is identified with the past, whether that past is remembered as wonderful or horrible. In this sense, learning to let-go or detaching yourself from past experiences is crucial for the most significant learning, active involvement and experiencing of reality.

In the Zen story, for example, Ekido became attached to the feeling of negativity from judging Tanzan's helping the young woman cross the muddy road and he could not let go of his negative judgment the entire way to the Temple. This thought was absorbed by his pain-body. Tanzan, on the other hand, just acted spontaneously from his innate desire to help others, in carrying the woman across the muddy road. His mind, heart and conscience were clear and untroubled from his action, in the present moment.

The mental and emotional baggage of negativity that we may carry with us throughout our lives is extremely damaging to our sense of Presence in the world. In fact, emotional and psychological pain from the past can be more crippling than even a physical disability to our capacity for happiness and well-being. This is confirmed by thousands of therapists and clinicians every day of their practice. And no amount of material goods or financial security that we may possess can make up for the emotional pain that we may suffer from, in our present lives.

It is commonly understood that our potentiality for Being in the present moment, fully and completely, is greatly handicapped by worry, regret, and negativity. 'Presence' is the ability to be fully involved and consciously present in a life-situation. Our potentiality, as sentient beings, is limited or finite, but our potentiality as Consciousness or the essence of who we are, is really infinite or unlimited. If we are fully present in the Now of experience, there is no limit to what we can perceive through our senses, feeling through our emotions, and accomplish through our actions. It is the great, empowering secret of the Human

Potential Movement—a social movement that has given hope and inspiration to countless millions of people; and one that has given new energy to the ethics of Human Rights, Civil Rights and Women's Rights, nearly everywhere in the world.

In sum, if you are unable to be in the present moment, you will not be able to fully experience or use your sensory, emotional, and intellectual capacities. Being fully present means that we can experience the living, ongoing and changing Presence of everything, which is the 'timeless, formless, and infinite' awareness of Being or what-is. This means that we can experience Life in its many forms deeply and fully through feelings, perceptions, and thoughts without any attachment, worry or regret.

The Pain-Body as Negative Energy

If you are severely imprisoned in the 'pain-body'—which everyone possesses to some degree—then no present thought, emotion, or sensation will be able to enter the iron-bars of your unfree self without having the key to unlock past traumas. Everyone has a past, and everyone has good and bad memories of their past, but an unknown number of people on the planet are suffering from an accumulation of negativity, pain, and disappointment from their past that is crippling them today, owing to their inability to detach themselves from negative, painful or shameful memories.

Tolle describes the pain-body as an 'entity' or field of energy that feeds upon our identification with past hurts, wrongs, pains, injuries of all kinds. The pain-body is an inner body that prevents us from being fully in the present moment of experience and Life. It is the dark side of our everyday self that 'clings' or attaches to everything that we do, say, think, and feel.

The pain-body forgets nothing negative and in fact, feeds upon negativity at every opportunity, for its own life-blood and survival. And if we are acutely afflicted by the tendencies of the pain-body, we cannot really experience our present life-form at all without 'permission' from its tyrannical presence and control. (4)

The Pain-Body and the Super-Ego

The pain-body is like Sigmund Freud's idea of a 'super-ego' that forms in the identity of everyone from an early age. It is the negative voice of a parent, teacher, or authority figure that we internalize and which controls our thoughts, feelings, and actions. It judges, censors, and establishes what is good or bad, on the basis of conventional morality. It is mostly formed unconsciously and against the ego's capacity for the enjoyment or spontaneous feelings especially for sexual experiencing and fulfillment. In this sense, the pain-body is like the super-ego since its development consists of "prohibitions and inhibitions, [and] all the rules of conduct which are impressed on the child by his parents and by parental substitutes." (5)

However, the pain-body is unlike the super-ego in us in that the pain-body is a totally negative force of demonic energy. Not everything that we learn through others is, of course, negative or painful. In Freudian psychology, the 'ego' represents the every-day personality or public face of a person, in a role, while the 'id' is the unconscious, hidden, and darker side of the total self. The ego is an embattled zone caught between the commands and inhibitions of the super-ego, on the upper side of the brain, with the primal, natural, and selfish energies of the id, on the lower side or primal brain.

In this regard, the pain-body can be seen as drawing on the energy of all three regions of the Freud's theory of the self, i.e. the super-ego, ego, and id; and these approximately correspond to the cerebral cortex, the limbic and stem regions of the human brain. Whereas there are necessary and positive aspects in these three realms of experience and functioning, the pain-body is nothing positive and symbolizes the accumulated negativity, hate, violence, and unhappiness that we have experienced and internalized in our lives. The pain-body lives within the everyday self and often judges others, events, and experiences of all kinds, in a sinister, alienated, and hostile way, due to an underlying unhappiness.

Habitual negativity is the worst aspect of our unconsciousness since its energy prevents us from being creatively present,
happy or fulfilled. Freud was lead to the conclusion that the
typical individual cannot be happy in modern society due to the
oppression of the super-ego's internalized demands from others.
Tolle thinks in a similar way about the tyranny of a pain-body; but
he is far more hopeful than Freud in believing that real happiness can be realized in the individual who has gotten rid of the
pain-body—through being fully present in the Eternal Now of
personal experience.

The Pain-bodies of Society: the Futility of Fighting

In philosophy and particularly in ethics courses, painful
human issues, life-situations, and social problems are often studied and discussed. I have spent many years studying the ethical,
moral, political, educational, and social problems of humankind.
And although I am clear about what can and cannot be done to
solve the perennial problems of humanity, i.e. war, poverty, racism, classism, sexism, speciesism (violence in general) I believe
that it is important for people of all ages to just be aware of these
problem.

The justification for the study of the unsolvable or systemic
moral problems of humanity lies in awareness; it is far better to
be aware or cognizant of a problem or issue that causes pain, suffering and unsatisfactoriness than not. When you are ignorant,
you are more vulnerable to pain and suffering and controllable
by others. Furthermore, when consciousness is focused upon a
'problem' or source of conflict and tension, a healing energy is
released in the body. Its tissues, muscles and tendons are flooded
with endorphins, enzymes, and chemicals agents that cause pleasurable sensations in the whole body.

Just knowing and understanding why certain complex social
problems have persisted without significant change over the centuries brings a settlement, a resolution to internal tensions. Even
if nothing is actually done, in an external sense, to resolve the

problem, an inward and essential movement of consciousness takes places.

Existentially, an individual can be changed for life through the essential educational movement of inner consciousness. In later life or following formal schooling, the awareness of the perennial problems of humanity may actually get acted upon by individual students of ethics, philosophy and society who may only be acquainted with them on intellectual levels. Significant social change occurs when individuals address the load of pain, negativity and tension that they perceive in the real world and at whatever stage of life.

The negative or dark side of human awareness and action occurs when persons take extreme positions and become obsessed with a certain idea or problem. Instead of a social or moral problem remaining worldwide or species-general, a given individual may so personalize or identify with a problem like war or human violence that it consumes or takes over his or her entire life-world. Instead of consciousness being a healing or resolving power, its movement is turned against the individual through extremely painful feelings, violent images and language. And this becomes yet another instance of the pain-body that crushes an individual's enthusiasm, joy, and love of life.

I have known many individuals who were so overwhelmed about a wrongful or 'evil' situation in the world that they could not think about or experience anything else. The pain-body or the existentially disturbed and stressed out sense of self, really thrives on distress, 'problems', and melodrama. Pain-bodies are attracted to violence, misery, and horror of all kinds. The subjects, problems, and conflicts of the world are like a continuous movie, a soap opera, or a CNN newscast in the mind that cannot be turned off.

News broadcasters create news from the violence of the world, through their pain-bodies and minds, for the entertainment of other pain-bodies and minds—the consumer. Everything that is the least bit conflict-laden or painful, fearful or hateful, alienating or negative becomes grist for the mill of the pain-body. The pain-body of the news consumer thrives on the violence and negativity, lies and distortions, stupidity and insanity of society. In such a climate of violent emotions and thoughts, fear and anxiety and waves of pain and suffering relentlessly break onto the shores of the everyday self, feeding the ravenous and insatiable appetite of the pain-body.

Although it is easy to wax melodramatic about pain-bodies, there is nothing theatrical about them. Pain-bodies are the basis for most if not all crime, corruption, and lawlessness in the world, and they are responsible for domestic abuse, gang violence, and other acts of random, senseless violence in society. In fact, just as the pain-body may dominate the inner life of mature individuals in its most developed forms—the accumulation of violence, hatred, and negativity within a group or nation-state erupts periodically in the ultimate horrors of war and genocide. In short, the parallels between individuals, groups, and nation-states are obvious ones, and the growth and development of a pain-body may well become a pandemic in its influences.

The pain-body, because it is basically fear-based and is nurtured by systemic cultural conflicts, is responsible for the persistence of racism, sexism, classism, and speciesism—the great moral scourges of the human species and real obstacles to the further evolution of a higher Consciousness in humanity. At the base of each and every one of these moral scourges, is the fear of non-being, death and oblivion. Although the world's religions do little to reduce the fear of people and heal the cultural divides that separate them, from *all otherness*, they will continue to be impotent in bringing Peace and Love to the world so long as they harbor dogmatic, absolutist and exclusivist doctrines and tendencies.

If individuals cannot free themselves of the pain-body and its negativity, it makes no difference what they believe, think, or do, since their actions will be undermined and guided by a psychological neurosis of the mind and its disturbed ego-structure. Once the unhappiness, dysfunction, and negativity of the ordinary self is recognized, then real work and progress towards

Self-realization can begin, at least in theory. Just as nearly every 'normal' person in society suffers from the internal presence of accumulated negative energy, in the pain-body, so does each and every person possess the infinite potentiality for self-realization and higher Consciousness.

Each of us is daily re-enacting the painful dramas of our personal past, powerfully conditioned by our families of origin, our immediate surroundings and the global society. The so-called real world with its neurotic and corrupted mass media, entertainment, and educational systems contain the essential qualities and experiences that build pain-bodies in everyone who makes some kind of contact with them.

Nature, society and existence condition everyone, everywhere to be strikingly similar in their instinctual needs, personal wants, and existential tendencies. That is to say, nature instills is us the desire for food, water and shelter which we mistakenly call *needs*; society shapes and influences us to such an extent that it difficult to say where personal needs ends and where social ones begin. Confusion in values, priorities and ends prevails in society that permeates human existence and creates profound contradictions and paradoxes within human consciousness, the everyday self and its action. Thus the virus of the pain-body is global in extent and transcends race, religion, and social class.

All people need to become vigilant in protecting themselves from the poisonous influence of pain-bodies. People in positions of authority and public influence need to be positive role models by promoting a nonviolent morality towards all sentient beings. The educational, moral, and spiritual influence of awakened individuals can make a great difference in any group—from the family unit, to a single community and to the entire world. And there are many such enlightened individuals to be found in history and the present society whose lives and teachings could serve as examples of nonviolence, creative intelligence, and an inspiration for millions.

The extent to which individuals can be conditioned by mass propaganda systems to hate, fear, and become aggressive towards an 'enemy' and start a hate campaign, war or genocide is all too-well documented. On the other hand, promoters of morally worthy causes, like feeding the poor, creating meaningful jobs for everyone, and taking real steps to brings about peace, justice and equality for all, receives a disproportionate degree of attention and support from the public.

Declaring '*war* on poverty' or anything else in the world is often completely counter-productive since it is based upon conflict, aggression and negativity. And fighting the natural tendencies of the inner self or body is wrong and will only end in failure and suffering; the total body knows much more about who we are than the mind does.

The reality is, when you begin to 'fight', become more aggressive, competitive, and make 'war' against others, you are creating a pain-body in yourself and others that will outlast the particular situation or social role, by years and even a lifetime. As Tolle wisely says over and over again, 'whatever you fight against, whatever the cause or reason, you only re-create it in fighting against it and make things worse'.

The Natural Goodness of the Self

Tolle is hopeful about the ability of each of us to 'stop adding to the pain-body that we already have' and stop identifying with those things, events, people, situations that formed it in the past. It was your unconscious mind, ego, and fearful self that created the pain-body in the first place; and if you cease giving energy and attention to those acts of thought, emotion, sensation, and speech that created the pain-body, then you can begin to purify, deconstruct, and dis-identify from it.

In other words, you have an inner presence or energy field within the physical body, neurologically, that can seriously interfere with or block your present functioning and experiencing of the world. If you get rid of the energy, habits, patterns and tendencies of the pain-body, greater happiness or a sense of well-being at the highest levels will inevitably follow. Your will experience your total self as being more creative, free to feel, think and act, without feeling guilt, shame or hostility towards others; and you will begin to feel the most powerful potentiality of the Self—its natural, innate and primordial Goodness.

Tolle is quite sensitive about the spheres of influence or relations with other people and the entire Earth that we each have. We are beings of energy, matter, and time that live in potential alignment with universal Being, the living Earth and the creative Now. If you want to think about Being as the creator 'God', Tolle has no objection except that 'God' should not be identified as a human form, condition or quality—as in anthropomorphic religions. Being—the more inclusive term for spirituality in Tolle's philosophy— is formless, unconditional, and impersonal, unlike many ideas of 'God' in the theistic religions of the world.

Because the emotional or affective dimension of self plays such a dominating role in our growth and development, throughout our lives, no 'problem' or challenge in life can ever be entirely separated from it. In this respect, the harm that negative emotions, such as a sense of loss, anger, sadness, regret, etc. can have is incalculable although not irreparable effect upon the present functioning of the self. However, the lingering effects of negative emotions often outlast the more positive experiences in life due to their predatory, addictive, and aggressive nature. Therefore, it is clear that any "negative emotion that is not fully faced and seen for what it is in the moment arises but it does not completely dissolve. It leaves behind a remnant of pain." (6)

But there are as many ways that pain and suffering can enter the world as there are ways of experiencing life. The 'problem' with pain and suffering is that it almost always prevents us from really experiencing Life, in the fullest, most pristine, and unitary sense, since it creates fear, anxiety, and even panic in us, while it grows like a cancer and dominates us or our ability to fully function in the world as real or fully functioning persons. In fact, there is ample evidence that depression, anger, and negativity experienced over long periods of time, and left untreated, make us physically, psychologically, and intellectually sick, and deeply influences our expressed opinions and judgments about other people, society, and life in general.

Typically, one pain-body feeds upon other pain-bodies and situations since pain-dominated people are unconsciously attracted to each other and become attached to each other's crippled sense of self. The psychological healing that pain-dominated people need can rarely be found through another crippled or injured self. Quite often, a close friend, a professional therapist or spiritual healer can help you get rid of the pain-body. However, there are other ways that anyone can get rid of the pain-body within, and even without the trust, love, and intimacy of other people.

For example, a close and loving relationship with non-human animals, reptiles, and plants, can have a rejuvenating and restorative effect upon the total self and feeling about the innate Goodness of Life. At the same time, many have found the natural Goodness that is within the Self as Consciousness, in a belief in the loving Presence that is formless, invisible, and spiritual. Whether natural Presence is called 'God' or not is irrelevant to the deeply ontological experience of our self-nature that is opened from an attitude of surrender, peace, and love.

Seeing and really experiencing the natural Goodness that is within all sentient beings and Nature is available everywhere, all-the-time. For example, Yoga philosophy and its many practices teach a holistic way of living that integrates all energy levels of the body, mind and Self through thought, feeling, and action. Every day that we are alive, breathing and perceiving the world of the body, nature and Spirit, is a miracle, a blessing and an opportunity for awakening to our true Being, the creative freedom and infinite potentiality of higher Consciousness.

When we understand 'reality' or the universe and our place in it, we can begin to make meaningful connections between ideas and things, relating them to real being or the body, the experiences of the present moment, and the on-going, ever-changing world of appearances. When we can 'feel our feelings' or experience our emotions, we gain a greater understanding of ourselves as moral and ethical persons or persons of conscience who know the difference between what right and wrong, good and evil, desirable and undesirable. It is not enough just to know something abstractly but to know how something could make a difference in someone's life, for the better, and protect all life-forms from violence, pain and suffering.

In sum, natural Goodness is already, always within the every-day self of everyone. Natural Goodness does not require technical knowledge, college degrees, or special training, to be known and experienced. We are born with Goodness as the essence or soul of our individual life-form. However, due to our vulnerability, impressionability, and plasticity as developing persons, we may only be aware of what we have acquired or learned from our 'upbringing', schooling and limited environment. We may have to endure many years of pain, negativity and hardship before we wake up to our full potentiality as a person who has gifts and something unique to offer the world.

The Ethics of Nonviolence and the Real World

The periodic political 'wars' against disease, poverty, evil, ignorance, etc. has only brought us more of the same. Or as has been repeated since biblical times and more recently by the inspiring Martin Luther King Jr. in the 20th century, 'an eye for an eye only makes us all blind' or 'violence only creates further violence' and so forth. This ancient teaching of *ahimsa* or nonviolence was based on the assumption of *himsa* or violence, suffering, and tragedy in the world; and these teachings of nonviolence can be seen in the religious philosophies of the Indic Jains, Buddhists, and Hindus to the Middle Eastern traditions of the Jews, Christians and Moslems to the more naturalistic and secular philosophies the Taoists and Confucians. -

Henry David Thoreau, Leo Tolstoy, and Mahatma Gandhi are other recent examples of lives that were committed to the ethics of nonviolence. For Thoreau, it was living a life based upon a closeness to and love of Nature and speaking and acting in Civil Disobedience against the destructive influences of civilization and technology. For Tolstoy, it was realizing in mid-life the Law of Love, Peace and Nonviolence that he discovered in the teachings of Christ and the New Testament. And for Gandhi, nonviolence meant the Power of Moral Truth (*Satyagraha*) in the universe; and he used the strategies and tactics of non-cooperation and nonviolence that led to the political overthrow of the British control of India, in 1948, without resorting to any form of violence against their authority.

Existentially and karmicly, pain arises from suffering—the suffering of birth, life, death, and re-birth. Or pain and suffering naturally arise from the human condition of ordinary consciousness and being-in-the-world. However, once we realize our common predicament and the paradox of existence, we can rise above it by affirming the *a priori* goodness of eternal Being that is infinitely stronger than the natural and social conditions of existence. There is really nothing that we cannot do, once we are aware of the Truth about reality and do not try to act against that Truth.

The sickness of civilization in the form of war-making, war and military aggression adds immeasurable pain and suffering to the human condition. There is usually only a small minority of individuals who joyfully participate in any war once it begins; but there are many more that choose to enlist or obey their government's draft to military service. There is another small minority of individuals who refuse to participate as combatants in war-making and become conscientious resisters.

In World War II, for example, there were over 45,000 American men who refused the draft into military service on religious, moral, and ethical grounds; and who eventually gained the right to volunteer for work in hospitals, prisons and human services. During the divisive Vietnam War of the 1960's, there were even more young men who found ways to refuse or 'dodge' military service and for similar reasons. In every war, civil or international, there have been many persons of conscience, nonviolence and peace-making who have refused military service, believing that violence only creates further violence and future wars. Yet there is a continuing mythology that 'winning' by fighting, aggression and violence is the only way to ensure peace, justice and happiness whereas the opposite consequences invariably occur.

There is a perennial ethical debate whether war—any war—can be moral. Is it wrong, absolutely wrong, to kill a sentient being—or not? The absolutist would answer that 'killing is always wrong' while the relativist would answer that 'killing can be morally justified' or words to that effect. The divide between these two views is quite profound in expressing differing meanings and values of Life itself.

From random acts of domestic homicide, to gang warfare, to a government's decision to execute convicted criminals, to the many forms of war-making, terrorism, and violence in society—the negative feelings, perceptions, and habits of the pain-body are expressed easily and readily on a daily basis. Nonviolence, on the other hand, is the absence of a pain-body within a person and affirmatively the Presence of kindness, compassion and understanding in our actions. Nonviolence is expressed in the personal sense of beauty, the feelings of love, pleasure and truth, and the whole range of social values that foster justice, equality and peace.

At economic, moral and political levels, the way of nonviolence can also express itself in the rejection of policies, laws and attitudes that discriminate against minorities, the poor and the powerless. For example, the civil rights movement in the United States established some of its greatest gains through nonviolent actions like the economic boycotts of white-owned stores, sit-ins at white-only restaurants and on apartheid public buses. Non-cooperation with racist authorities and institutions, organized mass marches and rallies, and others acts of 'civil disobedience' continue the 'struggle' against racially discriminating laws, hearts and minds of society; culminating in new legislation, policies and attitudes about equality, rights, and justice.

If there is one eternal Truth about human nature, it is this: there is a Life-force within each individual that is the same and it is Sacred. *Existence* or birth, Life, death and re-birth are immeasurable essences; and the difference between essence and existence is only made greater when individuals, groups, or institutions act from ignorance, negativity, and prejudice of the pain-body. On the other hand, when individuals act from an educated vision of humanity, equality, and fraternity, then the gap between individual existence and universal essence is closed through the harmony, compassion and light of nonviolence.

Although the power of Goodness may not be fully evident in the world, individually and institutionally, natural Goodness is present all-the-time in the soul or essence of individuals. When natural Goodness is felt, seen, and realized among individuals, the inner experience brings the purest kind of happiness into awareness. This experience is affective, perceptual, and intellectual all at once, from deeply within existence, in the Now of Consciousness. One does not have to read a book or attend a seminar to know what nonviolence 'is' since it can be experienced in our natural Goodness and Presence.

Once the experience and awareness of natural Goodness is present in our lives, then the human condition begins to look different, new, and more hopeful. In the materialistic society of Capitalism, an increase in happiness is often equated with making more money, acquiring more goods, and gaining more financial security. In the real world of human experience, 'more' is never enough since greed, selfish plunder and financial gain, can never be satisfied or fulfilled. If we really want to be happy, free spirited, and living the life that we desire—and not just hoping and praying—then we will realize that natural Goodness is the gift of Life and the most lasting basis for peace, justice and the truth of nonviolence.

The entire array of moral values—freedom, peace, happiness, justice, equality, etc.—are empty and meaningless abstractions apart from individual existence and a communitarian or social sense of Being-in-the-world. In other words, you cannot live as an individual in the pursuit of moral ideals entirely apart from others. Individual or personal ethics is necessarily and inevitably connected with one's social or public ethics. Too often there are times and cases where professional work, public responsibilities and social roles over-ride the values of one's personal relations and existence, with tragic consequences. For example, Eliot Spitzer, the attorney general of New York State, was caught in 2007 as a 'client' in the prostitution business while much of his career as a public prosecutor was built upon fighting corruption, illegality and racketeering on Wall Street! The discovery ended Spitzer's career as a politician as well as wrecking his family life.

Ideally, natural Goodness grounds you more solidly in existence because it connects you with essence, the active center or soul of existence. If you can build your life-world upon the living soul or consciousness of existence, then there will only be an intellectual difference between the private and public, personal and social realms of ethics. Confucius, the most famous ancient moral philosopher of China, based his vision of human excellence and moral character upon the precept that the heart and the mind work synergistically together, rather than in opposition to one another.

The Goodness of Life is really the natural perfection of all life-forms—a perfection that no human being, science or art can improve upon but only simulate, imitate or copy. If we realize universal Goodness, in a visionary insight, we can more easily cease our attachments to, obsessions with, and negativities towards the world of things and life-forms, and live more harmoniously and nonviolently. Change, evolution and becoming are universal characteristics of nature, existence, and the cosmos; yet the permanent or eternal dimension of everything—like natural Goodness—is nothing that we can ever directly or intellectually 'know' but only inwardly or intuitively realize.

People who are intellectually identified with a particular religion, ideology or point of view may be suffering from a pain-body. The pain-body comes in many forms, as Tolle says, and no two are exactly alike anymore than individuals are, although some are denser, heavier and more covered up, than others.

Getting rid of the pain-body by purging or cleansing ourselves of violent language, hateful thoughts and selfish habits is deeply

207

healing, educative and transformative. Indeed, the poisons and corruptions of existence are many and to maintain a pain-free self, require that we cultivate the habits of nonviolence which means overcoming ignorance in its many forms. Without self-knowledge, all other forms of knowledge are useless, superficial and dangerous; for a nonviolent person is a self-aware person who understands the emotions, thoughts and tendencies of the self that can undermine nonviolent behavior.

The refusal to be violent towards others implies an affirmation of Life in its many forms. It is the intention to align your everyday self with the sacred energy of Life in its individual life-forms. Nonviolence is the way of peace, harmony, and compassion since it comes from a profound faith in reason and human dialogue instead of brute force and armed aggression. It is the way of diplomacy in inter-national affairs rather than the way of war and hostility; and it is the way of communication and friendship in personal relations rather than the way of confusion, mis-understanding and enemies.

The refusal to speak, think or act violently in the world implies an intention to be nonviolent, peaceful, and harmonious. Nonviolence is learning how to be open, sensitive, and rational and developing a moral understanding of the world. It is refusing to fight others except in an extreme situation of self-defense and it is affirming the right to life, for all sentient beings. Nonviolence means the peace of mind, body, and soul that comes from faith, fearlessness or the courage to act and be nonviolent.

A completely or absolutely nonviolent Person is not possible in the real world given the weaknesses and imperfections of real human beings. Also, ordinary existence is uncertain, everything is constantly changing, and we are fallible beings. Therefore, the best that we can hope for in our lives and the wider world is to 'minimize violence and maximize nonviolence'; an individual life-form is brief and insignificant when compared to the age and vastness of the universe; but when seen in the frame of our own lives, we have the power to set in motion karmic or causal forces that can change the world, for the better.

The affirmation of Goodness, as a sacred value of Life, is the most supreme of moral acts. Affirmation strives to protect, nurture, and cherish each life-form, no matter how insignificant, corrupted, or imperfect, and respect its right to live and flourish in existence. If everyone practiced nonviolence, mindfully and compassionately, and established nonviolence in their habits of speech, thought, and action, there would be much less killing, stealing, lying or deception in the world. Given the 'nature the beast', weakness of the human will, and the power of the universe, it is unrealistic to think that humans will ever rid their world of violence without the help of Divine Intervention.

A nonviolent life is essentially a pain-free life since you live most fully in the Now when you do not fear, hate, or fight with others in anyway. It may sound incredible that anyone could live without pain and suffering and free of violent tendencies of any kind; but it is possible in the life-world of pure and perfect 'Being, Consciousness, Bliss' or *Sat, Chit, Ananda* in Hindu philosophy. Of course, since everything is Impermanent in the great, encircling universe of individual existence, it may be too much to expect that even enlightened states of Consciousness will last forever.

However, the most well-known historical examples are Socrates, Mahavira, Buddha, Abraham, Jesus, Mohammed, Lao-tzu, Confucius, etc. show that inspired, nonviolent and enlightened persons have lit up the philosophical and religious landscape ever since most ancient times. The more contemporary examples of a nonviolent Consciousness can be found in moral, economic and political philosophy. For example, enlightened ethical leaders advancing the ideals of universal equality, justice and nonviolence have appeared in the Feminist, Environmental, Civil and Human Rights movements with an increasing frequency in recent centuries.

As Martin Luther King Jr. has said, "the arch of history bends towards justice" and therefore nonviolence since one does not exist separately from the other. Thoughts and words have a power of their own and when they are linked or lead to action their power is increased exponentially. Thus we have only to change our way of thinking and speaking if we wish to change the world.

In essence, the choice to get rid of the pain-body begins with nonviolence, the affirmation of Life and its sacredness. However, this does not mean that freedom and the right to choose is less important than the 'right to life'. In the abortion disputes of the world, the 'right to life' and the woman's 'right to choose' are code phrases for false dichotomies. A nonviolent ethics fully recognizes the woman's absolute right to choose to have or not to have an abortion even though abortion is an act of terminating a life-form. Such moral cases are ridden with real-life choices, conditions or circumstances unique to each individual.

Metaphysically, universal Life is eternal or uncreated and thus it cannot be ended by human means. However, individual, organic life-forms are entirely contingent, conditional, and impermanent. Creation-destruction-transformation is the controlling dialectic of the universe, from the smallest to the largest forms of matter and energy. Killing occurs whenever a life-form is ended by willful means, legal or illegal, individual or institutional; and this applies to cases of Capital Punishment, Wars, Pogroms, acts of abortion, 'take no extreme measures', etc.

At the same time, it must be realized that Nature is thoroughly violent through its impersonal laws of creation, destruction and transformation. Birth, life, and death, is a continual process of cellular creation, division, and destruction. There would be no individual life-forms without this existential possibility. Yet on a scientific or empirical level of knowledge we have not the slightest understanding of 'why is there is Something rather than Nothing'? –The best answer has already been given by the 16th century scientific genius, Wilhelm Leibniz: God, the 'infinitely perfect Being' who set Heaven, Earth and the planets in elliptical orbits around the sun and planned for Eternity.

Becoming fully healthy, vital, and inspired begins with choosing to become an informed person. In this sense, nonviolence implies an enlightened awareness or education in the highest sense of the word. And since our freedom always implies taking responsibility for the consequences of our choices, we cannot hope to overcome the sickness, injustice, and violence of the world, by ignoring or repressing awareness of the real conditions of the world.

In sum, the transformation from painful awareness to a pain-free awareness is the most vital and healthy choice that we can make as conscious, responsible, and nonviolent persons. Becoming pain-free is to become a free and joyful spirit or some-one who experiences the natural Goodness of self and others. Ethics is rooted in the vision of nonviolence, the sacredness of all life-forms, and the universal Power of Nonviolence. Each of us has the power to re-make or reform the real world—the life-world we actually live in, in relation to others—and the wider or common world of human existence.

Divine Nature and Human Unconsciousness

"There is only one perpetrator of evil on the planet: *human unconsciousness*" asserts Tolle. Becoming a fully conscious person or one who lives in the Now and is not identified with the past through the painful memories of the mind, is the only way to "break-free" to the light of Being and the ability to be happy wherever you are and whatever you are doing. (7)

The difference between 'life-situations' and universal Life is that the former is contingent, limited, and conditional, whereas the latter is universal, unlimited, and unconditional. Universal Being is the most profound evolutionary force in nature, society, and history since it is responsible for the highest potentialities of humanity. However, humanity, individually and collectively, has the potentiality to determine its own destiny once it realizes the higher states of consciousness, innate freedom, and original Goodness.

Consciousness enables Being to become manifest from the unmanifested realm, on an everyday level of experience. Both ordinary and extraordinary states of consciousness all owe their Presence to manifested Being and the insights into reality that they make possible. The paradox deepens once we realize that Being is the primal source of Consciousness, on its many levels of experience and knowledge; but it is Consciousness that enables Being to be known, experienced, and revealed in its magnificent Radiance. The Truth is fully disclosed in the reciprocal relationship that Being and Consciousness enjoy with one another, quite independently of every other consideration. Yet it is a relationship of profound a-symmetry since human Consciousness can never fully realize the enormity and magnificence of radiant Being.

Awe, wonder, and incredulity are the extent of our emotional responses to the myriad manifestations of Being. Intellectually, we can penetrate the layers of reality that separate our daily existence from the innermost Presence of Being. But the concentration of mind through Consciousness is nothing that we can will through intention alone. Rather a tremendous commitment and sacrifice of self, time, and effort is required to 'glimpse' the ineffable totality of Being. And even when we glimpse the essential Totality, we can easily be deluded that we have arrived upon the shore of Freedom, once and for all.

Becoming a fully conscious person means being aware of our uniqueness in this life-form, in each life-situation of Now. Life as universal awareness means that we are aware of the relativity and contingency of our unique life-form. Knowing that we only have so many days, months and years to live in this life-form gives a perpetual sense of urgency and intensity to each moment and aligns us with the eternity of each moment. Awareness of the evanescent nature of this life-form imparts the need for inner purpose and meaning that is aligned with that of the universe. And this awareness is dynamic, evolving, and on-going with the events and circumstances of nature, society, and spiritual Being.

As the Hindus assert, our real nature is essentially Spiritual—not physical, existential or social—and we essentially exist at-one-with the creating, sustaining, transforming energy of Brahman or ultimate Being. In this context, what is transcendent (beyond the ordinary self) is also immanent (within the higher Self); and what is higher in Reality is present at the lower levels of experience, and what exists within subjective consciousness is also present in the object world. *Chitta*—Mind or Consciousness—exists as: 1, ordinary or everyday consciousness, 2, sub-consciousness or unconsciousness, and 3, super-consciousness or extraordinary consciousness, in potentiality at all times in the Now of personal experience. (8)

In sum, we possess the capacity for personal meanings, values, and purposes that are in potential alignment with the universal Mind of God—as philosophers from Aristotle to Einstein have realized—as the greatest of Truths. Our contingent, conditional, and mortal life-form possesses an innate potentiality for knowing what is Ultimate on an intuitively intellectual level of Being. This is due to the fact that we are at once divine-in-nature and evolving as organic beings through-h human consciousness or the manifestation of what is unmanifested. The major fly in the ointment is the *major perpetuator of evil in the world: human unconsciousness.*

Existence and the Healing Energy of Consciousness

The paradox and challenge of the pain-body is that it can be a real opportunity for awakening and transforming ordinary consciousness to a new sense of everyday life, a renewed awareness of who we are, and a fresh experience of Life. The unconsciousness that the pain-body thrives on—like a dark, dank, and dirty basement with no ventilation or light—can be opened up like any other life-form on Earth, to the daylight of Consciousness. Full awareness is the divine and ineffable experience of being human and feeling really alive in the world. Its energy is vital, creative, and oriented towards original Goodness in the Now.

Life is the perennial hope and basis for all new beginnings and changes in the world. But without a sense of inner purpose, we are wandering blindly in the world and are lead this way and that, by the slightest attraction, provocation, or familiarity. It is the nature of the pain-body, to continually look for those it can pry upon, infect, manipulate, or harm, often in the same devious ways that it has known. In its most extreme or psychopathic form, the pain-body is insane and even murderous in intent, so that the guilty one is often heard to say 'I did not know what came over me' in his or her defense of a criminal act.

"Forgive them Father for they know not what they do" Jesus famously said during the last moments of his Crucifixion. It is a statement that could be applied again and again to mass movements and individual actions that are motivated by the pain-body. Given the reality of the pain-body and the number of people who are in need of or seeking psychological help 'knowing not what they do' or acting without inner awareness is quite widespread. For example, it has often been observed by political scientists and pundits that the mass of people in a democracy will consistently and unhesitatingly vote for those candidates who appeal to the emotions and prejudices of the pain-body, rather than those candidates whose policies and philosophy may actually help them the most.

The power and influence of the pain-body or unconsciousness in humanity can never be underestimated, especially in times of greatest crisis or threat. However, once the threshold of higher awareness is crossed and one enters the light of Consciousness that illuminates the dark contours, habits, and tendencies of the pain-body, a real purging or dissolving of the pain-body from the total being of a person takes place. The result is a new sense of self, a clearer, more positive, optimistic, and hopeful sense of one's life-world and the wider, collective world.

It seems that mass movements, political parties, and armies are grounded in pain-bodies and ego-structures seeking gratification, admiration and recognition from others. Based upon many documented studies of War and statements taken from soldiers of all ranks, military life seems especially suited to the psychology of the pain-body. Gwynne Dyer has written as convincingly as anyone has—on the basis of his international study of soldiering and the military mind—about the insanity, irrationality, and unconsciousness with which warfare takes place. (9)

On an existential level, Tolle writes: "People with strong pain-bodies often reach a point where they feel their life is becoming unbearable, where they can't take any more pain, any more drama. One person expressed this by saying plainly and simply that she was 'fed up with being unhappy'. Some people may feel, as I did, that they cannot live with themselves anymore. Inner peace becomes their first priority." (10)

This realization drives most people who want to feel good again, to 'dis-identify' or disconnect from the emotional, psychological, and mental sources of the pain-body—whether these are persons, places, or things. Sometimes it may mean a physical or geographical separation from others persons, places, or things. Most often it is an important inner shift in consciousness, activating higher Consciousness, that must take place even after physical or environmental changes are made.

We are beings of Energy and the energy of self, mind, and ego comes from any person, place, or thing that we have identified with in the past. When we 'dis-identify' or detach ourselves from the main sources of pain, suffering and negativity in our lives, the pain-body within begins to die since it thrives upon any negative, unconscious, and painful memories. And dis-identification marks the true beginning of the healing process and getting rid of the pain-body that interferes with human happiness and higher Consciousness.

Prior to the experience of purification, purging, and healing of the total self, however, a pain-body can seemingly drain a normally healthy and peaceful person, of all natural Goodness. However, the initial realization of the most acute pain and unhappiness can often be the trigger for awakening us to the unequivocal desire to feel, see, and experience the original Goodness of Life again.

Breakthrough: a New Zeitgeist

Tolle believes that we are at the beginning of another cultural breakthrough—perhaps like that of the late 1960's and early 70's in the West—and he appears to be correct. It may be picking up where 1989-90 ending of the Cold War promised so much yet failed to deliver except to the rich class. The presidential election of 2008 in the United States could be the ending of the darkest international period of the United States foreign policy since 1945 and the ending of WWII. It also could spell the end of the worst presidential politics in United States history. These kinds of changes may seem irrelevant to deep pain-body changes in a given individual; but as volumes of scholarship tell us, individual existence cannot be entirely separated from the present social world or the historical times through which one lives.

Getting free of the pain-body is also freeing your existential self from the world 'out-there' as the empiricists say. Dis-identifying the self from the sources of the pain-body is the first step in healing the Self and restoring original Goodness; and the second step is not to be attached to your 'dis-identifications' since the intellect is blind to its conceptual forms without the perceptions of the body and Consciousness.

If you can give up your attachment to the pain-body for the sake of inner peace and tranquility, it will be immediately evident how much better you feel about yourself. The experience of feeling better, from the energetic centers or chakras of the body, will immediately spread to all your relationships with others and the world. You have nothing to loose and everything to gain in dis-identifying from the sources of pain and suffering in your present and past experiences. Remember that it is the nature of the pain-body to be attracted to, cling or be attached to other pain-bodies, 'problems' and sources of violence.

A completely pain-free self brings a happy and peaceful feeling to ordinary consciousness. It is just enough to feel and be alive in the present moment when you are pain-free. But if you begin piling on expectations about how great your life is going to be, in the future, you simply step out of the Now and begin erecting a new pain-body, all over again. The old habits of the pain-body within the nervous system are all too easy to re-establish if you are not consciously present in the Here-and-Now.

When you accept yourself at this moment, in the Now, you can feel whatever you feel without excuses, apologies, or conditions. When you are truly, deeply able to accept who you are, "Your true nature emerges, which is one with the nature of God." For Tolle, 'God' is synonymous with *Sat-Chit-Ananda* or perfect Being-Consciousness-Bliss—in the language of the *Advaita Vedanta* school of Hinduism. And forget about trying to pin down the meaning of 'God' or defining it conceptually; such definitions only create the illusion of understanding and deepen our ignorance with a false certainty of literal truth. (11)

'Being' expresses the Alpha and Omega of human knowledge by acknowledging our awesome and inspiring ignorance before the absolute totality of everything. Being or 'what-is' is entirely liberating when we admit that we often only 'know' reality through the symbols of intellectual understanding and such intellectual symbols represent the vaguest of realities. However, in Being-who-you-are, in the Now of awareness, you will know and experience all you can or need to know about yourself and real existence.

'Being' is the purest aesthetic, intellectual, and metaphysical expression of Higher Consciousness and marks the world with least possible trace of pain or suffering. In the context of emanative Being, the rays of light from yonder horizon fill the day and night of earthbound Consciousness in each of us. And 'you' as a separate, real being are just one of many who appears from and disappears into the mystery of Eternal Being; or like 'waves making their way relentlessly towards the ocean shore', we spend our lives watching and wondering.

What is required to make Being real are the sources of immediate experience that we have through the senses, emotions, and instincts of ordinary existence. We are not just intellectual or metaphysical beings, but persons with 'clay feet' persons with bones, blood and glands that make ordinary existence possible, in the first place. Indeed, it is the sublime hope and ideal that we all learn to connect our ordinary, everyday self with what is most enduring and meaningful in existence—whatever it is called.

It is in the present moment, in the Eternal Now, that the 'trans-mutation' of ordinary consciousness into higher Consciousness occurs. It is the ceasing of personal identification with all that gives pain and suffering. "Be-Here-Now" was the refrain of the nineteen-seventies and the Age of Aquarius and it could once again symbolize the *Zeitgeist* of the early twenty-first century.

PART IV

AWAKENING TO THE BODY,

MIND AND SOUL

We are whole beings, creatures of nature, an essence of Being. We can think, believe, walk, and make things. We can speak, listen, use language and communicate. We are caring, nonviolent beings and we are harming, violent beings. We can create and we can destroy. We can proliferate and we are everywhere on the Earth.

We are organisms with minds and souls. We are integrated systems with physical structures, functioning abilities and limitless potentialities. We are everywhere connected with Nature, a world existing apart from the human world and as miraculous and horrifying.

Atoms, cells and molecules make up the body, a wonder of design and parts, all doing as intended by the eternal Mind of All. Each life-form of the Earth is integral to the Whole, the universal Mind creating the infinite many; atoms and matter, energy and matter, each transmuting and transacting with the other, creating life-forms, forever and everywhere.

Minds creating meaning, wills creating purpose, actions creating consequences. Everywhere there are unities, small unities within greater ones, connections discovered, connections waiting to be discovered.

Meanwhile forms beautiful are being born, and more beautiful yet to come; each a carrier of the seed that went before and the one hereafter, with no end in sight; thoughts more numerous than stars in the sky, thoughts rising and falling in the great sky within; and knowledge growing, ever growing, changing, clarifying and expanding.

We awaken to a soul, the essence of All, the essence of Being. We awaken a world within the greater world, the world of earth, air, fire and water. We awaken the world of the elements within, with each breath, each moment in the Now. We awaken to *Sat, Chit, Ananda* or perfect Being, Consciousness and Bliss in our meditation.

Chapter 13

INTEGRATIVE STRUCTURES AND FUNCTIONS

OF THE WHOLE BODY

What is the whole body related to nature and existence? How are the subtle and gross, inner and outer, spiritual and material structures, functions and qualities related as a unified whole? How is the whole body related to the experiences of mind, ego and soul of ordinary existence? What do the chakra centers of Kundalini yoga symbolize in human experience and meaning? And why is an awakened consciousness of the whole body important to our sense of experience, happiness and Being-in-the-world?

"Liberation cannot be achieved except by the perception of the identity of the individual spirit with the universal Spirit. It can be achieved neither by Yoga (physical training) nor by Sankhya (speculative philosophy) nor by the practice of religious ceremonies, nor by mere learning...." Shankara, *The Crest Jewel of Wisdom*

"Now God, though He is absolutely immaterial, can alone by His own power produce matter by creation; and so He alone can produce a form in matter, without the aid of any preceding material form.... Therefore, as no-pre-existing body had been formed, through whose power another body of the same species could be generated, the first human body was of necessity made immediately by God." St Thomas Aquinas

"When I go back into the ground, into the depths, into the well-spring of the Godhead, no one will ask me whence I came or whither I went." Eckhart Tolle

"Yoga is restraining the mind-stuff (Chitta) from taking various forms (Vrittis) .... Control is by practice and non-attachment... That effect which comes to those who have given up their thirst after objects either seen or heard, and which wills to control the objects, is non-attachment. That is extreme non-attachment which gives up even the qualities and comes from the knowledge of Purusha." Patanjali

"Karma concealing wisdom...right insight; karma leading to pain and pleasure; karma creating complete delusion; karma determining the length of one's life...one's social status...one's birth into a particular family; karma that is generally obstructive." Georg Feurerstein

Feuerstein's interpretation of the Jain theory of karma is of course incomplete as quoted since he correctly reports upon the seven categories of existence and the fourteen rungs on the *Ladder of Liberation* in the pages that follow in his Yoga tradition text. The Jain theory of the soul is the secret key to their treasury of wisdom; and the Jain view of the soul (*jiva*) is composed of pure energy or *prana* which in its fall to embodiment and the world, is corrupted by atomic particles or the stuff of karma and causal determinism. The goal of Jain striving or seeking is called *moksa* or an absolute freedom-from all forms of *karma* which tradition teaches are nearly 150; and once the clinging net of existence is removed from the whole body and mind, the soul is then liberated from existence or karmic conditioning, and returns to its original purity or essence of Being. (1)

The Inner and Outer Body

Tolle emphasizes the importance of the body as the essential life-form of transformation. However, his emphasis is not upon the physical or outer body, but it is the inner body, the body of energy and formlessness, the body that is the basis for experience of all kinds.

The attempt to escape from the physical body, has, since the beginning of the various religious histories, been a record of failure, futility, and hypocrisy, since we cannot exist as human beings without a living body that has needs, structures and functions that are interactive with the mind and Consciousness and dependent upon the Life-force of the soul. Tolle wrote:

"The fact is that no one has ever become enlightened through denying or fighting the body or an out-of-body experience. Although such an experience can be fascinating and can give you a glimpse of the state of liberation from the material form, in the end you will always have to return to the body, where the essential work of transformation takes place. Transformation is through the body, not away from it. This is why no true master has ever advocated fighting or leaving the body, although their mind-based followers often have." (2)

Countless myths and fragments of teachings from ancient teachings have survived from the lives of Jesus, Buddha, Socrates, Mohammad, and other founders of the world's religions. 'You are not your body' 'I am in this world but not of it', 'you exist as a higher and not lower being' and other such half-truths have served as precepts advocating asceticism and monasticism or admonitions against life, the body, and our obvious animality. The effect of this falsifying attitude has been a culture of anti-life based upon an underlying fear of the body, nature, and death; and the evidence for this ancient feeling is the history of sacrifice, murderous rituals, and oppression against all those who would question the existence of unseen gods or goddesses.

A deep fear appears: the more intensely Life is felt, the more close death will appear to be. The fact is birth, Life, death co-exist in existence, and on a karmic plane of reality, so does re-birth or the continuation of Life in another form. The fear of Life and the love of life-forms cannot easily co-exist in the same internal space. The fact remains that Life is Presence or eternal Being and no conditional existence can ever interrupt its universality especially the extinction of one or more finite life-forms. However, death or non-being is an ever constant possibility for each human life-form of Now and *the existential threat* is present from biological conception in the womb and remains present throughout our worldly existence.

What we may not see is how a radical extinction comes to all life-forms, species, and life-conditions in time. As commonplace and natural as dying and death are to biological life-forms on the Earth, it is not inconceivable that very advanced species of life elsewhere in the universe die with less frequency than we do. Cryogenics, cyborg medical technology and the genetic sciences are already making life-extension dreams more theoretically plausible and doable. However, it is not plausible—from what we presently understanding about the manifested universe—that we could ever 'live forever' especially in anything resembling our present life-form.

Ontologically speaking, whatever comes into being, will sooner or later pass out of being. It is the law of constant change, transformation and impermanence that applies to all forms of existence, from the smallest atomic particles to the greatest galactic formations. In fact, one could view all of Creation as just one inconceivably vast Body of mathematical principles, atomic particles, chemical substances, electro-magnetic and gravitational fields of Energy, searching for the next planetary habitat to gain a fruitful footing on, in the name of their Creator Being and for all eternity. As such, all life-forms enjoy and suffer, by turns, the same existential destiny.

When outer space explorers visit and occupy other planets in our solar system and eventually colonize the planets in other star systems, they will be looking for evidence of the Life-force in specific chemical, mineralogical, and biological conditions of those planets. But since we know that Life and its creative, life-giving energy is universal and eternal, there is no reason to doubt that it could be present on planet X, given suitable, supportive chemical and geological conditions. Furthermore, we should not think that the creative Spirit or Life-force does not exist elsewhere in the universe; in fact, the Life-force is absolutely integral to the appearing, flourishing, and transforming of any life-forms, no matter how strange or alien they may appear to our terrestrial eyes.

Karma, Selfless Action, and Liberation

There is a sense in which a physical body is itself universal, given favorable supportive conditions for its development; but all physical bodies are finite, wherever they may be found, and however long they may survive. For where there is birth of a given life-form, death will inevitably follow, sooner or later, whether it is sixty seconds, sixty days, sixty years, or six hundred thousand years. The law of karma is a law of absolute causal predetermination on the levels of physical, human, and sentient existence and it indifferently operates in the past, present and future periods of time and space. However, the law of karma ceases the moment an 'enlightened' Consciousness ceases to identify with the processes, functions, and forms of temporal existence, and realizes 'God' or the Unmanifested realm of Eternal Being.

In Indigenous wisdom, the world religions, and *classical philosophy*—in the tradition of Socrates, Plato and Aristotle in the West— this momentous experience imparts a truly profound transformation in a person. The moment of 'enlightenment' or a breakthrough to Higher Consciousness, has been named, described and explained from many different points. Certainly one of the most well-known discourses on the enlightenment experience can be found in the *Bhagavad-Gita*, the most sacred text of Hindu literature. From Chapter Three of that text, it is written:

"For those of clear mind there is the path of knowledge, for those who work there is the path of selfless action. No one will attain perfection by refusing to work. No one can refuse to act; everyone is forced to act by the *gunas*. Therefore you must perform every action as a sacrifice to God, free from all attachment to the results thereof. In this way man attains the supreme truth through work, without care for its fruits. The ignorant act for the fruits of action; the wise act equally, but without desire for reward." (3)

The philosophical context for the ideal of selfless action is *Karma Yoga* or the realization of God through selfless action that looks for no reward. The three *gunas—fundamental qualities of existence*–are referred to here for the crucial role that they play in human existence at level of *prakriti* or nature. It is assumed quite generally in Indian religious philosophies, i.e. Hindu, Buddhist, and Jainist, that *gunas* compose the most basic, natural qualities of all manifestations of Reality, i.e. immobility (*tamas*), activity (*rajas*), purity and balance (*sattva*).

In Hindu philosophy, *Brahman* or the Supreme Creator put these qualities into the playful energy of *Maya*, a goddess imagined to veil or conceal the identity of *Brahman* with her fascinating dance and sexual beauty, as seen in many religious arts and philosophies of India. And since everything in this world is more or less out-of-balance due to *maya's* cosmic dance of veils, the best that we can do is work for the perfection of *sattva*—the most pure and subtle energy of creation which may be compared to the light from a star.

Although *sattva* is the most desirable quality for human development of the three *gunas, i.e. sattva, tamas, rajas,* the other two *gunas* are opposing /complementary forces for its fuller realization. The animal nature (*tamas*) of humans is often a source of inertia, laziness, and stupidity, which shows up in inactivity and the lack of consciousness. In order to realize the quality of *sattva*, a person must overcomes not only the heaviness and inertia of physical and mental being, but also activate the opposing natural energy, i.e. *rajas*, which is defined as passion, activity, and restlessness.

Unfortunately one extreme tendency only creates an opposite one and so in the quality of *sattva-consciousness* it is believed will reconcile or bring together in a perfect balance the extreme tendencies of existence. Again, the goal of *sattva-consciousness* is a foolish one since the liberation or freedom from warring tendencies in existence is only a temporary victory in the longer road to total liberation found only in the Consciousness of *Atman-Brahman*.

It is thought that the three *gunas* or qualities of existence control the feeling, thought, and action of a person at any given moment and that one quality tends to dominate the other tendencies. The three *gunas* have been fictionalized as the 'three thieves' who only steal one's potential for true Liberation from the identification with this body, mind, ego, and world, in various stories. The theme or assumption is that any identification with a quality in this world is only an occasion for further entrapment, desire, and lack of real freedom (*moksa*).

If we can learn how to be free ourselves from all desire or the source of karma, then the endless repetition on the wheel of existence (*samsara*) will cease and true Liberation (*Nirvana*) will follow. However, there is a practical difficulty in 'ceasing all desire' since it only brings death if followed to its biological extremes. For instance, if we cease to desire water and food for the body, we will soon die, and perhaps leave the mind or soul in no better condition than before the deliberate 'ceasing of all desire'; and if we cease the natural desire to breathe, a few minutes will suffice.

From the Buddhist perspective on karma, intention is the key ingredient in action and consciousness. What we 'hold' in our minds to do, whether we perform the deed or not, is the most significant factor in moral experience. To the Jains of India, *karma* of any kind is not desirable, whether it is deemed to be 'good' or 'bad' since the effects of all desire or intention merely bind one to existence and thus rebirth. Whether anyone can ever really claim to be absolutely free of all desire, *karma*, or even intention, is highly debatable, problematic, and at least paradoxical.

Assuming that many life-forms may be required to realize *moksa* or absolute freedom seems to take us all off the hook, at least temporarily; ultimately though there is no escape from the dilemma of existence except one, i.e. the freedom or the will. Almost every philosophy or religion known admits to the importance and reality of the free will except one: the scientific materialists, logical positivists or reductionists who will admit to nothing even remotely idealistic, monistic, or universal. Yet the freedom as articulated in Modern and Postmodern Existentialism still holds the strongest case for its Presence of the Will at the heart of our nature, i.e. body, mind, and soul. The most absolute ground for the reality of freedom is the divinity of Consciousness, i.e. its patent quasi-independence from the physical body and nature.

The will-to-Consciousness is entirely mobile, translucent, and the 'mover' of a self that enjoys the consequences of choosing and acting in the world. One does not have to follow Aristotle— who believed the Prime Mover is underlying *substance*—to believe in freedom. No higher goal exists than to be free from the pre-determining or limiting conditions of existence; and yet it would be impossible to accomplish anything of substance without the prior potentialities of Being that theists liken to 'God'. With or without the belief in 'God', each individual is endowed with seemingly infinite potentialities that can bring fulfillment when acted skillfully and wisely upon. And such courses of action can bring greater satisfaction to individuals, as well as improving the quality of living for others.

Choosing without a trace of self or ego may be impossible for mere mortals, but we can simulate the experience for sake of spiritual Liberation and closeness to eternal Being —in 'this very lifetime' as the Buddhists say. Or as the Hindus say, if we can real-ize Atman or the universal Self within all beings, then we can also become 'perfectly enlightened' or one with *Brahman.* On the other hand, the Jains insist that we are all, already blessed with an immortal, perfectly blissful, pure soul, within this decaying body, ridiculous ego, and imperfect mind. Thus, it is your simple task in Life to identify only with the soul or the Life-force which is eternal, infinite and omniscient like the soul of every *Tirthankara* or fully Enlightened and Self-realized Heroes of Indian history; then and only then can you count yourself among the 'Blessed'. (4)

In sum, Life is eternal and infinite while every life-form— including the 'Enlightened Ones'—in nature and existence is destined to die and be transformed into other life-forms (the many) or truly liberated (the few). The Higher Consciousness that human beings enjoy is the most essential fact of spiritual life.

It is the life of Consciousness that sustains us as human beings and gives us our higher potentialities for Being-in-the-world. This reality appears in the form of the Inner Body which exists through the structures and functions of physical, biological and metaphysical reality.

What, though, are the anatomical, neurological and physiological systems of the body that enable us to do transformational or healing work? To answer this question adequately brings us to *Kundalini Yoga*, a philosophical model for thinking about the totality of the inner (subtle) and outer (gross) body and acting upon these beliefs and ideas in everyday life

Kundalini Yoga: the Chakras of Wisdom

Tolle does little more than name the systems of the body due to his emphasis upon the inner body or body of Life-energy. In terms of the *chakra* (*chakra*=circle or wheel of energy) system of *Kundalini Yoga*, there are seven major sites where the Life-energy of the various biological and karmic systems are centered. These sites are situated from the lowest end of the spine, upwards to the crown of the head; and there are also energy sites at various joints, meridians, and pressure points of the body's limbs. In turn, these energy plexuses are the sites where the various anatomical and physiological systems of the body are contiguously located, through their most vital organs. In other words, you cannot separate the energy of the inner body from the outer body or the energetic and subtle body from the physical and gross body since it is the interactions between the biological and Yogic system that sustain the whole body of a living human being.

When Jesus said that 'your whole body will be filled with light' as you become one with God or the Source, he was referring to the inner energy body, soul or higher Self (Self=*Atman* in Hinduism). In terms of the *chakras* of Yoga philosophy, the Source or Self exists vertically at all levels of the body; and the mind, ego, and roles (all of which Tolle takes to task or critiques) merely occupy different *chakra* sites along the spine's energy currents or *nadis*. In the end, everything acquired in the temporal world of *Samsara*—the realm of 'interdependent origination' in Buddhism—is the stuff of illusion, impermanence, and mis-identification.

From most ancient times of India, *Kundalini Yoga* has recorded the names, images, and meanings for the various energy centers of the inner or subtle body. They are, beginning at the lowest end of the spine, 1, the *Muladhara-chakra*, at the lower end of the spine at the coccyx bone; 2, the *Svadhisthana-chakra*, opposite to the genitals; 3, the *Manipura-chakra*, at the solar plexus or navel region; 4, the *Anahata-chakra*, at the heart, lungs and chest region, 5, the *Vishuddha-chakra*, in the throat or neck region of the thyroid; 6, the *Ajna-chakra*, between the eyebrows of the forehead; 7, the *Sahasrara-chakra*, just above the crown of the head. Although these energy centers are mythic in nature, they have acquired a pragmatic significance owing to centuries of meditative practice, visualization, and yogic practices by mystics, yogis, and practitioners of many kinds. (5)

For example, the philosophical meanings of the chakra system have been understood by many diverse persons and they are essentially the same Starting from the lowest chakra center and moving slowly upwards along the spine to the crown of the head, the wisdom tradition of *Kundalini Yoga* teaches the values of: 1, Surviving, Adapting and Thriving; 2, Procreation, Joy and Pleasure; 3, Success, Power and Fulfillment; 4, Love, Compassion and Nonviolence, 5, Communication, Creativity and Intuition; 6, Intellect, Understanding and Meaning; 7, Self-realization, Enlightenment and Liberation. The establishing of these values, of course, did not just fall from heaven or the sky, but they have been discovered and experienced as real neuro-physiological processes of the body, mind, and soul, over many generations in different parts of the world.

Due to this tradition of yogic wisdom, we can awaken the inner Self of the *chakras* more quickly and efficiently than ever. Although the West is presently in the midst of an economic and financial collapse, it marks the dawning of a New Era of hope, healing, and promise symbolized by the election of the first brown-skinned President, Barack Obama (2008 and 2012). Every revolution in feeling, thought, and action is preceded by the collapse of the old cultural forms and beliefs, and the realization of new possibilities; and these changes are happening in the most subtle and gross forms of Being and culture nearly everywhere today.

Tolle does not use the chakras in his writings by name although the Presence of Life-giving energy in the *inner body* leaves little doubt as to his experience and belief. Their real existence in his unitary vision is implied through the fact that he extensively refers to the 'inner body of spiritual energy', 'pure consciousness', the 'enlightenment experience', 'Source', 'Yoga philosophy' and the like, throughout his two major books. And even if Tolle has little awareness of the chakra system in its technicalities, his Consciousness of the inner body and its obvious mutual dependence upon the functioning of biological systems and Life-giving energy from an infinite and eternal Source, puts him solidly on the ground of the Perennial wisdom of Yoga philosophy.

The *chakras* are used by meditators, psychologists, and other seekers of spiritual wisdom in many different ways, owing to differing existential assumptions and cultural values. In fact, there are at least as many traditions of Yoga philosophy as there are major chakras centers. Furthermore, the major world religions can be meaningfully compared to the various chakra centers, in their experiential and theoretical essentials. I am not making a case for this here, although I have written about this elsewhere.

Not only is it important to know the essential meanings of the *chakras*, but it is far more important to have personal or direct experience of the *chakras*, through meditation, visualization and behaviors associated with them. In this respect, starting from the lowest to the highest chakra centers, they represent the psychological experiences of freedom, power, and willing: 1, the will-to-survival, 2, the will-to-procreation, 3, the will-to-success, 4, the will-to-love, 5, the will-to-creativity, 6, the will-to-understanding, and 6, the will-to-liberation. In short, the Energy of the Will, effort and action lies at the center of the subtle body, encompassing the spine, brain and self.

It is through an individuated *Will-to-Power*, Arthur Schopenhauer and Friedrich Nietzsche asserted (in the 19th century) that humankind most fully realizes its most intimate relations with the eternal Life-energy and the universal Will. The enormity of this discovery drove both men to the extremes of their genius, albeit resulting in a profound critique of Christianity, Socratic philosophy and European culture (Nietzsche); and in the case of Schopenhauer, his dark, pessimistic view of the history and culture resulted in a profound insight about the connection between human sexuality and instinctive nature or the blind, unconscious drivenness of humans. Yet in both cases, their genius and troubled backgrounds resulted in their unhappiness and bitterness (Schopenhauer) and late-stage insanity (Nietzsche).

In sum, *Kundalini Yoga* is based upon an ancient, pre-historic and esoteric tradition of mythic and philosophic significance. Its various energy centers of the body point us to essential, timeless truths of Life and higher Consciousness, in the Now of experience and knowledge. In an age when information can transform consciousness at the speed of light through electricity, an individual can absorb thousands of years of Yogic wisdom and philosophical understanding about Life, the body, and human potentiality, through the new electronic technology and the re-discovery of ancient wisdom and its practices. (6)

Nature and Culture: Awakening to Total Being

Just as the chakras have been named, described, and explained by many practitioners and theorists over the centuries, the biological systems have ancient roots dating back to Aristotle and the atomists, materialists and naturalists of ancient Greece, India and China. Of course, the major scientific discoveries and medical advances in our understanding of the physical body have only occurred in the last 400 years or so; and even more recently as far as 'gee-whiz' medical breakthroughs go. In the fields of neuro-science and genetics, the advances in our understanding of the physical, microbiological, and energetic systems of the brain, consciousness, and unconsciousness, are occurring daily. And there are similar breakthroughs occurring in the natural sciences of geology, extraterrestrial science, biology, climatology, energy science, etc.

However, what many of these new fields of science lack, with some conspicuous exceptions, is an adequate metaphysics or vision of the ultimate questions of reality, i.e. the meaning and purpose of Life, the origin and destiny of Everything, immortality, and so forth. Eckhart Tolle, David Montgomery (a geologist) and Francis Collins (discussed below) could count as a modest beginning in filling the knowledge gap between the sciences and the ancient wisdom traditions (which includes the world religions).

It is not just a question of the 'gap' or 'lack' that afflicts the reductionist sciences and some of their major proponents—it is the negative, nay-saying attitude towards *anything spiritual or metaphysical*—that kills communication and promote ignorance on both sides. A proverbial blind spot exists in the physical, social, and behavioral sciences and it is the cause of a powerful prejudice against anything religious, metaphysical, or even ontological among large numbers of the educated class of the world. The intellectual distance between the various sciences and the religions of the world is now, almost but not quite unbridgeable, on philosophical and cultural levels. However, there are outstanding exceptions to this systemic prejudice among scientists and their apologists, towards anything remotely religious or 'spiritual'.

Among these exceptions is Francis Collins, the geneticist who headed the Human Genome Project in its early days, and wrote the remarkable book, *The Language of God*—a book that argues for the philosophical compatibility of science and religion. Collins affirms that the 'language of God' is the human genetic code itself—Now decoded and translated into the thirty thousand or so basic genes that account for the incredible complexity of the human body and its potentialities. If one desires empirical 'proof' for the existence of an infinitely creative Source of the life-forms found in nature, you need look no further than the human genetic structure and its many miraculous structures and functions in the natural body—so says Dr. Francis Collins. (7)

Gone in an instant could be all the age-old antagonisms and dualisms between Man and nature, God and nature, Spirit and nature—in the more inclusive, integrative perspective of knowledge. We are essentially spiritual beings of divine origin living through material bodies, becoming and evolving in a natural world. There are no dualisms between spirit and matter, mind and body, self and other, in divine Nature and its attunement with Consciousness. We are one integrated and whole being functioning in unison with nature and the Life-force. Nature, instead of being demonized by fear, illusion, and the dualistic 'indifference' or 'neutrality' of the scientific attitude, is translucent evidence of a caring, loving and sustaining Presence.

Instead of looking upon nature and the universe as an alien, threatening force in our lives, a more enlightened view sees it as a caring necessity for our total being and the very means by which we were created and have evolved to our present stage of consciousness and culture. The principle Idea that regulates or orders all forms in the universe is one set in three stages: creation, becoming, and transformation, in the material and spiritual dimensions of Being; and unless we go beyond the casual or material stages of necessity, we cannot see the phenomenal or possible levels of reality where Consciousness, the Will, and an essential Self exist and account for all that we call personal, cultural and sentient existence.

The Biological and Yogic Systems of the Body

Corresponding to the seven chakras are the twelve major biological systems of the human body. The first chakra level of adaptation for the sake of survival and security corresponds to the muscular, skeletal, integumentary, and neuro-sensory systems of the body. The second chakra level of sexuality and pleasure corresponds to procreative, urinary, and neuro-sensory systems of the body. The third chakra level of power and success corresponds to the digestive and periphery systems of the body. The fourth chakra level of love and compassion corresponds to circulatory, respiratory, and neurological systems of the body. The fifth chakra level of intuition and creativity corresponds to the immunological, lymphatic, and spinal-neurological systems of the body. The sixth chakra level of understanding and reason corresponds to the neurological and endocrine systems. And the seventh chakra level of transcendence and liberation corresponds to the entire nervous system, and the electro-magnetic, elemental and atomic forces of the universe. (8) (9)

It is these biological and physical systems and their chakra sites or nexes that are the material and organic manifestation of the Unmanifested Life-force that is eternally present. Without the manifested Presence of the Life-force, no life-form, human or otherwise, would exist on Earth or be possible! In fact, it is not plausible—assuming the Unity of the universe—that life-forms of any kind could appear independently of the universal Life-force on some other planet or realm of Being; but given the limits of human reason, understanding, and imagination, 'plausibility' may be an insufficient criterion for speculation.

The perennial precept of Wisdom is to love and cherish each moment of this life, in this body, and in this world, Now, as evidence of a divine Presence and an awesome universe! There is every reason to believe that innumerable other species, worlds, and life-forms exist throughout the universe, and if there are other 'universes', there too; since the Perennial Philosophy assumes that an infinitely creative and perfect Being has made all things real and possible. Unfortunately it is a creed eclipsed by fear, greed, and ignorance of self and 'difference' wherever it is found.

In sum, it is unlikely that a Life-force can appear independently of biological systems of some kind, whether they are

silicon or carbon- based or other. Also I am arguing for a completely unified and non-dualistic universe, one where spirit and
matter co-exist and give rise to one another from the Mystery
of creation—which means among other things, that we do not
understand everything.

In all becoming and Transformation, there is a neglected
Real or essence that 'saves' each of us from the oblivion of mate-
rial being. It is at once natural, divine, and evolving. The essence
of Being is the soul or Self that is not just immortal but eternal.
And it is this metaphysical fact or reality that is the essence or
Consciousness of experienced Being, in the Now of everyday life.

Death, Enlightenment, and Pragmatic Truth

If we intend to awaken the inner body where the Spirit
essentially dwells, we must begin in the material or real world
of contingent being. The enlightenment process is a matter of
'letting go' of everything, at least once a day, and more often if
you can. We must think about 'enlightenment' first as getting rid
of old, negative, pain-body habits of mind, body and soul. It may
be a long, difficult, psycho-ontological path to travel, where others undoubtedly can help but which you alone must tread and
undergo. Second, there is a need to be frugal, thoughtful, and
simple in your living habits, and giving everything that you think
of as your 'own', away, to others who may need it more than you
do, long before you die.

Generosity or a spirit of giving rather than one that is 'taking', possessive and fearful, is a virtue in every major religion or
spiritual path. On the material level, generosity means detaching
yourself from everything you own and not caring what happens to
your things or money, since the entire Capitalistic form of Being
is a sad and sick delusion of ownership, that only creates divisions
between people, i.e. the economic class system, enslavement, sexism, speciesism, etc. On a more spiritual level, generosity means
'giving up' negative emotions from the past, expectations about
the future, and relations in your present life-world. Morally,

generosity refers to detaching yourself from any and all relations of identification or feelings that you are 'invested' in a role or ego-state that entitles you to benefits and privileges.

Much of the preceding precepts are extremely difficult for the vast majority of people to ever fully actualize. And that is why the 'enlightenment experience'—the fully developed feeling of a liberated Consciousness and way of living—is so elusive and difficult to establish, once and for all. It is one thing for someone to realize, in momentary glimpses of higher Consciousness the radiance of Being; but it is something very different to establish a higher Consciousness as the basis for one's way of living in the real world. And this is also why so many religions, philosophies and sciences seem to have so little to do with social problems, mass values and pursuits, and the whole materialistically driven, global nightmare.

Facing death, there are many who believe that they will never die. For the rest of us—Realists and Existentialists—we may anticipate the end of our life-form all-too-much, and hope that we are not surprised or shocked when our body is assaulted by a disorder for which there is no cure. However, what may come as either a surprise or nothing at all is the aftermath of this life-form. As Tolle has said, we will just have to 'wait and see' for the full truth about death. The Perennial or metaphysical Truth about death is that we will know a condition far more perfect, blissful, and fulfilling than anything that we have experienced on Earth, following the big collapse of this body. And the means by which this occurs is through the same Life-force or divine energy that gave rise to our birth (from eternal Being) into the realm of material existence, in the first place.

Or as William James and the Pragmatists say, you are free to believe, choose and act upon whatever 'works' or brings satisfaction in your life. If believing that there is only oblivion following our natural death seems right to you, then freely choose it without any illusion or hope that it could be any different. But if believing in the possibility that there is infinitely more to Life than we can now know seems right and true for you, then choose that Path and follow it for as long as it seems right to you. Either way, you are entirely on your own, as a solitary subject in the vast universe; but you are also deeply and profoundly connected with every other life-form and element in the universe. (10)

As Emile Pascal of the 16th century has written, you really have nothing to loose in believing in the divinity of Christ. Christians like Pascal reason as follows: since Christianity only requires you to 'believe' in the divinity of Christ to be saved from Hell and enjoy a Heavenly existence at the side of God following death, why not believe? If the Christians are wrong about the divinity of Christ, you have lost nothing, but if they are right, then you will have gained eternal happiness by merely believing. It is a 'wager' or bet well-worth the risk of taking, and potentially a 'win-win' situation even if the belief only gives you hope in this life-time. (11)

Buddhists and other skeptics of Christian doctrines would typically counter that Pascal's Wager only creates a delusion about the afterlife and especially the existence of God and the divinity of Christ. However, there is a pragmatic sense in which any religious doctrine can be valuable to a person, group, and nation-state, even if it may be judged to be false by the criterion of verification. Following William James, an idea or belief may be valuable or true if it 'works' in satisfying the desire to end doubt, uncertainty, or a perceived difficulty. Or the truth of an idea or belief is known in the consequences that it may bring from a particular course of action.

Letting-Go and the Philosophic Adventure

As remarked before, although Tolle did not speak directly about the chakras, they are implicated in his concept of *the inner or subtle body*. Similarly, his comments and references to the bio-logical systems of the body, give further evidence that he wishes to use empirical knowledge like that of the biological systems of the body, for awakening us to the depths of Being. At the same, such knowledge and that of reason and the mind, Tolle insists can get in the way of experiencing Being; consequently thoughts of any kind merely create the illusion of reality—not the underlying, Unmanifested continuum of Being.

Meanwhile, there are many ways that we can awaken to real Being; perhaps no ways are more vital than the perception, feelings, moods, and intuition. Usually, these phenomena are thought to be soft, unsubstantial and unreliable phenomena of experience; but if they are removed from experience, you are only left with the shell of a person; in fact, no person at all.

If we remain only in our abstract thoughts, reasoning and logical mind, we will become entranced or cemented in our intellectual views, remembered wrongs, and expected outcomes. Furthermore, the hardening of thought, reason and feeling invariably find their way into linguistic forms of kind or another; and words not only harden thought processes, they can misinform, deceive, hurt and even kill.

Of course, forgiveness can soften the blow of unkind, lying words but memories may always linger and haunt us in the present moment. An act of forgiveness or an apology, whether it is inwardly acknowledged or outwardly confessed to another, is the beginning of 'getting over' or 'letting go' of remembered or imagined, perceived or judged, wrongs and hurts. Even more broadly, Tolle offers:

'Forgiveness means to offer no resistance to Life and to surrender to the wholeness of Being in the body', he writes. If we do not forgive ourselves and others, for mistakes made or wrongs felt, we will begin to hold grudges, harbor resentments, and cultivate anger, all of which are poisonous or toxic to the body, mind and soul. Such attachments and negativity only bring physical diseases and mental disorders in their train, if held onto long enough; and they are corrupting to the soul, adding to our karmic debt. (12)

The mind feeds on conflict, negativity, and feelings of strife. If there is a conflict, doubt, or uncertainty—a 'problem'—in your life, then the mind and its thinking processes set to work on it. Oftentimes, when the mind is working on a problem for which there is no ready solution, it easily becomes obsessed with it, and a distortion in the experience of Life inevitably occurs. Since so much of modern technocratic life is based upon thinking, problem-solving, and machinery, we tend to be dominated by the mind and its abstracting, symbol-using processes; and the Inner Body—the yogic, spiritual Body is the subtle and organic ground of real Experience—tends to pushed aside, forgotten and eventually sinks into total Unconsciousness.

In reality, 'you' or the inner being of Consciousness has virtually infinite power to intervene when there are blockages or real problems in the energy of the Body. Since the most important 'problem' in Life is the condition of your energy or inner body, you must attend to its cerebral vibrations and emotional states. If you are feeling 'low' or depressed, alienated or unbalanced, or badly for no apparent, external reason, the chances are that the pain-body is flaring up and looking for a fight; and you may be fighting on the outside with someone whom you love, while on the inside, you are engaged in the real fight with demons from your past, and projections from them upon innocent others in your present world.

If you can bring full Consciousness to a pain-body, whether in yourself or with others, you can destroy that negativity by just witnessing and not judging it. The pain-body is essentially sick, irrational, and unconscious, and thrives on negativity, judging, and violence of any kind. If you can rid yourself of its ghostly presence, you will immediately notice a big difference in your life-world and feelings about Life. And it is important to realize that the energy or inner body intuitively knows far more than we can readily understand, intellectually.

The 'ego' or the essential mind-created form that functions as a personality in the world, can be the greatest obstacle to forgiving others since the ego wants to hold onto everything that we experience and build up the energy of self-importance, being right, and more than often, pain and the memory of suffering. As we earlier saw, the ego thrives on pain and suffering, and does everything to keep us attending and focusing upon any past hurts or felt wrongs by others, to our detriment, since it interferes with our easy, harmonious, and more peaceful experiencing in the Now.

The mind and its potentiality for learning, thinking, and remembering is like a double-edged sword when it comes to forgiving or letting-go. Many ideas or concepts that we learn in life and particularly in formal schooling may become like lead sinkers in living that may only keep us weighed down with useless knowledge and deadened to what is new and alive, cripple our creativity and stifle our spontaneity in the Now.

The American pragmatic philosopher Alfred North Whitehead made a distinction between inert and dynamic ideas in the 20th century and it is still a good distinction when using knowledge to problem-solve. Whitehead wrote that

"Nothing is more curious than the self-satisfied dogmatism with which mankind at each period of its history cherishes the delusion of the finality of its existing modes of knowledge. Skeptics and believers are all alike. At this moment scientists and skeptics are the leading dogmatists. Advance in detail is not admitted; fundamental novelty is barred. This dogmatic 'common sense' is the death of philosophic adventure. The Universe is vast...." (13)

Any idea, attitude, or belief that is not subject to re-vision or change is potentially crippling to the 'philosophic adventure' and the love of Life. 'The Universe is vast' means to underscore the smallness of human knowledge and the immensity of the universe. Whitehead was a highly respected and accomplished philosopher of science, during his long tenure at Harvard University, but he was also profoundly humbled by his effort to comprehend the 'vast Universe' and the Life-force thereof. He famously said that a 'philosopher is an ignorant person speaking in public' private thoughts and feelings that would be better left in private life. Yet he spent a life-time teaching, writing, and trying to communicate what his innermost thoughts and feelings.

We have considered some of the extreme tendencies of human experience, thus far, and they are never more evident than with questions that are philosophical. In philosophy, skeptics and believers, scientists and religionists, fatalists and possibilists occupy some of these extreme tendencies. According to Whitehead, both may fail in the 'philosophic adventure' due to their dogmatism; and we must guard against new dogmatisms that the mind and its ego may smuggle into our thoughts.

Among believers or possibilists, the Unmanifested dimension of the body is your direct link with Source-Being or the creative Energy of the universe. Anything—especially the negative thoughts, memories, and emotions of the pain-body—can poison the physical body and sicken the mind and its ego states. This can create a neurological blockage in your ability to experience the most superlative states of Being through higher Consciousness.

Readiness, maturity, and the build-up of positive karmic energy, can ripen your Consciousness for the harvest of maturity. It is one of the benefits from aging or living through several developmental stages of existence. Aging alone, however, is no measure of wisdom since children are endowed with the power of insight and intuition.

Tolle states: "when you have reached a certain stage of inner connectedness, you recognize the truth when you hear it. If you haven't reached that stage yet, the practice of body awareness can bring about the deepening that is necessary" in order to experience Being, Now, and the Truth of divine Oneness. (14)

When you feel moved by the flow of Life, deeply within you, then you will know that your blessed time has come, and you will feel the Presence of the deepest Truth—no matter how short or long its duration in the Now.

Chapter 14

ATOMIC, ORGANIC AND SENSORY

CONNECTIONS WITH NATURE

What are the relations between nature, the self and civilization? How can we experience and know nature as physical or objectively and Nature as spiritual or intuitively? What are the relations between organic nature, human nature and spiritual Nature? And why is a sense of attunement or aesthetic oneness with Nature important to our health, well-being and sense of liberation?

"The world of Nature is many forms in One Mirror; no, One Form in diverse mirrors. Bewilderment arises from the difference of view, but those who perceive the truth... are not bewildered." Ibn Arabi

"Wherever you look, you will see that one unique Presence, indivisible and eternal, is manifested in all the universe, but that it is very difficult to perceive it. This is because God impregnates all things." Ananda Moyi

"I did not arrive at the fundamental laws of the universe by purely rational means." Albert Einstein

"Unity is in multiplicity and multiplicity in Unity." Sufi formula

"To think is the same as the thought that Being Is; for you will not find thinking without Being.... For nothing else either is or shall be except Being, since Fate has tied it down to be whole and motionless; therefore all things that mortals have established, believing in their truth, are just a name: becoming, perishing... and changing...." Parmenides

Parmenides of Elea in Sicily is one of the most *enigmatic* of ancient philosophers—*except to mystics and Perennialists*; for he believed in the eternity of Being and that real thinking only

245

occurs in relation to Eternal Being or what-is—prior to all change, forms, and opinions. Truth is the realization of the necessity that *something exists prior to everything else;* and Being is *permanent, indivisible, motionless, perfect, spherical, the same everywhere, whole, unique, unified, and balanced in every direction*—Parmenides wrote. Since Being represents the eternal Truth about everything, thinking separated from Being is impossible since Being interpenetrates all that we do, say and think.

Implied in Parmenides' intuition about Being is that *Being cannot not be (or something does not come from nothing)*; and that the whole of civilization and our names for, opinions and ideas of the entire phenomenal world, are the flotsam-and-jetsam on an infinite ocean with no boundaries. (1)

Martin Heidegger, among other modern Existentialists, was deeply persuaded by Parmenides' *vision* of eternal Being and wrote extensively about Being, arguing that Western philosophers have forgotten about integrative and spiritual Being in their quest to be scientific, analytical and empirical. As Heidegger passionately writes in *What is Metaphysics*:

"The spiritual decline of the earth is so far advanced that the nations are in danger of losing the last bit of spiritual energy that it makes it possible to see the decline (taken in relation to the history of 'being')....This simple observation has nothing to do with *Kulturpessimismus* [cultural pessimism], and of course it has nothing to do with any sort of optimism either; for the darkening of the world, the flight of the gods, the destruction of the earth, the transformation of men into a mass, the hatred and suspicion of everything free and creative, have assumed such proportions throughout the earth that such childish categories as pessimism and optimism have long since been absurd." (2)

The spiritual decline is not merely about philosophers and philosophy, it is the systemic condition of modern civilization and which the nations of the world must take responsibility for. Heidegger's critique of the horror of modern science and technology is expressed in a similar vein, which only *meditative thinking* about Being can remove us from—on a scale that is difficult to even imagine, given the depth and complexity of the problem—the *lack or distance* from Being.

Yet there are many who have been influenced by Heidegger's critique of the modern world and its destructive effects upon the sanity and well-being of human persons, nature and all sentient beings. Perhaps the greatest loss from our loss of Being is the potentiality of authentic existence which is uncovered in the paradox of death, our *ownmost possibility*.

As Heidegger writes in *Being and Time*, his *magnum opus*: "*The closest closeness which one may have in Being towards death as a possibility, is as far as possible from anything actual.* The more unveiledly this possibility gets understood, the more purely does the understanding penetrate into it as the possibility of the impossibility of any existence at all. Death, as possibility, gives *Dasein* nothing to be 'actualized' nothing which *Dasein*, as actual, could itself be.... Anticipation turns out to be the possibility of understanding one's *ownmost* and uttermost potentiality-for-Being—*the possibility of authentic existence....* Death is *Dasein's ownmost* possibility." (3)

Among other things, *authentic existence* is a redemptive possibility for Dasein, the human person, in being oriented towards our ownmost possibility, death, which in other contexts, he describes through his rather lurid concept of *freedom-towards-death*. In announcing the spiritual decline of earth and humanity Heidegger gives us a critique of human existence that is perhaps second to none except his philosophic muse, Friedrich Nietzsche.—Unfortunately, Heidegger's ontological genius did not extend to politics and the Second Reich of Nazi Germany.

Ancient and Contemporary Atomism

It is uncanny how the public, external, and physical world of visible and sensed phenomena later becomes the invisible, subtle reality of the unconscious mind. However, human experience is a compound or transformed mixture of various levels of illusion, intuitively synthesized by the mind, and later made sense of by Consciousness through language. What is strange and unfamiliar, in one context, often has a way of becoming the most familiar and commonplace reality in due time and under the influence of repetition and habit.

What we call 'real' in the sensory world is indeed real at the physical and atomic levels of reality. However, as physicists tell us, the material world brought to us by the outer senses is only an illusion of solidity since 99.99% of the material world is empty space. The space both within atoms, at the subatomic level, and between atoms is so vast that they can easily re-configure themselves, at atomic and chemical levels, into other forms once the initial forms that they constitute age or decay and are destroyed and disappear by natural or artificial conditions.

Even atoms and our intellectual models of them are partly fictions of their actual or real structure. No one can detect atoms through the eyes unless our perception is aided by elaborate electronic devices and/or experimental conditions. What we then see are abstract images, recorded at subatomic levels, of atomic particles, patterns, and waves of energy. Fascinating though they are, subatomic phenomena actually constitute an infinitesimal degree of any human and interactive situation, reducing their relevance in ordinary experience to the realms of mathematics and quantum physics.

At everyday levels, we experience the effects of atomic phenomena through the senses in hearing, seeing, tasting, smelling, and touching. As we shall see with the Roman poet, Lucretius, and his view of atoms and the Void, the birth of atoms and forms builds upon the death of others. Before Lucretius, there was the genius of Leucippus, Democritus and Epicurus of ancient Greece, all of whom intuited without the language and technology of modern atomists, that atoms make up every physical form of the universe, constantly moving and changing, giving shape and substance to our ideas, feelings, and perceptions. Furthermore, as modern neuro-science informs us, we can only experience or know material phenomena through the myriad networks of neurons within the brain that we later call *appearances or reality*. (4)

Similarly, atomistic philosophy appeared in India, particularly among the Jains in their concept of the eternal soul. In its pre-karmic or pre-existential form, the soul is pure, i.e. without any worldly corruption from experience. Once embodied, the soul (*jiva*) is in constant interaction with the body (*a-jiva*). The soul constitutes the higher Consciousness of potential *Omniscience*, in the Jain theory of knowledge; while the body represents unconsciousness, nature (*prakriti*) and spirit (purusha) appear from the unmanifested realm, at conception, to create each individual person.

A person is the spiritual form of the soul in material existence shaped by the causal interactions of nature, society and cosmos. The moral corruption of a person results from violent (and therefore *wrong*) 'beliefs, thoughts and actions' or negative karma. Violence (*himsa*) occurs through the motion of atoms that are not perfectly controlled by the Consciousness of the yogi —or one who has awakened the *Inner Body* through meditative practices. Absolutely perfect nonviolence (*ahimsa*) *can only be realized approximately* by fallible and finite human beings; while minimizing violence moves us ever closer to this ultimate, moral goal and the purity of the soul.

It is miraculous (and mysterious) how such extremely small phenomena as atoms can be known and manipulated at all by the mind and Consciousness of finite human beings. If we could learn how atoms came to be in the universe, in the first place, and the Void that presumably 'moves' them, then we could know with greater certainty why and how we are here.

Lucretius: *On the Nature of Things*

The early European empiricists articulated a theory of knowledge that had been clearly nascent in the history of knowledge for a long time. Anticipation of this development can be found in the early Greek Naturalists, Skeptics, and Sophists; and in the Roman Stoics, Epicureans and Hedonists of the ancient era. Of these broad grouping none perhaps has better survived the rages

of time and decay than Lucretius, and his long, lyrical and persuasive poem, *On the Nature of Things*.

The remarkable Latin poet, Lucretius (99BCE—55BCE)
articulated the thought of the Epicurus, the earlier founder of
the school of ethics (Epicureanism) that bears his name, perhaps better than anyone before or after his brief life. Of Epicurus
writings, only fragments remain but of Lucretius' justly famous
poem, the entire text was recovered by relentless searching during the late medieval period in a Christian monastery.

We must imagine that somewhere on the island of Pompeii,
shortly before it was buried by the eruption of Mt. Vesuvius,
Lucretius holding forth before his group of admirers and fel-
low artists, about the Roman gods whom he grudgingly paid his
respect to, for Lucretius was an atheist and saw in the structure
of Nature, a sufficient cause for the world's immense, prodigal
variety and abundance. For instance, take the following passage
from Book I, *The Nature of Things*:

"Whence Nature all creates, and multiplies
And fosters all, and whither she resolves
Each in the end when each is overthrown.
This ultimate stock we have devised to name
Procreant atoms, matter, seeds of things,
Or primal bodies, as primal to the world." (5)

In other words, Nature is both a necessary and sufficient
cause of all life-forms. No 'external agency' or god is necessary to explain the whole of creation. Gone are the gods of the
Greeks and the Romans and all those to come in the cosmology
of Lucretius and the naturalists. This view is quite consistent with
Tolle's vision of Life since both Nature and Life are elevated to
Universals or eternal, causal Forces. Lucretius continues:

"Each birth goes forth upon the shores of light
From its own stuff, from its own primal bodies.
And all from all cannot become, because
In each resides a secret power its own.
"...All things, were they not still together held
By matter eternal, shackled through its parts,

Now more, now less.

"...Nature ever up builds one thing from other, suffering naught

To come to birth but through some other's death." (6)

Each life-form is unique and is born from its likeness or species of Nature (Life) and possesses a potentiality ('secret power its own'). Matter is eternal and although death is the fate of all, death is necessary for future births and the progress (up building) of Nature. Much the same is assumed by Tolle who has a superbly naturalistic view of life-forms (see *The New Earth*) that is consistent with his inspired universalism.

Finally, when Lucretius is discussing the primacy of the void of each atom or material 'stuff', he assumed that without the void the atoms do not move. In other words, the void and atoms are co-equal in existence, within the material stuff of each form.

Experience in the Modern World

The five senses of sight, sound, taste, smell, and taste are so natural to our daily experiencing of reality that we are virtually unconscious of them. Instead what we see in the process of using our innate, primary senses are the objects and life-forms to which they individually connect us in the external environment. In part, the autonomic processing by the five senses of the outer world becomes the basis, once internalized, for the subconscious phenomena of the unconscious mind.

John Locke and David Hume of the 17th century gave us the scientific basis for Empiricism, so far as human experience is concerned. They reasoned that experience is the primary basis for knowledge and we experience reality initially through the five external senses. Once internalized by the nervous system and the glands of the five senses, *experience* initially appears to us through *impressions* formed by the brain or the cerebral regions associated with the five senses. Thus, sensory experience provides us with the primary neural network of the world, from which higher, more abstract phenomena are formed.

When we *reflect* upon our impressions of sensed phenomena in the environment we begin to form *ideas* from the sensory impressions first formed in the mind. Our ideas thus represent objects of the mind that are twice removed from the physical objects sensed in our environment. In this context, *mind* is merely a global term constitutive of facts, ideas and values taken initially from the surrounding world of experience. *Mind* does not add anything new to our understanding of how our ideas initially take root in Consciousness, except that it represents a clearly independent space-time to the impressions furnished by the five senses of physical appearances.

In this context, experience is the total inner sense that we have about gained through our engagement or involvement in the world. And as the empiricists of modern times remind us, we experience things first through our senses, the impressions that are formed by them in the brain and later by the reflections made upon our impressions by the mind or consciousness. Experience, in this modern sense of the word, is formed by the body, the mind and the real world *and* the inner, intuitive sense that is ultimately shaped by Consciousness. Thus, our sense of experience is interactive, constantly changing and transformative since it is necessarily connected with the inner body in the most essential way and the total sense of our place in the universe.

The Body as a Philosophical Touchstone

From the viewpoint of scientific naturalism, *we are our bodies.* The philosophy of naturalism reduces our identity or self to biological processes, structures, and functions. This more reductionist form of naturalism reduces the self and particularly the body to a machine rather than an organism. Whether this viewpoint should be granted any philosophical or holistic truth is at least debatable since it merely supports the mechanistic approach to human nature—an extreme view of the self that merely echoes medieval dualistic theories separating Spirit and matter.

To adequately establish the intellectual content for our identity as organisms, we must study the findings of the anatomist and physiologist of biology, and explore the various systems of the body, their structures, functions and interactive relationships with one another, that constitute the miracle and wonder of a particular life-form. Second, and no less importantly, we must study the psychological and sociological dimensions of personal growth and development, and the extent to which we can understand the totality of the self's interactions and developments in nature and society. Third, the higher self or cognitive dimensions of a person are moral, ethical, aesthetic, intellectual and spiritual represent our innate potentialities.

A cursory study of the body's many neuro-physiological and anatomical systems will reveal the extent to which we are dependent upon the outer, real environment for the life of the organism. Breathing and fresh oxygen are taken for granted in living, but nowhere is it in shorter supply than at high altitudes or polluted atmospheres. In fact, we—in the privileged parts of the world—take for granted that we will have an environment that supplies us with adequate oxygen, water, and food with which to sustain our bodily existence. But take away any of these three vital life-supported elements for very long, beginning with oxygen, and the organism will soon die.

At the same time, the outer five senses play a major role in developing knowledge and experience, and sustaining the human organism. From a reductionist or empirical viewpoint, the mind, personality and intellect are seen as mere 'by-products' or consequences of the human body's life, health, and integrity. Whether or not and to what degree other animal organisms possess personalities and a reasoning mind, is at least a debatable proposition although it is certainly not among pet owners and advocates for animal rights. The empirical or materialist viewpoint, if too narrowly defined, leaves out of consideration everything traditionally called religious or metaphysical in our make-up like the 'soul', 'Self, or 'Consciousness' since these phenomena are seen as superstitious, super-natural, and pre-scientific objects of belief.

Last, the metaphor of a *touchstone* as source of magic and meaning is ancient in origin. If nothing else, the body is a philosophical touchstone for experience and the grounding of knowledge. Furthermore, if there is any ultimate meaning and purpose in existence, it must be found in the *total* structure and function of the body; and this includes the inner and outer, spiritual and physical body.

Pragmatism and Re-Configuration

In our contemporary sensational, materialistic, and mechanistic world—sense realism, naturalism, and pragmatism have a growing appeal to the masses—especially 'pragmatism'. But in its classical form, Pragmatic philosophy, as it historically developed in America during nineteenth century and early part of the twentieth century, became a synonym for all kinds of differing tendencies in thought, action, and belief; and these differing tendencies we can find in the philosophies of Charles Sanders Peirce, William James, John Dewey, George Mead, and Alfred North Whitehead—to name a few.

For example, Peirce's initial definition of pragmatism from the essay titled "The Fixation of Belief" describes four chief methods of fixing or establishing belief in human thought and action. Although he clearly favors the empirical or *a posteriori* way of thinking, now associated with scientific thinking and the inductive method, Peirce respects the other three—the methods of *authority, tenacity, and a priori* —for their strengths over the empirical method of science. James, the naturalistic psychologist, medical doctor, and scholar of religious mysticism, left the door wide open to the individual's need and right to believe in something Absolute. At the same time, he developed a framework for thinking about the truthfulness of our ideas through the actual consequences of actions in experience. Dewey, the professional philosopher and educator, developed his pragmatic philosophy on the basis of a highly generalized scientific method that he proposed philosophers and educators should use in thinking about the problems of society, education and cultural life. Mead enriched the psychological perspective of pragmatism through his knowledge of sociology, developing the necessary contexts for thinking about the experiences of individuals caught in the juggernaut of society. Whitehead, the professional mathematician and philosopher of science, developed a highly speculative view of scientific cosmology that borrowed from the metaphysics of essentialism.

And there were others like Josiah Royce whose pragmatic idealism most closely resembles Tolle's Perennial philosophy in his view on the necessity of a religious Absolute. His Christian ethics of the community sought to reconcile individual meaning, purpose and existence with the life of community, in the divine frame of Absoluteness. There is no ultimate meaning or purpose in life without the sense of loyalty and hope that each individual can experience through the divine membership in community. All and all, American Pragmatism expressed the cultural pluralism and diversity of views better than any other prevailing viewpoint in the twentieth century, even though it was largely ignored by the establishment's analytical and positivistic philosophers. (7)

Diversity and pluralism is the cultural strength of pragmatism owing to its lack of doctrine-based dogmatism and presence of a *humanistic* toleration of human differences. In its method of thinking, there is certainly a stronger bias towards the empiricism of scientific thinking than any other. To others, however, it is the broader *naturalism* of Pragmatic philosophy that distinguishes it from other, competing postmodern philosophies more than anything else. Yet others view pragmatism as being strongly influenced by traditional *rationalism,* owing to its emphasis upon human reason, questioning and the method of doubt. Lastly, if modern *empiricism* is taken as the full gospel of pragmatism, then its more generously spirited, broad-minded, and open-ended views of self and the universe, may be in jeopardy.

It is probably no exaggeration to say that pragmatism is the dominant, yet unconsciously acquired philosophy for most people in America. That is, without ever consciously studied this philosophy as a unique historical development in American thought, pragmatism is referenced in all kinds of ways without a speaker or writer being fully aware of 'sources' within the history of pragmatism. And so it is, one argue, with much of our thought and utterances, i.e. we are not usually, fully aware of where our ideas or beliefs come from in the history of thought. Albeit, the pragmatic way of thinking seems particularly popular among politicians, television and radio broadcasters, engineers, mechanics, lawyers, administrators, reporters, teachers, doctors, entrepreneurs, etc., in our mass culture.

Whoever has gone through a period of formal education beyond high school, and became settled in an identifiable professional role, uses the language and the methods of pragmatism, often without knowing or much caring how one has acquired so much good sense and reliable intelligence. What marks the pragmatic way of thinking is its tendency to define a belief, idea, policy or practice in terms of what 'works' or brings greater 'satisfaction' and 'success' to an individual life or entire nation-state. And the pragmatic habit of thought is usually separated from all procrustean ideologies or dogmatic positions—so far as the moral, economic, and political issues of the day are concerned.

Tolle is highly critical of a materialistic, mechanistic and reductionist philosophy since it is not possible to understand 'who we are' or our relation to eternal Being merely through the physical body and thingy, social world. In pragmatism, what really 'works' in experience is confirmed by emotional satisfaction or the consequences of our actions. Ideas are true or false, valuable or not, according to their success in enabling us to realize our goals, whether in an individual or a societal context.

For Tolle, what most accurately describes his position with respect to the physical body, pragmatic action, and the existential world, is the principle of what he terms, *re-configuration or re-organization*. And pragmatism is a philosophy of change, re-vision and re-construction of the existing world if nothing else.

"In the West," Tolle wrote "it is the physical appearance of the body that contributes greatly to the sense of who you think you are.... [Consequently] Many feel a diminished sense of self-worth because they perceive their body as ugly or imperfect.... At the root of this condition lies identification with the mind." The problem of judging, objectifying and reducing reality to mere sensory appearances is at the root of this tendency or habit of mind. (8)

Tolle goes on the say that the therapeutic approach to this disorder or dysfunction is the ability to 'feel the body from within' and thus to dis-identify from judgments that the mind makes of a physical body—yours or others. In the process, we learn to awaken to the Inner Body or the real, yogic body, where Consciousness, the soul or the essence of Being dwell authentically and purely.

Re-organization or 're-configuration' of the total self occurs whenever there is a radical shift in consciousness that recognizes the contingent, conditional and existential becoming of the life-form. Birth and death are the two most radically re-ordering natural events in a person's life-time; but so are our most significant life choices, i.e. marrying, having children, choosing a career role, making friends, living in foreign countries, acquiring a formal education, reading great books, camping in the wilderness, so forth and so on.

In thinking about who 'you' are or your relation to Being as you essentially exist, it is important to remember that the view formed by the senses and the physical body is no more than a material image or surface appearance of who you or others really are. It is like looking into the mirror and believing that the mirror can give you a real understanding of who or anyone else is, without the interpreting the image, applying other knowledge of the person, etc.

If you realize how directly (and *indirectly* in terms of the mind and soul) we are connected with the external world through the senses and how the experiences of the object world influences the egoic mind and the judging self, then the stranglehold that the world has upon us can be interrupted and eventually broken. Indeed, this is the initial, necessary stage for self-realization or true self-knowledge.

Realizing the complex of relations and influences that are formed by the object world upon your emotional self and the judging voice in the head may occur gradually and suddenly. Much depends upon the intensity, depth and duration of your *awakening experience* and the *breakthrough* to a higher Consciousness or real self-knowledge. The important thing is that the realization occurs and brings you back to your authentic being or who you really are.

In this context, Tolle wrote: "Ego is always identification with form, seeking yourself and thereby losing yourself in some form. Forms are not just material objects and physical bodies. They are energy formations, finer and less dense than physical matter, but they are forms nonetheless....Ego arises when your sense of Beingness, of 'I Am', which is formless consciousness, gets mixed up with form. This is the meaning of identification. This is the forgetfulness of Being, the primary error, the illusion of absolute separation that turns reality into a nightmare." (9)

Indeed, volumes of explication of the metaphysical kind have been written on the confusion between forms and formlessness, appearances and reality, things and persons, etc. It is an existential distinction of the most basic kind, i.e. existence and essence or a pragmatic distinction between knowledge and experience. When 'reality becomes a nightmare', we forget who we are, know not where we are, or why we do what we do. Our reason flees from our passion, free will and soul.

The Senses, Consciousness, and Paradoxical Existence

The really fascinating truth about the senses, at an epistemological or empirical level, is their individual connections with the brain through the nervous system. The key to understanding how this is possible can only be explained by consciousness or the essential means by which meaning arises in the self and world. Without consciousness and the information, understanding, and wisdom that it absorbs and transacts, our sensory experiences are dumb, blind, and without meaning in our lives. Although consciousness remains one of the great mysteries of existence, it is genetically pre-wired to act through each of the five senses of the body and yet exists in phenomenal independence of them; as the sixth sense of intuition and reason, consciousness enables us to understand, appreciate, and acquire wisdom from the information that the senses bring to us. This experienced fact of daily life is nothing short of miraculous and a source of constant wonder.

There are at five, differing and interrelated dimensions or 'levels' of phenomena in the external world of Nature. Broadly speaking, they are: 1, the subatomic world of energy and material phenomena having electro-magnetic properties; 2, the macro-biological world of living organisms, evolutionary processes, and the interactions between species of various kinds; 3, the psycho-social world of human relationships and institutions existing within larger configurations of communities, nation-states, and international relationships; 4, planetary and inter-stellar realms of the physical universe that exceed experience and real understanding due to the incredible distances and magnitudes of planets, stars, and galaxies; and 5, the extraterrestrial existence of other intelligent, compassionate species of life-forms living beyond our solar system and as yet unknown to us, save through speculation, imagination and creative media.

These differing levels of consciousness bring forth the obvious complexity of the self and universe. The complexity, mystery, and miracle of existence can be most readily understood through the various chakra centers of yoga philosophy. Nature, as given to consciousness through the senses of inner and outer reality, intersects with Being or universal Consciousness at virtually every level of the body-Self.

For example, at the sixth level or dimension of Being and Nature, we can begin to see pure consciousness or the formless Self within each person, in the *Ajna-chakra*. Speculative though it may be, we can find ourselves suddenly freed from the conditions of mundane existence which are observable through the five senses, the body, and lower chakra fields of Nature. The seventh or highest dimension of reality offers a greater clearing of Being—the island of sunlight, radiance, and luminous splendor—made real by higher Consciousness or *Sahasrara-chakra center* at the crown of the head.

We have repeatedly seen throughout our study of Tolle's philosophy how frequently he returns to a Perennial theme of spiritual wisdom: knowing and experiencing 'who you really are' and its central importance in all living. The five senses and their connections with higher Consciousness are absolutely vital elements in the quest of Perennial Wisdom or true understanding. Of the many things that are subject to change, doubt and uncertainty, this much is not.

Similarly, we exist and experience the world inwardly and outwardly, subjectively and objectively, and as higher and lower sentient beings. We exist as a totality wherever we are or whatever we are doing. However, the full or total truth about who we are cannot be known much less experienced until we have lived to the end of our earthly existence. Hence, we exist as a totality that is at the same time unknown to us—the paradox of existence.

The Unmanifested or Formless Source of Reality

Tolle's answer is one that comes from the 'empty space' approach to Life found in several religious traditions. He wrote in *A New Earth*, "Empty space is life in its fullness, the unmanifested Source out of which all manifestation flows. The traditional word for that Source is God." (10)

Over and over again Tolle reminds us that 'words and thoughts belong to the world of form'. Words can do little more than merely express or give articulate form to the formless realm of existence. Beyond pointing to the formless realm or Emptiness of everything, words and thoughts also mediate between the formed and formless realms. They give expression and representation to the inner body or the essence that lies within the physical or external body. In this sense, words, reason, and thought can take us to the threshold of Truth but it is the deeper, intuitive processes that take us to the inner sanctum of mysterious Being.

At the deepest level of 'Being', 'God' or 'Source-Being' exists in the Emptiness and fullness of everything. Yet Tolle and most other metaphysical philosophers are emphatic about the impossibility of given anything like a final expression to this 'hypothesis'. As elusive as the unmanifested realm is, many search for a life-time to find that the Hiddenness of Being is the Truth itself. When we look in all the wrong places, we cannot hope to find what we may be looking for.

Or, the 'riddle of the universe' is not a riddle at all, but only a question or a hypothesis that cannot be answered by words or rational means. Or as one sage said to me long ago, 'there is Truth for those who are looking for Truth and no-Truth for those who have given up looking'. Tolle is one who has found Truth because he has ceased looking or searching for it.

The most important datum of experience is our own immediate existence—'I Am' or 'I Exist'. We exist as both an object-in-space and a subject-in-time in the real world. The outer realm of nature is an abstraction from the totality which is the inner-outer, higher-lower, and subject-object unity of existence. Everything that we call 'reality', as Alfred North Whitehead wrote, is an 'undifferentiated aesthetic continuum' that cannot be totally described or explained in language or symbol, partly because language 'differentiates' and it is not continuous with 'reality'.

Meanwhile, there is yet another gem in Tolle's wisdom that 'you need to lose yourself to find yourself'. The human self—a concept of who we are that has been analyzed to death by psychologists, sociologists and ontologists—is still the most dynamic of realities since it refers directly to this 'body-mind-soul' as a totality.

For example, the Buddhists describe the self in terms of 'sheaths' or circular spheres of the body and mind, with only

Emptiness at the center of this and every other form. The Freudians describe the self as composed of the id, ego, and super-ego, with the unconsciousness (rather than consciousness) providing the energy that holds it all together. Evolutionists, when they bother to define the human self at all, tend to reduce it to an organism-in-an-environment that behaves little differently from other animals, with no intrinsic soul, conscience, or even mind, to redeem its violently adaptive, changeable ways.

The Ocean, the Sky, and the Land

As the poets have said, just to name the things of experience and put them together in a way that Nature could not, is a wondrous thing! And yet it is actually greater to use our senses in seeing, hearing, smelling, tasting and feeling a seascape, say, on a soft, summer day. Outside my window, there is a soft warm wind blowing through the sea grass and bamboo close to the house. I feel the ocean air coming through the open window while on the radio there are the liquid sounds of a concert piano playing before the wind. Birds are chattering and flying in all directions with one another; and on the salt marsh pond there are two swans floating peacefully on the tidal current.

Meanwhile, somewhere distant a chain-saw sounds, muffled by the intervening groves of pine trees. On the nearby beach road, cars move slowly by from their gasoline engines and make swishing sounds in their airy wake. The sound of a nearby lawn mover is most clearly and urgently heard and then stops abruptly as if it had struck an obstruction.

The smells, tastes, and feelings from being at the ocean, where the land meets the waves and currents from afar is an experience of synaesthesia or a synthesis of all the senses. The integration or unity of the external senses can cause a change of mood or orientation of the whole organism. The experience of unity is made possible by higher Consciousness or an awakened sense of self-in-nature, time and space. And the whole scene seems to arrange itself for my self-centered benefit, only to suddenly reverse itself in an overwhelming cascade of sensations, emotions and surrounding phenomena.

It may be the case that our most distant, non-human ancestors swam from the ocean and morphed into land animals many millions of years ago. I have walked beside the ocean and played in its waves for many years, thinking that this evolutionary theory could be completely true. It could account for the magnetic attraction that the ocean holds for most people; and it gives an even deeper connection with my sensory love for the ocean where its horizon of endless waves meet the sand, rocks, and surrounding sky.

The Earth and its Life-forms

The Earth is the Great Mother or Gaia of us all. No sense of home is greater than the Earth yet we continually take it for granted. The Earth gives us our cosmic journey through time-space and physical forces of gravity, electro-magnetism and the atoms.

Our ticket is from birth to death and transformation—from one unknown to another. Our passport is existence—an absolutely free, paradoxical freedom. Existence is an intersecting point in space-time where a triangulation of forces, i.e. Life, Being, and Nature, meet and create our precious life-forms; and then after a certain period of time, we disappear or *de-materialize*, as Tolle says.

In Indic culture, the sun is the ultimate basis for *Prakriti*—the Hindu goddess of Nature and matter—and the necessary natural condition conducive to all life-forms of the Earth; but it is *Gaia* or the Earth goddess that is the most holy or sacred energy in the natural order of things. Without *Gaia* or the living Consciousness of the Earth, life-forms and the natural elements would not be. In the end, of course, nature requires no deities or myths to awaken our inner being to its miraculous life-forms and to stand in awe at its power, beauty, and creativity. Wherever we may travel and explore on the Earth's surface or nearby in the solar system,

Nature is beautiful, miraculous, and undergoing continuous and fascinating transformations.

Purusha or the principle of the Life-force is the other necessary condition of all life-forms on Earth. Purusha (Spirit) and Prakriti (Nature) work together, dialectically, in creating the life-forms of Earth. When life-forms are discovered elsewhere, the same physics, chemistry, and biology will be seen there too, but in new, wondrous combinations beyond present imagining and scientific speculation. The universe is more beautiful, miraculous and weird than we can even imagine.

The same natural, life-supporting conditions may not exist in the geology and climatology of other planetary worlds. The hills, valleys, forests, mountains, skies, and rivers, will exceed all present experience and knowledge. Different life-forms have populated the universe as numerously as sands upon the beaches of the Earth and more numerously than the stars that populate the galaxies of the universe. Multiply by any number conceivable and you will not exceed the possible forms of life in our universe since it may only be the beginning of infinite number of galaxies!

Here, on a hill, near the end of a country road, and amid luxurious summer trees, the blue sky startles me with its blueness. Now, there are low-floating, tropical, and misty clouds appearing above the green ocean of leafy trees. The birds are sounding throughout the nearby forest, and occasionally they are seen flying across the cut meadows and valleys that separate the trees. My senses can only reveal the glittering, sunlit leaves that cover and cast dark shadows over the tall trunks of maples, oaks, and pines; the greater unmanifested reality of the forest extends beyond yonder hills and valleys and even hides in the darkness beyond my line of sight and sense of sound.

Who would believe, who can know or even say, what riches and complexities are present to the external and internal sense of experience in just one moment of time and space! No camera can capture what the unaided senses can bring to inner

Consciousness; no dream can do justice to the most ordinary or mundane experiences gained through all seven senses; and there is no time or place that is better for loving the Earth and surrendering to its sacred Presence, than in the present moment of Now.

I have walked for hours and whole days at a time in the forests where I live, in New England. The trees, plants, and flowers are by every measure or quality of Life, the friends and lovers of my senses. Plant-life embodies the *Satori* experience of awakening to the infinite perfection of Nature. In fact, all life-forms obey the same laws and cycles of Nature with perfect equality, harmony and absorption. And the plants, animals and inanimate things of Nature are every bit as sacred and miraculous as that of humans and usually less violent and cruel.

The fact that we do not completely understand the languages and ways of mineral, plants, and other animals of the Earth is our loss. We see birds in the air all the time yet we cannot fly like they do. We see fish in the water all the time yet we cannot swim alongside them to their depths. And we see and look for the tracks of land animals all the time, and we do not know their languages, habits, and fears.

Artists have represented in words, paints, and musical sounds—the hills, valleys, and forests in their perfect beauty, wonder, and mystery. I have seen single great mountains represented over and over again by writers and painters; but none has succeeding in representing any mountain more perfectly than Gaia herself. The value of most art lies in elevating consciousness to a higher, spiritual level of awareness and creating the illusion of a different and higher reality; Nature is continually doing this without even trying.

Yet through the arts, sciences, and humanities, we participate in the discovery of the unmanifested-in-the-manifested world and deepen our love and sense of wonder before Nature. All our simulations, discoveries and representations of Nature are refined, mediated, and artificial in the end.

Philosophical Questions and Speculations

Nature is complete and perfect in all ways. No science can exceed its boundaries of 'knowing'. No philosophy can achieve anything without Nature's Consciousness. And no religion can realize what is ultimate and present in Nature, at this moment.

Nature is the basis for society, history, this moment and place. Without nature and our sensing of it, we would not experience or know what we can. We can know the Perfection of nature in our inwardness and outwardness of Consciousness. When we experience things as 'higher' or 'lower' we are merely recognizing the various dimensions, depths and heights of Being. Virtually, all adjectives and constructions that orient us in time and space are merely metaphors for knowing Being more completely. And when we discover something new about Being, we discover something new about ourselves, the natural world and existence.

Life is new at every moment of time and space. We live on a natural space-ship called Earth and it is showing us a new unfolding of Life at every moment. 'God' is an image, model, or hypothesis of what a 'completely perfect Being' could look like; or 'God' is the Idea that you have in your Consciousness about 'What-is' in its absolute Perfection. If 'God' has merely planted the Idea of His own existence in the mind at the moment of our creation, it only begs the questions:

Does 'God' exist? Does God exist only in our thinking about God? Which came first: Eternal Being, God, or my thinking about these things? Since my thinking is in no way 'eternal', is God merely another finite being like me, invented by humans to account for the universe? And even if this is true, something does not come from nothing; thus we are left with Eternal Being as the creative Force of everything.

Other questions arise: What is the difference between reflection and speculation? I 'reflect' upon or use my intellect rather than imagination, to understand a form of reality like society, a rock or a person. Is reflection more real, true, and valuable than speculation? In speculating, we form hypotheses, educated guesses or intuitions about what could be true. Are our reflections and speculations merely projections of our prior values, biases, and points of view? Can we ever separate subjectivity, i.e. the first person singular point of view, from what we claim to know through the intellect or imagination?

What such questions of a philosophical kind suggest is the highly ambiguous nature of reality, knowledge and values. Tolle avoids many philosophical questions by remaining steadfast in the Now of experience where eternity and temporality meet. This means that the present moment is fully available to us at anytime in waking consciousness when we empty our minds of past and future time and live fully in the Now. And this also means that many of the questions that philosophers are trained to raise just dissolve into the emptiness of words and the formlessness of mind, when we stop thinking, reflecting and speculating and just be present to our senses, aesthetic feelings, and immediate experience.

Perception is the waking consciousness of experience made possible by the sensory functions of the everyday self. Perception 'embodies' reality for Consciousness, giving it material substance or 'concreteness'. If we were suddenly unable to perceive reality and found ourselves without the normal five external senses and the internal ones of proprioception, intuition, etc., our conceptual knowledge would be 'empty, blind, and unconscious', as Immanuel Kant centuries ago opined. But when perception and conception are joined together, real understanding of the self and world is more likely to occur. Such understanding—'right understanding' as Shakyamuni Buddha expressed it in the first of the Noble Eight Steps on the Path to Enlightenment—is the real beginning of Consciousness.

Or we can ask: what is space? (Space=the unmanifested that is made manifest in the Now.) Without space, no life-form can appear in perception. Space is an intuitive reality that perception alone cannot detect. We perceive (see, hear, smell, feel, taste) things and forms all the time in our waking Consciousness, but who sees the space that pervades our perception of things?

Answer: we are only able to perceive the objects and events of the world, because we are blessed with the *a priori*, intuitive understanding of Consciousness.

Intuition is the most vital function of the ordinary mind and higher Consciousness since it enables us to experience spatial, temporal, and causal relations as we perceive, conceive, remember, imagine, etc. More technically, 'intuition is a non-inferential form of knowledge' since it enables us to grasp or immediately understand a proposition, condition, or entity without the aid of perception, memory, or 'reasoning' which depends upon reflective and conceptual processes. Even though intuition is so vital to all functions of the mind there is a distinct prejudice against it that comes from a narrow and reductive empiricism.

Tolle trusts in his intuitive intelligence although not to the point of silliness or stupidity in the face of contrary evidence. The mark of genius is a trust and confidence in one's native intelligence balanced with the sober realization that individual intelligence—no matter how highly 'trained' or disciplined—requires knowledge, experience, and honest reflection to lead us to the truth of any state of affairs. Asking a genius in one field of expertise to give us his wisdom about another that he may have no knowledge or experience about is often ridiculous and disappointing.

The emptiness or formlessness of reality is one of the most elusive of Buddhist truths. If you realize that all forms are finite, impermanent, and co-arise with everything else, from the unmanifested formlessness or Void, then you can more readily 'see' or intuit this reality. Emptiness is the unmanifested reality from which the manifested plenum of forms in the world arises. Formlessness is a close synonym for emptiness which denotes that forms do not arise from an absence of something. Emptiness pervades life-forms as the most vital energy of nature, at the atomic level, and it is the space through which universal Life-force travels; and it is the totality of who we are in our formed and Conscious potentiality.

In sum, the senses, their structures and functions, unify the inner and outer realms of Consciousness through intuitive

processes. Subjectivity and the so-called objective world are inseparably linked through the senses, emotions, and thoughts of ordinary consciousness. 'Right understanding' is the most important
first step in the Path to Enlightenment or higher Consciousness.
Individual existence unfolds through natural processes of the
mind, body and soul in the Now of eternal Being; thus existence
is contingent, conditional, and dependent upon the natural elements of air, water, food, earth, and fire. Emptiness, the Life-
force, and Consciousness exist in the most extensive realms of
unmanifested reality. (11)

On Being Present

The activity of the senses—touching, tasting, feeling, hearing, and seeing—is the natural life of Consciousness and the
experienced presence of Being. How is it that something so ordinary like our sensory experience can lead us to the infinity and
eternity of Now? The answer lies in the following generalized
description of the senses, by Tolle:

"Use your senses fully. Be where you are. Look around. Just
look, don't interpret. See the light, shapes, colors, textures. Be
aware of the silent presence of each thing. Be aware of the space
that allows everything to be. Listen to the sounds; don't judge
them. Listen to the silence underneath the sounds. Touch something—anything—and feel and acknowledge its Being. Observe
the rhythm of your breathing; feel the air flowing in and out,
feel the life energy in your body. Allow everything to be, within
and without. Allow the 'isness' of all things. Move deeply into the
Now." (12)

Right now, for example, I am writing in an old farm house
where there is a thunderous rainstorm all around it. The rain is
dripping off the high roof and onto the lawn and stone steps. The
sky is very dark and so are the leafed out trees around the fields.
There is a silence between the thunderclaps and there is a silence
between raindrops falling on the window sills and ground and
there is a silence in my thoughts and there is a silence in the house.

I am aware of breathing deeply in and out from my abdomen. I feel a strong energy in my body. I close my eyes to an invisible Presence that is everywhere. I sit very still for a few alert moments. I open my eyes and write these few words. I know that these words will distance me from the things that I perceive. I am at peace with this.

Chapter 15

THE UNITY OF THE BRAIN, MIND AND

CONSCIOUSNESS

What is the mind in relation to the brain and ordinary consciousness? How is the mind related to the brain, knowledge and higher Consciousness? Why is it important to realize the natural connections between the brain, mind and higher Consciousness?

"When mind is nowhere it is everywhere. When it occupies one tenth, it is absent in the other nine tenths." Takuan

"He who is learned is not wise / He who is wise is not learned." Tao Te Ching

"To know all things in the cause of their existence I must soar beyond all lights, temporal and eternal, and plunge into the causeless essence which gives mind and being to my soul. Drowned in this being, aware of self and things merely as being, my soul has lost her name." Meister Eckhart

"Wisdom will not enter into a malicious soul nor dwell in a body subject to sins." Anonymous

"The learned who perceive the truth say that the mind is ignorance, by which alone the world is moved about, like cloud banks by the wind; [thus] the seeker of liberation should diligently effect the purification of the mind. When it is purified, liberation is as a fruit in one's hand." Shankara, *Crest Jewel of Discernment*

Shankara (788-820) was one of India's major philosophers and saints. At a time when the sacred writings and practices of the Hindus were being challenged by the Buddhists (and early

271

Moslems) he renewed their authority and wisdom among the people by establishing *ashrams* (spiritual centers) and writing numerous, insightful commentaries on *Vedanta-Sutra, Bhagavad-Gita* and the *Upanishads* of the Hindu *Vedas.* In the above quotation, he suggests that the mind is very vulnerable, suggestible and constantly needing *purification* due to its corruptibility. However, with *diligence* or constant attention and effort, liberation will occur like 'a fruit in one's hand'. It was a reassuring message to the majority of India and one which has had a lasting influence throughout the world. (1)

Brain, Mind, and the Unknown

What is the mind? How does it differ from the brain? Is there a necessary connection between the two phenomena? Is the relation between the brain and the mind such that it reveals the secret, the hidden truth about our identity? If one is only speaking about the basis for consciousness and functions of the mind—yes; but if one is thinking about the wholeness of personal being, then more must be considered.

First, the brain is the central organ of the human nervous system. The brain is empirically knowable, operable, an object of observation. It is also, arguably, the most important organ in the activity of the mind which, in turn, accounts for thinking, symbol-using and understanding. Even though we now know much about the brain through electronic imaging techniques, the Human Genome project, brain surgery, and even certain techniques of psychotherapy, the vast complexity and architecture of the brain reveals much more than we comprehend. Furthermore, there is a significant difference between the brain and the mind, since the mind denotes an extremely subtle field of energy i.e. consciousness in its many manifestations and potentialities.

Second, we know that the mind exists since it is the basis for our awareness of real and imagined states of reality. Awareness is consciousness in its ordinariness or the necessary intellectual connection that we have with what perceivably exists. The connection between the mind, our reasoning capacities and higher Consciousness is one that has evolved over unknown millennia. At the same time, the development of language and symbolization has contributed immensely to the growth of the mind and higher Consciousness; and as importantly is the evolution of our relation to Nature or the sacred origin and destiny of all sentient beings, consciously experienced in the Now.

Third, since there is a necessary relation between the brain and mind it is evident that the mind or consciousness as such cannot exist independently of the brain. Whether consciousness, in any of its various forms, can exist independently of the brain, its structures and functions in the body, is not known for sure although both common sense and empirical science tell us that it cannot. However, since we have asserted that a soul or higher Self exists, it is entirely possible that higher Consciousness or its deepest, inner connection, the soul, can exist independently of our individual life-form.

Four, there is no perspective in philosophy, science, or religion that can adequately answer 'all possible questions' even assuming that we know what they are. However, on the basis of metaphysical faith and reason, we can assert that 'something'— whether we name it consciousness, soul, or Self— survives the death of the brain and the neuro-physiological functions of the body. At least this is the fundamental premise allowed for in virtually every major religious and spiritual tradition of the world. Whether true or not, the proposition of 'survival' is based upon faith, reason and hope; but if the former (faith) is lacking, the latter (reason) becomes meaningless; and hopelessness if not despair may often replace hope.

The *existential* way of confirming the truths of religion is through personal experience or a subjective, affective, and organismic response that can transform a person from a state of uncertainty and doubt to certainty in belief and feeling. The existential way finds personal transformation and hope in possibility—the possibility of *ultimate* meaning and purpose, the possibility that the improbable is possible in an uncertain universe. In this perspective, subjectivity trumps objectivity, just as experience is the most obvious basis and test for truth of all kinds.

Although atheistic existentialism is based upon the lack of any absolute foundation or basis for our choices or being-in-the-world, theistic existentialism posits the existence of a divine or absolute basis for our moral relationships and individual choices in the world. Soren Kierkegaard and Friedrich Nietzsche represent these two branches of Existential philosophy in the nineteenth century; and this philosophy has significantly developed in Europe, the United States and elsewhere in the twentieth and twenty-first century along these and other lines.

Fifth, the traditional support for faith or belief in the soul's survival of death exists in the practices, habits, and rituals of the world's religions; and the philosophical support for survival is and has always been divided and contentious. Arguably there is no greater issue or value of religion than that of the belief in immortality if not Eternal Being for the individual. Considering that personal existence is fraught with mystery and uncertainty save it will end in the annihilation of the physical body, we may have no better choice but to live courageously towards the Unknown—if we lack *faith* in the possibility of individual survival.

The Survival of Death: Choosing to Be or Not to Be

Given the possibility of a conscious survival of death, our practices, habits, and rituals of daily life may become the necessary basis for a transcendental or liberated Consciousness, in the here-and-now. 'To be', in a liberated way, means to live with faith and the awareness—a soul, Consciousness or Self—that survives the death of the body. To 'not be' is to have no faith, feelings or practices that serve the ends of the *survival of death*. The survival of death then becomes a choice or an act of the *will* that each person makes or refuses to make, based upon prior faith or its lack.

Although it may be consoling to think that we can survive death merely through belief, an act of will *and* right moral action, an irrational degree of faith is required to transcend the uncertainty of existence. Intellectual appeals to history, karmic theory, or scientific materialism, cannot alone settle the metaphysical questions of life and death, meaning and meaninglessness in personal existence. Similarly, a systematic religious or theological education cannot bring us any closer to the Truth, in an absolute form, if prior faith is lacking.

If one wishes to die and die completely and absolutely to the universal Life-force, then Nature has made this intention and expectation of consciousness an easy one to realize. But if one wishes to live in a fully conscious and Transcendental way following the death of the body, then the Life-force of Being has made this alternative available to us without discrimination owing to the potentiality of the free will. Of course, prior to both possible outcomes of eventful or physical death, there is the immediate, existential and ethical question about 'how we should live', in the here-and-now.

Answers to the ethical question of existence has been given in numerous ways—by atheistic science and theistic religion, by the New Age spiritual paths to the more academic and philosophical moralities. Whatever your choice may be, you have nothing to lose and everything to gain by living in a fully conscious way towards the Unknown, aware of the possible consequences of present intentions, actions, and choices and what they may lead to, without illusions or expectations.

If you wish only to take each moment as it comes and goes, rises and falls, in the various modes of being, and in the light of changing circumstances, the ontological choice is readily available. The ontological choice (based upon Being) is superior to the metaphysical one (based upon the Beyond) in that it makes no judgments about existing conditions as they unfold in nature, culture, and personal being. To those of a metaphysical persuasion, the ontological choice is an act of bad faith in that no position is taken about final or ultimate matters.

Whether we ultimately survive death or not, may not depend upon our choosing one way or the other about survival. Of course, the process of the aging, dying and eventual death of the body is an entirely natural process. Similarly, the developmental transformations of consciousness are sometimes intimately linked to biological stages of the body. The power of faith, intention and will, however, are reflective of deeper, unmanifested processes and structures of the inner body, soul and the heart center of a person.

However, since the wholeness of existence is shrouded in uncertainty, ambiguity and the Great Mystery, we are ultimately at the mercy of forces vastly beyond our capacity to really understand or comprehend. Thus, ontological uncertainty and psychological insecurity have more often than not led to personal action, faith and spirituality that have little to do with religious forms or philosophical reasoning and speculation.

In sum, if we choose a lesser way of living—disengaging ourselves from the possibility of higher Consciousness, in the Now—we may miss the experience and opportunity of flourishing in the light of eternal Being. On the other hand, we may choose to live entirely without illusions and expectations, and live in the conditional or real world and with an open, clear mind about the future. Both ways seem to be based upon a common and largely unknown Ground of possibility.

Thinking as an Obstacle to the Sense of Being

The 'problem' with the mind in Tolle's philosophy is that it often blocks our experience of Now (or Being) through the habit of identifying with thoughts, roles, and memories. This happens primarily through the habit of 'thinking' which is most often an unconscious pattern formed by certain negative experiences from the past that are brought into the present moment of awareness. If we are emotionally attached to painful experiences and memories, awareness is blocked or prevented from experiencing Being.

Tolle further asserts that 'undifferentiated and primordial emotion' exists more deeply than pain, fear, or anxiety within our nervous system, which in turn causes the mind to fight against such emotions, but to no avail, since 'fighting' only creates antagonism in the other. Thus unless we become Conscious of the primordial and undifferentiated emotion that interferes with the harmonious functioning of the mind, our thought processes will remain in the 'stuck' position, focusing upon the emotions of fear, pain, and anxiety whose intellectual consequences are doubt, uncertainty, and endless questioning.

Such forms of thought are endlessly circular and like the mythic snake who swallows his own tail, thinking creates a threatening 'other'. There is a potentially vicious circle existing between your 'thinking' mind and the ocean of primordial emotion buried deeply and unconsciously within the brain. Furthermore, there is no ordinary thought process or philosophy that can hope to resolve or relieve the tension from this relationship. As Tolle asserts: "the harder the mind struggles to get rid of the pain, the greater the pain. The mind can never find the solution, nor can it afford to allow you to find the solution, because it is itself an intrinsic part of the 'problem'." (2)

Your true nature will not reveal itself until you find those emotions and experiences within that are positive, Life-giving, and affirming of 'who you are'. Tolle expresses the depth of his own faith when he says that "glimpses of love and joy or brief moments of deep peace are possible when a gap occurs in the stream of thought." In other words, it is the phenomenal, internal openings or 'gaps' within the unconscious stream of thought that afford us 'glimpses' into Being or the positive experiences of the Life-force within us that reveal our true nature, our sacred Self. (3)

But it is important to realize that the positive emotional states cannot alone 'flourish' until you have freed yourself from the dominance or tyranny of the mind. True 'love, joy, and peace' lie beyond the usual emotions of daily life, on a deeper level of existence; but you must 'become fully conscious' of the wide range of emotions that may block your Path and Consciousness. For 'emotion literally means disturbance' from the Latin *emovere*, and

Tolle affirms that we must learn to break our 'addiction to negative emotion' as well as the pleasure-pain cycle that is unending, in order to experience the real love, joy, and peace that is the essence of Unconditional Being. (4)

The glimpses that we can experience of Being, even in the midst of painful, addictive, and toxic relationships, are not illusions at all, but the strength of you natural Self or will suddenly revealing your Path to the real you. Even when the sun is obscured by the darkest of clouds, the other side is always brightly lighted. The analogy can be likened to the luminous experience of Being that may often seem to be obscured or darkened by the 'problems', 'evil' and violence of the world, only to be suddenly revealed by a breakthrough or clearing within awareness.

Overcoming the Alienation of the Mind

Tolle has written about the internal frustration that many people feel from a primordial event that occurred eons ago, but which still directly affects us at the deepest levels of unconsciousness. The problem or perceived lack in us occurred when humans "fell from grace, entered the realm of time and mind, and lost awareness of Being. At that point, they started to perceive themselves as meaningless fragments in an alien universe, unconnected to the Source and to each other." (5)

Exactly when this unhappy state of affairs first occurred, and to whom, in the cloud-bursts of pre-history, we have no reliable evidence to go on. The attachment that many may feel to this prior event—the 'Fall from Grace'—is partly mythological and but most completely existential or ontological in origin. What this means is that a few unknown mystics awakened to a felt sense of 'lack' within their consciousness, here and there, at first, and then the awareness spread like wildfire throughout the tribe or kingdom of nomadic groups.

The primal consciousness of humankind attached itself to every perceived, imagined, and conceived of object in experience. The sense of 'loss', 'lack', or 'Fall' was in losing a sense of the Wholeness and eventually the sacredness, mystery, and Unity of everything. The universe seemed a 'meaningless' and purposeless place since no dimensionality or even directionality of Presence was experienced. Primal 'man' was open only through the surfaces of experience and refused to surrender to the depths, heights, and fullness of Being. However, there were exceptional individuals even during the 'Fall of man' whose potentiality fully awakened to the mystery and wonder of the universe.

The subject of alienation has been the focus, in recent times, of philosophers and materialists whose consciousness awakened to the ontological and social dimensions of humanity. Such philosophers have not always seen the present state of alienated consciousness in anything other than personal, intersubjective, and inter-human relationships. However, the terrible sense of loss or lack of meaning and connection with Something in the depths of Being and ordinary life cannot always be explained or understood through life-histories or even cultural analysis. Of course, there is no end to the mind's suggestibility and vulnerability to environmental influences that invariably occur below the level of everyday consciousness.

On the other hand, the 'Fall from Grace' is a dreadful and true image of our existential condition. Existential alienation may not be the entire answer or explanation of the 'problem' of Being that so many individuals and groups suffer from, but it goes a long way in explaining much that is felt on an ontological or everyday level of Life in society. It is one of the root sources of the pain-body—the experience that comes from identifying with the mind and its abstract objects, the roles of the ego, and the negatives memories and situations that we drag with us into the present moment of existence and interferes with the experience of Presence.

Tolle believes that every pleasure or emotional high contains within itself the seed of pain which will only manifest itself in time. On one level, Tolle's belief may seem like a gloomy assessment of existence. But if you consider what most people are looking for in a sensate, materialistic, and narcissistic culture like our own, his view is psychologically realistic.

And what are 'most people' looking for? Perhaps they do not know themselves given the dominance of the unconscious mind and the irrational ego-structures that sustain it. We pride ourselves on being intelligent, rational, and even humane beings. But are we really rational or humane beings when so many members of our species periodically slaughter each other by the millions to protect a 'way of life', a 'leader', 'democracy', 'freedom', or the belief in a personal 'God'?

Contributing to our lack of critical or analytic thinking is the hectic pace with which most people in the postmodern, media-driven society live. Generally speaking, we do not take the time that is necessary for deep thinking, feeling or much less, concentration and meditation. Consciousness may not be the answer to everything, but it can contribute immensely to the habits of mind, body and soul that orient us towards Being or what is deepest and most profound in Life.

Typically, we value fast-talking, worldly people like news media pundits and television comedians, who can process situations of pain, suffering, and human loss like so much sausage or baloney in a fast-food bar. As a consequence, human life becomes devalued, and the tragic or comedic sense of life becomes banal and superficial in the habit of mind that reduces everything to a sound bite, slogan, or ego-trip.

Whether it is drugs, sex, or money, the 'mind identified egoic state' of unconsciousness simply turns into some form of pain, in time. We can only get out of the pain and negativity cycle that we are in, when we become conscious of Now, confront the pain-body through conscious watching and detach ourselves from its negativity and tendency to project our pain into the future, in visions of Armageddon, catastrophic events and horrific imaginings.

For example, one need only switch on the television during Prime Time and see what a steady diet of violence, horror, and crime shows the public is fed to keep the pain-body alive and 'healthy'. Is it any wonder that so many people feel helpless and impotent to 'make a difference' in society or even their own lives when they are constantly exposed to a steady diet of negative, immoral and violent images of 'life in society'?

American culture is the most violent culture in the world, by almost all social measures, and nothing is newsworthy or entertaining unless it shows blood, murder, thefts, lies, corruption and violence of every kind. It would make more sense to speak about 'death in society' rather than 'life in society' since there are so many people who appear to be miserable in their work, unhappy in their families, and situations of hopeless pain and suffering.

In Existential Philosophy, 'alienation' is typically used to describe the disconnection of the individual from primordial Being. It is this dis-ease or syndrome that Tolle uses to describe how the pain-body initially arises in the world. A human being instinctively values connection, unity, and the wholeness of Being yet civilization has developed in ways that fragment and cut off our connections with Being or sacred wholeness. The formation of the pain-body is a reaction to the fragmentation, compartmentalization, and identifications of mass society and *anomie* or the modern experience of meaninglessness.

A Christian View of Being: Emile Pascal

Tolle's solution to the ontological crisis of modern man—to the extent that there can be one—is to become Conscious of the pain-body that has paradoxically formed between consciousness and our primal sense of Being. The dis-content, dis-connection, and dis-ease of modern and now postmodern man is a symptom of the pain-body within the self that makes it virtually impossible for the average individual to 'sit quietly in an empty room and be contented'—to paraphrase Emile Pascal of the 16th century and the beginning of modern European culture.

Remarkably, Pascal apparently experienced the most profound states of transformation in the inner Fire of a Christ Consciousness lasting nearly four days. It bore all the signs of what the Zen Buddhists refer to as *Satori* or a profoundly deep and intuitive connection with formless Being. In fact, Pascal's awakened Consciousness is strongly indicated by his many writings in the *Pensees* (*Thoughts*) one of the world's greatest philosophical journals. A sampling from this classic amply shows the deeply mystical 'range' of Pascal's mind, heart, and soul:

"Let us then acknowledge our range: we are something, and we are not everything. What we have of being hides from us the knowledge of the first principles which emerge from nothingness. The scant being that we have hides from us the sight of infinity." (6)

On Plato and Aristotle's politics and ethics:

"We imagine Plato and Aristotle [as] upright people like everyone else....And when they were amusing themselves [they wrote] their Laws and Politics [and] they did it light-heartedly. It was the least philosophical and serious part of their lives, the more philosophical part being to live simply and calmly.... If they wrote about politics, it was as if to provide rules for a madhouse." (#457)

On the importance of the soul and its absence in modern ethics:

"There can be no doubt that whether the soul is mortal or immortal ought to make the whole difference in ethics. And yet philosophers have drawn up their ethics independently of this!" (#507)

On the priority of faith (heartfelt and divine) over proof (of human origin):

"Faith is different from proof. One is human, the other is a gift of God.... It is faith that God places in man's heart and the proof is often the instrument." ("Order" #41)

On the superficiality, pretense and hypocrisy of society:

"Mankind is...nothing but disguises, lies, and hypocrisy, both as individuals and with regard to others. They...do not want to be told the truth. They avoid telling it to others." (#649)

On the fear of nothingness, tranquility and the soul:

"Boredom: Nothing is so intolerable for man as to be in a state of complete tranquility, without passions, without business, without diversion, without effort. Then he feels his nothingness, his abandonment, his inadequacy, his dependence, his helplessness, his emptiness. At once from the depths of his soul arise boredom, gloom, sadness, grief, vexation, despair." (#515)

On the alienation from the present moment of experience:

"Everyone should study their thoughts. They will find them all centered on the past or the future. We almost never think of the present, and if we do it is simply to shed some light on the future. The present is never our end. Past and present are only means, only the future is our end. And so we never actually live, though we hope to, and in constantly striving for happiness it is inevitable that we will never achieve it." ("Vanity" #80)

On the vanity and distractions of the world:

"Anyone who does not see the vanity of the world is very vain himself. And so who does not see it apart from the young who are preoccupied with bustle, distractions, and plans for the future? But take away their distractions and you will see them wither from boredom. Then they feel their hollowness without understanding it...." (from "Vanity" #70)

On the fear of self-awareness:

"It is certain that the more awareness we have the more we will find both greatness and wretchedness in ourselves." (from "Contradictions" #155)

On the ignorance of the void and the infinite:

"What is humanity in nature? A nothingness compared to the infinite, everything compared to a nothingness, a mid-point between nothing and everything, infinitely far from understanding the extremes; the end of things and their beginning are insuperably hidden from him in an impenetrable secret....All things derive from a void and are swept on to the infinite." (from "Knowledge" #230)

On the Wager that reason cannot answer:

"Let us therefore examine this point and say: God is, or is not. But towards which side will we lean? Reason cannot decide anything. There is an infinite chaos separating us. At the far end of this infinite distance a game is being played and the coin will come down heads or tails. How will you wager? Reason cannot make you choose one way or the other; reason cannot make you defend either of the two choices?" (#680)

On his enlightenment experience:

"The year of grace 1654, Monday 23 November, feast of Saint Clement, Pope and martyr, and others of the Roman Arthrology. Eve of Saint Chrsogonus, martyr, and others, from about half past ten in the evening until about half past midnight: FIRE.

"God of Abraham, God of Isaac, God of Jacob, not of philosophers and scholars. Certainty, joy, certainty, emotion, sight, joy, God of Jesus Christ. Your God will be my God. Ruth. Oblivious to the world and to everything except God...." from *The Memorial.* (7)

The philosophic depth and breadth of Pascal's vision is obvious as is his intense Christian belief and the metaphysical experience that he underwent on November 23, 1654. His genius for geometry, mathematics, philosophy, and theology was exceeded only by his intuitive understanding of human nature and the human condition. One can certainty argue with his theology and metaphysics; but his depth of understanding human nature and our primal relation to Being and the extent to which it is conflicted with everyday experience and civilization is of Perennial significance. And there is also little in Pascal' philosophy that an admirer of Tolle's thought would find unacceptable.

Buddhist Mindfulness: the Awareness of Now

The Buddhist view of existence, like most philosophies of the world, is divided between Transcendental and empirical or more religious and scientific viewpoints. Importantly though both branches of Buddhism emphasize the central role that ethics play in the goal of liberation from karmic or cyclic existence. And central to ethics especially personal ethics is the Middle Path between the extremes of existence or asceticism and hedonism.

The four noble truths or 'facts' of existence—as some prefer to call the four main doctrines of Buddhism—are: 1, the truth of *duhkha* or negativity, dissatisfaction and violence 2, the truth of *karma* or causation, reason and pre-determination, 3, the truth of *moksa* or freedom from violence, negativity and violence and 4, the truth of the Middle Way which is based upon the eightfold path of liberation and enlightenment.

The Middle Way of ethics offers eight steps towards self-realization or awakening to who we are as existing beings. They are; right understanding, right intention, right speech, right action, right livelihood, right effort, right mindfulness, and right concentration. The aim of Buddhist practice is to perfect the sense of rightness and so to bring one's self into alignment with the most fundamental laws of the universe.

All of this must be done in the frame of understanding that all existing forms (*dharmas*) are: 1, lack independence and thus are empty of intrinsic essence *(Shunyata)* 2, totally interdependent and mutually arise in the real world 3, all phenomena arise as an expression of the absolute (*suchness*). This view was made popular by the *T'ien-t'ai* school of Chinese Buddhism in the 6th century and it is mainly based upon the philosophy of Nagarjuna or the somewhat paradoxical and profound philosophy that all viewpoints and forms are relative, conditional and lack in essence or absoluteness; yet at the same time, they naturally arise in relation to something Absolute like Emptiness! (8)

Mindfulness or the seventh step in the eightfold Path of the Middle Way is simply being fully conscious or perfected in the observation of phenomenal existence. Mindfulness is thus an inclusive perspective of existing phenomena, physical, emotional and mental, and recognizes the dialectical law that controls all forms in relation to absoluteness or what can only be known interdependently as 'the emptiness of forms and the forms of emptiness'.

Like Yoga, the aim of mindfulness is to bring the mind under control and it is based upon the elaborate four foundations of mindfulness found in the *Satipatthana*-sutra of Buddhist Theravada. Briefly, this consists of awareness of the body and its thirty-two parts, the feelings (*vedana*) of pleasant, unpleasant and neutral, the five sense organs and interpenetrating consciousness that creates impressions upon the brain, etc. In general, feelings are a vital part of the Buddhist and Existential views of Life and the phenomenology of consciousness. (9)

Since experience and knowledge are derived from *observation* or perception, conception and intuition, all forms of reality exist on the ground of formlessness or absolute suchness. Here, the limits of knowing are realized and the possibility of intuitive experience or omniscience is glimpsed deeply within higher Consciousness. Strictly speaking, all forms of experience and knowledge are observed in the Now of eternity and time.

Meditative mindfulness is meant to be practiced in everyday life, in every situation of Life, in relation to inner, outer, higher and deeper phenomena. In theory, mindfulness exploits the fact of consciousness in its everydayness and elevates, perfects and deepens awareness in all occasions and experiences. In practice, humans almost always fall just shy of absolute perfection or a perfection that is permanent.

Observing or 'watching' is being fully conscious of the here-and-now. We may never be absolutely perfect in 'watching' but we can approximate the ideal condition with practice and establishing the habit. In the privacy of your own awareness, you can watch for or observe any negative energy from the pain-body that arises and pull it up before it takes root. And this habit of meditation can be brought to your awareness of immediate conversation, a news broadcast, a television or radio program, literature, etc., and watch for negative energy, emotion, or thought that may be present and feeds the pain-body.

What is particularly interesting is how the energy of the pain-body reduces your Consciousness from the Now. Typically, the pain-body feeds upon the past and the future and all things distant in space and time. The mind- body-soul—its perceptions, thoughts, emotions, images and memories—has immense power in our lives and the potential goodness that it can effect is unlimited; but so too is the pain-body's violence, negativity, and attachment to existing things. However, higher Consciousness has the

286

power to control the dialectical tendencies of the mind- body and its conditioned habits of experience and knowledge through the soul's perfection.

Consciousness has the power to burn up negative energy or karma through the act of healing awareness. Its power works like magic in helping us to get rid of the pain-body that everyone suffers from, to some degree. Of course there are no 'magic bullets' when it comes to contingent or real being since self-being is conditioned, habit-ridden and resists quick or easy change. Hence, we must develop good habits of awareness; and learn to detect the signs and evidence of the pain-body in ourselves, other persons, and the media-saturated, institutions of society.

Vigilance or mindfulness—as the 7th step of the 8-fold Path of Buddhism asserts—is crucial for maintaining the Middle Way or Path between the extremes of experience. Mindfulness is the panoramic view of the mountains and valleys of personal experience. Mindfulness is noticing everything as it happens in the here-and-now, without the judging, comparing, and analyzing mind. When we are 'watching mindfully' we can see things as they appear, persist and disappear; and we can experience the things, habits and roles that may interfere with or alienate us from the wisdom of Being. (10)

The Sense of Being: Happiness and Peace

The experience of Being occurs in the here-and-now; and even if Being is only 'glimpsed' or experienced in a brief period of time, the experience of timelessness and formlessness or eternal Presence is life-changing. In fact, any experience of Being should be cherished like a beautiful flower, smile, or summer day. For the experience of Being or divine Goodness is the experience of everything holy, sacred, and valuable in Life.

Human happiness, good feeling and positive thought is the readiness to relate to others openly and with a warm heart and it is the real beginning of *Nirvana* or the experience of release, openness and *moksa* (freedom). Happiness is the door through which you can walk and experience the spaciousness of Being or the feeling of being alive, happy, and peaceful.

There is really only one cure for the domination or tyranny of a mind that is unconsciously conditioned by a pain-body. The cure or healing comes from our sense of Being, the Higher Consciousness that is the path for happiness, peace, and the free will. And once we have made our peace with 'who we are' or the essence of Being, the soul, then we can really feel at home in the world—wherever we are.

No one ever said that living meaningfully and purposefully was going to be easy—or if they did they were not telling you the Truth; but once realized, then you can use your mind and its reasoning power with confidence and feel at one with the wholeness of the total Self.

The ethical consequence of the awareness and experience of Being is that fighting, aggression, and needless suffering will eventually cease. Peace will come to your heart, mind, and soul when you become fully conscious of divine Presence. And there will be 'nothing to die for' because there will be everything to live for.

Chuangzi: Forgetting the Words

The wit of the Taoist philosopher, Chuangzi, comes from a place of great insight. In the following series of statements, Chuangzi draws some humorous parallels between very different phenomena. Does his question suggest that we cannot 'exist' without words?

"The fish trap exists because of the fish; once you've gotten the fish, you can forget the trap. The rabbit snare exists because of the rabbit; once you've gotten the rabbit, you can forget the snare. Words exist because of meaning; once you've gotten the meaning, you can forget the words. Where can I find a man who has forgotten the words so I can have a word with him?" (11)

Chapter 16

THINGS, THOUGHTS AND HUMAN BEINGS

What is thought in relation to a word or a physical thing? How are thoughts related to the mind or consciousness of a human being? What kind of thoughts lead to knowledge, wisdom and the Truth about existence? And why is it important to see thoughts as just momentary forms of the mind created from reason, perception and ignorance of the Divine Ground?

"He is a miserable man who knows all things and does not know God; and he is happy who knows God even though he knows nothing else." St Augustine

"This universe ... is both One and Many." Dionysius

"Christ is all, and in all." Colossians

"Any knowledge that does not bring us to supreme bliss and freedom is not worth acquiring. We stuff our minds with knowledge of so many facts and things gained from all and sundry, or reading all kinds of books. The brain becomes a repository of learning about all the ephemeral and passing phases of life. Naturally such a man becomes a restless being— unbalanced, confused and erratic in his behavior and conduct. Seek, therefore, to know the true source of your life—God. That is why you are here." Swami Ramdass

"Wisdom is better than the weapons of war." Ecclesiastes, xi.18

Ecclesiastes, a Jewish Preacher in the Old Testament, is *a sacred book* in the wisdom tradition of the Bible. This is an intensely written book by a sincere believer in God who sees nothing but futility in the efforts of humans, especially fools. However, it is not clear where the difference lies between the wise and the foolish

289

since 'All is vanity and futility and a striving after wind' in human action. Furthermore, *Ecclesiastes* does not offer any solution to the problem of seeking after wisdom since "What is crooked cannot be made straight, and what is lacking cannot be numbered.... For in much wisdom is much vexation and he who increases knowledge increases sorrow." The Preacher offers some hope in Chapter 7: 23-29 when he says that the essence of his wisdom lies far, "far off and deep, very deep; who can find it?" But the answer is foiled by the "wickedness of folly and the foolishness which is madness." *Ecclesiastes* supports his general feeling of the lack of justice in that "the race is not to the swift, nor the battle to the strong, nor bread to the wise, nor riches to the intelligent, nor favor to the men of skill; but time and chance happen to them all" which seems generally true. Again the "words of the wise heard in quiet are better than the shouting of a ruler among fools. [And most importantly] Wisdom is better than weapons of war, but one sinner destroys much good." There is much wisdom to be gained in closely reading *Ecclesiastes* even though it may sound the note of "the futility of being good" once too often for the faint of heart. Finally, *Ecclesiastes*, in Chapter 10, darkly assures us that it is futile to do almost anything: "He who digs a pit will fall into it; and a serpent will bit him who breaks through a wall. He who quarries stones is hurt by them; and he who splits logs is endangered by them." The one consolation and paradox against all odds is that "wisdom helps one to succeed." (1)

Words, Meanings and Language Users

The most trustworthy anchor in the world of the experience is the physical world of real, perceivable things. In fact, it appears to be so real that I wonder why our distant ancestors ever invented language. As the Zen masters of silence and meditation teach, it is best never to open your mouth and say anything sometime since words often cover up the truth as much as they may uncover it. A brief exchange between a Zen monk and his disciple illustrates this point:

"Master" the disciple asked "What is the most basic Principle of everything?" And the Zen teacher replied, "If I told you what it is, it would be the second principle."

What this bit of dialogue shows is the double-nature of a word: it covers over, creating an illusion of reality of its own, as much as it uncovers or discloses what is real or true. In this case, the Zen teacher refused to use the word for the one Principle, knowing the difference between words and what they merely symbolize. If the Zen teacher had replied "Mind" or "Emptiness" the chances are that his student would become attached to the word and taken it for the Truth; whereas the struggle in silence and nonverbally could awaken him to the Truth that is beyond words.

The paradoxes of language should make sense to everyone—not just hermits, monks or ascetics, since communication is such a big part of human communities of all kinds. Yet most of our direct experiences of reality are mediated nonverbally or without language or communication with others. For example, our daily experiences of reality are mediated by the five, external senses of seeing, hearing, tasting, smelling and touching. Furthermore, our five senses are interpenetrated by consciousness, the unseen witness and source of meaning and satisfaction for the mind and body.

Language is the proverbial double-edged sword since it cuts through whoever uses it and it can also cut or harm the user as well when words are used in haste, anger or a lack of understanding and empathy. The meaning of words is a very subtle matter determined by a myriad of conditions in a communication situation of persons and things. The clarity of word meanings is typically only skin-deep since words do not have to penetrate to the complexities of emotion, memory or imagination to be intellectually clear.

The technical use or meaning of words, as from a dictionary, is a good example of conventional usage that may make clear but limited meaning in terms of human experience and language users. In other words, there is the experience of depth in the use of language when words make connections with our total sense of experience. And there are many communication situations where language is necessarily vague, ambiguous and lacking in clear referents yet are aesthetically, emotionally and spiritually satisfying.

I emphasize the ambiguity and doubled-nature of language since this is where insanity creeps in, cat-like. Decades ago, general semanticists warned that not understanding the metaphorical and symbolic nature of language can lead to the insanity, in thought and action. For example, the mind and its forms of thought and emotion seize upon a word or a slogan, a tag or a label, and before we know it, the word becomes the thing, person or event that it merely represents or points to. The result is a confusion between word and and thing or what merely exists in the neurological structures and functions of a language-user. (2)

Meaning is an immediate and intuitive response to words in the learned vocabulary of the mind. If we do not know the language that we hear or read, the words or sounds are meaningless. So meaning is an experience that we have from knowing one or more languages; and this subjective experience becomes a social, cultural and existential one when we learns to share and communicate with others. But there are real limits to the experience of meaning since there are many experiences in living and just being-in-the-world, nature and the universe, that may not mean anything but which bring great satisfaction, enjoyment and happiness to us.

Illusion, Identification and Ownership

We have nearly all been conditioned to believe in capitalism and the goodness of being rich; but we soon discover how few ever do. Still, it is the dominant myth and goal of many young, poor and middle class people. But what does being rich really mean?

The illusion of ownership derives from having or possessing many things; and feeling that these possessions define who you are. If I have a lot of things, particularly money, then I may feel more secure even important in the world. You quite profoundly become what you own or possess and that thing identifies who you are.

The subtlety or unconscious way that things of ownership invade our inner being is insidious and beyond awareness. Instead of us owning things, things that we possess begin to own us. And you only need to reflect upon the number of things or stuff that you collect over time in your life to verify this.

What does it mean, for example, to have 'health and well-being', 'money and security', 'friends and family', or 'knowledge and wisdom'? For sure, everyone is going to the question in a different way. And we could debate forever what these things and possessions really mean; but we could probably agree that they are all important for people who live a somewhat normal, well-balanced and ordinary life.

In a Capitalistic society where Life is reduced to 'having' or the possessive mode of being, the conditioning of the ego by thoughts of ownership and consumption are very powerful; and too often they tend to override all other values and concerns in living. A person's whole life-time of work and monthly paychecks may often be nearly exhausted on paying-off a loan, for a house, a car, or a family member's college education. Houses are notorious for mortgages that may last for thirty years and are often re-mortgaged or leveraged for their equity value so that more things can be bought and owned.

The more existential view is that no one ever really owns anything since we are born into the world naked, and naked, solitary and penniless, we shall die. Yet the entire experience of living in a Capitalistic society is one that reduces everything to ownership, capital, and investment, whether it is our relationship with another person, a career, house, or education. In turn, the more we have of these phenomena, the more the illusion of who we are grows and feeds the ego or individual sense of self and alienation from Nature and authentic Being.

Concerning the 'illusion of ownership', Tolle cites Jesus: "'Blessed are the poor in spirit, for theirs is the kingdom of heaven'. What does 'poor in spirit' mean? No inner baggage, no identification. Not with things, or with any mental concepts that have a sense of self in them. And what is the 'kingdom of heaven'? The simple but profound joy of Being that is there when you let go of identifications and so become 'poor in spirit'." (3)

Just giving up your money, assets and material things will not bring you the 'kingdom of heaven' or peace that you seek unless you give up the ego, its identifications and thought processes that are the cause of ownership in the first place. You must reconsider the state of your inner being or soul no matter what you do—especially if your actions are to have a transformative effect. Thinking that you will feel more secure, happy and fulfilled with more money, stuff and roles in society is the basic illusion of consumerism and the capitalistic economy. (4)

Desire, Sexuality, and Spirituality

Desire is a natural part of being human, as natural as having a body and mind. Problems, conflicts and antagonisms arise when we crave, cling, and become attached to our desires—whatever they may be. There may be no greater desire than the longing for a union with eternal, formless and undifferentiated Unity of everything. This spiritual craving can be infinitely greater than that of sexual longing which we are naturally pre-wired to experience although it is not uncommon that sexual and spiritual longings are confused with one another, resulting in psychopathic disorders.

In fact, the sexual longing, craving, and drivenness of persons—especially during early and middle adulthood—may often be a symptom of a repressed desire for spiritual union with what is Ultimate. There are many other reasons why people may be sexually driven, i.e. karmic past life conditioning, negative sexual experiences occasioned by older siblings or relatives, and being born into a sexually obsessed, narcissistic culture like the United States.

Whatever all the reasons for adult sexual behavior in contemporary culture, it is obvious that the body or the organismic unconsciousness and the mind or conscious intentionality play reciprocating or co-equal roles; and following puberty, in the teens and early adulthood and when the procreative and irrational, will-to-lust blinds young men and women—all reason, judgment and wisdom is useless and unheard. When the irrational sexual behavior of youth continues into adulthood and even old age is when pathos becomes absurdity.

The relationship between human sexuality and what is termed 'spirituality' has always been fraught with dangers—at every age except old age and early childhood. The term 'spirit' is notorious for its vagueness of meaning since its contexts and referents are often thought to be supernatural ones. If the term is to be rescued from total emptiness of meaning in the postmodern world, it must be thought about as having an organic, energetic, and naturalistic origin in experience.

'Spirit' and 'spirituality' must be thought about in relation to Being or the Life-force of present experience. Eternity, temporality, and organic nature constitute the Inner Body or Spirit while its conscious or rational aspects exist at higher levels of potentiality, i.e. the *Ajna-chakra*. In fact, no better model exists for thinking about the subtle relationship of sexuality with spirituality than the theory of human nature that is embedded in the theory and practices of Kundalini Yoga.

In this philosophy, the aim of Life is to awaken the yogi (or anyone) to the sacred energy or Life-force that sustains ordinary existence. Although the Life-force constitutes the Inner Body or life-world of the person, its structures and functions are atomic, chemical and cellular in nature, and creates the powerful, unconscious and blind currents of passion associated with the energy of sexual experience. The experience of adult sexuality is so strong due to its primary aim, procreation; and ancient yogis viewed the control of sexual energy as the basis for the experience leading to spiritual liberation.

Whether this use of sexuality makes any sense for normal adults who are not practitioners of Kundalini yoga, is highly debatable and controversial in some circles. If and perhaps 'only if' sufficient intelligence and maturity is brought to the practice of awakening the subtle body of sexuality, could Kundalini yoga be considered a pathway or means of higher Consciousness or spiritual Awakening.

Since I have introduced the outline of this theory elsewhere in this study, I will not discuss it any further here except to say that historical persons believed to be the most perfected 'spiritual' beings among us have often been deified by the masses as if they could 'walk on water' or perform supernatural miracles. Rather than dismissing such phenomena out-of-hand, the attainments associated with Siddhartha, Socrates, Jesus, Mahavira, Mohammad, Lao-tzu, et al, should be thought of as persons who awakened fully to the Life-force within the body raising their consciousness to the highest levels of potentiality.

The History of Religion, War, and Delusion

Spiritual fulfillment can be realized by 'becoming' who you really are. The perfection of Being cannot be improved upon and realized at some later date. The inner perfection of who we are– is Now; and all our becoming or stages of development as persons are superficial in relation to the inner perfection of your own present Being.

Rather than constantly wanting or desiring fulfillment in spiritual matters, the followers of the Buddha, Jesus, Mahavira or Mohammad—or whoever your spiritual ideal is—have often identified with such persons. As Tolle has well-cautioned, there is a psychological danger in identifying with or following anyone— whether that person is deemed a 'god' or someone rich, famous or wise.

As the Buddha allegedly said before dying, 'Be a lamp unto yourself'. Or the atheist, Friedrich Nietzsche advised his readers, 'I have found my way; now what is yours?' Or the last words spoken by Christ on the cross, 'Forgive them Father for they know not what they do'. Or Tolle's spoken words about the question of death, 'Let's wait and see'.

In the history of religion, 'spiritual' development is practically synonymous with moral development; and both have been seen as constantly evolving, on-going, and contingent. The only constant or universal is the inner condition of spirituality, i.e. that which is free, transcendent, and unconditional.

Even though there are relatively few famous persons or founders and shapers of the world's major religions, one can attain a degree of personal, moral and spiritual development by cautiously identifying with the thought of such persons. Becoming a follower or disciple of a master, guru or 'Enlightened One' is not recommended by most people who have spent much time around spiritual or religious teachers. Certainly, Tolle condemns the practice and so do I.—That said, there is something to be learned from everyone and especially, sometimes, people who have identified themselves as teachers of a religious or spiritual tradition.

Although it is an extremely risky, dangerous, and sometimes deadly choice to follow a so-called 'religious' or 'spiritual' leader who is only realized at the egoic or mental level of consciousness—a similar danger, equally sinister, exists with leaders or teachers who have no beliefs in anything—save their ego, and are intent upon gathering followers or votes of support, for their nihilistic creed.

History has shown that fraudulent, self-deceived, and inauthentic persons are often attracted to the role of becoming a spiritual leader since the psychological conditions are always ripe for the exploitation of gullible, poorly educated, and needy persons. The tragedy at Jonestown, South Africa is only one such recent tragedy in 1990's in which over 900 people died in a single act of 'suicide' or mass murder, perpetrated by a pathological and charismatic leader who preyed on the most primal fears and needs of his devoted followers.

The history of religion is replete with similar tragic stories of mass violence, war, and genocide that were created by murderous leaders who used religion and the belief of eternal happiness in a Heavenly realm to attract the masses. Absolute morality, metaphysical Certainty, and extreme Nationalism or Patriotism, have often been used as a sufficient justification for the most horrific of crimes against humanity. A mere glance at the history of warfare since the Crusades of the Middle Ages to the oil wars of the Middle East in the 1990's and since 9/11/2001, discloses an unscrupulous, murderous, and self-righteous delusion among many followers and leaders who have only left a long trail of blood and sorrow.

That said, the ideals, precepts, and means for becoming virtuous or 'spiritual' are readily available through the wisdom traditions of the world. Not all of the 'wisdom' traditions of the world are religious or metaphysical. For example, the histories of Naturalism, Existentialism, Jainism, Pragmatism, Marxism, Freudianism, and Buddhism, are conspicuous for their having no known 'God' or metaphysical Agent who is known to witness the mundane affairs of humanity much less protect humanity in times of great need and tragedy. Such philosophies should be studied for the truthful assessment that they have made of human existence.

Although no one viewpoint can be said to contain the whole or complete truth about Life and death, good and evil, creation and human destiny, there are many viewpoints in the history of philosophy, religion, and science, which enable us to climb to ever higher vantage points in reality, and to gaze down upon the wholeness of things, to ever deeper depths of Being. These views which exist always in the visions and Consciousness of single individuals, initially and originally, are Perennial so far as their depth and scope of understanding is concerned, and are the most enduring and valuable testimonies to the Truth.

As Tolle has written, personal striving and desiring, 'wanting' and struggling, begins and ends in the Now. We often create the most serious obstacles to our fulfillment or happiness, by constantly fighting and refusing to surrender to the deepest challenge, i.e. being peaceful in the sacred present. It is more therapeutic to surrender to eternal Presence than to fight against problems that are merely imaginary in the end. As has been implied on every theatrical billboard of the world, 'death cancels everything' which should remind us of the importance of the real play. (5)

Dis-identifying from Things, Thoughts, and Meanings

Existentially, we never really 'own' anything even the body which is the most precious object or thing in the world. The body really owns us in that the ego, mind, and thoughts are entirely dependent upon the body's health or capacity to sustain our life-form. However, we *are* also a higher Consciousness and the essence (*soul*) of Being. The truth is we cannot even say or describe adequately 'who we are' since Being is ineffable or beyond the power of language and thought.

As the Existentialists, mystics and Perennialists have known, *Being* is an intuitive feeling rather than a thought or intellectual concept. *Being* is, importantly, a sublime illusion created by language and thought that is ambiguous and dialectical. Being is the unseen Unity, the unmanifested realm within the manifested realm of consciousness, nature and society. The changing forms of the world are merely illusions from the perspective of primal Being.

Higher Consciousness is like an opening or a great doorway into the hidden or unseen dimensions of the universe. Non-possession is the attitude of not really owning anything even if you legally do; and non-attachment is a consequence of the feeling of non-possession that sees all ownership as temporary, precarious and an illusion of the ego; and if non-possession and non-attachment co-exist in the same consciousness, we are witnessing an increase of nonviolence.

Being is the Light of the universe, the Sun beyond all suns that shines through time, nature, and knowledge. Being is entirely indifferent to the mind, its thoughts, and other ego states, since it is infinite, eternal, and cannot be known through thought. *If the essence of who we are is eternal like Being, infinite like Being and absolutely free of limiting roles and conditions, then our essence is already, always saved from the corruptions of worldly existence.*

What is the meaning of this one life-form or individual self? Meaning is just another trap or illusion of thought. Life cannot be adequately expressed in words, as a thought or idea since all thoughts and concepts are limiting abstractions. Dis–identifying from the effort to describe or explain Life is the beginning of philosophical liberation and the end of existential analysis and the illusions of meaning. It clears the path to Being and living fully in the here-and-now of Consciousness or absolute freedom.

Dis-identifying from things, thoughts, and meanings is the beginning of complete liberation. It is re-claiming your life-form for a more universal sense of Life. It is freeing yourself of obstacles that block your path to Being and Truth. And it is *the way* to restore the original power, Goodness and will that you lost while you were in the process of adapting to an insane, unbalanced and dehumanizing world.

Dis-identifying is learning to *intuitively feel* your way back to universal sense of Life rather than constantly thinking that you have to figure everything out or understand something before you can experience it. In reality, *experience precedes knowledge and understanding* for it is our needs, feelings and perceptions that are the most real or basic ingredients of knowledge while our ideas, thoughts and concepts are the more abstract parts of understanding.

Finally, experience and knowledge are dialectical ideas that emerge from the cauldron of existence. We are subjective organisms, first and foremost, and all our efforts to be 'objective' and 'scientific' in thought and speech, are little more than abstract glosses upon the totality of experience. *From our view of the vast and starry heavens beyond the Earth to the wonder of the human Genome within the body, all our perspectives and articulations only express the mystery of Consciousness in its subjective unity with the objective world of material existence, in approximate, ambiguous and incomplete forms.*

Dis-engaging from Philosophy

'Life is short and philosophy long' just about sums up the existential dilemma of knowing and living. If you assume that philosophy means the 'love of wisdom' then the activity is virtually unending. And from ancient times, in Greece, India and China, at least, philosophers have been raising the same questions and giving similar answers.

Today, almost three thousand years later and counting, we are little closer to answers for the Big or Ultimate Questions like: Who are we? What do we know and how do we know it? What is the Truth? Where did we come from? Where are we going? And why are we here?

Pragmatic or real world thought gives mostly practical, useful and verifiable answers to ultimate questions. Exceptions exist to this rule even among the Pragmatists. Some Existential philosophers give more subjective, humanistic and literary answers the ultimate questions while others are more academic, formal and technical. Existentialists tend to focus upon existence-as-lived at a persona level and ask questions about meaning, ethics and politics. And there is a variety of other philosophies currently in play like Analytic philosophy, Marxism, Feminism, and Environmentalism; and there are numerous branches of philosophy like metaphysics, linguistics, logic, ethics and politics that matter in the whole spectrum of philosophy: the world religions, the physical and social sciences, the arts and the humanities, human existence and Life.

Perennialists, we have seen, make up a group of thinkers who have faith in a universal or ultimate purpose in human existence and the universe; and Tolle must be counted among them. Following the Chinese Taoists, we may not know the right word or really understand the concept of *Something Ultimate*, but it is the faith or belief that matters in the feelings, thoughts and practices of religious and spiritual philosophies.

Just now, in the twenty-first century, the spectrum of philosophical perspectives is vast, multidimensional and multidisciplinary—as it has always been. For example, there are symbolic, logical and scientific perspectives in philosophy which tend to dominate more contemporary, Eurocentric, Western cultures; and in India, China, Africa, South America, and the indigenous peoples of the world, the possibilities are broader in scope, deeper in experience, and closer to our most distant origins as a species. These are only broad generalizations but useful for a more detailed description and analysis.

The opportunities for thinking, meaning and identification with the manifestations of ego, thought and mind are rife and endless in philosophy as an academic activity. If you wish to build up your ego, get hung up on the forms of thought and the abstract categories and concepts of the mind, philosophy is an abyss, a dizzying whirlwind of abstractions and distinctions, a maze that no one should be forced to go through or even introduced to without strong warnings and clear notices of the dangers that philosophy poses to one's physical, emotional, mental, and spiritual health!

For example, one is apt to become so absorbed, entrenched and rooted in one viewpoint or another—that the avowed goals of 'learning how to problem solve' 'acquiring knowledge and understanding' 'finding wisdom' 'becoming enlightened'—may be in some superficial sense, realized; but the belief that the soul or consciousness survives death, that God may exist or that a free will is not an illusion, all this and more is summarily dismissed as 'pre-scientific nonsense', 'intellectual rubbish' or words to that effect. If one enters the deserts of philosophy with the expectation that prior beliefs will be respected, a terrible shock awaits them. Every thought, feeling or practice is sliced, diced and ground to its smallest visible particles of matter; and what is not visible is condemned as illusion, superstition, religion or worse!

What is objectionable in philosophy or any other category of knowledge is the egotistical pretense and dogmatism that 'I know the Truth about 'X'—X in this case representing Ultimate Questions about the meaning of existence, life and death. For sure, the philosophy of Perennialism is grounded in the faith traditions of the world or the world's major religions; but the same criteria that are used in scientific problem-solving to determine the truth or falsity of a proposition are simply not applicable to religious or spiritual propositions.

For example, propositions like 'God exists', 'the soul is eternal', 'Being is infinite', 'there is life after death', and so on and so forth, are statements of faith, subjectivity and human feeling; and the scientific or empirical criteria for 'knowledge' like observation, testing and experimentation, induction, and verifiable evidence, simply do not apply to beliefs of 'faith and reason'.

For many centuries, St. Thomas Aquinas "Five Proofs for the Existence of God" have been the bedrock among Catholics for their belief in the existence of God. But in spite of Aquinas' impeccable a priori logic and deductive reasoning about God's existence, those who have no belief or faith in the existence of a Supreme God remain un-persuaded. Thus reason, no matter how well used, is no match for faith or the lack of it, when it comes to such emotional subjects like God. (6)

Anything of a religious, metaphysical or spiritual nature is simply thrown out the small windows of science. Yet the rooms of science have given us tremendous insights, technologies and advances in our understanding of matter, energy and the vast spatial-temporal universe in which we all live. Science has taken us far beyond the vague, intuitive, and ambiguous propositions and beliefs of mythology, theology and spirituality. But science does not exist independently of human subjectivity, values, and the same limits of reason and understanding that plague all other fields of experience and knowledge. Science is limited by the same conditions of knowing and being that are present everywhere else in human existence. In short, there is no escape from human finitude, mortality and tragedy.

So what's the answer? Actually there are none that you can 'take to the bank' and be absolutely certain and secure about—except one: what you feel, believe and know is true until it is proven otherwise by your actions in experience. It is *experience* or the values that we hold, consciously and unconsciously, that make us all different from one another; and even if we all had the same experiences, what is given through the human genome and the meta-genetics of identity—the soul—makes us all essentially different at the moment of conception and continuously through gestation, birth and thereafter. Following our live birth, things become more complicated due to the exercise of the free will, our relations with others, and the total influence of the natural, social and cultural environment.

So what is left of *philosophy*—the esoteric, jargon-ridden, and academic subject of colleges and universities—and beyond it? It is just the billions of ordinary, non-philosophical people who struggle, suffer and live their lives in anonymity from the limelight of popular culture and higher education. Academic philosophy is something cloistered, elitist and alienated from the daily experiences of ordinary people and the real world. It is an activity that suffers from a shortness of breath, prone to panic attacks and heart palpitations, a sclerosis of the liver and kidneys, and a paralysis of the limbs.

The best cure for academic philosophy is early retirement, the open air and fresh winds, sunshine and a retreat to the most peaceful place of the Earth. And that place is where you are and it is the present moment.

Becoming an Authentic Human Being

As Shakespeare wrote in *Hamlet*, "There is nothing either good or bad, but thinking makes it so." Real thinking takes place within the neural pathways of the mind and the logical means by which we solve problems and arrive at conclusions based upon verifiable or falsifiable evidence. Otherwise, much of what is called thinking is really something like day-dreaming, random and unfocused awareness, unconscious action, and role-playing. That said the deeper, more revolutionary forms of thinking take place with unconscious thought processes where insight and intuition are able to see through received truths, norms and values and take humankind to new depths of understanding where the Truth prevails.

The pain, suffering and alienation from the whole body, Nature and Being are far more extensive than most people realize. The trouble with thinking is that it often separates us from real experience, higher Consciousness and the *Truth of Being*. Tolle has written in several places about *genuine or authentic Awareness* which is known when we experience ourselves as completely natural, integrated and spontaneous persons and *beyond* the social roles and agendas that we may have. Tolle wrote:

"Mother, father, husband, wife, young, old, the roles you play, the functions you fulfill, whatever you do—all that belongs to the human dimension. It has its place and needs to be honored, but in itself it is not enough for a fulfilled, truly meaningful relationship or life. Human roles alone are never enough, no matter how hard you try or what you achieve. There is Being. It is found in the still, alert presence of Consciousness itself, the Consciousness that you are. Human is form. Being is formless. Human and Being are not separate but interwoven."(7)

'Human roles are never enough'—needs to be repeated like a sacred *mantra* to overcome the identifications that we have with social roles. Consciousness and Being, Human and Being are dialectically related—one cannot be separated one concept or sense of reality from the other for they co-arise and co-exist in our actual experience of self and the universe. Furthermore, the reason why so many rarely experience the sense of fulfillment that they feel capable of, in role-playing or being this or that in society, is their felt lack of higher Consciousness and the sense of Being. Awakening to the meditative stillness, silence and concentrating upon just-being-who-we-are—and not what-we-are— we are suddenly liberated from any inauthentic being-in-the-world.

One of the most fundamental assumptions of Tolle's philosophy is that you can never be more than you are, as a total person of Being—no matter what you accomplish, how wealthy, wise, or famous you might become. To play a variation on Shakespeare's statement about thinking, role-playing is neither good nor bad;

it is only thinking and the absence of Awareness that makes it so. However, if we can *truly think*, i.e. *meditate upon just-being-who-we-are*, then the possibilities are endless, the horizons of experience unlimited.

If we only rather unconsciously play a role, perform a necessary function in society that tradition, training or professionalism merely dictate, there is a good chance that your experience will only bring dissatisfaction to you and others. Furthermore, no amount of money, status, or recognition from others is going to set things right from a lifetime of alienated role-playing or actions that lack a closeness to or Consciousness of authentic Being; and *of crucial importance to the authentic sense of Being-in-a-role is the closeness that you enjoy with other human beings.*

Acting with a divided or absent sense of a deeper, higher and more inclusive Consciousness or Being, in your ego's role-playing only guarantees that you add to your *pain-body*—the inner, hidden body that remembers every nuance of feeling, thought and sensation that registers your pain and dissatisfaction, albeit unconsciously. The only cure for it is to step away from it and begin to dis-identify from the region of pain, alienation and lack that you may feel, within the self, and just give up role-playing.

About this, Tolle has written: "If you can be absolutely comfortable with not knowing who you are, then what's left is who you are—the Being behind the human, a field of pure potentiality rather than something that is already defined." (8)

This is the essential Truth about our human sense of Being: 'pure potentiality rather than something that is already defined'. In other words, we are capable of acting dualistically or destructively towards ourselves when we *just role-play*; and we do so separated from who we really are—our essence. When we act from who we are, we experience ourselves from within the body as a whole self. And when we experience and know who we are, we experience ourselves as the formless Presence that *we always, everywhere are.*

Or, as Tolle has written about our relations with others: "Whenever you interact with people, don't be there primarily as a function or role, but as a field of conscious Presence." (9)

And this means really listening and being-with-others in their Presence as whole persons. The ego or the way that we are collectively conditioned to behave in society, is too often a source of *pathos* or suffering—no matter how successfully we may perform for their recognition. If you are only behaving or playing a role for social recognition, you have already missed an opportunity to be-with-others as an authentic Being in the *mutuality of I and Thou or Presence.*

The ego that we develop and the roles that we play are usually just creations from thought or the cognitive activity of the mind and not from our deeper, more spontaneous self. Unless we meet the other in human situations we miss Being or the reciprocal, mutual, trusting openness that is pure potentiality of sacred Presence. Although we are subject to powerful conditioning in growing up, schooling, and living in society, we are ultimately responsible for the way that we internalize, hold and act out our conditioned self and roles. (10)

If we were not absolutely free beings at our core, then no one could be held responsible for what they do, as separate, willful individuals. For sure, we are quite impressionable beings from the earliest age on; for the brain and its neural matter is quite malleable and vulnerable to shaping by others in society; which means that we are both subjects and objects in existence. From the beginning to the very end of our time on Earth, we are either living from the free, authentic and responsible core of an individual will, or we are not, be degree of difference; and the difference is of crucial importance to who we are and become.

One can argue that we are both free and not free, at the same time; yet the existential fact of ambiguous and paradoxical freedom remains only so long as we delay or refuse to act. In other words, the potentiality of the free will, which is the gift of Consciousness, exists in the Presence of who we are, and acting from this awareness is real, true and good, no matter what consequences may follow.

As the Existentialists of the 20th century have emphasized, especially Jean-Paul Sartre, Albert Camus, et al, there is no excuse for not choosing what is right or good especially when everything is on the line, as in the threats to human freedom, justice, and existence. When we live a life that is authentic, we are living a life that we freely and responsibly choose—free from alienation, ill-will or cowardice. And when we live a life that is inauthentic, we are merely 'seeking happiness' and covering up the inner sense of Being-an-authentic person or subjectivity that is fully present in this moment of Consciousness.

The problem with human society, generally, is that it creates the delusion that happiness or well-being can only be known or experienced on a materialistic, financial and social basis. Add to this, the competitive, militaristic, and consumerist ethic of the present globalized world, and all trace of inner Being or anything transcendental is either ridiculed or ignored by the technocratic and scientific mind-speak of the Establishment.

In the collective or public world, intelligent, sensitive and descent-minded young people can grow to adulthood, doing and accomplishing all that society, their parents and peers expect of them, and wonder why they are not happy like the American Dream promises. There really is an alternative to the sickening way that too many people live and die, get married, have children and perform at their workplaces the way that they are expected. And you do not have to go through twenty years of formal schooling to learn it since that is where most people in the privileged classes of the world learn to become alienated from their authentic, spontaneous and joyful self.

We often substitute our egoic mind and role-playing selves for authentic, free and spontaneous sense of reality that is the true source of happiness. Awareness is the basis for all important change in ourselves. Unless we are not aware of who we are or what we are doing, we cannot find that precious space where the free will engages our higher and more creative Consciousness, and our actions are doomed to nearly constant dissatisfaction, negativity, and misery. When we are truly *conscious*, we can bring an infinite sense of being into our life-world, its actions, thoughts and feelings, and transmute them into a source of true happiness or well-being. When we are happy, we are also balanced, healthy, and peaceful.

The most important thoughts are those that bring joy, peace, and love into the world. To avoid living a life that is a "tale told by an idiot, full of sound and fury, signifying nothing," you need to learn to become fully Conscious of who you are, in the eternal Now of Being. Circumstances or our life-situation is constantly changing as our body, mind and soul move ever closer to the final stages of our life-form—aging, dying, death, and eternal Being.

If we forget about inner, deep Being and only focus on the external, superficial and temporal aspects of Life, we cease living in the Now. When we use the mind and its thought processes to align ourselves with eternal Being, we can discover our inner life purpose. Nothing may guarantee our happiness more than to realize that authentic wellness is an inner experiencing of the *soul*, the essence of Being, and not just the physical or gross body.

The Inner Body is where the *soul* essentially lives although it is sustained by the biological body or the structures and functions of a total, living organism. Make no mistake about it: without the health of the body, we as life-forms will surely die; but there is only one part of the story. The other part is the Life of the soul which is eternal, pure and perfect owing to its divine Source. And the awakened yogis, saints and sages of the ages have skillfully controlled the energy of the inner Will to realize the highest potentialities of the ordinary human self.

Learning how to play a role without becoming or identifying with that role is one of life's most difficult and essential lessons—as Tolle has said. When we learn how to do this, we are at the same time living a life that is authentic, natural, and fully conscious—no matter what we may think about and do. (11)

Story: The Lost Ring

In the story called "The Lost Ring," Tolle relates how a woman was dying from cancer. Tolle saw her in the role of a spiritual teacher and she became very upset one day after losing her grandmother's ring and she suspected her housekeeper of taking it. The experience became an important moment in the evolution of the woman's consciousness since it enabled Tolle to confront her habits of attachment and identification with things of the world that distorted her sense of Being.

After a series of questions from Tolle, the woman suddenly awoke from her unconscious mental-habits. The woman said: "Suddenly I could feel my 'Am-ness'. I have never felt that before. If I can feel 'I am' so strongly, then 'I am' hasn't been diminished at all. I can feel it now, something peaceful but very alive."

Tolle then responded to his client: "This is the joy of Being....You can only feel it when you get out of your head. Being must be felt. It can't be thought. The ego doesn't know about it because thought is what it consists of. The ring was really in your head as a thought that you confused with the sense of 'I Am'. You thought that the 'I Am' or a part of it was in the ring."

"Whatever the ego seeks and gets attached to are substitutes for the Being that it cannot feel. You can value and care for things, but whenever you get attached to them, you will know it's the ego. And you are never really attached to a thing but to a thought that has 'I', 'me', or 'mine' in it. Whenever you accept a loss, you go beyond ego, and who you are, the 'I am' which is consciousness itself, emerges."

Tolle adds that after the woman died, the ring was found in the medicine cabinet of her apartment. Was the ring there all the time or did a thief return it? One thing is certain: Life will provide experiences that are helpful for the evolution of our consciousness if and only if we are present to Being. (12)

In our personal journey through Life, we will know that an experience is *right* if it is occurring in the present moment or the natural unfolding of everything. In the story of the Lost Ring, Tolle helped the dying woman awaken to her full sense of Being, for one precious moment, and her habit of attachment to the things of the world like the ring.

Chapter 17

THE SOUL OR ESSENCE OF BEING,

CONSCIOUSNESS AND BLISS

What is the soul in relation to Eternal Being? How is the soul related to the body, mind and higher Consciousness? How can we awaken to the subtle and pure energy of the soul and know it as the essence of Being? And why is an experience of the soul important to self-knowledge and experiences of *Being, Consciousness and Bliss?*

"The power of the soul, which is in the semen through the Spirit enclosed therein, fashions the body." St Thomas Aquinas

"It is only when you hunt for it that you lose it; you cannot take hold of it, but equally you cannot get rid of it." Yung-chia Ta-shih

"The limits of the soul you could not discover though traversing every path." Heraclitus

"The soul which is attempting to rise to the height of knowledge must make self-knowledge its first and chief concern. The high peace of knowledge is perfect self-knowledge." Richard of Saint-Victor

"The Way (of the Sufis) can only be reached by immediate experience and ecstasy and inner transformation." Al-Ghazali

Al-Ghazali (1058-1111) held a prestigious position in philosophy at Baghdad University for several years until he resigned and began a solitary journey as a Sufi mystic. He wandered from city to city being convinced that the mystics were men who had 'real experiences and not just men of words. ' From his autobiography, he wrote: "It had already become clear to me that I had no hope of the bliss of the world to come save through a God-fearing life and the withdrawal of myself from vain desire. It was clear to me too that the key to all this was to sever the attachment of the heart to worldly things by leaving the mansion of deception and returning to that of eternity, and to advance towards God most high with all earnestness. It was also clear that this was only to be achieved by turning away from wealth and position and fleeing from all time-consuming entanglements." This statement puts into personal context the Al-Ghazali's laudable desire to experience the 'ecstasy and inner transformation' that is commonly associated with the mystical sense of eternal Being. (1)

Metaphysics and the Real World

What is the soul? Is the soul the essence of our Being-in-the-world as persons? Is the soul the essence of the energy of Creation? Is the soul integrative of past time, present time, and future time in its essential Now? What is the truth about the soul and how can we experience, know and express the truth of its reality? And is the soul the ultimate answer to the *why* question?

The soul is the essence of the Life-force or Being itself. It contains the karmic code for our DNA and RNA identity as persons. Its sacred energy is a karmic transaction of male and female chromosomes at conception. The soul is the essential karmic basis of the body-mind and its potentialities. It is the necessary and sufficient condition for the individual's survival of death, just as it accounts for our birth in a human life-form.

The soul is the means by which we survive death whether fully liberated or not. The soul is worldly to the extent that it is attracted to the material, human and spiritual forms of the world. It sought and found embodiment at conception owing to its *karma* or causal condition from previous incarnations. Its embodied energy is driven to seek union with others souls, on this plane of existence, for its earthly fulfillment and happiness.

The soul cannot exist separately from the body and mind once embodied. It carries the potentialities of reason, imagination, and higher Consciousness. In fact, it embodies all the potentialities of sentient existence through its atomic structure. The soul needs the physical body for its earthly fulfillment or worldly being; however, its needs are ontological not just biological like the body. In these respects, the soul is a dialectical phenomenon due to its acquired worldliness.

The soul exists continuously in the Now through the body-mind or total self. However, a person can become alienated from the soul like one can be alienated or cut off from the Now or the field of interaction between time and eternity. The soul creates our ordinary sense of continuity through the interactions of the mind and body, which orient, balance and ground us in everyday experience.

The soul exists invisibly beyond ordinary perception and reason through the energy fields that structure the neuro-physiology and anatomy of the body. In Hindu mythology, the soul exists as *Purusha* or the God of pure Spirit in a dialectical relation with *Prakriti* or the Goddess of Nature. The soul is the formless essence that is karmicly embodied in each sentient being, from the infinite and eternal Energy of the cosmos—whether that sentient being is human or not.

The soul is the essential key to the mystery of Being existing in the language of sound and silence, movement and stillness, in the visible and the invisible realms of existence. The soul gives us the miracle of language, in a myriad of human and animal forms, due to its infinite creativity, power of the will-to-meaning and communication. The soul is absolutely free and possesses all the potentialities for ordinary thought, action, and feeling as well as the most extraordinary potentialities for insight, intuition, and psychic powers of humans. The soul enables us to have prior knowledge and the recognition of Truth owing to its karmic journey through other realms and life-forms of the cosmos.

None of the most ordinary emotions, thoughts, or memories of the everyday self exists entirely separately from the power and influence of the soul. Every act of perception, memory, imagination and intellect gives existential and pragmatic knowledge and understanding of the real world; but the soul exists continuously and identically as higher Consciousness or the intuitive knowledge of Being. The power and loving Presence of the soul is strongest through the innate conscience or *Good Will* of each person which exists absolutely even when it is hidden and corrupted by the pain-body in Unconsciousness.

'Dust to dust' is certainly true of the physical body or the formlessness of *Prakriti*. But from 'eternity to eternity' must be spoken about the soul in its mundane or existential journey and the potentialities of the body, mind and ego. When we leave this body and existence by means of the spiritual energy of the soul, we will take with us whatever understanding, wisdom, and enlightenment that we have acquired while living in this world. Everything in this world depends upon the well-being, integrity, and power of the *soul* to free us from ignorance and corruption, through its will and intellectual omniscience of higher Consciousness.

Doubting, Believing and Acting

The soul does not and cannot exist separately from Being or the absolute and eternal mystery of unity and wholeness. Yet no one can really comprehend how the soul—whose *dharmic* essence is eternal— can exist in a universe that is constantly changing and uncertain. More generally, why is there Being at all and not just a Void? Or why does anything exist as it does?

Doubt is possible about the soul's existence and it occurs on the basis of perception and physical being. Although doubt may be the father of modern European philosophy—on the basis of Rene Descartes *Meditations*—its mother is faith, intuition, and feeling that are stronger than mere thinking. If there is no soul or means whereby a person survives death, either as a *soul* (Jains, Jews, Christians, Moslems), *consciousness* (Buddhists) or a higher *Self* (Hindus), then the faith in immortality is an illusion, a fiction, and false basis for a spiritual existence.

Having it both ways is really the only way that faith can be reconciled to reason and doubt. The stand-off between religion and science is a ridiculous battle between conflicting egos and thought processes that has fueled centuries of philosophical debate and cultural conflict. Their common ground is the divine Oneness or Unity that transforms the infinite energy of the universe into the dialectic of reason and faith, perception and conception, subjectivity and objectivity.

Albeit, the skeptical, naturalistic, and perceptual view of the world is a necessary dimension of the soul's worldly Being. However, no soul can be entirely satisfied with the experience and knowledge of the manifested realm of the world. The origin of the soul is the *unmanifested* realm of reality from which persons are born, and into which they return after their journey on planet Earth and others like it.

The existence of the *soul* (*jiva* in Jainism; *purusha* in Samkhya yoga) is the only adequate answer to the 'why' question of Life. We are here to purify the soul of its moral corruption and liberate it from cyclic existence. This can be accomplished in this lifetime through meditative absorption in the Now and living with right understanding, right action and right concentration upon Truth and Goodness. Acting courageously and having complete faith in the inner purpose and universal meaning of Life is a constant challenge for everyone.

Finally, as the American Pragmatists have taught, most notably John Dewey and William James, if you really believe in a cause, another person or yourself, you will be willing and ready to act on your belief. Even if there is a lingering doubt in your mind about the worth of a belief or idea, acting on your belief is the best way to test its strength and discovering what its true worth or value may be. Pragmatic certainty is knowledge that is tested by personal experience and the satisfaction that a certain course of action may bring to you and / or others.

There is no one golden road or Path to fulfillment or liberation in Life. Each person must find his or her own unique way to the Truth. If you merely follow another person, no matter how brilliant or admirable that person may be, you have not made your own way. The world is infinite in its possibilities even though we are finite beings and it is only up to each of us to act on that way which is right for you.

Awakening to Corruption and Violence

From the standpoint of the soul, the human world is violent, irrational, and insane. Each soul struggles to remain vital and healthy against the contingent forces of the body, mind, and world. It is very difficult to be completely nonviolent, reasonable, and harmonious in the real, morally corrupted world. However, it is far easier to be in the real world as an awakened soul with a higher or liberated Consciousness than it is to be unconscious, irrationally attached, and obsessively driven.

There are innumerable forces and conditions of negativity, violence, and irrationality that presently threaten the wholeness, freedom, and well-being of the person. Throughout the history of humanity, there have been murders, wars, and genocides taking place all over the world, at one time or another; it is also evident that people lie, steal, and kill without thinking of the consequences to their souls. But it is often useless to preach morality or quote from Scripture when the layers of negative conditioning and violence cover the original Goodness of the soul.

Thus, the question naturally arises, how can we reach the extremists of humanity or those who are willing to kill others, for whatever reason or belief? Is the conscience or empathy of some humans so weak and impotent that it cannot activate the soul? Or are some souls so corrupted, burdened and crippled by previous experience—from this and previous life-times of pain and negativity—that they are unable to act otherwise?

We cannot blame the immorality of human beings solely upon worldly attractions and corruptions since it is corrupted souls that bring the residual wrongs or violence from former incarnations and times, to this world. Although the soul contains the innate power of conscience or sense of right and wrong, goodness and evil, etc., the soul is not absolutely pure due to its karmic contamination from its former incarnations and present attraction to this world. The soul is in this life-form in order to purify itself of all worldly or existential corruption and then to ascend to an absolutely pure and perfect state of being, which is its original or primal Goodness.

The Ultimate Purpose of Existence

The body, mind, ego, and world exist only in order to free the soul from *Samsara* or karmic birth, life, death, and re-birth. It is the living paradox of creation that all sentient beings are cycled through an embodied existence in order to learn who they are, at the depth of the soul, and to help others learn the Truth about their own karmic souls. We each have a moral obligation, assigned by creative Being, to become the best persons that we know how to be and to help others become their best moral selves. In doing so, we can free ourselves from the misery, suffering, and unhappiness that affects so many people of the Earth.

From the viewpoint of the individual soul, just one unhappy, sick, or immoral person is one too many. But each person has the innate or natural potentiality to become an absolutely good, caring, and loving person, free from doubt and negativity, free from a sickness of the soul, free from the insanity of mind, free from any illness of the body, and free from worldly corruption and immorality. Of all of these 'freedoms from', none is so precious as a freedom from the sickness of the soul, since this freedom can inspire, guide, and lead the mind and body to its most rational, moral, and healthy ends.

Without the Life-force flowing through *prakriti* or divine Nature, there would be no life-forms in the world; in fact, it would nothing but the energy of atoms which will swerve and weave, with electrons jumping rings and transforming each other, in an undifferentiated, absolute Void. Yet this is an entirely meaningless picture of the world since it is a world without sentient life-forms of any kind and thus lacking in the potentialities of consciousness and an embodied soul.

Thus if there is an ultimate purpose and meaning for the 'whole shebang' as the science writer Timothy Ferris calls the universe, it is for the creation of consciousness in an embodied form and all that naturally goes with it. And we are here to awaken to the total truth and knowledge of our individual and collective condition and to do all that we can to heal, enable and elevate each other to our highest potentiality.

Selfish Ego, Altruism and Justice

A meaningful and fulfilling life, one informed by inner purpose and vitality, cannot occur if the soul is suffering from a karmic sickness brought on by the body, mind, and ego-attachments. The ego is the person's separate sense of self, the feeling that 'I am great', 'I am superior', 'I should be treated differently from all others', etc,—when in fact, we are all the same and unique in potentiality due to the existence of the individual soul, consciousness and the universal Self.

The ego is a creation of the worldly personality, an alienated and divisive force of arrogance, greed, and self-centeredness that demands to be seen, heard, and recognized. The ego takes, seizes and does not readily give or share unless it sees an increase in its selfish power. It has no real comprehension of morality or ethics except the distortions of greed, selfishness and control which it mistakes for what is right.

As Tolle says, quoting Shakespeare, a person needs to see that the world of the ego is "a tale told by an idiot, full of sound and fury, signifying nothing." The human relationships that come from the role-playing of egos are sickening, idiotic, and unbalanced, and serve only to create similar role-playing and egoic living patterns in the world. The extreme self-centeredness of an ego-dominated personality easily extents to the relationships of an immediate family, tribe, Corporation, and Nation-state, and then to the present global Corporatocracy with its unending civil wars, international antagonisms, and the continuing threats of a nuclear holocaust.

Egoic selfishness, greed, and ethnocentricity have taken on new and extremely complicated configurations during the first decade of the 21st century and beyond. The lack of regulation and legal oversight upon officials who with egoic cunning manipulated ignorant, needy and vulnerable populations of consumers; meanwhile, consumer who were driven by unquenchable desires for 'more', bigger, and newer, created a monster in the economy that greatly increased the profits of entrepreneurs, officials and investors alike while seizing and destroying the illusory things unwary consumers acquired in the 'bull' and bubble economy.

Capitalism or a system of greed, economic injustice and environmental plunder, is a natural consequence of an ego-based social system. We will not have a change in the economic, moral and social circumstances until the immorality of a self-centered, ego-dominated personality is fully seen. The power of the present wasteful, polluting and threatening system will continue as long as individuals do not wake up to the harm that it is doing to their innate potentiality for goodness and happiness.

Finally, justice has been the central value in ethics, politics and metaphysics from ancient times. If we are really serious about equality and fairness in society, we would be stemming the tide of greed and corruption that is sweeping the world in the wake of Capitalism. Perhaps no symbol is more fitting for the fever of Capitalism than the Chinese Dragon which represents nine different animals and reptiles of pry. It represents omnipotent power, plunder and control.

The way free from the economic paralysis and growing gap between the rich and the poor is through awakening to the truth of existence and an altruistic ethics and politics. It really does not matter what name or slogan a system of government has, what matters are its actions, its policies and readiness to serve all the people and not just special interest groups—the rich—as is presently the case. Until that joyful time, we will continue to live in a plutocracy—a government by the rich and for the rich.

The Potentiality of Goodness

The soul is like a single precious atom of energy dropped from the cosmos by the mysterious Life-force that is directing this world and all others. If the human species as a collective body of wills does not make the necessary life-decisions and moral corrections that must be made to survive and flourish on this plane of existence, then it will surely destroy itself in a thermonuclear holocaust. No amount of exhorting, lecturing or moralizing by our leaders will alone awaken the people to their self-destructive ways of Being-in-the-world. 'The People' must be awakened to the infinite power of their souls and realize that their own life-forms embody a Goodness of Being that is infinitely creative, nonviolent and loving in potentiality.

So often in mass culture and the sickness of the entertainment industry, we hear only about how bad things are and how violent the world has become. Goodness is hardly ever spoken about or described as the underlying structure and condition of the world; instead, the sensational manifestations of the world are given nearly exclusive airing and discussion, i.e. murder, violence, injustice, greed and so forth. The frequent pairing of opposites often hides a deeper truth, namely the soul's presence in experience as a messenger from other worlds, other lives, and other possibilities. We must begin to think about the Presence of divinity within us, as the soul and inner body that is the basis for a new Earth, a new World.

Awakening to essential Goodness is the third stage in the fulfillment of the soul's freedom-in-existence. The goodness of the soul is grounded in its own infinite potentiality for perfect Being, Consciousness, and Bliss or *Sat-Chit-Ananda* in the Hindu faith. However, it is the soul's solitary journey through this world and in this body that is most important in realizing the higher Consciousness of spiritual Liberation. The absolute freedom or *Moksa* that is so highly valued in Indian religious philosophies has its historic parallel in the Platonic Goodness of ancient Greek philosophy. And both philosophies are echoed in the Chinese

Taoist belief of the mysterious and mystical Tao that is formless, eternal, and beyond intellectual comprehension.

God, Love and Happiness

'God' is the probably the greatest hot button word or trigger of emotion among both believers and doubters. The negativity surrounding the word among doubters and skeptics of religious truth really exceeds all rationality. On one side of the iron curtain are believers and religionists who use the word in declarative, analytic, and exclamatory ways, by turns, without reservation or qualification; and other side is equally absolute, dogmatic and certain in its beliefs.

The two opposing groups of believers and non-believers are as polarized as they have ever been so far as meaningful and empathic communication is concerned, with little hope that the divide will be easily or soon bridged between them. Meanwhile, between the two camps in the DMZ zone, a calm truce has been declared and it is rigidly enforced by the lack of reason, humility and meaningful dialogue. The fuller truth about 'God' and all such absolutes is that no one can know for sure—since human reason is limited, the future is unknowable, and there can be no complete, final or total answers in a universe that is constantly changing.

The high voltage or electricity that the word 'God' generates between opposing groups doubtlessly has much to do with its historical contexts of usage and the extent to which it has been used as a sufficient justification for the most horrendous of murderous acts and carnage against humanity. What is usually missed in the justifiable condemnation of many religious institutions of past and present history is the fact that 'God'—the symbol for what is Ultimate, Absolute, Perfect and the Source of all—represents the *absolute limit of human reason and understanding.* In this sense, Ignorance or Agnosticism—not Theism or Atheism— would be a far more fitting symbol for what the word 'God' philosophically signifies.

Tolle himself is quite clear about just who or what 'God' is and is not. He wrote: "It has been said 'God is love' but this is not

absolutely correct. God is the One Life in and beyond the countless forms of life. Love implies duality: love and beloved, subject
and object. So love is the recognition of the oneness in the world
of duality. This is the birth of God into the world of form. Love
makes the world less worldly, less dense, more transparent to the
divine dimension, the light of consciousness itself." (2)

In defining 'God' as the 'One Life', Tolle asserts that Life is
universal and eternal whereas its myriad life-forms are not. The
second point that Tolle is making is not as obvious as the universal
One God that is beyond the duality of the love. In claiming that
God is 'born' into the dualistic world of forms, where humans
dwell in love, at least potentially, we experience the divinity of
'God' through our human love. At the same time, human love
reduces the density, weight, and darkness of the world by disclosing the hidden, inner realm where the light of 'God' can be seen.

In a related passage, Tolle writes about happiness—arguably
the highest end of human life-forms—as an experience that
comes from the realization of universal Life or the divine reality. Happiness is also something which cannot be sought after or
fought for. Tolle expresses his viewpoint this way:

"Don't seek happiness. If you seek it, you won't find it, because
seeking is the anti-thesis of happiness. Happiness is ever-elusive,
but freedom from unhappiness is attainable now, by facing what-
is rather than making up stories about it. Unhappiness covers up
your natural state of well-being and inner peace, the source of
true happiness." (3)

Seeking, fighting, striving, struggling, etc. are essentially
antagonistic acts against nature and Being. In 'seeking', we admit
to a 'lack' and then want to fill or complete it. But the experience of happiness comes in realizing that the 'natural state of
well-being and inner peace' is now and not in the future or past.
It is the experience of intrinsic Goodness that is the 'source of
true happiness'. And if you wish to term this reality *God*, it is your
existential right to do so.

In the Christian tradition, few theologians loom greater than
St Thomas Aquinas. He has written: "If God's essence is to be

seen at all, it must be that the intellect sees it through the divine essence itself; in that vision the divine essence is both the object and the medium of vision." And it is certain that the soul within a person is nothing other than the essence of God or what Tolle refers to as Being. If you have perfect faith in this divine union than your salvation from corruption and liberation from suffering is assured. (4)

Soul as the Way to Inner Peace

Finally, there is the soul or the basis for the survival of death. If one grants the existence of something transcendental or spiritual within the self, then all is not lost at death. On the other hand, as we have argued and seen throughout this study, doubt can always be raised. The true believer though has no doubts left and all metaphysical questions have been answered.

The Hindus of India proclaim that the goal of this life is 'perfect Being, Consciousness and Bliss' or *Sat-Chit-Ananda.* The natural question always arises, 'How can I realize that'? The answer is, just as simply, 'You already, always have *perfect Being, Consciousness and Bliss* and yet you do not know it! You embody *Sat-Chit-Ananda* in your individual essence or soul.

The bridge or way to awaken the soul is through the chanting or repetition of *OM (A-U-M)* the hidden sound or vibration of every atom in the material universe. When you chant *OM* you awaken the atoms that constitute or structure your individual soul. In chanting *OM* we simulate the most basic sound or vibration of the material universe. And this is the way to awaken the soul or the universal Life-force of the body. (5)

Once you experience the presence of the soul, in and as true Awareness, then this cognition is the basis for genuine faith. The proof that you seek lies in the heart of compassion where you can feel oneness or connection with all other sentient beings. Faith awakens the heart, sustains us in the here-and-now, and restores reason to living. It is the Way to peace, love, and genuine happiness, for humanity and the Earth.

PART V

AWAKENING TO DESIRE, EMOTIONS

AND RELATIONSHIPS

Desire is the will-to-live, to endure, to dominate. Needs and wants are its allies, its offspring and manifestations. Desire undermines the attitude of surrender, submission and giving in to what is greater. We may desire to be happy but fail to know how. We may desire to be rich, famous or important in society but fail to know how. And what desire most fatally misses and is ignorant of, is how to just be and be at peace with what-is.

Nature is the unseen work of divinity, the infinite knowledge and wisdom that shapes all forms. The emotions of the body are the DNA of the mind; while thoughts and ideas are merely faint copies of the original. Society is simply the extension in human terms of what primordially exists in nature, twisted and corrupted and in pain. If humans are ever to improve their world, it will have to be through the love of Nature and the sacredness of all sentient beings.

The experiences that we most desire are beyond desires, wants, and needs. It is the recognition of something greater than the self, this world, and forms. The most primal experiences of the self are those of Being or what is formless, unmanifested and sacred. Beyond the wonder of the senses, emotions and ideas is the soul, the pure essence of Being— already perfect and eternal. The peace of the soul is the supreme peace of the world.

We desire to experience relationships since everything is already related or unified. We desire confirmation, proof of what-is, evidence that we are here-and-now. We love since the energy of love relates us to what-is, universally. If we truly experience love with one being, the feeling spreads to the world of others. We see, understand and intuit that the self is necessarily related to all other beings, through karma, evolution and creative Being, the One Source. When we begin to *really see*, through the soul, mind and heart, we can really begin to see everything.

Chapter 18

DESIRE, ENTHUSIASM AND PEACE

What is desire? What is the difference between need and want, having and being? What is most desirable and why? What are the causes of desire and the growth to greed? How is desire related to working in the real world of material, financial and human relationships? Can we ever not desire anything? And why is the control of desire important for the moral, intellectual and spiritual sense of peace and happiness?

"We may live for thousands of years and may obtain whatever we desire of the world but we shall never be happy so long as our hunger for earthly things does not perish." Swami Ramdas

"The best knowledge is that which enables one to put an end to birth and death and to attain freedom from the world." Udana

"Just as there can be no ice without water, so Nirvana is immediately present." Hakuin

"The one and only thing required is to free oneself from the bondage of mind and body alike; putting the Buddha's own seal upon yourself. If you do this as you sit in ecstatic meditation, the whole universe itself scattered through the infinities of space and turns into enlightenment. This is what I mean by the Buddha's seal." Dogen

"The eternal peace is your real existence—it is not a state of truth to be attained but to be realized; because you are always That Peace." Swami Ramdas

Swami Ramdas makes the distinction between attaining something *and* realizing it. *Attainment* marks the end of a goal after a period of striving while *realization* is seeing who you already are,

331

inwardly, and thus realizing the Peace of true self-knowledge. Inward self-realization is the real beginning of the mystical Way to *wisdom*. Swami Ramdas' words express a typical attitude among mystics, namely that it is the realization of the inner existence of Being, as the soul, which awakens you to the truth of Presence; and this experience is sufficient in realizing the Peace of eternal Being.

Three Realms of Being

Buddhist philosophy describes three realms of human experience i.e., the realm of forms, the realm of desires, and the realm of formlessness. Only the formless realm is ultimate or supreme since it pervades all forms and desires in ordinary existence. The formed realm includes all physical and mental objects, 'things' that exist inwardly and outwardly through the body, mind and consciousness. The realm of desire is the region of existence that most directly accounts for human action in ordinary life, i.e. means and ends, desired and desirable values, actual and possible life-worlds.

Three Realms of Yoga

In Kundalini Yoga, the desire realm constitutes the: 1, biological, 2, psychological, 3, social, 4, ethical, 5, aesthetic, 6, intellectual, and 7, metaphysical backbone of human thought and behavior. In terms of the chakra system previously discussed, the desire realm constitutes the first three levels of Being, i.e. the biological, psychological, and social. The realm of forms constitutes higher three levels, i.e. the ethical, aesthetic, and intellectual levels, and the formless realm is the basis for the seventh level, i.e. the spiritual or metaphysical level of the higher Self. The formless level is actually no-level since it pervades the form and desire realms, just as spirit or the Life-force pervades all levels of reality in yoga philosophy. (1)

I have described the seven levels of being as corresponding to the seven classical centers (chakras) of divine energy constituting the human self and Consciousness (see chapter thirteen). They can be seen as representing the totality of who we are, our essence (soul) and the real existence (temporal, spatial and material dimensions) of Being. Although Tolle does not make explicit reference to the chakra system of Kundalini Yoga, he does refer to yoga philosophy or the most ancient tradition of Indian philosophy on which the chakras are based. In fact, the chakra theory of Kundalini Yoga enhances Tolle's theory of values and knowledge by giving a systematic model for awakening to the Perennial Wisdom.

Desire: Intrinsic, Extrinsic, and Mixed

The body is the most obvious context or field of energy for appreciating the Presence or Nowness of desires—desires of all kinds. The range or spectrum of human desires is as great as the scope of actual and possible experience. Initially, we must define 'desire'—although like many qualitative phenomena that help us understand self-Being, desire is very elusive, ambiguous and difficult to fully grasp.

The *Cambridge Dictionary of Philosophy* divides desire into 'intrinsic' and 'extrinsic' categories of difference. Intrinsic desires are those desires that we have for their own sake, as in the Now of Being. For example, we may want no gain, profit or end that the fulfillment of a particular desire may hold, other than to enjoy it here-and-now. In other words, intrinsic desires have no object or state external to them. Finally, the experiences of love, beauty, and goodness are said to be intrinsic desires and values although the experience of these values may imply an external referent or object.

Extrinsic desires may lead us to some other contingent state of Being, i.e. one desired for future fulfillment but which is not now present. Hence, extrinsic desires may lead us to a condition or something external to us, in time and space. For example, the desire to produce a product or construct an object of some kind, such as a book or a house, are said to be extrinsic desires. (2)

Experientially, if the process or means for working towards an extrinsic object or end is not intrinsically valuable or desirable, it is doubtful that the realized goal will ever be entirely fulfilling or satisfactory. The disjunction or dualism between process and product, means and ends, desire and satisfaction, cannot always be foreseen in everyday experience; but it really does exist owing to the duality of superficial awareness and conditioning. Intuition can clarify and cut through confusion and experience faster and more deeply than reason alone.

Many if not most of our desires are said to be 'mixed' desires, that is we desire something or another that is 'in the future' so far as their satisfaction or fulfillment is concerned; we may also realize that certain means are necessary to that end. For example, in a very Capitalistic and materialistic society such as our own, many desire to make a lot of money and may desire money for its own sake, independently of what good it may enable them to do in reducing the suffering of all sentient life-forms.

Most people appear to believe that you cannot be happy unless they have enough money to live comfortably and without worry. But in a Capitalistic society the desire for money is so great that it often becomes both the means and the ends of living; and the worry of not having enough becomes endless. Happiness or one's sense of well-being, in an essential sense, is often not even considered or thought about, in the quest for material wealth and financial security. However, the meaninglessness of wealth beyond the need to fulfill the basic needs of existence is all too evident to those who are wise in the ways of living. Consequently, human existence in a Capitalistic society is often experienced in a quite irrational and psychologically dysfunctional way.

More is *never* Enough

'More' is never enough no matter what kind of desire is involved. We cannot build a life of meaning, happiness, or fulfillment upon quantitative measures; the essence or qualitative experience in living is immeasurable, non-quantitative, and ineffable.

If we do not learn to live in the Now and accept whatever condition, external or internal, that we are faced with, as real and unavoidable, we may never really have a fulfilling experience in Life. Measuring out sugar or milk with tea spoons may be fine for our tea or coffee, but it will not do for the qualitative or intrinsic experience of living, in the immeasurable Goodness of Now.

The pessimistic English poet, T.S. Eliot once wrote that he 'measured out his life with coffee spoons'. He implied in the rest of the poem "The Wasteland" that modern civilization is full of misery and unhappiness. In Tolle's language, most suffer to some degree due to a 'pain-body' that dogs their days on Earth. It is no wonder if one merely measures the quality or worthwhileness of their lives by their bank accounts or stock market profits. By *that measure*, the vast majority of people may be living lives that are much less than desirable or worthwhile, owing to their less than 'rich' or even 'wealthy' status in the world; and by the values of Capitalism, billionaires should be the happiest people in the world!

The world is mad from the disease of making or desiring money. The disorder has now spread from the developed postmodern world to every developing country in the global marketplace. We live in a world, as Noam Chomsky of the New Left wrote, where Profit is more important than People. You can see this sickness wherever you look—in the way that the U.S. Health Insurance Industry treats the uninsured and the underinsured; the low pay that U.S. and Western Corporations give to their workers everywhere; and the readiness of Corporations to lay off workers in the U.S. to maintain their *bottom line* and to cancel worker pensions whenever the profit margins to stock holders are threatened. (3)

The desire for 'more' is the result of a moral culture that values greed over frugality and simplicity in living and considers greed *good* as seen in the popular movie *Wall Street*. There is nothing inherently evil in desire, as metaphysical cynics may think, but there is a sickness abroad in all fields of business and human experience, most often based upon a ruthless competition as in professional athletics where 'winning is everything' or in politics where it is the 'winner takes all' no matter how much it brutalizes players and degrades humanity.

The problem with economic competition in a Capitalistic society is its inherent lack of justice or fairness. No one is really worth the kind of 'salaries' that CEO's enjoy in the typical American Corporation today. Inheritance, cunning, luck or being at the 'right place at the right time' and rarely genius usually account for the fabulous fortunes of the few. And there are a few Corporations where real profit-sharing among the workers may take place and worker rights and the environment are protected by its policies and the public from dangerous and toxic products.

Whatever the full truth is about correlations between great wealth, big business and human happiness, there is far too much wealth at the very top of the economic pyramid (1% of 1% control half of the world's wealth) and *a conspicuous lack* of justice in a living wage and equal pay for equal work, health, well-being and happiness, for everyone. The small consolation of the poor is that aging, disease and death are quite indifferent to the possession of great riches or material and financial wealth. And according to the sayings of Jesus, the heavenly Father favors the poor over the rich: for 'the rich man has as much chance of entering the gates of Heaven as a camel can go through the eye of a needle'.

In the spirit of Tolle and other Perennialists, nothing can exceed the sheer pleasure and enjoyment of being with your friends and loved ones and sharing time and space together. The most precious things in Life are still free, like breathing, talking, walking and laughing; or enjoying a warm summer day at the shore of an ocean. And the existential truth about 'more' is that 'less' is better and the peace of mind that it brings.

Living, Working and Money

On an existential level of Life, most people desire to live in this body and this world, for as long as possible. We may not have consciously desired or chosen to live in this life-form, but we nevertheless do exist in it. The best way to ameliorate your life-situation is by becoming aware of your total situation, accept it and embrace it even if you may not entirely like it. Liking and disliking, however, are judgments that only divide existence into dualistic and antagonistic parts.

Of course, you may decide to drop out from a negative situation, leave an undesirable relationship, take a trip to somewhere desirable, retire from an unfulfilling career, and do whatever you may deem positive, healthy, and freeing. The most important thing is that you can and must decide for yourself and not let others or external conditions merely drive you to unconscious action and living. Perhaps nothing is worse in one's personal existence than to realize that you may have wasted portions of your life in futile, frustrating and painful situations.

Whether you believe in the reality of a soul or essence of your nature is secondary or tertiary in importance to living a meaningful and good life. The primary thing in Life is to act consciously and deliberately on the basis of how you really feel, no matter how long you have been stuck in an unfulfilling role or routine. Most people in the developed countries of the world are driven by the financial and material conditions of existence like their salaries, bank accounts, bills, things and more things. Many middle class and even working class people own so much 'stuff' that they have to rent special cubicles for storage—after their basements, attics, and garages are filled with useless 'stuff'. And it does not really matter what kind of things you are in the habit of collecting, the end result is always the same: more stuff than you will ever need or use.

The same is true for money. There are many people in the world who have more money than they know what to do with, so they gamble in the stock market or the many casinos of the world, and spend most of their waking time in frivolous activities that only serve for self-amusement or distraction from the underlying anxiety and boredom of their lives. The touted global market-place thrives on the 'surplus' labor-value or money—as

Karl Marx called it—money that the wealthy, rich, and super-rich possess and do not know what to do with. Of course, the actual labor or work that the 'haves' engage in for their incomes is nothing like the labor or alienated work that the 'have-nots' are forced to undergo. The 'have-nots' of the world are controlled by clock-time and the hourly wage, while many of the 'haves' of the world may only need to even show up in their workplaces, to draw their inflated salaries.

There are serious signs that all of this is about to undergo a big change with many people falling through the 'gap' between the haves and the have-nots which in recent years has greatly widened. For example, the salaries of CEO's are often hundreds and even thousands of times larger than the average wage-earner in the same Corporation. Such discrepancies in income cannot stand for long without revolutionary sentiments growing in the proletariat or the working classes.

Meanwhile the so-called professional classes of the world will continue to be paid off to do the 'devil's bidding' even though they know that they are only 'part of the problem', i.e. the injustice of the world economic system. Ironically, it is the members of the professional class who complain most vociferously about their low pay while hardly a word is heard from the real 'have-nots' of society, the minimum wage-earning workers who clean the toilets, collect the garbage, empty the bed pans, dig the ditches, and in general fill the jobs that no one else wants.

In the end, you have to decide why and how you want to live. If you first have a compelling or motivating reason for living, you have answered the 'why' question. And once you know why you are living and not just surviving or existing, then the how becomes much easier and secondary.

Just living to make money and more and more of it, is the way of too many people in society. Like Socrates, I believe that if you are not putting the 'well-being of your soul' before all other values in existence, you are wasting your life. It may be that we will have many other opportunities to purify our soul and live a fully meaningful life, but I am not placing bets on it.

Finding Fulfillment in Your Work

The experience of the inner will is the experience of desiring, acting and choosing freely. If you can experience yourself as a conscious person or being-in-the-world, it can make all the difference in the quality of your life. But if we are just constantly compromising our values, it is only a matter of time before we will discover our essence or soul has been darkened by the corruption, injustice and violence of the world.

It all comes down to meaning and purpose in Life, particularly what Tolle calls your 'inner purpose in Life" and not necessarily all those purposes that a particular role or career track determines for you. But the sense of congruence and harmony between inner and outer purposes of Life are the most important sign that you are where you really desire to be. No one has to reward you or tell you how good you are when you realize or actualize the alignment between the inner and outer purposes of living; you will know because you feel it before any extrinsic rewards may be given to you. In fact, when you are doing what you really want to do with your life, it does not matter what you are making for a salary since you will have realized the inner purposes and intrinsic value of personal being.

In the language of Yoga philosophy, when you are living in harmony with your intrinsic being or who you are, the chakras or energy nexuses of the inner body are open, dynamic, and circulating their energies throughout your total being. Such times of congruence may fluctuate with changing circumstances; but when your sense of attunement with the *Tao* or sacred Life-force of existence is present and most acute, you can reach the highest states of consciousness.

In *A New Earth*, Tolle makes this all quite clear. He writes: "Consciousness is already conscious. It is the unmanifested, the eternal." I prefer to call Consciousness, in this context, the soul; but the words do not really matter. It is the reality, the experience of something eternal and incorruptible that counts. Rational or philosophical argument will often never persuade someone who is not open-minded-and-hearted, to believe or have faith in the invisible or intangible values of Life. The culprit, in more cases than not, is a cynical, negative and doubting attitude that is shaped by years of similar thinking along corrupted, sick and distorting neurological pathways. For just as the so-called lower animals wear pathways in the 'forest primeval' so do our thoughts, feelings, and tendencies of mind wear pathways along the ganglions and neurons of our nervous system. (4)

What Tolle calls 'awakened doing'—a brilliant phrase—can be experienced through three 'modalities', i.e. acceptance, enjoyment, and enthusiasm. He writes that you can consider these experiences as "the underlying energy-frequency that flows into what you do and connects your action with the awakened consciousness that is emerging into this world." It is all essential to the creation of *A New Earth*—that is Now happening through your essence or soul. (5)

"Acceptance means: for now, this is what this situation, this moment, requires me to do, and so I do it willingly." Most importantly for a world at war with itself, "Performing an action in the state of acceptance means you are at peace while you do it. That peace is a subtle energy vibration which then flows into what you do." The peace is consciousness or the soul, your essence, which connects with Being or what is Ultimate. Your state of consciousness, as it connects in mood and emotion to everything else, is the key to real peace in the Now. (6)

Beyond Wanting to the Joy of Being

If the acceptance of a situation brings you a high of peacefulness or serenity, enjoyment really kicks it into gear. "In *A New Earth*," Tolle tells us, "Enjoyment will replace wanting as the motivating power behind people's actions." Or "enjoyment is the dynamic aspect of Being." For the philosopher in everyone, "there is more meaning in joy than you will ever need." Joy simply starts you on living whether you are ready or not. (7)

Because we are connecting with our essence in the emotion of joy, the flow of feeling comes from deep within us, rather from what we do in the physical or social. Again it is the intrinsic desire for Life that always matters the most. "You will enjoy any activity in which you are fully present, any activity that is not just a means to an end." This 'deep sense of aliveness' that is joy itself brings you to the doorway and inner house of Being where the great power of creation can be experienced. (9)

If you want to test yourself in joyful experiencing, choose an activity that is boring or stressful to you, and "Be absolutely present in what you do and sense the alert, alive stillness within you in the background of your activity." And it does not matter what the activity is, since it is the inner dimension of Consciousness that flows into your behavior and enables you to find the 'Joy of Being'.

The 'joy of Being' is the light of Consciousness, the eternal, infinite dimension of everything shining through the essence of you, Now, in whatever activity or situation that involves you. This is also like the 'breath of Christ' Tolle says, quoting the Sufi master, Hafiz, that everyone is heir to. And it is music as extraordinary as anything ever composed, since it is the Life-soul showing itself through your present, real-time actions. (10)

Enthusiasm and Empowerment in Life

Enthusiasm is connecting your life's inner purpose with your everyday or external actions. Enthusiasm is when the Now is extended to the future without any distortion in the experience of Now. It occurs due to a vision, goal, or life-plan that comes from your discovered essence. Enthusiasm amplifies the 'energy-field of frequency vibration' in consciousness, building on the emotions of acceptance, peacefulness, and enjoyment. It gives direction and outer purpose to these emotions, connecting them to the greater world which is seen as part of the total self. (11)

The word 'enthusiasm' comes from the Greek language—'*en*' and '*theos*, meaning 'enthused with the energy of 'God'.

We become quite literally 'possessed by a god' such as found in many mythologies and religions of the world. Tolle quotes Ralph Waldo Emerson that "Nothing great has ever been achieved without enthusiasm." Whatever the true Source may be, in the experience of enthusiasm you are transformed by a higher energy, a 'wave of creative energy' that carries you to new heights in your consciousness. It is what the yogis have experienced and describe as the higher chakra centers of consciousness. (12)

The sense of empowerment—so important to Feminists and other oppressed *and* minority groups—is palpable in the experience of enthusiasm. Tolle cites Jesus when he said "I can of my own self do nothing." Unlike ordinary ego-driven, competitive, and aggressive action, enthusiasm is based upon the 'inclusion not the exclusion of others'. "Enthusiasm and the ego cannot coexist. One implies the absence of the other. Enthusiasm knows where it is going, but at the same time, it is deeply at one with the present moment, the source of its aliveness, its joy, and its power. Enthusiasm 'wants' nothing since it lacks nothing. It is at one with life...." (11)

The 'Peace that Surpasses Reason'

A 'core of peace exists in the midst of activity' when we align our inner purpose of life with the outgoing creative movement of the universe. When we can create with no attachment, no ego, no expectations of results or profits, enthusiasm does its work. Sooner or later though, all inspiration wanes and dissolves into the formless realm. Then it is only through a 'surrender' to the greater forces of the universe that we can ride the wave home, back to the beginning, the Now of eternity.

The danger with any great purpose or work is that we may construct inflated images of self like a "movie star, a famous writer, or a wealthy entrepreneur." And even if we realize these images, the stress and work involved is too often destructive to self and others. When it comes to the use of mind—an important consideration in any project of substance—you can only "manifest what you already have" and wanting what is lacking is only the way of stress and unhappiness. And if you seek a worthwhile image of life's inner purpose, Tolle suggests that you "see yourself inspiring countless people with your work." (13)

Tolle ends his discussion of empowerment through enthusiasm with a quotation from the Christian Gospel of Mark 11:24: "Whatever you ask in prayer, believe that you have received it, and it will be yours." A reasonless peace is perhaps the most precious of gifts that we can receive from any activity, enabling us to experience the most superlative emotions and thoughts, without attachment to them or wanting 'more'. It is important to remember that we are all equal to one another in potentiality for joy and the experience of freedom; knowing these things, we can then find our way safely home, wherever we are, to the 'peace that surpasses reason'.

Chapter 19

EXPERIENCES OF THE BODY, MIND AND SOUL

What are the most important experiences of the body, mind and soul? How can we free ourselves from the pain-body, the ego, and other corruptions of the mind, body and soul? And why are the virtues of love, nonviolence and goodness crucial for the knowledge of wisdom?

"*Good men spiritualize their bodies; bad men incarnate their souls.*" *Benjamin* Whichcotc

"*Knowledge comes about insofar as the object known is within the knower.*" *St* Thomas Aquinas

"*Knowledge is the ultimate perfection of the soul, in which consists our ultimate felicity.*" Dante

"*If one contemplates things in mystical meditation, everything is revealed as one.*" Zohar"

'*We go round and round in a circle game*'. Joni Mitchel

By changing our minds we can change the outer aspects of our lives." *William James*

William James, the American *Pragmatist*, puts emphasis upon the mind and its potentiality for directing our lives outwardly, in action. For the pragmatists, the truth or the value of an idea is to be found in the results or consequences of our actions and not in *a priori* knowledge or metaphysical truth. Historically, the traditions of idealism and realism, rationalism and empiricism, mysticism and skepticism have played important roles in the philosophies of pragmatists like James, Dewey and Peirce; and the distinction between *a priori* Truth and *a posterior* truth is the logical difference between mystical and pragmatic views of knowledge and wisdom—for these and other pragmatists. (1)

Experiencing the Peace of Just-Being

In *The Power of Now*, Tolle raises our consciousness to a new level when he discusses the emotion of happiness in relation to Being. He does this by making the simple distinction between superficial happiness and the deep sense of peace that comes from the simple 'joy of Being':

"The happiness that is derived from some secondary source is never very deep. It is only a pale reflection of the joy of Being, the vibrant peace that you find within as you enter the state of nonresistance. Being takes you beyond the polar opposites of the mind and frees you from dependency on form. Even if everything were to collapse and crumble all around you, you would still feel a deep inner core of peace. You may not be happy, but you will be at peace." (2)

Hidden within this paragraph is a strong critique of contemporary culture and the cult of happiness. The happiness that we may find from this or that experience, relationship, or possession, is a momentary and superficial reflection of a deeper and ultimate reality. Happiness—the psychological experience—is generally a derivative emotional state of changing circumstances. The deeper, primordial experience of Being reveals a condition that is always available to us no matter what happens relationally or externally.

The deeper experience is the 'peace of Being' that surpasses the various emotional or material states of happiness. In the intuitive, felt experience of Being, we can know a 'deep inner core of peace' amid the negativity of the oppositional world. Being resides deeply within, beyond the surface layers of intellectual ideas, the ego, and worldly roles. It brings us the greatest sense of happiness, peace and joy. The peace of Being brings us to the formless, inner, subtle body of the self where the Eternal Now is experienced and really known.

346

The full range or spectrum of emotions within human experience is greater than our thoughts or ideas. In actuality, we cannot entirely separate our emotions or passions from our deepest thoughts and understandings. Sometimes, it may be useful to make semantic distinctions and clarify our concepts, but this analytic activity cannot close the gap between thought and emotion or consciousness and Being—no matter how exhaustive the analysis. In fact, intellectual analysis often distances us from the internal sense of Now, especially when we lose touch with 'who we are' and only experience Consciousness as the abstract 'witness' of thought and action.

Tolle explores, discusses, and relates the full range of human emotions, positive and negative, to natural processes, mental forms, and primal Being. His vision lights the Path that can help us become liberated from negativity, conflict, and antagonism in this life. Of course, it is true that none of us can become 'absolutely perfect beings' in this life-form; a 'residue' of corruption and imperfection remains even among the 'enlightened'—until *par-nirvana* or a death without conditionality occurs.

Tolle's vision emphatically pointed the Way of an enlightened existence, perhaps as clearly as the founder of any school of philosophy, and in an updated, postmodern language. Each person, however, has to find his or her own way to liberation, and honor their own subjectivity or point of view that is the true basis for experience, meaning and purpose. And however liberation is struggled with and finally won, it is always in the Now or present moment of experience.

The 'I' of Consciousness, if it is a genuine witness to experience and knowledge, is able to see how our emotions, thoughts, and perceptions, condition our actions and help or hinder us in 'surrendering' to Being. So much of human history is a record of strife, conflict, and misery that it is remarkable that the human species has survived and flourished for as long as it has. The lack of prudence or real foresight about actions and their consequences has been an obvious 'lack' or problem in human history.

Even more than the lack of foresight or prudence, and even the ignorance of the past and human folly, is the lack of mindfulness or attention to the Present. If we cannot perceive what is happening in the Now and become absorbed in the present moment, its relations, events and changes, we cannot live in a fulfilling or meaningful way. The problem with so much 'knowledge' is that it lacks a vital connection with the living present, where Life is constantly unfolding and happening, in ever new and unpredictable ways.

In *this* sense, the moral, political and educational leadership of the human species has been a nearly continuous story of stupidity, unconsciousness, and violence from its earliest beginnings to the Present, with only brief periods when leaders of genuine vision and moral excellence brought peace, justice, and liberty to 'The People'—or the great, unknown majority of 'have-nots' who are ignored and taken for granted in the decision-making of the so-called 'leaders'.

The Pain-body as Resistance to Being

Tolle states that "All negativity is resistance....Negativity ranges from irritation or impatience to fierce anger, from a depressed mood or sullen resentment to suicidal despair. Sometimes the resistance triggers the emotional pain-body, in which case even a minor situation may produce intense negativity, such as anger, depression, or deep grief." (3)

Tolle's concept of the pain-body can enable us to become liberated from the extensive range of negative emotions. The pain-body is constituted by a field of energy from past experience that is negative, aggressive, and conflict-ridden, remaining mostly below the level of waking consciousness as the unconscious mind. A person may typically live with a pain-body within the energy field of the self that is unconscious to his or her waking consciousness, but evident to others when it expresses itself in aggression, negativity, or melodramatic outbursts. Unconsciously, the pain-body causes great psychological misery, both to the host self and others who may come into contact with its negative, aggressive and violent field of energy.

Getting-Rid of the Ego's Tendency to Fight

The ego feeds on negativity; the more negativity the better. "The ego believes that through negativity it can manipulate reality and get what it wants." But it cannot ultimately and the energy of the pain-body is profoundly unhealthy and insane. There is nothing really healthy or good about the pain-body and the controlling ego; in fact, there is probably no other animal on Earth that can so intensely poison its own body, mind and soul and project their psychic pollution upon their environment.

Tolle writes that "The only other animals that may occasionally experience something akin to negativity or show signs of neurotic behavior are those that live in close contact with humans and so link into the human mind and its insanity." (4)

The 'I am' of subjective consciousness is intimately connected with the emotional or limbic brain of the total self. The mind and its thoughts, the ego and its roles, are among the most significantly expressions and forms of the emotional brain and its subjective states of consciousness. There is a somewhat popular myth that purely objective thought, knowledge, or even consciousness can exist apart from the subjectivity of the total self, its body and the nervous system.

In fact, the existential phenomenologists of the late 19th and early 20th century may have destroyed the belief once and for all about *totally* 'objective knowledge'. They affirmed that subjectivity or the first person singular structure of ordinary consciousness, i.e. our *perspective* of the world, is not only the basis of experience but the natural 'bias' and interpretation that we bring to the objective or real world. Or, in the language of phenomenology, 'subjectivity and objectivity are inextricably linked or unified through consciousness itself'; and I have found this to have a liberating effect upon what I presume to 'know'!

If we were not nearly always in a battle with ourselves, we could more easily rise above the self in the clarity of higher Consciousness and just watch what is going on. The rising and falling of emotions from the unconsciousness of the brain, confirms our animal self, if nothing else—not to mention the whole autonomic system of the stem brain. In fact, plants and animals instinctively surrender to and respond to the Nowness of natural events and changes in their surroundings, often more readily than humans do.

The human 'tendency to fight' and not just eat and procreate, as our kin in the animal world are seen to do, is probably being corrupted by the increasingly close contact that they have with humans. As their habitats shrink and their numbers diminish from the increase in our numbers, non-humans animals have to defend themselves as perhaps never before, for survival. Not just this, but they are probably developing their own pain-bodies from our violent habits towards them, for the questionable habits of meat-eating, entertainment and experimentation.

At this point, a few questions need raising, like: How can we meet the challenge of the pain-body that is now institutionalized? Can we meet it head on without creating more violence and aggression in the world? If the human nervous system and its habits of mind, body and egoic actions are the biological, psychological and social basis for the pain-body, what is the best means for getting rid of the pain-body, individually and collectively?

Obviously, a virulent phenomenon like the pain-body—and the *ego* which is the social face of the inwardly dwelling pain-body— needs to be thought about as a deadly pathogen that is spreading throughout the world. Thus the ego and the pain-body need to be thought about and acted upon as a public health issue, morally, medically and pharmacologically, as well as psychologically and philosophically. For if we ever hope to change global society for the better, we will have to cure it of the pandemic that is already in place, i.e. an ego whose only justification for existing is to control, fight and destroy whatever or whoever stands in its way.

In sum, the desire and habit of 'fighting' or intellectually competing with others may be acceptable within the rules and regulations of a debate, a political contest, athletics, or the business world; but if the ego-dominated habit of mind and behavior becomes the only norm or standard for human relationships—which it too often now is—we will be no better than our most barbaric predecessors of civilization and possibly much worse. The solution—if there is a universal one—is to begin with your own sense of Being and ferret out the pain-body in which the fighting ego is rooted, and take the necessary steps, one at a time, towards a more Nonviolent way of living.

The Nonviolent Solution: Do Not Fight

Accept, forgive, and surrender. Do not resist what may aggravate you. Let negative emotions pass through you, without ego, resistance or the tendency to fight. Tolle wrote:

"Offer no resistance. It is as if there is nobody there to get hurt anymore. That is forgiveness. In this way, you become invulnerable." And instead of getting constantly bent out of shape by things that "should be happening" and are not, let them go, and just let things pass through you as if 'you are not there'. (5)

This is as useful an insight for the *peace* that is 'beyond happiness and unhappiness' as any I know. 'Offer no resistance' to negativity or the energy and acts of the pain-body that may be coming from other people. Just learn to be present and listen to others with empathy rather than judging or reacting with aggression. Let any negativity or violence from others just pass through you as if you are not even there! The precept of non-aggression or not-fighting is the most important principle in the theory of nonviolent ethics.

Any habits of aggression, fighting, and violence action do not easily disappear in the typical individual. Our primal conditioning and genetic pre-dispossession is partly that of a hunter and fighter in the hostile and life-threatening environments of our most distant ancestors in Africa and elsewhere when wild, man-eating animal were commonplace. Now in the 21st century and 50, 000 years or so after the last important migration out of Africa, most civilized areas of the world are nearly completely clear of threatening non-human animals. The paradox is that we are still fighting the ghosts of wild, man-eating animals in our urban, suburban, and rural areas of societies around the world.

Tolle raises the important question: what is the purpose of irritation, negativity, and anger? There is no good purpose or reason whatsoever, since it only makes us and others feel worse. But it is vital to realize that it is the unconscious mind or ego—and not Consciousness or true awareness—that causes negativity since the individual ego always wants to be right and control others. And the aggressive instinct of the ego is based upon a basic and pervasive fear of the other, where the threat is known or not. (6)

The connections between the physical, emotional, and social dimensions of the self are quite evident when we look at corporations, hedge funds, and the greedy practices of Wall Street and Investment Banks. The root of greed is the ego that has an emotional and mental structure of desire and 'wanting' that no profit or acquisition can fulfill. The condition that most disturbs the ego is the present moment of Being, causing constant restlessness and anxiety. At the same time, there is a basic dysfunction in the ego's obsessive mind that fails to see or appreciate basic needs—needs of the inner body or to live in a tranquil, balanced and worry-free state of Being.

The ignorance and lack of caring of the ego-dominated self is reflected in the living and working conditions of the working class and poor people of the world. It is not a direct causal relationships so much as it is a symptom of the systemic injustice, selfishness and lack of ethics in the business, financial and commercial sectors of developed, Capitalistic societies around the world. 'Egoic entities' such as Corporations cannot see beyond their wanting more for their 'bottom line' even if it means less or nothing for the working poor.

Tolle writes about Corporations, in the Marxist and existential vein:

"Their only blind aim is profit. They pursue that aim with absolute ruthlessness. Nature, animals, people, even their own employees are no more than digits on a balance sheet, lifeless objects to be used, and then discarded." (7)

The criminality of most corporations is exceeded only by their destructiveness and insanity. Raised by a Federal Court decision in 1890's to the status of a super-person, the 'rights' of a Corporation imply no corresponding responsibilities for those whom it oppresses, exploits, and enslaves. And although it may seen inappropriate to ascribe a pain-body to inanimate things like National Banks, Insurance, Oil and Communication Corporations, their contaminating influence upon the population at large, leaves little doubt about their diseased structure and functioning.

It may be too idealistic to think that those who are owners, shareholders, and managers of the great Corporations of the world could begin to assume moral responsibility for the consequences of their systemic greed and predatory practices in the public realm. It has been nearly two hundred years since one of the first critiques of the Capitalist system and its levers of corporate power and exploitation were written, *The Communist Manifesto*, by Karl Marx and Friedrick Engels.

Since then, Capitalism and its Corporations have only grown larger, stronger and more dominating in the global world. Indeed, 'Globalism' may be here to stay but so is the psychological, environmental and international violence that it has fostered. It is far past time for them to assume moral responsibility for their harm to the world. It is naïve to think that they ever will on their own without a world-wide catastrophe that would bring them down.

The Power of the People, the 'Have-nots' will have to since Corporations control the levers of government, the military, education, etc. This time the Revolution must be inspired by *nonviolent* strategies and tactics like boycotts, strikes, sit-outs and other forms of non-cooperation, and not the violence of guns, bombs and soldiers. The Will of the People must prevail or else the few will continue to exploit the many, and destroy the perfection, beauty and abundance of the Earth.

The Primary Obstacle to Love

Whether your love is felt in solitude or with someone else, you cannot expect glimpses of true love to grow or flourish unless you get rid of the pain-body or your own history of negative relationships, experiences, and illusions. The pain-body exists as an energy-field, a ghostly presence of the past within your life-form that weakens, poisons, and undermines your feelings of well-being, positive emotion, and the ability to be Present to others and the world. It is largely unconscious to your everyday awareness—although you are fully able to get rid of the pain-body by dis-identifying from old toxic and painful patterns that undermine your present relationships and ability to be fully in the Now.

Consciousness or the pure essence of Being possesses the power to destroy the pain-body just by 'Watching' whatever arises within the self without judging or analyzing it. The awareness of Consciousness brings us genuine self-knowledge; and the pain-body cannot endure the positive energy of pure consciousness since its reality is developed from the negative, painful, and violent energy of the past. In fact, when 'resistance', fighting or violence begins to appear in your present moment of awareness, it is a sign that the pain-body is threatened by Consciousness or the healing truth of loving Being.

In the searing gaze of higher Consciousness, the pain-body can be reduced to ashes, a mere trace of its former false 'self' or ghostly identity. The recognition of a pain-body within one's self is the beginning of the real cure that higher Consciousness can bring. Friends, lovers, teachers, and therapists can further enable anyone to be fully cured of the dysfunctional energy of the pain-body that prevents one from being fully alive and peaceful in the present moment.

Love as the Way and Truth

Of all the emotions of human life, none surpasses the experience of true or universal love. Plato uses the god of love or *Eros* as the messenger that brings Truth to the philosopher's consciousness from beyond this changing world of material forms. Christ refers to a Divine Love of the heavenly God, the Father, who accepts and forgives all without any discrimination. The Buddha implies that an infinite form of Love exists in the Four *Brahma-Viharas or Immeasurables,* i.e. Loving Kindness, Unlimited Compassion, Infinite Joy, and Perfect Equanimity. Each Chapter or *Surah* of the *Koran* begins with "In the name of God, the Benevolent, the Merciful" implying that the One 'Benevolent and Merciful' God of Abraham and Adam is omnipresent and omnipotent.

References to a divine and creative love are as widespread as the major world religions and the cultures of humanity and with good reason: the experience of love connects us to the infinite and eternal perfection of universal Life. The experience of love is the true basis for the moral sense of Being and a higher Consciousness. Love's philosophical message of Universality brings us closer to the Source of all life-forms than any other experience-in-existence.

In the context of "Enlightened Relationships," Tolle discusses the true state of love or Being itself. True love differs from the negative, co-dependent, and unconscious patterns of relationships that ordinarily pass for love, in moving us more deeply into the Now. 'It is that simple' since we bypass melodrama, role-playing, and the pain-body when we move toward Being—alone and together. Truly experiencing Being-with another person is an act of transparency, transmutation, and the transcendence of separateness in which we experience the eternal Now in Oneness. (8)

Tolle has written as profoundly as anyone on the subject of love—true love and not the delusion, attachment, and romantic madness that usually pass for love. He wrote: "Love is not selective, just as the light of the sun is not selective. It does not make one person special. It is not exclusive. Exclusivity is not the love of God but the 'love' of ego."

The intensely empathic energy that may be felt with one person, more than others, can also be the "same bond that connects you with the person sitting next to you on a bus, or with a bird, a tree, a flower. Only the degree of intensity with which it is felt differs." For once the experience of love is awakened it can readily flow to any person or thing and eventually spread universally to include the whole of nature, humanity and the universe. (9)

A Story of Zen Enlightenment: just-as-it-is

Tolle relates the story of Zen master, Banzan, who for many years sought enlightenment, but to no avail. Then one day he walked into a marketplace where he overheard a conversation between a butcher and his customer. "I want the best piece of meat that you have," the customer requested. And the Butcher replied, "Every piece of meat that I have is the best. There is no bad piece of meat here." Upon hearing this, Banzan became fully enlightened. (10)

The moral or explanation of this story is that when you accept what-is, 'every piece of meat'—or every moment just-as-it-is—you can become enlightened in an instant. You do not need to keep seeking for the next best technique, book, or guru, just learn to accept each moment, inner state of Being or relationship just as it comes to you, in the Now, as the best. After a while, you will realize the continual miracle and mystery that Life is, just-as-it-is.

Chapter 20

ADDICTIVE AND ENLIGHTENED

HUMAN RELATIONS

What do addiction and enlightenment mean in human relationships? How do intersubjective relations, feelings and understandings contribute to the breakthroughs and shifts of consciousness? What are the obstacles to harmony, kindness and enlightenment in our relations with others? And why is self-knowledge important for enlightened relationships with people—and all other life-forms?

"Only the truly intelligent understand the principle of the identity of all things. They do not view things as apprehended by themselves, subjectively; but transfer themselves into the position of the things viewed.... So it is to place oneself in subjective relation with externals, without consciousness of their objectivity,–this is TAO." Chuang-tzu

"The world is a passing show; we are the sun of Truth and the world a flitting panorama like the clouds. Whatever has name and form must change and vanish. It is only that immortal Truth, Spirit or God, that nameless, formless, birthless and deathless Reality—with which we are one—that never changes and ever exists." Swami Ramdas

"One who truly realizes that all women are manifestations of the Divine Mother may lead a spiritual life in the world. Without realizing God one cannot know what a woman is...." Sri Ramakrishna

"The Thought of Enlightenment has arisen in me I know not how even as a gem might be gotten by a blind man in a dunghill; it is...for the caravan of beings who wander through life's paths hungering to taste

357

of happiness this banquet of bliss is prepared that will satisfy all creatures coming to it." Santi-deva

"Shall I not inform you of a better act than fasting, alms and prayers? [It is] making peace between one another: enmity and malice tear up heavenly rewards by the roots." Muhammad

Muhammad, the founding Prophet of Islam, gives us a taste of his divine wisdom about our relations with others. If you have hatred in your heart and ill-will of mind and soul, your rewards in the heavenly realm will be destroyed. Not separating this life from what follows in afterlife states is a crucial assumption in Islam and mystical *wisdom.* Muhammad's words are an important corrective to the current extremist groups of Muslims who believe violence and terrorism will win them a place in Paradise. In general, the dualistic habit of mind can cause great harm and violence to self and others. (1)

Enlightened Relationships: There is Nothing Else to Attain

Tolle writes in the context of "Enlightened Relationships" that "There is nothing you can ever do or attain that will get you closer to salvation than it is at this moment." Or you find salvation, happiness, or enlightenment, the moment you realize that 'you are there already'. So often persons think that self-realization or the peace of Being can only be known when some external or future condition is obtained—whether it is graduating from school, getting a certain job, retiring or whatever. (2)

If you are religious in a theistic sense, transcending the dualistic world is seeing that God is not some external or future something, but exists as your innermost essence. Quite typically when you ask someone about God or the truth of the afterlife, the response will be 'we will know *that* only after we die' or words to that effect. In the pragmatic or real world of material relations, it is true that we cannot know with certainty the truth about future events or the consequences of our actions until they occur.

Self-fulfillment or the *Truth* about Being occurs in the experience of here-and-now—an eternal, immediate reality. We are *always, already* enlightened beings, just-as-we-are. When we see that *seeking* just creates more problems, tensions, and conflicts, we will learn to give up seeking something that is not-yet, not present already. We enter the Goodness, Perfection, and Truth of everything from wherever we are, since the universe and all beings in it are essentially unified and related to universal Being. If human beings became *aware* of their absolute equality in universal Being, their pain, suffering, and unhappiness would soon disappear.

Relationships of the Body, Consciousness and Soul

Inwardly, we exist separately from the natural environment, other people, and the institutions of civilization. The skin is the natural, physical boundary between the inner sense of the self and the external natural and social world. The skin is not just a biological condition of the body; it is also symbolic in separating one person from another in the real world. The skin is not only the largest organ system of the body, in covering its entire form, it is also a unity of processes, tissues and cells, protecting the whole self from injury, invading pathogens and regulating the body's temperature. Thus, no matter what kind of relationship exists between persons, the skin and other organic systems of the body, function beyond awareness, daily interactions, and ultimate control.

The body is also the home to an eternal *soul*—the atomistic *jiva* in Jain philosophy—and the soul is our most essential connection to the unknown Source-Being. That these metaphysical truths can be doubted and questioned only points to the essential freedom of the *will* in all human beings. And when we think about subjective and intersubjective relationships, it is important to keep these metaphysical questions in consideration since they represent and point to the underlying Unmanifested dimension of the self as the unconsciousness.

Phenomenology is the theory that consciousness is a natural unity between subjective or inward being and objectivity or outer being. In other words, what we call the 'inner self or being' is only a figment of thought or abstraction since no parts of the self can *exist* separately from the whole, organic, functioning body. Although most people are normally born through the sexual copulation of a man and a woman and the union of a male sperm cell and a female egg cell, medical intervention and procreative procedures have greatly expanded the means by which the natural process of conception can be actualized.

As much as we may extol the mind, soul, or Consciousness, the human organism or the physical body is still the commanding, sacred Presence of the person. If we did not possess a living, functioning body, we would not exist at all! In fact, all of our relationships with others and roles in society completely depend upon this one given fact.

Our social relationships are as natural as having a body, mind, and soul. However, owing to the complexity of the body's emotions like love and hate, generosity and greed, faith and doubt, human relations are never uncomplicated or without conflict. Furthermore, when there are habitual, delusional tendencies of the mind and ego, such as addiction, identification, and the loss of self-control, powerful negativities subtly develop in relationships at the unconscious level of everyday life. And when we lose awareness or consciousness of our thoughts and actions, these addictive or irrational patterns of behavior and emotion undermine our ability to control or change our behavior.

Negative Patterns of Addiction in Human Relationships

Identifications of the self with others are the fodder for negative energy patterns or addictions of many kinds. For example, in intimate relationships involving sex, addiction grows exponentially from sexual desire, awakened emotions and orgasmic acts. Typically, control patterns, attachments, possessive roles and emotions sprout up around sexual relationships with others. Instinctively, the will of the other begins to constrict and withdraws to defend the wholeness or integrity of the self. Before either lover 'knows' or is conscious of what has happened, a pattern of action and re-action, aggression and response, develops around a formerly loving relationship.

The forms of emotional negativity found in human relationships are many and the pain-body formed in periods of negativity, violence, and unconsciousness is their common denominator. Tolle lists a few traits or qualities found in negative patterns and relationships:

"possessiveness, jealousy, control, withdrawal and unspoken resentment, the need to be right, insensitivity and self-absorption, emotional demands and manipulation, the urge to argue, criticize, judge, blame, or attack, anger, unconscious revenge for past pain inflicted by a parent, rage and physical violence." (3)

Addiction can form around any negative or positive emotional tendency and especially clinging attachments such as are found in romantic love and relationships based upon sexual lust. The early common experience of 'falling in love' occurs when unconscious emotional processes engulf consciousness or one's essence and free will. At first, 'falling in love' is intoxication, a rush of feeling and emotion, and a natural 'high' or inspiration; and then there is the discovery of the other beyond the sexual lust and affective high. The result is—rather commonly—that such 'loving' attention leads to suffocation in the relationship causing a loss of integrity, will, and freedom on both sides. In romantic love, the experience of 'love' is often confused with natural lust and/or reduced to possessiveness to such a degree that a person cannot live without the other, as depicted in such romantic tragedies as Romeo and Juliet.

Addictive love is sick, crazy and unbalanced love since it desires a total possession of the other. It never lasts for very long or if it does, it may become psychotic, obsessive, and violent. Addictive love destroys the wholeness of Being in the self and others since its energies come from the most desperate, anxious, and irrational sources, the unconscious and negative emotions of the pain-body such as fear and insecurity.

The best cure for addictive love—no matter how satisfying the sex or the *hook* may be—*may be* to end the relationship. Of course this is easier said than done and many who are in harmful relationships have many defenses based on denial and self-loathing that keep them in such relations. Addiction thrives on paradox since what is eating at one's soul is often ignored and adapted to even though it, like most forms of cellular cancer, will eventually destroy the health of the body, mind and soul on which it thrives.

If you are healthy and sensitive to the real needs of your self—and not your addictive tendencies—you will happily 'let-go' of relationships that are based upon patterns of addiction, selfishness and insecurity. Having friends who are drug-addicted to alcohol, tobacco and marijuana can be just as unhealthy and corrosive to your emotional, intellectual and spiritual well-being as addictive sexual relations. So choose your friends wisely and with a view to your body's health and the well-being of your soul, mind and heart.

In general, addiction is usually a sign that we refuse to confront the pain-body and choose a drug of some kind—alcohol, nicotine, sex, food, money, another person—to sustain the pain-body's energy in unconsciousness. After the initial euphoria that an additive behavior may cause, the pain-body returns with a vengeance, looking for additional fuel or sustenance for its desires. The cycle of pain-addiction is completed when co-dependent subjects search for the renewal of their additive behaviors in other pain-bodies—thus avoiding the restlessness, boredom, and emptiness where it all begins. (4)

Freeing Ourselves from Addictive Relationships

How can we free ourselves from addictive and painful relationships? We have only one primary or primordial relationship in existence, i.e. our attunement or oneness with the inner, deeper sense of existence. When we learn that true love is grounded in our relationship with the universal Life-force and not just exclusive love—addictive relationships, irrational patterns and other negativities fall away on their own; and the clinging, possessive, and fearful nature of loving relations is undermined at the roots of existence and they are replaced by a deep and abiding oneness with all life-forms and the universal Life-force. Tolle wrote:

"To know yourself as the Being underneath the thinker, the stillness underneath the mental noise, the love and joy underneath the pain, is freedom, salvation, enlightenment." (5)

This may sound all-too-easy but it is perhaps the most challenging and worthwhile experience that we can realize in this life-form i.e. becoming a self-realized being or one who feels universally connected in the here-and-now, without pain, addition, or delusion. And when you can bring this universal knowledge of the self 'home' and into your relationships with others, you will be able to form enduring, loving and fulfilling relationships that transcend the pain-body and its negative, dualistic and sickening patterns of emotion, thought and behavior.

In a state of transcendence or enlightenment, all relationships become love relationships. Why? The space, gap, or *sense of lack* that you feel in dualistic relationships dissolves and disappears from self-awareness and you become naturally grounded in your higher Consciousness and the essence of Being; and you begin to see new connections everywhere and feel them in your body, mind and soul—where before only addictively created dualities, separations, and boundaries existed.

What actually exists in the immediate Now of personal experience is the Light of Being where your sense as a separate self disappears and dissolves into the universal Life-force flowing and sustaining everything, everywhere and all-the-time. Of course, you may object, I do not want to dissolve! I want to exist!' But exist you will when you experience the Light of Being, as perhaps never before! The light of free being brings a sense of certainty to yourself that is the most true and enduring basis for spiritual liberation or enlightenment.

Friendships, Social Recognition and Salvation

A really lasting, healthy and positive relationship is one based upon friendship. A friend is another person, animal or imagined being who is always present for you and ready to help you. A living, breathing and active person is more able to be a full, supportive and trusting friend than a person or being who is merely imagined. Having friends or trusting persons in your life-world for all occasions could be a good thing but it takes time and effort and you must be ready to present for them too when they need your help or support. So be discriminating and careful about who you spend your time with and as conscious as possible about your motive; but it is always best not to be calculating in friendships least you destroy them in your score-keeping and calculations! In general, you will know your friends by the company that they keep and you can read your own wellness of the soul or the deepest part of you, by your own friendships.

Meanwhile, the sense of wholeness is important since we continue to exist as separate, unique persons even when we are in the best of relationships. However, it is the case that our identity or wholeness as persons is also a relational one that feeds upon social recognition and simple attention from others. And because we exist biologically or continuously in and through this body, a sense of continuity is organically built into our psychological expectations of others; but this is somewhat unrealistic since others, no matter how close or trusting the relationship, cannot always be at our 'beck and call' since they exist as separate beings too!

Thus as externally derived sense of wholeness as in relations that 'cannot live without the other' are counterfactual, biologically, and unbalanced and addictive, psychologically. The most vital, natural sign that we exist separately with natural boundaries between us is the skin that covers each body with its protective layers of tissue and hair. Nature is wise beyond our comprehension and technology to improve upon what we have been gifted from conception and birth. And there are few other things in this life-form, if anything, that exceeds the health and wellness of the whole body—its inner, subtle and outer, gross parts.

Social recognition is arguably the most powerful and compelling reason why we do much of what we do; we desire and even crave recognition or simple attention from others for who we are and what we may do; and most importantly, *that* we are and even exist in the first place! Of course, one can easily become addicted to social recognition too and ignore everything else in your life-world just for the sake of a look, a smile, cheers and clapping from others. Whether we can ever give up some form of attention from others, and still remain fully healthy, well and creative, is questionable. The starving artist in the attic of an abandoned house or the monk, who meditates alone in a Himalayan cave for years, may sound romantic and appealing to a few persons, but it may also be impossible and unhealthy in the extreme for most people.

Finally, it is debatable whether social recognition and the creativity that is sometimes implied by it can ever be a substitute for salvation or the survival of the soul. Like so many abstract questions and conditionals, it all depends upon the individual person and his or her karmic journey. Each person has a different cross to bear and the quest for social recognition may only be just one more timber in our eyes that prevents us from seeing the whole Truth of our situation as existing beings. For if we really were only concentrated upon Being or the essence of who we are— the soul—we would most certainly not be so hell-bent on gaining social recognition for our little ego.

After all, is it not salvation or the well-being of the soul—to quote Socrates—that deepest part of ourselves that we should be concerned about, in the present moment? After the clapping ends and the curtain falls, who are we and where are, with our souls? Should we count on an unseen, unknown, and invisible God to save us? Or are we all alone, in our karmic journey through heaven and hell, to an unknown destination, at an unknown time and place? And the answer, as with so many metaphysical questions is 'yes', 'no' and 'maybe' since it up to each of us to decide what is real, true and right—for us.

Enlightenment: Theory and Practice

Since enlightened beings continue to exist in the real or natural and social world, there is no absolute or total liberation for a contingently related, finite life-form. That is, even enlightened beings continue to have real needs and interests, psychological desires and tendencies towards addiction in the external world. But the additions of an enlightened person—as opposed to one who is not an enlightened person—are those that can be given up, through new choices, new possibilities, and a sense of release. In other words, a greater degree of self-control exists in enlightened beings as opposed to unenlightened ones.

Even if we feel totally and completely at-one- with primal Being, we still need this body, its wants and desires, to continue living or existing. In short, we may have an infinite potentiality for realizing Being or the Source of everything, through a higher Consciousness, but we still need this body, mind, and soul to continue living, just-as-we-do or any other way. Thus the enlightenment experience, even in its most realized forms, is contingent, conditional, and relative to who we are, in our personal sense of Being-in-the-world.

The essential basis for the experience of enlightenment is the higher Consciousness of subjectivity. In the spiritual literature, this is called 'Transcendental Subjectivity' where the sense of universal Being or Mind is realized; and this is true for someone like Ken Wilber who thought can be traced back to Plato of Greece or the *Upanishads* of India. The delusions of ordinary consciousness are many and the difference between conventional and Extraordinary states of consciousness is often a matter of degree rather than kind. Furthermore, there presently exists no empirical way of measuring or quantifying such differences of degree, much less kind.

Thus the experience of Enlightenment (with a capital 'E') is always undergone uniquely by a particular subject—one who may report upon a Revelation, profound insight, or an illuminating surge of energy. The phenomenology of the enlightenment experience is notoriously ambiguous and always subject to meta-physical and psychological interpretation; and whatever else is said about it, the enlightenment experience is subjective, idio-syncratic and social. Yet in no way do these conditions and quali-fications negate the possible value or existential truthfulness of the enlightenment experience itself.

Enlightenment may initially only be a state of awareness or consciousness, a purely inward state like being able to perform an advanced level of calculus or solving a complex ethical dilemma. Enlightenment, in its metaphysical framing, is a purely medita-tive experience of higher Consciousness and only secondarily does it involve the body-mind, or social tasks and roles in the social world. However, these secondary or practical and worldly aspects of the enlightenment experience can become occasions or opportunities for awakening to our innermost, deepest and highest potentialities, too.

In other words, the enlightenment experience or insight into soulful being has the distinct value of freeing us from addictive, toxic and sickening relationships of many kinds—those brought on by the conditions of the world, other people, and the total self. Among the sources of addition are our attachments to symbols, things and persons, and our inability to free ourselves from condi-tions and patterns of feeling, thought and desire. When we awaken, we can see the way forward—the way that solves a dilemma, begins a new course of action and ends any pain and suffering.

Even the most enlightened, famous beings who have lived like Socrates, Siddhartha, Mahavira, Chuangzi, Confucius, Jesus, Mohammad, et al, continued to have a body, mind and soul with real needs, interests and desires—following their enlightenment experiences. The real difference between us and them, in actu-ality and not potentiality, may only be their fame and historical significance as world leaders or founders of religious and philo-sophical traditions. We may admire them and perhaps use them as role models in our own lives; but there is a serious philosophi-cal and psychological question whether we should ever *deify* a human being even if that tradition teaches otherwise.

In the enlightenment experience, you may become more aware than ever at just how irrational, self-destructive, and violent human beings can be in their relations to one another; or even how in the more intimate or close relationships, any trace of a pain-body tries to seize control of the other. The experience of enlightenment comes from our closeness to Being or the Light and Clarity of higher Consciousness. In the experience of non-addictive or non-attached awareness, all negativity is absent and joy, peace, and love are supremely present. And if two or more enlightened persons are related through their friendship and more intimate relationships, then their individual creativity and power for Goodness is greater due to their divine energy and loving Presence in the world.

We are instinctively and ontologically attracted to enlightened persons or liberated, intelligent and pain-free beings; beings that live fully in the Now. Spirituality exists individually, mutually and collectively; and the divine energy of the creative Life-force exists everywhere in the world. The spark that lights the fire of the collective ethos or Spirit in society can be ignited by a single, enlightened, and impassioned individual or many such individuals in union, support and interaction with one another. And history has examples of many such persons in every generation and society, and in all walks of Life.

The energy of enlightenment or salvation is like a contagious fire-storm of Goodness that engulfs the whole person, inwardly and outwardly through an inclusive sense of Being. The danger in the group or herd experience of spirituality is that it may only affect us superficially and addictively especially when there is no inner readiness or removal of the pain-body and purification of the soul. Without a purified inner body that removes the underlying negativity or resentment of a pain-body, even the most liberating of experiences may only be quite temporary or skin-deep.

In the model of Yoga philosophy, the enlightenment experience activates and opens the full spectrum of chakra centers connected with the inner body of the Life-force. It is an experience that awakens us to the most profound truths of humanity and timeless Being. From the *Muladhara-chakra* at the lower end of the spine to the *Sahasrara-chakra* at the crown of the head, the energy of the higher Self becomes fully illuminated in the enlightenment experience.

Under the influence of enlightenment, the formless or unmanifested realm is awakened and shows itself in the experiences of everydayness. The mundane world is transformed and the most ordinary objects or phenomena of existence appear as the most extraordinary miracles of Life.

Paradoxical Freedom and Human Rights

The 'slave morality' of the masses that Nietzsche spoke about in 19th century Europe is still widespread throughout the world. Nietzsche's view of the masses may have come from an elitist prejudice, but it is one that remains as true today about the human condition as it did then. What has not significantly changed, as yet, is intellectual understanding of the masses about the structure of human freedom and the extent to which it enslaves us all.

The faiths of religion still divide the world into us and everybody else, and the egoic delusion that only 'we' are saved and everyone else is damned. An intellectual, emotional and semantic *duality* is the cause of many human problems and conflicts in the world; and the cause lies in its distortion of universal existence or the oneness of Life.

If we really valued Life and protected its many life-forms because they are all equal and sacred, we would end all sources of slavery, war and violence; instead, we glorify war and violence in our mass media, or cover it up as in the cases of poverty, slavery and the other forms of exploitation. When we cease to be entertained by the pain and suffering of others, it will be a clear sign that we have freed our inner self of the pain-body. (6)

'Self' and 'other', 'subject' and 'object', 'us' and 'them' are the root semantic causes of mentally created dualities which split us apart just as surely as addictive, unconscious, and pain-ridden relationships do. There is really only one primary relationship in Life and that is our oneness-with-Being or who we are. When we see who we are, individually and universally, we can know and accept ourselves as we exist, warts and all. We are all unique, equal and universally related due to our origin in primordial Being, the Source of all life-forms and the universal Goodness of Life.

The highly politicized freedom of human beings is due to the real Presence of the universal Will in every individual although nature, society and the contingencies of existence have developed us differently. We 'prove' the existence of free will every moment in the choices that we make and through the reality of experience, in the here-and-now. Thus, an inner sense of freedom exists at the core of our Being and it is the means by which we create a meaningful and purposeful life-world.

When our inner purpose or reason for being is in alignment with the outer or objective purpose of the universe, we become self-realized or enlightened persons. The enlightenment experience should be thought of as an educational or developmental process rather than one divides us from the body, mind and soul of total being; and on the other side of the imaginary or intellectual divide, the self and the real world of inter-subjective relationships, and the totality of natural and social conditions that make up our personal lives.

Intersubjective relationships exist due to their discrete and unique life-forms in existence; and subject-object relationships exist simultaneously with intersubjective ones. We exist simultaneously on many levels and in many dimensions of reality due to our infinite potentiality for self-actualization. The unity of self, others, and the world is due to the greater, more inclusive unity of nature, society and the cosmos. Each life-form is a unified totality within ever greater realms of unity and totality; and no experience or knowledge of the totality can be greater than the totality of universal Being.

The life-world of each of us is unique, situational, and self-chosen. Human freedom implies responsibility for the exercise of the will; and we cannot escape from the necessity to choose our way in existence. Therefore, freedom is a living paradox in that we cannot, *not choose,* for in passively *not* choosing, we have chosen just as surely as in active choosing. As Jean-Paul Sartre has stated, 'we are condemned to freedom' and it is a paradox that makes us peculiarly human in that we may be the only species that realizes the nature of paradoxical existence.

As absolute and paradoxical will implies that the *actions* of the human will have consequences in the real world of material and social relations; and consequences are of two kinds, those that are intended by the intentionality of consciousness and those that are not or the unintended consequences of experience. Both kinds of consequences found in experience, derive from human willing and intending or not, and make up the structure or character of human glory and folly, success and failure, comedy and tragedy. Such extreme tendencies in existence and all gradations between cannot be avoided in the story of history and the solitary journey of an individual's life.

If you believe in the inherent or naturally endowed 'rights' of humanity, such as can be found in the United Nations "Universal Declaration of Human Rights" or its founding Charter, then you may need no convincing about a free will. Of course, as nearly everyone realizes, the Rights of humanity are quite unevenly and unjustly distributed between the nation-states of the world and within each of them. And these rights are found unjustly conditioned by class, race, gender, age, nationality, religion, language, etc. in the common world.

Below I have included the first six Articles of the U.N. Charter as a reference for what the majority opinion of educated leaders from the nations of the world hold to be the 'endowed' or natural birthright of all human beings:

"Article 1. All human beings are born free and equal in dignity and rights. They are endowed with reason and conscience and should act towards one another in a spirit of brotherhood.

Article 2. Everyone is entitled to all the rights and freedoms set forth in this Declaration, without distinction of any kind, such as race, color, sex, language, religion, political or other opinion, national or social origin, property, birth or other status.

Furthermore, no distinction shall be made on the basis of the political, jurisdictional or international status of the country or territory to which a person belongs, whether it be independent, trust, non-self-governing or under any other limitation of sovereignty.

Article 3. Everyone has the right to life, liberty and security of person.

Article 4. No one shall be held in slavery or servitude; slavery and the slave trade shall be prohibited in all their forms.

Article 5. No one shall be subjected to torture or to cruel, inhuman or degrading treatment or punishment.

Article 6. Everyone has the right to recognition everywhere as a person before the law."

I encourage everyone to read the remainder of these *thirty articles* since they speak volumes about the ideals that most men and women cherish and the extent to which the present real world has fallen short of them. The Charter is also a distinctly secular document avoiding the religious traditions that so unnaturally divide too many human beings against each other. (7)

Finally, I only wish to add to the Charter that the free will is the gift of the Designer that keeps on giving. The free will is innate, absolute and translucent within the higher Consciousness found in each human being. It gives us the power to shape and direct our own lives. And it is the means by which we can sometimes overcome external conditions or forces in our lives.

Whereas the will is limited, contingent and conditional, the soul is not; it exists unconditionally or infinitely in potentiality for transforming the ordinary self from one life-form into another life-form; and the power of the soul remains inscrutable and beyond the power of reason to comprehend or understand. Yet its sacred Presence is all that we need to see the paradoxical truth of the Right and will-to- choose.

PART VI

AWAKENING TO CHANGE,

CONSCIOUSNESS AND WISDOM

What is philosophy in relation to change and permanence? How can philosophy enable us to know the truth of change and the Truth of permanence? Why is philosophy valuable in everyday life and human existence?

In Western civilization, philosophy is based mostly upon reason, knowledge and science; in Asia and the Middle East, philosophy is based mostly upon intuition, experience and religion. A fuller, more adequate view of philosophy combines both perspectives and is non-dualistic and integrative of such oppositions; and this is the basis for a more holistic, humanistic and *perennial Wisdom*.

There are innumerable visionaries in history who have possessed an integrative, holistic and unitary view of Wisdom. The founders of the major world religions and generations of philosophers, theologians and scientists are prominent among them. Today, there are increasing numbers of scientists who realize the limits of scientific thinking and see the need for a more ontological, pragmatic and existential perspective of human knowledge and experience.

Meanwhile, change is a universal fact of individual existence, society and the universe. Change is caused by the gravitational movement of matter in time and space, from sub-atomic to cosmological dimensions of reality. Change implies impermanence, uncertainty and the probability that knowledge can only be conditional, tentative and ambiguous. From an ontological perspective, change and forms co-arise with the actuality of *permanence* or eternal Being; and Being exists as the essence of Consciousness that transcends the relative and changing world of forms.

Finally, information, knowledge and wisdom constitute the progressive, developmental stages of consciousness, culminating in the experience of Enlightenment or true liberation. The quest for liberation from the pain-body, negativity and violence of experience is the essential means for acquiring *perennial or universal* Wisdom. The analytic, pragmatic, and existential perspectives of experience and knowledge are necessary and relevant to the full awakening to Being or who you really are.

Chapter 21

LIFE, LIFE-FORMS AND GOODNESS

What is Life in relation to life-forms? How is universal Life related to finite, changing and mortal life-forms? And why should we believe that universal Goodness is the ultimate origin of sentient life-forms and the universe?

"You know, my Friends, with what a brave Carouse / I took a Second Marriage in my house; / divorced old barren Reason from my Bed / and took the Daughter of the Vine to Spouse." Omar Khayyam

"This is the air; that is the glorious sun; / This pearl she gave me, I do feel and see it; And though it is wonder that enwraps me thus; / Yet it is not madness." Shakespeare (*Twelfth-Night*)

"The madness of love is the greatest of heaven's blessings." Plato (*Phaedrus*)

"Even if the gnostic were cast into the fire, he would not feel it, because of his absorption, and if the delights of Paradise were spread out before him, he would not turn towards them, because of the perfection of the grace that is in him and his perfect attainment, which is above all else that can be attained." Al-Ghazali

"Do not desert your home to live somewhere else. The wonderful Tao exists not far away from your own body. It is not necessarily found in high mountains or in unknown waters." Chang Po-tuan

Chang Po-tuan, the Chinese *Taoist*, gives his sage advice about where and perhaps how to live based upon his knowledge of the *Tao* or the eternal Unity of All. Our physical being and worldly existence cannot be separated from the *Tao* since it links every form equally upon the Earth. Thus do not be too hasty to 'live

377

somewhere else' just because it may look different or even better, geographically. The *Taoist* form of *Wisdom* is everywhere in nature and existence since you carry it with you in your bones, flesh and blood.

Chang-Po-tuan is known in Taoist circles for his quest of spiritual immortality. He combined elements of Zen Buddhist and Confucian thought with the Taoist doctrine of Yin and Yang in the awakening of the inner body. Meditations upon the essences of certain metals during the solstice times of the year are said to grow a new, non-dualistic sense of the body where subject and object disappear and only the truth of immortality remains. It is reported that Chang-Po lived for ninety-eight years in his material body, during the 11ᵗʰ century. (1)

Life, life-forms, and Nature

In *The Power of Now* Tolle writes that "Past and future form an uninterrupted continuum, unless the redeeming power of the Now is activated through your conscious presence. As you know, underneath the various conditions that make up your life situation, which exists in time, there is something deeper, more essential: your Life, your very Being in the timeless Now." (2)

The experience of Life differs from a life-form or worldly self, in that it is formless, eternal, and essentially spiritual. The life-form or body-self is contingently situated in space, time, and the material world, and there is no 'exit' or safe escape from the body-self or situational life-world. In the living experience of the timeless Now, you are already aligned and vitally present to Life; otherwise your soul or essential self would have no life-form or real existence.

Life, in its existential relation to physical nature and its various elements, is the universal basis for your life-form; otherwise you would have no spiritual relation to Being much less a material form in nature. Life and Consciousness are formless, eternal, and infinite in their universality; they really exist beyond our conceptual or intellectual understanding as the eternal essences of

Being. They are approximately understood through our insights, intuitions, and deeper perceptions of reality.

The various elements, laws, and material conditions of nature can be scientifically understood through observation, experiment, and testing. However, the essence or universality of nature cannot be absolutely known; our knowledge of nature is always relative, approximate and conditional. Nature is informed and transformed by the Life-force in the dialectical creativity of knowledge and life-forms. Being is the divinely creative center (that is everywhere) in the universe and like the God of theism, Being is infinitely perfect, omnipotent, and omnipresent in reality. However, unlike the conventional God of theism, Being is formless, hidden and intellectually unknowable.

In sum, life-forms and ordinary consciousness is finite and dependently related to nature and its elements. Life is infinite, timeless, and generative of life-forms through their material relations of nature. The forms of organic nature are constantly changing—although at a universal and formless level, Nature does not change due to its essential relation to Being. Because of the infinite, eternal, and unchanging essences of Being and Life, nature cannot be comprehensively understood. However, existential life-forms in their structures and functions can be approximately understood although their essences can only be experienced; and experience is always mediated through intuitive, affective, and cellular processes of the body, nature, and Being.

Becoming Adventurous and Getting Unstuck

Being is the formless totality of Life, Nature and Consciousness in their myriad and changing relationships. When humankind journeys to other planets in the solar system and then to the stars and other worlds, they will discover with a new sense of wonder the miracle and mystery of Life and Nature working together and creating other life-forms in other worlds. At the same time, the emotions of fear, anxiety, and terror will co-exist with fearlessness, curiosity and wonder in the new explorations of the space age, since humankind will be pushing past the boundaries of mythic, conventional, and scientific knowledge, to worlds that are more incredible than the most imaginative science fiction.

You or the *Thou of spirituality* are spoken about often by Tolle. It refers to the conscious presence of Life or the 'pure consciousness' of the *soul*. When you experience an illness, physical pain, or disability, it is your life-form or body-self that is most directly affected. Your higher Consciousness or sense of universal Life is only indirectly involved. If you learn to surrender to the condition of pain and not fight it, the result is an essential liberation from the illness and a transformation of your ordinary consciousness and life-world into a higher and extraordinary Consciousness.

You or the sacred *Thou* of Being is the most intimate experience and feeling of peace that you can have in this finite life-form. 'You' are a *soul* or essence of Being in your innermost self that is vibrating energetically at atomic levels. The problems or conflicts of everyday existence have created contingencies, conflicts, and doubts about the meanings of Life, Being and nature that are extrinsic to the intrinsic essence or soul that *you are*. If you learn to surrender to your *deepest sense of self or soul*, you will discover the infinite reservoir of peace, goodness, and potentiality that lies at the heart of your own and every other sentient life-form.

When two or more persons have the same *noetic* or intuitive experience in their relationships with each other, it is one of true love, empathy, and attunement. There are many other words in every language that refer to the empathic relationship or infinite potentiality that all life-forms embody owing to the Life-force; and there are few experiences in Nature, in its biological and universal senses, that have more spiritual and moral significance. However, great potentialities and relationships also carry great risks with them and persons in relationships of any kind must be flexible, open to change, and aware of the dangers and possibilities.

Potentially, our deepest, intimate and evolving relationships with others can enable individuals to make vital and exciting connections with the unconditional nature of Being and the ordinary world. We are positioned in the limitless and timeless energy of Life, as adventurers or space-time explorers on the planet Earth, through our present life-form. 'Life is an adventure or it is nothing' wrote Alfred North Whitehead; and we can never know, for sure, what the future holds for us since we and the natural, social and existential conditions of Life are ever-changing, in the here-and-now.

What is needed to maintain the 'sense of adventure' in Life, is to look beyond the myriad changes of subjective-objective existence, the reasoning and thinking mind, and the forms of the cunning ego, to *experience the perfection of what-is* or Being itself. If we get stuck in the various forms, relations, and roles of Life, whose origins are temporal, worldly, and organic in nature, we may miss the higher Consciousness, perfect Being, and universal Life-force, that have made everything possible.

'Getting unstuck' means to get free of the many hang-ups that we all acquire in the possessive, petty, and narrow-minded habits of the selfish body, mind and ego. Getting unstuck means being able to easily change or break old toxic habits that deaden our creativity and spirituality and ruin our relationships with others.

No one is born knowing how to live a perfectly moral, practical and spiritual existence. We all must learn how to live; and in the process of living, we make choices that are sometimes wrong and hurtful ones; and if we are living intelligently or mindfully, we learn from them. And in the end if we have not learned to be humble before nature and ordinary existence, we have probably learned little that is useful, healing or liberating.

Becoming Aware of your Life-Situation: the Courage to Be

If you are present in the Now you will realize that the memories, thoughts, and feelings of the past are often triggered by present situations. Our memories and present perceptions interact with each other, in psychological, associative, and mysterious ways. If you are really consciously present to your perceptions, memories and expectations, there need not be any problem with reflecting upon the past or 'thinking' about events, persons, and experiences, in the here-and-now.

Becoming fully present in the Now where eternity intersects time-space and material existence, is realizing that we never really separate ourselves from the past or even the future, since the eternal Now implies that the three dimensions of time continuously co-exist. We may wonder how is it possible that everything is Now present, everywhere, and the answer is through infinite and divine Presence. Because no one can know the total, final and absolute answer to ultimate questions, we can only provide rather long, complicated answers that just approximate an answer—like the present one!

Becoming a fully conscious person means: you can be present to every contingency in existence without being threatened or lessened by it. You exist as a mortal, sentient being or one who is limited and finite and that you experience pain and joy, fear and fearlessness, and the courage to be, wherever you are and whatever you are doing. Becoming fully human and conscious means to accept your finitude as a person but also to recognize your potentiality for a higher Consciousness and a sublime sense of Being.

When the existential theologian, Paul Tillich, published *The Courage to Be*, in 1951, the world was just emerging from the horror of World War II. Although the book quickly became popular and a best seller, it was a time when some of the worse paranoia was loose in the world; it was the beginning of the Cold War between the Soviet Union and the West, the McCarthy era and its witch-hunts for Communists—or the new enemies for the United States government.

Since *The Courage to Be* is an important text in 20th century existential philosophy, I will quote directly from it since I believe that Tillich's and Tolle's philosophies are quite similar.

In Tillich's philosophy, the power of a single individual is derived from Being-itself or God, ultimately. *Courage* is a subtle and deep form of power in the ontological sense or as primal Being; and ultimate Being transcends the world and the ordinary, finite self and can only be known or Revealed in rare, mystical moments of courage. This means that we have the Power to bring divinity into the world through our fearless and courageous actions, even if our acts could bring the ultimate sacrifice, or the end of our life-form. Tillich wrote:

"Man is not necessarily aware of this source [the courage to be]. In situations of cynicism and indifference he is not aware of it. But it works in him as long as he maintains the courage to take his anxiety upon himself. In the act of the courage to be, the power of being is effective in us, whether we recognize it or not. Every act of courage is a manifestation of the ground of being, however questionable the content of the act may be....There are no valid arguments for the existence of God, but there are acts of courage in which we affirm the power of being whether we know it or not....Courage has revealing power, the courage to be is the key to being-itself." (3)

The affirmative 'Yes' character of the *Courage to Be*, in the here-and-now, is evident here. Tillich takes into account the questions and doubts about the existence of God, and even summarily dismisses rationalistic efforts to 'prove' the existence of God, as spurious distractions to the requirements of Being-itself. Certainly, Tolle takes a similar stand, seeing the arguments against divinity or Being as the blindness of a pain-body and folly, futility and hubris of the intellectual mind.

Tillich's feeling about the power of courage is clear in linking it to the existence of God—'whether we know it or not'; and the same attitude exists in Tolle who sees the denial of divinity or the sacred related to the fear of the unknown and ultimate meaninglessness.

"Theism transcended: the courage to take meaninglessness into itself presupposes a relation to the ground of being which we have called 'absolute faith'....The content of absolute faith is the God beyond God. It is absolute faith and its consequence, the courage that takes the radical doubt, the doubt about God, into itself, transcends the theistic idea of God." (4)

This is a mystical concept of God—reminiscent of Meister Eckhart's thinking about the 'God beyond God'. That said, Tillich believed that mysticism does not cure modern humans of alienation and their sense of emptiness and meaninglessness. This is where Tillich and Tolle really differ since Tolle affirms that if you are really living in the Now, the sense of emptiness or meaninglessness does not arise. Being or What-is is synonymous with God and there is no room in Tolle's vision for the existential nihilist who haunts the castle of Tillich's Protestant theism.

Living with Meaning and Purpose: Some Moral Precepts

Living with meaning and purpose means that you have recognized and accepted responsibility for your freedom as a sentient being. It means that you are a conscientious, responsible and courageous person who is willing to take chances in living since you realize that 'playing it safe' is a recipe for missing some of Life's most precious opportunities for actualizing your potentiality for happiness and self-realization.

Living with purpose and meaning means that *you are* an infinite Consciousness, soulful and related to a universal Self; and it is realizing the difference between *being and having*. When you live with meaning and purpose, you see how utterly contingent, conditional, and precarious each life-form is situated in the world. Then you realize that each life-form is sacred and it should be protected, revered, and nurtured due to its divine essence or embodied sense of Being.

Life, as it is manifesting, unfolding, and evolving through Nature, is a continual miracle and a mystery, *just as it-is*; and there is no meaning or sense in judging or condemning its various conditions just because they do not meet with your expectations or approval. However, the real human world of artifacts, institutions, and policies, is filled with innumerable horrors, stupidities, miseries, and misjudgments, all the time, everywhere. And no one can be entirely immune from making mistakes, trivial and tragic, that may change your life-situation and impact others negatively.

Becoming fully conscious in our Life-situation is all that we can do to become liberated or enlightened beings. If you are really present in this life-form, there is never a question of who am I, where am I going, or the meaning and purpose of Life. When 'you' are really present to and Conscious of your unique Life-form, its relations with others and the world, you can live more peacefully and harmoniously wherever you are. Life, nature, and the unknown Source of the universe, have created the Earth and all creatures upon it with infinite perfection, intelligence, and creativity.

The rest is really up to us since we have been given the potentiality, intelligence and creativity to shape our individual and collective existence on the Earth, as we desire it to be. And rather than being just a by-product of evolution, we can, to some degree, shape and determine our destiny in the world.

For example, there are many precepts and ideals for living a peaceful, loving, and joyful Life: Be Present; Stay Conscious; Love all sentient beings; and Perceive, cherish, and nurture human differences. Think deeply and meditate in total absorption. Feel the emotions of your body, mind and soul. Understand all that you can. Nurture your body, mind, and soul. Cherish all relationships. Actualize your potentialities for living and being. Be nonviolent, compassionate, and peaceful.

Even though we may have many moral precepts does not mean or 'prove' that we are moral beings. *Goodness* is not something we merely create on a whim, memorize precepts or maxims of, or pass a school exam about. Goodness exists naturally and ontologically or as the essence of our real being; and we can honor, recognize, and strive to cultivate Goodness in our everyday actions—just as we can learn to cultivate a garden of vegetables or flowers.

Goodness exists because Being exists and Being is the eternal Source and essence of Goodness. Evil, violence and injustice are the lack of Goodness due to the weakness of the will and failure of reason among human beings in society; and unlike universal Goodness, actual human goodness is dependent upon many functions of the self, the conditions of society, and the totality of relations in an individual's personal life. However, the potentiality of Goodness remains universal even though individuals and societies may fall into absolute violence, evil and injustice.

When we see radiant Goodness through our intuitive desire to know the truth, we awaken to the most profound reality of the universe. There is nothing that exceeds the power of Goodness when it is grounded in hope and the renewal of life. It enables us to overcome doubt, negativity, and the anxiety of existence, and to live with a courage-to-Be, no matter what horror, loses, and heartbreak we may suffer.

Absolute Goodness and a 'Nuclear Winter'

This life-form or existence is an incredible opportunity to experience who you are and get connected with Being or the Absolute Goodness that many seers, saints, and yogis have envisioned. There is really nothing that you should be embarrassed by or ashamed of, in believing that Something Absolute really exists. The only problem from an intellectual or empirical viewpoint is that Goodness in its absolute or timeless Form cannot be known—at least not in the so-called real world of things, ideas and persons.

The reason why Goodness cannot be known intellectually or perceptually is because it exists as an 'essence' of Being or a universal. Goodness in its absolute essence can only be 'known' intuitively or through a Revelation of Being. So if knowledge or intellectual understanding is less important to you than believing something absolute like Goodness, really exists in a higher dimension of reality, then there is no reason to reject Absolute Goodness.

If you imagine the most horrible thing that humans could do to one another—a 'Nuclear Winter' or Armageddon is one of those things. The major world powers are currently armed with Weapons of Mass Destruction that could completely destroy all life-forms of the Earth. Various studies by scientists have been conducted proving that a deadly Nuclear Winter would follow from only thirty medium sized nuclear bombs being exploded over as many major cities of the planet.

Assuming that you survived the initial attack and incineration of the thirty cities—a Nuclear Winter would make Life as we know it impossible on the Earth owing to poisonous gases in the atmosphere, a heavy cloud of pollution circling the Earth blocking off sunlight to the surface, and extremely cold temperatures that would follow everywhere, making human life unbearable if not impossible. The growing of food would be very difficult owing to the freezing temperatures and the darkness; and other food resources would be scarce to non-existent.

The madness of possessing such weapons is impossible to understand or morally justify. Of course, one can talk endlessly about National Security, Nuclear Deterrence and the Right of Self-Defense. But none of these moral, political and military claims is based upon a metaphysical absolute such as absolute Goodness or the sacred Life-force. Rather they are based upon fear, paranoia, distrust, power, ego, ideology, and greed.

It was essentially the inherent madness of the doctrine of Mutually Assured Destruction that brought the end to the Cold War in the Post World War II era, in 1989; that and the bankruptcy of the former Soviet Union to maintain the Arms Race with the West. Of course, it was Premier Gorbychev's vision of *Perestroika* or an open, free, and democratic Russia that would bring down the fragile dictatorship of the Soviet Union. Such courage and vision are rare among leaders, but it brought down the Berlin Wall, the symbol of division, antagonism and paranoia between the East and West, for over fifty years.

In addition to the political and psychological factors of the madness concerning nuclear weaponry are the cultural and educational systems of the world that are mired in relativistic, materialistic, and competitive values. 'Popular culture'—although globally connected through the Internet—remains distracted, entertained, and distanced from the underlying political, international, and military threats to human civilization. The 'higher culture' of education, the sciences, arts, and humanities is biased towards 'scientific materialism' or the intellectual model of skepticism, atheism, and dogmatic empiricism. And the religions of the world remain as divisive as they ever have been, especially since 9/11 and the new *Jihad* against the West among the extreme factions of Islam.

In the 5th century BCE, Plato gave us a view of eternal Goodness or what he believed to be the most perfect Republic, led by an 'enlightened philosopher' or one who has a vision of absolute Goodness. If you think of absolute Goodness present in this moment and world and not in some other world or Heavenly realm as Plato did, you can have an intuitive experience of Goodness and really see it everywhere existing by degree of perfection in various life-forms. If you remain open to the reality of absolute Goodness in the Now—in its essential Formlessness and relations to Being, Life, and Nature—you will begin to see how many beautiful, wonderful, and perfect life-forms there are in this world, and without your having to lift a finger, speak a word, or change a single thing.

Goodness and Morality

From the smallest subatomic forms to the largest galactic forms of the universe, there is the wonder of eternal Goodness, existing relatively, conditionally, and contingently, in the Now. The fluctuating power of 'evil' or what causes violence, pain and suffering in this world is evidence that Goodness—for whatever reasons, conditions, and contingencies—also fluctuates and changes through the cosmic Will. Goodness is supremely strong over all other tendencies of nature, society and humanity; and its dominance in this world fluctuates owing to the atavistic and retarded evolution of civilization, education, and our moral intelligence.

> 'Vice' or what is not right, healthy or conducive to 'virtue' are not independent forces in the world, but they arise mutually and reciprocally owing to their dialectical nature. The Life-force of spiritual energy exists in essential relation to nature or the primal ground of all life-forms. Goodness is the underlying or invisible moral condition of the real world, the world that is natural, social, and immediately present. Our moral judgments and decisions about right and wrong, undesirable or desirable, etc. tend to be superficial, reductionist, and distancing our acts of conscience from primal being and its inherent, absolute Goodness.

No matter how 'bad', violent, and insane an individual life-form, a group of individuals or and an entire nation-State may become, eternal Goodness or the Spirit of Being will eventually prevail and return human life-forms to more virtuous, nonviolent, and sane conditions of existence. Life is eternally cyclical throughout the karmic universe; Love and Strife are cosmic forces dialectically locked in an eternal struggle for the domination of history on Earth, as the ancient Greek philosopher, Empedocles, speculated; and just now, we are dominated by Strife.

If and when the Earth itself is destroyed by natural or cosmological forces—which the astronomers tell us is inevitable—or even by human means, universal Goodness or the moral essence of existence, will continue to exist in the universe; and the souls or essences of all sentient life-forms will persist until their karmic follies are extinguished by the transformative power of absolute Goodness and universal Love.

Acceptance and Nonviolence

Acceptance is one of the most important moral and psychological qualities of existence since it enables us to get along harmoniously with others. If you look in a mirror and do not like what you see, and then begin attacking the mirror, your madness will be evident. But as Tolle says, this is precisely the situation with people who cannot accept human differences or are intolerant towards the beliefs, ideas, or opinions of others. Their lives are one unending hell merely due to the habits of non-acceptance, intolerance, and prejudice. (5)

If we learn to accept ourselves as a totality—flawed, imperfect, or only relatively 'Good'—we can more readily see and accept other people and even non-human or animal beings. Acceptance may very well be the most important initial condition of *moral* action and thought, since the attitude of openness and trust is so basic to morality of any kind. In fact, whatever sense of goodness or virtue we express or seek, virtue always exists in relation to the primordial and eternal Goodness of existence. Thus, it is highly important that you are a morally sensitive person since Goodness is the essential, underlying condition of existence that has created and maintains the world.

Finally, if you are an accepting person, by habit, you have a much better chance of reducing the violence of the world. Accepting does not mean that you just roll over and play dead whenever trouble or conflict arises. It means that you do not resort to violence in your speech, thoughts and actions, to defend your ground or place in the world. If you find yourself in a threatened position, you may have every reason to defend yourself. But if you just threaten back, attack and fight with someone, you are only increasing the violence of your situation. And fighting in any form has only increased the violence of society and history is only a long nightmare due to the habit of violence that begins individually and spreads like a pandemic.

Truth as Naturalistic and Transcendental

The universal truth about earthly and cosmic existence is that all forms, whether life-forms or not, will be completely transformed by time and change. Certainty—of a naturalistic or empirical kind—is limited to the present moment of time and can only be known through the perceptions of consciousness and the various senses of the body. Consciousness is a byproduct of a healthy body and mind, but it disappears with death. In fact, birth, life, and death are absolute conditions of existence from the atheistic, naturalistic and scientific- materialist viewpoint. For the skeptic or materialist, there is no re-birth or survival of a soul, consciousness or transcendental Self since awareness, of any kind, cannot survive the death of a body or organism.

If you fully realize that this vital, healthy body will someday become a rotting corpse, which turns to dust, and then back into the elements of the Earth, in time, you will become aware of what human existence in its purely natural form means. Of course one must see that the whole panoply of emotions, thoughts, and relationships of each sentient life-form exists through the life-world of consciousness and its unique interior dialogue. Although great Mother Nature holds all sentient beings in her loving and sustaining embrace, their longevity is strictly limited, conditional and precarious. It is as if Nature herself has a divided mind about her human off-spring and that the experiment that she is condemned to endlessly repeat has little hope or prospect for a different outcome.

Thus, truth is temporal, organic, and historical on a natural plane of existence, and the Transcendence of death or nonbeing is non-existent. If we take the more inclusive view of reality i.e. that the naturalistic theory of truth is integral to universal Being or Life, then the myriad life-forms of the world are essences of the universal Life-force in ways that we may never completely understand.

Meanwhile, the empirical, behavioral and naturalistic sciences have separated themselves from the humanistic, contemplative and transcendental sciences in modern times. This has given the Great Divide between scientific and humanistic cultures in higher education. Most scientists avoid any reference to an Absolute of any substance like the plague; just as the humanists avoid the mathematics and measurements of the scientists for the contamination that it might bring to their disciplines. The truth is that both camps flail at a darkness of their own rather than nature's making. And for sake of an imaginary purity in their cognitive claims, they sacrifice a more inclusive sense of reality to dualistic roles and the illusion of a cloistered superiority.

Nature in general has no ultimate basis in reality beyond the presence of spirituality or Being itself. But the Truth about existence is not a question of either/or, i.e. nature or Spirit, existence or Transcendence, consciousness or Consciousness; both realms of experience and knowledge are needed for a genuine understanding of existential being. In short, deep understanding or Wisdom comes from the most inclusive view of reality—as incomplete as it always is—or one that is 'many-sided', as George Hegel of the 18th century held.

The Perennial problem in philosophy is that honest, educated and thinking persons will not agree about the many sides, faces or essences of Truth; and final answers are never as final as we may think since everything is always changing in ways that we cannot foresee with certainty.

An Existential View of Life

The emotion of sadness and even tragedy hangs over the mortality of each individual who is born, lives and dies; and no matter how insignificant or great the journey of individual existence, death is inevitable, natural or the 'Way of all things'. Whether a single human life is tragic, absurd, or insignificant is a matter of perspective and interpretation. Subjectivity or a transcendental view of Truth is inevitably biased, perspectival, and situated in the first person singular viewpoint; and this is a basic presupposition of phenomenology or the theory of consciousness that assumes consciousness is always embodied, situated in time and space, and privileges perception over conception, feeling over thinking and nature over transcendence.

The so-called 'pure consciousness' or Consciousness (capitalized) in existence, is inevitably tainted, corrupted or contaminated by human subjectivity and existence in its supposed subtlety. Friedrich Nietzsche, the atheistic existentialist, saw this natural (existential) condition of knowledge as clearly as anyone has, but it failed to free him from the tyranny of his own language, thought and delusion. In fact, the intensity with which Nietzsche gazed into his own soul, will and deep self eventually drove him insane.

Nietzsche's well-known madness cannot be understood through conventional or biographical evidence. We must recognize that both he and Soren Kierkegaard saw into the abyss of human existence and saw the same deep and unshakable, human-all-too human truths: 1, that the split or division between the physical and spiritual dimensions of experience, is a byproduct of several historical causes; 2, a dualistic language, 3, a conditioned consciousness split between subjectivity and objectivity, 3, finite reason and passion, 4, and the individual structure and function of consciousness which renders our knowledge limited and incomplete, in a word, *perspectival.*

Religion, for Kierkegaard and other existentialists, exists on the basis of faith and passion—not reason or the intellect. Reason can 'prove' something like the existence of God true or false, if and only if there is a prior emotional disposition supporting the conclusion; but *reason alone* can prove nothing that can overturn the passion of the true believer. For example, Kierkegaard has written that to believe in God requires a leap of irrational faith that a 'finite being can be infinitely happy'—and *that in the face of the objective uncertainty about God's existence.*

Tolle's genius is that he is able to see through the whole confusion and despair of human knowledge. His vision of Being integrates the wholeness of existence, knowledge, and experience in the great net of a higher Consciousness that is God-like. He does this with great ease and a genuine humility, grace, and balance. He has found the secret to Life through his heart and sense of Consciousness, without sacrificing reason or faith and with a pain-free body or one that is free of negativity and violence.

The Way and Nowness of Chinese Philosophies

Rather than despairing over the relativity of human bias, we must learn to celebrate, protect and cultivate our own Way in the world. This obsession with excellence is central to the humanistic philosophy of Confucius, China's most important philosopher, who was pre-eminent in scholarship, education, and citizenship. Confucius believed that human nature is primarily social and only secondarily individual—since only hermits, saints and animals can live in isolation from others. By contrast, Confucius extolled form and ritual, *roles* and group-belonging, family and loyalty to the ruler—collectively termed *li*. In contrast to the Taoists, one's participation in society became all important in Confucian China; and this ideology that dominated the former imperial ruling class of China for over two-thousand years, is still ghostly present in the Chinese central government that is guided by a Maoist dictatorship.

What Confucian philosophy lacked was a sufficient inner life of individual consciousness that Indian Buddhism importantly provided by the 5th century CE. At the same time, indigenous Chinese Taoism added the cosmic or ontological dimension (*Tao*=Being) to the social philosophy of Confucian education. Meditation or concentration experiences upon the *Tao, Emptiness, and Buddha nature*—all experienced in the present moment or Now—are central experiences to the Taoists and the Buddhists which became even most evident in *Chan* Buddhism (or Zen) or their synthesis in medieval China.

An even greater synthesis occurred by the 12th century, when Chu Hsi appeared, purifying and clarifying Confucian philosophy with a bold interpretation and synthesis of key traditional concepts: the Great Ultimate (*T'ien*), humanity (*jen*), material-force or energy (*chi*), the social principle (*li*), natural and cosmic energy (*wu-wei*), and the investigation of things (*ko-wu*). This synthesis of concepts became known as neo-Confucianism, a tradition that is alive and well today. Master Chu Hsi wrote:

"Throughout the universe there are both principle (li) and material-force. Principle refers to the Way [the *Tao* of nature] which is above the realm of corporeality and is the Source from which all things are produced. Material-force refers to material objects, which are within the realm of corporeality; it is the instrument by which things [the 10,000 things of the world] evolved. Therefore in the production of man and things, they must be endowed with principle before they have material force, and they must be endowed with material force before they have corporeal form." (6)

Chu Hsi also made the case for a Perennial philosophy from the major elements of the Taoist, Buddhist and Confucian philosophies in his vision of a sublime Unity. And although his preference for the Confucian tradition is obvious, his neo-Confucian philosophy of the twelfth century is a rather modern view of much older philosophies.

Twentieth Century China and Western Capitalism

Due to the revolutionary changes of 20th century China, the old philosophies of China have been largely forgotten. The extent to which modern Chinese society—and especially since the rise of the 'People's Republic of China' (the PRC) in 1949— has embraced Marxist and Capitalist ideologies of the West, is strikingly contradictory. On the surface, at least, 21st century China appears to be obsessed with the Nowness of economic, technological and cultural change. The new China enthusiastically embraces the ideology of western Capitalism which justifies great wealth and privilege to the few, and struggle, poverty and sacrifice for everyone else; while the official political ideology or propaganda favors the needs and interests of the *proletariat* or the working class over the bourgeoisie.

Compared with the humanistic philosophies of ancient China, i.e. Taoism, Confucianism and Buddhism—the Communistic *and* Capitalistic philosophies of China are pragmatic, scientific, and materialistic. The points of difference, friction and outright contradiction between these philoso-phies and ideologies of contemporary China are outstanding. However, a similar cultural pluralism exists in other major nation-states of the world, reinforcing the *Perennial Wisdom* that ideologies and philosophies may come and go like the tidal changes of a great ocean, but an Eternal Matrix, Life-force or Oneness exists just beneath of the surface changes of every-thing and it remains the Same.

In 1973, Chairman Mao zi Tung and U.S. President Richard Nixon opened the Chinese gates to Western Capitalism; and as if to seal the deal, Mao's successor, Premier Deng Xiao Ping, declared that it is 'good to get rich'. Although the old philoso-phies of Taoism, Confucianism and Buddhism are present in Capitalistic China, they are destined to all but disappear in time unless members of the present and future generations of Chinese people re-consider their goal of 'getting rich'. Of course, the same criticism about contemporary China could be made about Western societies, in spades, where the Capitalistic ideology con-trols the political, legal and social institutions and which reflects the hierarchical, economic class system.

Capitalism unchecked, unregulated, and lawless, is the rule of the jungle—'one against all and all against one— as is evi-dent on Wall Street or the major gambling Casino of the world. Capitalism t is the extension of Machiavelli to every sphere of Life-in-society. In Capitalism, it is the end result or product that matters, i.e. financial power, the accumulation of wealth, and the elevation of personal or institutional status; and among the many means that Corporate Capitalism has of maintaining its power in the real, social world are: the control and manipulation of workers, a passive and brain-washed population of consum-ers, the control of manufacturing, marketing and distribution of products and services, the exploitation of publicly owned, natu-ral resources, the ownership of banks, financial systems, and the mass media, and an advertising system that aims at the rich, the indebted and the poor to desire products that are often shoddy, dangerous and useless.

If Capitalism was based upon serving human needs and elevating interests above the material and financial levels of existence, it would be one thing. Its primary aim is anything but the welfare of the people or the health of the Earth unless these values could be seen serve its bottom-line mentality for profits.

Although greed is perhaps too banal and worn-out a term to apply to the chief emotion directing Capitalism, there is no term that more accurately represents its motivation; of course, there are similar psychological and moral terms that condemn the motivations of the typical entrepreneur like selfishness, self-centeredness and narcissism. Arguably, these terms also characterize human beings everywhere, to varying degrees; and in a cultural system that values appearance, status and material things as much as it does, the narcissistic personality is bound to be endemic.

Capitalism is more ruthless than the raw-toothed hunger of the jungle since it is based upon appetites that cannot be satisfied. If animals in the wild are hungry, they instinctively go after the kill to satisfy their hunger pains. But human beings, caught in the juggernaut of Capitalism, are brain-washed and manipulated by its advertising system to believe that they have to have X, Y and Z to be happy; and of course the advertisers and promoters of Capitalism are right, to a limited degree: the typical human being can be persuaded to consume what they do not need to be happy. But what the consumer is left with, at the end of the day or his entire life, are debts that he or she has worked a life-time to pay off.

The solution to the problem of Capitalism must come from the counter-emotions and ideals of economic justice or fairness which means, if you are poor, paying workers at the bottom of the social pyramid a wage that they can live and thrive on; this and the moral empathy for the have-nots or the victims of the class-based hierarchies of power and privilege.

Last, China's political philosophy is based upon a Marxist utopian ideology from 1949 to 1976, where the working classes of the world were imagined to overthrow the ruling class and seize control of a world government that is truly democratic or classless; but if and only if there is a total collapse or destruction of the Capitalist economic system is a Marxist utopia conceivable; and that possibility is increasingly unlikely given the new financial wealth and material success, especially in countries like China and India and the rest of the developing world.

In Mao tzu Dung's memorable words, in his first speech to the Congress of the People's Republic of China, in 1949, he wrote that 'China is not yet ready for a democracy' and according to the silent members of China's ruling political and economic elite, it still is not. In the coming years and decades, China seems destined to solidity the economic, political and technocratic elite that rule the country with an iron fist. And once the rich and powerful are sufficiently insulated from the resentful many, it is only a matter of dribble-down economics and the credit system that pacifies the hungry masses and guards the elite against all revolutionary intentions. (7)

Agape, Compassion and the Designer

Human compassion or *Agape*—the caring for others that is actively engaged—is the moral and psychological way of really Being-with-others. When we see that we all live in 'a yellow submarine' and on the same spaceship, Earth, we begin to feel that wealth and the pursuit of it, for its own sake, becomes meaningless, futile, and a waste of precious life-time. *Now* is forever or eternal; but in this life-form, body, and world, we are entirely mortal, finite beings.

The fear of death or non-being is first experienced deeply by every sensitive child who is seven or eight year old; and it is this fear that persists and grows underground in the self into adulthood, influencing many habits, strategies and adaptations to deny its hold on us in the unconsciousness.

The many forms of material and immaterial existence are grounded in the formless realm of Being; yet even beyond the realms of desire, form and formlessness—the eternal Mystery is ubiquitous. We can only know or intuit and experience the Mystery of Being through the act of surrendering or letting-go of the mind, ego, and worldliness. The sensing of what is ultimate or mysterious may have little to show for itself at cognitive or intellectual levels; yet the mystical impulse in human beings everywhere has persisted throughout the last five thousand years, with no end in sight since it brings the most inclusive or integrative perspective into Life and living.

No one should expect that academics are going to come to rescue of the established religions which are nearly everywhere collapsing, in disarray and conflict with each other. In fact, the nihilistic and atheistic tendencies of most academics dover-tails quite well with the prevailing materialistic and financial frenzy on the right side of the political system. Considering how much propaganda has been spread the apologists of Pragmatism and similar secular philosophies that tout science as the only way to truth and knowledge, one wonders why a science of spirituality has not been rushed in to replace the ailing religion of spirituality.

The beauty of Now is that it makes all of us—the most stupid, ill-informed, wise, and talented among us—equal and the same, before existential Being. The savant, the scholar, the prescient— all are leveled by finite being and yet elevated to infinite degrees of Consciousness, at the same time. In the Now, all knowledge is collapsed into Being and nothingness, infinity and finitude, eternity and temporality. Formal or merely academic education is exposed at its roots and branches in serious decay owing to its clerical and bureaucratic forms of knowledge that dominate society through the methods of quantification, verbal analysis, and abstract reasoning; and in the obsession with grades, degrees and careers in higher education, the immediate needs, interests and truths of subjective experience are all but ignored and passed over as merely personal and irrelevant to the educational process.

The *evolution of consciousness* can be traced back to animal instincts, drives, and needs; but its ultimate origin cannot be. Today's neuro-and-cognitive scientists enthusiastically mine the brain for new knowledge about how we think, but too few ever think or see that much more can be discerned from such activity. One exception to the rule among neuro-scientists is Dr. Francis Collins who successfully headed the Human Genome Project; and Collins wrote the book titled *The Language of God.* Collins quickly realized that the human genome could not have just randomly or by blind chance happened in nature or through evolutionary processes alone. He reasoned that there had to be a master-Designer, super-Intelligence and infinite Consciousness supplying the original intention or plan the human *genome,* and *Evolution* or the energy of organic nature (*prakriti*) did the rest.

Deeply embedded in the 'Language of God' or the human genome is the Perennial Wisdom of the universe. It is the God of nonviolence, the Reverence for Life, and a universal Compassion for all sentient beings. It is this Wisdom that returns after all wars and genocides, periods of despair and hopelessness, with a stronger desire for the ideals of peace, justice and equality. The wisdom of the human body is sacred because the body, soul and mind are of divine origin in design and intention. There is a Perennial Wisdom of spirituality in the body and soul of all sentient beings is a treasure that can be discovered and experienced by everyone.

In sum, nature—caring, conscious and compassionate— is a gift to the Earth and all sentient beings, by the One God of Abraham, Moses, Jesus, Mohammad and the Vedas. Truth, change, and morality are all for the glory of an unknown God, the creator and liberator of human beings who seek to free themselves from the tyranny of the doubting mind, the de-humanizing masks of the ego and the violent world. The image of finitude, mortality and re-birth is symbolized in the flight of the arrow that always returns to the Earth; but it is Creation as transformation and transmutation that transcends mortality, through higher Consciousness or the universal Self of the infinite Designer.

Chapter 22

BEING, CONSCIOUSNESS AND WISDOM

What is the relation of Being to ordinary consciousness and the Perennial Wisdom? How does intellectual understanding enable one to experience higher Consciousness and the mystical Unity of Being? How can Being remain the same or eternal while everything else is constantly changing? And why is Being manifested through higher Consciousness and *ordinary* experience and knowledge and wisdom of the present moment?

"With all their science, those people in Paris are not able to discern what God is in the least of creatures—not even a fly." Meister Eckhart

"It is by the power of Buddha only that one can see that pure land (of Buddhas) as clear as one sees the image of one's face reflected in the transparent mirror held up before one." Amitayur-Dhyana-Sutra

"Let nobody presume upon his own powers for such exaltation or uplifting of the heart or ascribe it to his own merits. For it is certain that this comes not from human deserving but is a divine gift." Richard of Saint-Victor

"When the source of immortal joy is opened within us, it flows and saturates every fiber of our being, internal and external, and makes our life at once a waveless peace and ceaseless thrill of ecstasy. Death, fear and grief have no significance for us." Swami Ramdass

"If once a man in intellectual vision did really glimpse the bliss and joy therein, then all his sufferings, all God intends that he should suffer, would be a trifle, a mere nothing to him; nay, I say more, it would be pure joy and pleasure." Eckhart

Meister Eckhart, the Christian mystic and visionary thinker, beautifully expresses his view of the *intellectual vision that really glimpses the joy and bliss* within; then and perhaps only then will we realize that human suffering is nothing compared to the perfect joy and bliss that God has intended that we can experience and know. Eckhart's view of the intellectual vision compares quite favorably with that of the Zen Buddhist mystic according to D.T. Suzuki.

Detachment in Zen and Christian Mysticism

In D.T. Suzuki's incisive essay on Christian and Buddhist mysticism, he compares the writings of the Christian mystic, Meister Eckhart, to his own Zen Buddhist philosophy. What he finds is remarkably insightful for both traditions since he discovers places where they seem to perfectly agree. Early in the essay, Suzuki comments: "Eckhart's experiences are deeply, basically, abundantly rooted in God as Being which is at once being and not-being; he sees in the meanest thing among God's creatures all the glories of his is-ness. The Buddhist enlightenment is nothing more than this experience of is-ness or suchness which in itself has all the possible values we humans can conceive." (1)

The parallel between God's is-ness and Buddha's enlightenment becomes even more in a similar comparison; a Zen master asked a monk: "'Where does this monk want to find the Buddha? Is this not a silly question?' Indeed, we are all apt to forget that every one of us is Buddha himself. In the Christian way of saying, in the Christian way of saying, this means that we are all made in the likeness of God or, in Eckhart's words, that 'God's is-ness is my is-ness and neither more nor less.'" (2)

Meanwhile, there is a clear distinction between 'God' and 'Godhead' in Meister Eckhart's vision of things. In the former, 'God comes and goes in the world, works and rests and is becoming something or another all the time; and in this activity, that humans name, describe and conceive of 'God' as their Savior of everything.' But 'Godhead' is above and beyond the

'God', the image, symbol and object of worship; and Godhead is "immovable, imperturbable, inaccessible" in Suzuki's words. It is 'God' who humans perceive and conceive of, but Godhead remains Eternal within and beyond time in the Now of ownmost inwardness.

Or consider the view of the Indian philosopher, Coomaraswamy, about cultural comparisons and eternity itself. "Eckhart presents an astonishingly close parallel to Indian modes of thought; some whole passages and many single sentences read like a direct translation from Sanskrit....But what is proved by analogies is not the influence of one system of thought upon another, but the coherence of the metaphysical tradition in the world and at all times." (3)

Finally, to detachment itself; Eckhart says that any desire, wanting or preferences creates difference and separation and thus the dualities of alienation. "Perfect detachment...is minded to be master of itself, loving none and hating none, having neither likeness nor unlikeness, neither this nor that, to any creature; the only thing it desires is to be one and the same. For to be either this or that is to want something. He who is this or that is somebody; but detachment wants altogether nothing." And Suzuki comments that where there is 'God' there is movement, work, somebody and something. 'Perfect detachment' or liberation is impossible in the real world; but where there is 'Godhead' we find the unmoved, a nothing where there is no path to reach. It is absolute nothingness; therefore it is the ground of being from whence all beings come." (4)

The Buddhist doctrine of *Shunyata* or absolute nothingness and formless being and Eckhart's mystical vision of the 'Godhead' seem a nearly perfect match—once the symbols drop away and the only eternity remains; and the really wise are speechless.

The Dialectical Dimensions of Being

We are accustomed or conditioned to believe that only forms exist; and if we define a form as that which is impermanent, it is true. But if we reflect upon the essence of consciousness rather than its 'nature' (material conditions) we find ourselves in the higher dimensions of Being or who we are. Existence means that forms with all their structures, functions, and essences dominate our awareness or what we ordinarily call reality.

To speak about the realm of formlessness, we need to enter an altogether different dimension of reality, a more pervasive one from which all forms arise and to which they return. Many have referred to it as the meta-physical realm because it is assumed to lie beyond or apart from the physical realm of forms. Another way of referring to formlessness—and one which Tolle seems to prefer—is the unmanifested realm of Being. However else you may think about a formless realm of reality, it does not exist separately from the realm of forms.

An analogy can be used of a great ocean—this one as large or larger than the formed universe itself—that is the realm of formlessness, an oceanic dimension of pure energy out of which the various orders of the known universe eventually evolve and to which they devolve or return. The physical, mental, and spiritual phenomena that we know from experience, both actual and possible, remembered and imagined, perceived and conceived, etc., are only so many differing orders of forms, appearing to us like the endless waves upon the surface of the ocean, and dissolving into foam when they crash upon our shores of existence.

Another analogy for the dialectical ('dia'=twofold or dual) relationship between the formed and formless realms of Being, is to think about the Taoist symbol of the *Yin and Yang.* A circle is divided by a curved line, and within the two halves of the circle are two smaller circles. Each of the large halves of the great circle are shaded dark and white, and the small circle within each half is shaded an opposite shade from its surroundings.

The most basic assumption about form and formlessness is that opposites are contained within each other and thus they complement or complete each other. The principle that opposites co-arise and complete each other can be applied to nature, human existence, and Being. And it can be seen in everything that we do, think about, and desire since there is always a hidden, deeper, and unmanifested dimension in the forms of reality.

Knowledge, Meditation, and Everyday Existence

The knowing process is a continual pushing against the known boundaries of experience and perception into the unknown that is formless and infinite. If calculated against the magnitudes of nature, time, and the universe, our present knowledge of reality is peppered by many more questions than we can adequately answer. By analogy, the space within atoms and between atoms— the Void or Emptiness— is far greater than the 'weights' of atomic particles; and the number of neurons or cells in our brain may exceed the number of stars in our galaxy by several orders of magnitude.

Numbers and quantities aside, it is the *qualities* of Being or the moral, aesthetic, intellectual and spiritual totality that mostly matter to us. If you raise the question of origin and destiny, i.e. where do things come from and where do they go?—you can begin to see and experience the formless realm in the present moment. There are also the riddles known as 'koans' in the Zen Buddhist tradition that will have a similar effect: Which came first, the chicken or the egg? A tree falls in the forest and there is no one around to hear it; does it make a sound? What is the sound of one hand clapping? And so forth.

There is an unorthodox form of negative knowledge known as no-knowledge in Buddhist literature. It is the result of meditating upon the profound emptiness or nothingness of forms that rise and fall within the field of mind. No-mind or no-self is the negation of the inveterate tendency to conceptualize and think thoughts in the endless stream of meaning and meaninglessness. No-knowledge is simply a way of 'emptying the mind' of perceptions, thoughts, and desires or all forms of experience and knowledge and engaging the deepest dimension of all—profound emptiness, stillness, and formlessness.

Thus defined, no-knowledge is a negation of the formed world experienced in the surfaces and depths of consciousness and it has no attachment to forms or their meanings. No-knowledge is this same consciousness, experience, and quality of awareness brought to the everyday world of life that can make the most profound difference to self-being-in-the-world. In this context or frame of experience, *meditation* is the gentle art of turning inwardly in the awareness of Being and learning to let-go of all forms of existence.

Awakening to the self of higher Consciousness can make the most significant difference in the life-world of the meditating yogi, especially if the yogi is serious in intention, good-hearted, and guided by noble purpose. Of course, the most subtle benefits of meditating are not measurable although they are knowable through qualitative consciousness or the subjective states of awareness. The main goal of meditating is to awaken the total self to Being-in-existence, at perceptual, conceptual and intuitive levels of experience.

Albeit, there are many reasons or aims of meditation—from the mundane to the most ethereal. Essentially, the experience allows us to know what is called 'Cosmic Consciousness' or the farthest reaches of experience. In mystical philosophy, meditation is a direct, immediate and *noetic* (intuitive) experience of the formless realm beyond the raucous noise and clamor of daily existence. In existential philosophy, meditation allows us to awaken to personal existence, the experiences and qualities of body and consciousness, problems of society, and conflicts of Being-in-the-world.

Meditation makes possible intuitive experiences or 'glimpses' of primal Being. It is an essential means for intuiting Being through an absorption of the soul. Meditation is the inward turning of consciousness upon the body-Self or the essence (soul) of who you are; and it is a phenomenal discovery of the Unity of self and other, meaning and purpose, and the inner and outer realms of existence.

Although the meditative *glimpses* of Being are precious and insightful, they are not a substitute for dealing with the continuous, ongoing challenge of life-situations that arise in the journey of the soul in everyday existence.

Meaning and the Formless Realm of Being

The knowledge of forms is relative, contingent, and conditional whereas the formless realm of Being is 'unknowable' through ordinary consciousness or means. If we claim that the realm of formlessness is absolute, necessary, and unconditional, we would use words that are empty of ordinary cognitive meaning. It is assumed that the manifested realm of Being is the visible side of the formless or unmanifested realm. In other words, physical, psychological, social, and higher forms of consciousness are the perceived, experienced, and symbolic manifestations of the unmanifested realm which is formless, infinite, and eternal.

In reality, eternity and temporality, infinity and finitude, etc., cannot be separated in the seamless web of universal Being. They co-exist in all experiences of consciousness and everyday reality. We cannot know and experience the realm of formlessness in the same way that we know and experience the realm of forms; similarly, we can stand on the shore of a great ocean (the formless realm) and observe its surface waves (forms) building, breaking, and crashing to the shore, at our feet; but we cannot know the formless realm through ordinary perception, sensation and conception.

The difference between the realm of forms and the realm of formlessness is that the former can have intellectual content and symbolic value while the latter is neither perceived nor conceived but only assumed to exist. The formless realm is almost entirely resistant to our usual habits of mind, i.e., perceiving, conceptualizing and meaning-making; yet it is the Source of everything that is known and knowable in the material, intellectual and spiritual world of forms.

Any analogy of formlessness like an 'ocean' can be misleading since it is 'formless'. In reality, the energy of formlessness is *chaotic, irrational, and unseen* compared to the visible order of the everyday world. To call the formless realm 'chaotic' may be misleading too, but the word denotes only an unformed or *inchoate* state of Being, so far as we can know. It does appear to be 'irrational' or absurd even since we cannot comprehend formlessness through the intellect. What we are left with is only an inference, an intuitive and noetic glimpse or insight of what could be true, until we awaken to the highest level of Consciousness.

Consciousness, Self-knowledge and Evolution

What is evolution? Does consciousness evolve or grow and develop through time and experience? Or is consciousness, in its highest potentiality, something permanent and unchanging? And what is the function of consciousness in self-knowledge?

It may well be that consciousness in its myriad connections with the human nervous system of the body is pre-wired or connected with the Perennial or cyclic wisdom of the universe—as the ancients believed. Tolle implies that higher Consciousness, i.e. the essence (soul) of existence—is the perfection of Being in its embodied or changing form. He asserts that Consciousness (God?) is permanent or changing and it does not evolve or grow and develop in complexity or potentiality. Thus, the 'evolution is consciousness' is just another popular myth or illusion of mind.

We are intuitively aware that we exist as a total or real self; and that everything else may be uncertain or only approximately known by comparison. In this sense, the certainty of self-awareness is the most important basis for knowledge of any kind since if we doubt that we really exist then everything else is also subject to doubt. Thus the forms of knowledge that we are most certain about are ones that require no 'proof' beyond *intuition* or a felt certainty involving insight.

If we ask what is the basis for consciousness?—we may be staggered by the possibilities. For example, 'chit' refers to absolute consciousness in Hindu Vedanta or 'chitta' refers to the totality of mental processes in same tradition; and in the construction 'Chit-Shakti', it refers to consciousness as the supreme energy of the universe. In the phenomenal relativism of Western materialism, consciousness always has an object in the formed or manifested world that it refers to; in other words, consciousness does not arise independently of the objective world or subjective being of personal experience.

From a materialistic perspective, if we attribute qualities like 'pure', 'precious', 'translucent' or 'absolute' to Consciousness, these words may sound alluring and exotic but they are also rather empty of meaning or real significance. In this context (the materialist), the 'evolution of consciousness' must refer to the progressive growth and development of a person in the context of real existence since personal being is inextricably linked to consciousness—in a relative and not an absolute sense.

If we speak pragmatically or even existentially about the evolution of consciousness, we are left standing and holding an empty bag. We simply cannot know the growth of consciousness except through the quantitative measures and qualitative experiences of the formed and changing world and the inferences that we make thereof.

On the other hand, if we meditate or just 'watch' how intangible forms rise and fall within the field of awareness—or how tangible things come and go, appear and disappear in the so-called real world, we will not necessarily get any closer to understanding what the evolution or growth of consciousness means. Our view of consciousness as 'permanent and unchanging' or 'evolving and changing' can be resolved if and only if we make the distinction between ordinary and Extra-ordinary consciousness or conventional and Transcendental consciousness.

If we admit that everything in the realm of forms evolves and devolves, grows and declines, in time and existence, why would consciousness be an exception to this truth? At a conventional or ordinary level of existence, consciousness grows, changes, develops in complexity of functions and richness of understandings;

in a word, consciousness evolves at the manifested level of existence. However, at a transcendental level, consciousness is absolute, pure, or *Isvara*-like in its Unmanifested states; and at this level, consciousness exists as a potentiality of the soul or the essence of who we are.

In sum, consciousness arises through the sacred, infinite energy of the unmanifested realm of existence. In its various situations of existence, consciousness is necessarily linked to subjective being and the objective world through its inherently unifying energy. At a transcendental and infinite level, it is eternal, higher, and absolute, embodying the knowledge of creative Being; while at mundane, empirical and ordinary levels, it is finite, fallible and relatively situated in the real world.

The Perennial aim of existence is to discover, learn and evolve through ordinary consciousness— the transcendental source of the universe, and so to liberate ourselves from cyclic existence. Our means for accomplishing this heroic goal or purpose are through the various and sundry functions of body-Consciousness, the roles that people choose to play in society, and the use, enjoyment, and potentialities of total Being.

Breakthrough to Higher Consciousness

If you believe in the lawful repulsion and attraction of cosmic forces, i.e. gravity and anti-gravity, electromagnetism, weak and strong atomic forces, then there is good reason to believe that the realm of formlessness may be quite different from what we have thought. Although the biblical God of final judgments and cosmic justice may only be a quaint fiction or image of how things are—recent discoveries in astrophysics gives us an image of how weird reality appears to be, which means that anything may be possible from the quantum and relativistic perspectives.

Unfortunately we do not yet have a comparable science of morality to that of astrophysics. But neither science nor religion can give us a complete understanding of reality. The present uncertainty in human knowing is only a new interpretation of some old dilemmas and conundrums. The new forms of knowledge and data are the result of advanced technology from the digital age. And although there have been some impressive breakthroughs in our factual knowledge of human genetics, the brain and many functions in the body, no one really knows or understands what 'it all means'.

The real 'breakthroughs' in human understanding will occur from those who know enough to put it all together into a coherent vision and express it in a form that can readily be comprehended. The term 'breakthrough' assumes that there is an obstacle or barrier to greater understanding or insight that has been overcome or penetrated. In Tolle's philosophy and that of other Perennialists, the 'breakthrough' is the realization of a deep Being-in-the-world.

In the New Age culture of human potentiality, from the late 1960's, higher consciousness, self-actualization and guru-worship have been somewhat cultist in nature. Even though 'higher consciousness' has become merely another consumable object of the market place, there is a philosophical basis for it—if one can surrender the ego and its delusional states of mind—in the interpenetration of the manifested and unmanifested realms of real Being. The chakras or energy sources of the inner body are involved in such experiences, and the anatomical and physiological systems of the body play their parts in the creation of this this unique and liberating experience.

There are no flashing lights, pyrotechnic storms, or neon-signs within awareness pointing the way to the spirituality of a 'higher consciousness'. In fact, it is in the realm of ordinary, everyday awareness and experience where 'breakthroughs' can only occur. In this context—the pragmatic one—there is something inherently ridiculous in speaking about 'higher' or 'lower' consciousness, since these are only metaphors or symbols for differing states of awareness. Furthermore, the totality of Now, in Tolle's philosophy, implies present time, Life, and the essences of Being.

Of course, one can dress up the insight into the formless realm of Being in all kinds of ways —as has been done in the history of metaphysics and religious spirituality. But the 'break-throughs' of consciousness, vision or speculative knowledge have not significantly increased our fund of wisdom as the result of the recent visions of extraordinary individuals. Rather most if not all of them have only served to reinforce the inherited wisdom from the past, which exists for all those with the seriousness of mind, sufficient time and commitment to fathom or comprehend through the sacred Texts, lives, and experiences that reveal the essential truths about reality.

History is only the beginning of philosophy and real understanding. One must go beyond names, dates, and events, to the why, what, and wherefore of life-situations, to the essence and Being of wisdom, for insight and the growth of consciousness. One must bring wisdom to events or what actually happens to see the Truth that lies beyond them. 'Facts' always require consciousness of understanding that people bring to data and events. The beginning, middle, and ending of any human life-form is strongly influenced by values or fulfilled needs and interests that serve or take-away from consciousness the character of human bias and perspective.

Of course, one can level a similar criticism at other areas of 'knowledge' especially ethics and politics, and wonder why these areas of knowledge have remained so stagnant and non-progressive. Much of this has to do with the herd factor or mass consciousness in human knowledge. It is the consciousness of conventional morality that determines the anatomy of a given culture and the cunning of leaders to manipulate human emotions and desires. Thus in speaking about a 'higher' Consciousness or any consciousness whatsoever, we need to see the truths about society as a whole to understand why a 'higher' Consciousness is always deemed to be so 'extraordinary'; in fact, enlightened consciousness exists as a potentiality in every human being.

The truth may be that humankind is too given to inertia of the will that stifles striving for values any higher than are absolutely necessary for survival, procreation, and adaptation to the status quo in society. In Yogic terms, the mass of human beings are often stuck in the bottom three chakras of experience and living, owing to the hierarchical and oppressive nature of civilization. The spiritual or higher Consciousness that Tolle and other extraordinary individuals like him articulate and embody is the actualized, evolutionary potentiality of everyone; yet it remains largely a well-kept secret among the comparatively few persons who study philosophy and other such matters.

However, Tolle and others like him, are doing their best to inform the public at large that the Truth that redeems our time on Earth, is available, in Here-and-Now, and it is within your awareness in the form of higher Consciousness. The experience brings us the most intimate knowledge of Being or the perennial Truth about existence, an essential aspect of which teaches that you, as an embodied soul of eternity, are a sacred part of divine Creation.

This comparatively simple awareness when it is not hedged in by philosophical doubts and questions is one that can deliver us from the worst tribulations that this worldly existence can bring to us and free us, once and for all, from metaphysical terror.

Consciousness as Creative

The essential way in which we can know, on an intuitive level, that formlessness is real and not an imaginary construct is through the experience of everyday consciousness and our total life-form. Just hold up your hand and look at it; and just consider how it is possible that you can even see it, and that the appearance of your hand, 'out-there' in space, is separate from 'you' or Consciousness. Is it not a Mystery that 'you', the essential, timeless, and infinite 'you' is this very Consciousness? And it is this Consciousness that possesses the power to re-make or destroy the world.

Once you awake from the sleep of everyday life, and see the world through an awakened consciousness, you can decide with an entirely new sense of the world, what to do with the rest of your life. It is an experience that occurs over and over again in the course of most people's lives and its significance is great for the breakthroughs in creative consciousness that can occur. Imagine beginning to start your whole life over again, as quickly as the insight occurs! Yet it is the power of creativity that everyone possesses through the miracle of an awakened consciousness.

Tolle writes about creative consciousness in many places. Below is one of the most significant passages:

"The primary factor in creation is consciousness. No matter how active we are, how much effort we make, our state of consciousness creates the world, and if there is no change on that inner level, no amount of action will make any difference. We would only re-create modified versions of the same world again and again, a world that is an external reflection of the ego." (5)

Language often misleads and confuses us into believing certain realities that are only distortions or exaggerations of reality. At one level all language creates a separate sense of reality that is purely symbolic and metaphoric. For example, the words 'pure' 'impure' 'inner' 'outer' 'higher' 'lower' etc. can be quite misleading since there is nothing existing entirely separately from contingent, conditional, and formed reality; and for all that we can know about reality, it is essentially and existentially determined by the first person viewpoint of subjective Consciousness—meaning 'You'; and therefore the unmanifested, unseen, and hidden realm of existence may all be an illusion, a mere *bewitching* of language.

Remember too, that when Siddhartha, the Buddha, had his famous breakthrough of consciousness at Bodh-gaya after continuously meditating for 49 days, he merely discovered 'who he was' or awakened to 'Bodhi', a perfected knowledge of reality. And although many interpretations and numerous schools of thought have arisen from this one historic, world-changing event, you possess that same potentiality of the historic Buddha! –So what are you waiting for? (6)

Consciousness and Evolution

We are temporal, spatial, and organic life-forms. The perspective of formlessness or eternity and infinity arises when we begin to think about ultimate ends or beginnings. There is an obvious difference between contingent life-forms and formlessness. However, this is not seen as a 'problem' but only as a challenge to Consciousness to remain Present in the eternal Now where life-forms and formlessness co-exist continuously and in a seamless unity.

Consciousness is the unmanifested, eternal realm of formlessness. It is the appearance of the changing world as we know and create it, in the meta-region of experience. But due to the Presence of Spirit in the real world, Consciousness appears or manifests at all levels, structures, and functions of a life-form; and it can also be known through the energies, structures, and functions of the chakra centers experienced in Yoga philosophy.—Consciousness follows the Path of the 'One' manifesting into the 'many' forms of the world.

We evolve or grow through activities of many kinds and yet it is only the inner state of Being that remains most important in the midst of any other activity. In conventional terms, if we have a positive state of awareness and believe that we are doing the right thing, in our active doing, then progress can be realized on a personal level. It—or any notion of 'progress' or creative development—becomes far more complex in our relations and roles with others since we exist as separate, unique, and self-centered beings with differing values and interests that must be recognized for real growth or evolution to occur. It remains a truism though that ordinary people can do extraordinary things; and we all possess the potentiality for shared good, self-actualization and enlightened states of Being that could benefit others.

What is the implication of this for existence—as we live our precious lives, from moment to moment, in the Now? Tolle gives us the 'Perennial Wisdom' of the ages about eternal Being while summing up some of his earlier points:

"There is an even deeper level to the whole than the interconnectedness of everything in existence. At the deeper level, all things are one. It is the Source, the unmanifested one Life. It is the timeless intelligence that manifests as a universe unfolding in time." (7)

It is also 'You', 'I' and every other sentient being with a life-form, vibrating at the frequency level of the natural species that we belongs to. As an individual consciousness we are related to the Universal Consciousness or Mind that is the manifested essence of the Unmanifested or formless realm of existence. However, the formless realm is only an abstract reality in relation to the organic life-form that we inhabit or have sacred Presence within as a sentient, existing being. Life, as universal and shared by all, is essentially Present in each evolving, creative life-form, 'looking out' upon the world in the present moment of time, space and causation.

Finally, higher Consciousness is assumed to be irrevocably timeless or eternal and beyond the reach of all material conditions then it does not evolve, grow or develop in some progressive or even regressive fashion; at least, this appears to be Tolle's bias. But it is really unclear why the critically important condition of growth and development should not apply to lower forms of consciousness and thus be like the rest of organic nature.

After all, can we really say that the consciousness of our so-called leaders of the world is all that it could be and that human society is as perfected as it could ever be? Anyway I rest my criticism of Tolle's assumption about 'consciousness' as it evolves towards higher Consciousness, on individual and collective levels of reality.

Consciousness, Re-birth, and Resurrection

The realm of Formlessness is similar to the Christian belief of Heaven and Hell. However, formlessness as Heaven or Hell is not a realm or region of Being that we can safely visit and hope to return from, in this life-form. This is why in many religious traditions of Asian and throughout the non-Christian world, there is the well-known doctrine and belief in re-incarnation or re-birth, which requires an energetic means by which we can journey to other regions of the universe, and back, again and again, without perhaps the slightest alteration in our Consciousness, but which spells one *catastrophe* after another for our Being, which we call 'birth', 'life' and 'death'.

Traditionally, the energetic means for surviving death is the 'soul' among the Hindus, Jains, Jews, Christians, Moslems and numerous others, throughout history. Among the Hindus and Sikhs of India, it is the higher or universal Self; and for many Buddhists and others, it is *consciousness*—in some form— that makes re-birth a possibility. Philosophically, the survival of death in any form is a debatable subject since the empirical evidence for 'survival' is ambiguous. However, philosophy and empirical science aside, there is no debate or uncertainty for those with sufficient insight, faith, and experience of the Truth.

The belief in re-birth or transmigration (of the soul) was widespread among the ancient Greeks, Pagans and at least one early Christian group, the Gnostics. The belief in some form of resurrection through the soul in order to join a world Redeemer or Savior in Heaven is the most widespread belief among Catholics, Moslems, and some Jews. Since it has been impossible to empirically 'prove' that either re-birth or resurrection is true, one is always free to believe in either doctrine, or nothing at all, and just 'see what happens' following death—as Tolle has said. (8)

Emile Pascal of the 17th century argued that one has nothing to loose and everything to gain by *merely believing* in the Divinity and Resurrection of Christ, since if it is not true, you have lost nothing. But if what Christians believe about Christ is true, and you are a true believer, then you will gain eternal Life and enjoy eternal happiness in God's Heaven. What have you to loose— Pascal asks—except the time required to fulfill the 'wager'? (9)

Critics argue that Pascal's wager requires far too little from believers, since living the Christian life of nonviolence, love, the forgiveness of sins, keeping the Ten Commandments, etc., are the necessary pre-requisites of a true Christian. Of course, there is no empirical way to settle the argument except the pragmatic one that bets on a certain outcome that no one can be absolutely sure about, one way or the other.

If and when any form of 'enlightenment' or breakthrough of consciousness occur, we will wake up from the dream-states of existence and begin to 'smell the coffee', 'see the flowers', and 'hear the wind in the trees'. In other words, we experience the changes occurring in the eternal Now through our individual sense of Being. Whether this life-form leads inevitably and necessarily to a heavenly, hellish or oblivious state of Being, we cannot know for sure. However, we remain free to believe or not in whatever appears most true for ourselves.

In sum, re-birth or resurrection can only occur within the innermost regions of the universal Life-force where the eternal energy of the soul, Self and Consciousness exists. In this sense, the Indian Jains (due to a soul), Hindus (due to the Self), and Buddhists (due to consciousness) have a philosophical stake in the outcome of our earthly existence—say what you will about its joys and sorrows, etc. One way or another we know that this life-form will cease functioning one day and then we *may* know more than we now do.

The Perennial Wisdom exists—confirmed by subatomic physics—that the energy of the universe is constantly being transformed from one state of Being into another. *Change or transformation is a universal principle of all material forms; while Permanence or Eternity appears to be the universal principle of Life, Being and Consciousness—at the highest levels.*

Is the universal Life-force eternal? Yes, it is. Can we know the Truth about our earthly existence? Yes, we can. Will we enjoy Life everlasting as many religious *Scriptures* promise?—In a universe where *anything is possible*, why not? As Tolle has said, hedging his own bets, 'we will just have to wait and see'.

Chuangzi: the Way that is Formless

If you think that you have understood what Formlessness is, think again—so the Taoist Chuangzi implies when he wrote about the eternal Way of Nature. His words are as clear as any can be about this abstract subject, but their meanings may escape the finest of minds. The only means of knowing the Way, Chuangzi implies in the following passage and other writings, is through a deeply intuitive and mystical experience of the soul.

He wrote:

'The Way has its reality and its signs but is without action or form. You can hand it down but you cannot receive it; you can get it but you cannot see it. It is its own source, its own root. Before Heaven and earth existed it was there, firm from ancient times. It gave spirituality to the spirits and to God; it gave birth to Heaven and to earth. It exists beyond the highest point, and yet you cannot call it lofty; it exists beneath the limit of the six directions, and yet you cannot call it deep. It was born before Heaven and earth, and yet you cannot call it long; it is earlier than the earliest time, and yet you cannot call it old." (10)

Is there a sense of reality that Chuangzi's words awaken in you that is entirely beyond words? If so, then perhaps you already 'know' with an intuitive awareness of the soul what he is referring to. But if not, then perhaps you may want to read the passage again with a deeper, non-cognitive part of your brain that has nothing to do with words, meanings, or forms. It is liberating to realize that although we cannot conceptually 'understand' certain things we can know these same things—like Life, the Way, and Formlessness—with the deeper and more intuitive function of Consciousness.

PART VII

AWAKENING TO GOODNESS, WISDOM

AND ENLIGHTENMENT

"The breakthrough of *pratyahara* [non-attachment] is a pivotal experience for a *yogi* [one who is transformed by the discovery of the soul]. (Tambe, 245)

"Ultimately, it is not possible to describe terms like *Isvara* (form or image of *Brahman*, or formless Supreme God], *Purusha* [eternal, original Person who witnesses everything] and *soul* in words; and it is worse to try to grasp them with our conditioned minds. They all represent pure energy.... *Soul* is the core inside of the subtle causal/atomic body, but it is distinct from it. Unlike the bodies [physical, astral and causal bodies], the soul is indestructible.... *Soul* does not have a personality...it is a fragment of the divine, and any part of the infinite is infinite too. It has no beginning or no end. It is timeless because 'time' is born as a product of the mind that belongs to existence, into which the omnipresent soul has descended only *for the time being!*"

These are the words of Suhas Tambe, an Indian born scholar who has translated and interpreted, Patanjali's *Yoga Sutras*. Tambe's book, *The Making of a Yoga Master*, is one of the most insightful and illuminating studies of the '*Yogik Path of Self-realization*'. (1)

In this Part of *The Perennial Wisdom*, I have discussed how the insight of universal Goodness can be considered (Chapter 24); and in Chapter 25, what the 'Experience of Enlightenment' means. Most crucial to both Chapters is the belief in an eternal, pure soul that has fallen into this world and become corrupted by it. When we discover the soul within the subtle, inner body, we intuitively awaken to the physical world and understand the myriad conditions that have 'entrapped' it.

Tambe has interpreted a *Yoga-Sutra* (4.7/1.25) in the following way: "*In* Isvara [the energetic soul within each person] *the germ of all knowledge expands into infinity.*" The freedom from karma or all conditioning is the essential or innate nature of the soul. One's personal existence should be about liberating the soul from the corruption and karma of self and world. Learning this, we become enlightened beings.

Chapter 23

GOODNESS, TRUTH, AND EXISTENCE

What is original Goodness and how is it related to evil? How is Goodness related to ordinary existence and knowledge? And why do we possess the capacity to experience and know divine Truth, Goodness and Wisdom?

"The universe is both... One and Many." Dionysius

"There is only One Truth whose existence has no need of proof since it is itself its own proof for those who are able to perceive it." Henry Madathanas

"The truly learned man is he who understands that what he knows is but little in comparison with what he does not know." Ali

"I am better off than he (a man reputed for wisdom) is—for he knows nothing and (only) thinks that he knows; I neither know nor think that I know.... The truth is, O men of Athens, that only God is wise." Socrates in Plato's *Apology*

"The mind of the philosopher alone has wings; and this is just, for he is always, according to the measure of his abilities, clinging in recollection to those things in which God abides, and in beholding which He is what He is. And he who employs aright these memories is ever being initiated into perfect mysteries and alone becomes truly perfect. But, as he forgets earthly interests and is rapt in the divine, the vulgar deem him mad, and rebuke him; they do not see that he is inspired." Plato (*Phaedrus*)

Plato, the most famous student of Socrates in ancient Greece, gave us the paradoxical wisdom of Socrates in his many *Dialogues*. Socrates is characterized by Plato in the *Apology* as a paradoxical *agnostic* who 'knows that he knows not' whereas others *merely think* that they know—the divine Wisdom of the Greek sages. In other contexts, Socrates affirmed that the 'unexamined life is not worth living'—a critique of those who lived to make money and pursue wealth, in his own times.

While Plato's early picture of Socrates shows him focused upon moral questions like 'what is virtue?' and 'what is the best way to live?' the middle and late periods of Plato's writings show Socrates as mystical, speculative and metaphysical. In most of these writings, Socrates' assumption that virtue is the result of knowledge, especially of intellectual goodness, is not seriously challenged by others.

In the quotation above, Plato probably had Socrates in mind when he wrote about the 'mind of the philosopher' in the *Phaedrus,* a middle period *Dialogue.* Socrates belief of reincarnation, the transmigration of the soul and its *recollections* and *memories* from the heavenly realm of *Ideas*—Plato's controversial metaphysical doctrine—is referred to in several contexts, especially *The Allegory of the Cave* in the *Republic.* Although one could fault Socrates, the husband and father, for his poverty—a life of poverty seemed to be an authentic choice about how to live his single-minded devotion to philosophy, the best path to self-knowledge, the examined life, and the preparation for death.

Finally, there is Socrates the mystic, rationalist *and* moralist. Finding congruence between these polarizing tendencies has been a perennial problem in human thought and civilization. The depiction of Socrates by Plato is one who believed in a metaphysical—and not merely intellectual—*Good,* the controlling *Idea* of the universe. If one *sees,* in a mystical state of Consciousness, the Truth that is eternal, then one cannot fail to do and be a good person. On the contrary, if one fails to do and be good, that person is simply *ignorant* of divine Goodness and therefore must be considered *evil.*

At least this is the *rational* Socrates, who believed in the dominating power of reason and its capacity to control the emotions, appetites and senses of narrow self-interest and greed. This Stoic doctrine of self-control through reason was questioned by many after Socrates, beginning with Plato, Aristotle and especially the Existentialists of the 19th and 20th centuries. Plato, the loving follower of Socrates, was forgiving of his teacher when he wrote: "*the philosopher... forgets earthly interests and is rapt in the divine, the vulgar deem him mad, and rebuke him; they do not see that he is inspired.*"

In the end, Socrates' *mystical* tendencies made him vulnerable to satirical writing as in Aristophanes' play, *Clouds,* and more seriously it was a source of confusion and suspicion among his conservative Athenians that Socrates was an atheist. This and the ridiculous charge of 'corrupting the youth' in his teaching them to question the existence of the official gods, was enough for the 'democratic' assembly to condemn him to death. (1)

God and Disbelief

Among the many meanings of Being or 'God' the image that humans have of 'an infinitely perfect Being' must be counted among them. Yet asserting this says little about the identity of God and whether anything believed to be 'infinitely perfect' can be understood through reason or the intellect. Furthermore, empirical grounds for believing in the existence of God are notoriously lacking for the skeptic.

To assert that the universe and all that we can actually experience is *real, true and good* is not the stuff of illusion. Such beliefs do not usually stress our readiness to accept unsupported claims; rather personal beliefs are those that express a code or creed for living and thinking, and should not be judged or considered beyond the existential right to believe.

Abstract or logical claims have their origin in 'higher cognitive processes' of the intellect; thus such claims are of a rational or analytic kind and little more. However, it is on the basis of the heart and soul of intuitive and affective knowing that religious believers are persuaded about the divine origin and destiny of everything. In other words, spiritual beliefs *and* disbeliefs have their basis in the different hemispheres of the brain, the left hemisphere for the skeptics and the right hemisphere for the believers in spiritual Truth. As well, believers and skeptics activate the energies of different chakra centers in articulating their viewpoints.

For example, believers typically actualize the affective energy and nerve networks of the *heart or Anahata-chakra located in heart-lung nexus* while skeptics actualize the intellectual energy of the *Ajna-chakra in the cerebrum or forebrain of higher brain functions.* Meanwhile, both believers and skeptics of religious Truth are known to actualize the creative energy of the *Vishuddha-chakra at the throat region* that activates speech and communication connecting the heart and brain chakra centers; and the three lower chakra centers, controlling energies of survival skills and adaptability, pleasure and procreative seeking, the will-to-power and success, are common to both points of view. Thus the existential differences between believers and skeptics are subtle, intellectual and subjective since both positions in the debate over religion and spirituality begin their arguments from differing assumptions or anatomical centers of the body-heart-mind connections.

Disbelievers or skeptics see only the impersonal, heartless, and soulless nature of the material world; while believers typically see nature and existence in spiritual terms. To disbelievers, the empirical or physical level of reality lacks any vital connections with a soul, Self or higher Consciousness; while believers look upon the world and see one miracle, mystery and wonder after another that can only be explained by a Creator Being. To the skeptic or disbeliever, nature and the universe may appear to be entirely indifferent if not hostile, to our personal life-form and its various situations; while to the believer, we live in a friendly universe with a sacred Life-force that gives birth to, sustains and transforms all life-forms. And so forth.

There is really little that one side of the religion / science divide can say or do to persuade the other side of the merits of its viewpoint. The problem lies in the fact that both sides begin from differing starting points, with different assumptions, logically, leading to entirely different conclusions and through differing neural connections in the brain. Whether the universe 'cares' or not what we think may be irrelevant to what we believe is true; what matters is how we feel and the organic and felt difference that it makes in our lives.

If skeptics, materialists, and other scoundrels of philosophy are asked about ultimate origins, they will usually answer in the negative and remain closed off to any rational debate. On the other hand, since few individuals remain unchanging in their philosophical and religious views about mundane or ultimate matters during their life-time, the transformation of consciousness and underlying beliefs—even among the most hardened skeptics—to an attitude of faith is always a possibility; and of course the opposite sort of transformation is also possible among believers.

In sum, much of what we presently know about the world points to a constantly changing universe, from one state of being to another, at all levels of Life and becoming—human or otherwise. It is merely the prejudice of *anthropomorphism*, first realized by the poet-philosopher Xenophanes of ancient Greece that prompted some to believe God must be *formless and impersonal.* Perhaps someday if we ever make contact with extraterrestrial life-forms that are more developed than we are, we may put an end to the self-serving delusion about our moral, intellectual and spiritual superiority.

Existence, Essence and Consciousness

Our knowledge or intellectual constructions about the self and world are constantly changing compounds of ideas, images, and memories, held together by the will, mind, and ego. There is nothing eternal or ever-lasting about knowledge even though our educational and cultural system is based upon their fictional and fragmentary forms. What has been sorely neglected in the recent history of knowledge is the notion of essence or the intuitive insight that bring us closer to the truth about reality than the knowledge that is acquired solely through abstract reason.

The attempt to define, describe or explain 'essence' is a fool's game—in the view of the skeptic—since we can know almost nothing about infinite and eternal Being. However, since none of us is perfect except in desiring to be so, acting the fool is often synonymous with being human since without 'daring to be wrong or in error' we may well cease to know anything that is genuinely new or different from old forms of belief and thought.

In this context, 'essence' may only appear as an insight into what is true in contingent existence and never independent of it. In other words, *existence and essence co-arise* in experience although reason may seize upon the latter as eternal and independent of existence. It is certainly true that humans create 'essences' or personal meanings throughout their lives; yet eternal essences are those which appear solely as objective 'qualities' of Being. Thus contingently real or existential essences cannot then function as eternal ones; and eternal essences are necessarily universal, infinite, and binding upon all sentient beings, while existential essences are finite, individual, conditional and subject to universal change.

Essence is what distinguishes us as a species-being from other species since we create—through the will of conscious Being—'who we are' from the wholeness or matrix of real existence, as we live our individual lives. Whether a person becomes a 'doctor, lawyer, or candlestick maker' is sometimes a matter of choice as much as supportive circumstances; or whether we marry, have children or not; or live our lives serving others or not, can be circumstantial as often as willful or freely chosen. Conversely, whether a person is born with the potentialities of a certain body type, sexual identity, or certain moral and intellectual predispositions (of being) is not a matter of human choosing, socialization or environmental circumstances.

Or more metaphorically speaking, *essence, existence and consciousness* are in a dance together, inseparably connected by reason of nature and Being, self and culture, in most instances. The result is the rather bewildering and unpredictable complexity of how people 'turn out' and against the odds or guesses about their destiny. There is simply no way of predicting, in the majority of cases, what people will do, how they will respond to different circumstances, and what influences within and beyond a family of origin in time and place, to different people and events.

Thus, it remains existentially true that we possess the power to create ourselves in a variety of quite different ways. In fact, we must do so to become truly or fully human. Although it may be true that we are of divine origin, in an ultimate sense, we are not condemned to our existential or social circumstances of birth and upbringing. If we are born into existence by means of an individuated soul that is karmicly or causally conditioned—as most Jains, Hindus and Buddhists believe—we create ourselves in the Now of time and space through the infinite potentialities of Consciousness or an eternal soul.

Philosophically, then, if you believe that essence is prior to existence, you will tend to think in mystical and metaphysical ways; or if you believe that existence or organic being precedes essence then you will tend to think in more existential and pragmatic ways. In real life-circumstances, both essence and existence are inseparably linked since *body-mind-soul* are not just hyphenated! but they are necessarily or lawfully connected and different. It is a dance, a game in real time and space, that we only vaguely understand with teleological (ultimate) and pragmatic (real world) consequences.

In the metaphysical framing of existence, essence, and Consciousness, reincarnation (or more pragmatically *re-birth*) is a circular or cyclical pattern of *essence or a soul* that enables us to learn and grow towards greater universality, albeit from one finite life-time to another, until we realize who we are and learn to live in attunement with the highest spiritual Reality which the Hindus name and chant: *Sat-Chit-Ananda* (perfect Being, Consciousness and Bliss or the real existence of *Atman-Brahman*). Whatever way that you take or conceive of it, Life is an enduring process *existentially* and an eternal one, *metaphysically*; and if you choose to believe one way or the other, may be as circumstantial and it is karmic and pre-determined.

431

Three *Darshanas* of India: Hindu, Buddhist and Jain

From the humbling perspective of Indian philosophy, existence is *Samara* or a condition of successive life-times conditioned or poisoned by 'hatred, greed, and delusion' (Buddhism). Until we awaken from our ignorance and experience our essential sameness with *Brahman* or Supreme Oneness, we will remain in ignorance, cyclic existence and suffering (Hinduism). *Nirvana* is the 'released' or freed condition of Consciousness, i.e. *moksa* or liberation, which is the final or highest goal of existence; the other three goals are *artha* (wealth), *kama* (pleasure), and *dharma* (duty). And among the Jains, a soul (*jiva*) exists in an atomic or energetic form with the body and mind, in real time-space and place; but then mysteriously gains complete independence at death until it reincarnates in another life-form.

In some texts, the Hindus also have a belief in an independent soul from the *Atman-Brahman* identity; but it is not emphasized nor is an individual soul as clearly independent of *Brahman* or God; and more importantly, Jainism is an atheistic and materialistic philosophy of spirituality; while Hinduism is clearly theistic, idealistic and only superficially materialistic. Meanwhile, the scholarship of all three religious philosophies express an embrace of the new *Zeitgeist* of science, especially the more esoteric reaches of mathematics, physics and biology. Only contemporary Buddhism and Jainism have a basis for fully embracing the sciences of the mind, body and existence provided they both clear the decks of ideas about metaphysical karma, reincarnation, rebirth, soul or consciousness; but this is not very likely without jeopardizing their exotic appeal to Westerners.

On a social level, a person's life-time is consumed by *the three* worldly values of Hindu origin; but it is the goal of *moksa* that ultimately delivers us from the madness, confusion, and violence of the world. In the Jain and Buddhist religious philosophies, *Ahimsa* or *nonviolence* is the means or Way that delivers us from the violence and corruption of the world if we live a life of non-attachment, compassion, and right understanding.

432

In the Jainism, it is *Anakantavada* or the *many-sidedness of existence reflected in the perspectival nature of consciousness* that most importantly conditions our experience and knowledge of everything.

Realizing the truth of perspectival consciousness and knowledge, a certain freedom of mind, heart and soul can certainly be experience leading to greater non-attachment to 'name and form', rank and file, etc. In other words, from the Jain view, if we live in a non-absolute, non-attached and non-violence way we can realize the absolute purity of the soul and actualize the infinite potentiality of *moksa* or *ultimate liberation.* `

All three *Darshanas* or philosophic viewpoints—Hindu, Jain and Buddhist— teach that re-birth or re-incarnation is not the ultimate goal of spiritual development or realization; rather it is the ending of re-birth and all *karmic becoming that is the goal*; and it is the transformation of awareness from worldliness to non-worldliness that brings final liberation or *moksa.* This has been described as realizing the perfect union of the Higher Self (the *Atman*) in each person with the infinite perfection of universal *Brahman* for the Hindus; and for the Buddhists of the Pure Land sect of China, it is *Brahma-vihara* or the realized states of *immeasurable kindness, compassion, joy, and equanimity*; and among the Jains, it is the attainment of *Nirvakalpa Samadhi* or the highest consciousness on the Ladder of Freedom (*Gunsthanaks*) that finally frees one from cyclic existence or *samsara.*

That said, ordinary existence is a continuous mystery, wonder and miracle to the extent that it has the power to manifest what is Unmanifested through Consciousness or the free will of individuals. Whatever *Darshana,* philosophy or viewpoint that we may follow in existence, it is limited at a conceptual or rational level; and therefore incomplete and simplified at practical, human and social levels. And at a mystical level, we must be willing to 'kick the ladder of philosophy away' as the skeptic Ludwig Wittgenstein once said, to see a Truth that he could only be silent before: the *infinitely perfect Being or Supreme Identity* of Perennial Philosophy

Acceptance and Surrender

Acceptance and surrender are critically important acts in Tolle's philosophy of Being. 'Acceptance' is like *ahimsa* or non-violence and the refusal to 'fight' a perceived evil with violence. Although acceptance may seem like 'giving up' it is really different since in acceptance you affirm Life—not death, violence, or disease—and go with the sacred flow of energy that is Life. It is the conscious decision to give up fighting or resisting on a surface level of reality in order to affirm a deeper level and connect with the healing power of nonviolence and the divine energy of the Life-force.

Acceptance transforms ordinary consciousness into the attitude of surrender or the deeper phase of Consciousness. When ordinary consciousness is experienced as surrender, it is transformed by the *loving and caring energy of Being*. This is the inner, deeper, subtle body of the soul where the higher or collective Self can be intuitively realized. The experience of essence or the soul is also found through this intuitive and *noetic* process of Consciousness which transcends intellectual concepts and analytic distinctions. It is like the Islamic injunction to 'surrender' to the infinite Mercy and Compassion of Allah for the final seal of faith.

The experience of essence as surrender moves consciousness from the cerebral region of reason and intellect to the heart region of love and compassion. Surrendering is an act of higher Consciousness that makes the most profound difference in a person's life. The difference cannot be measured but it is experienced as a greater degree of harmony, peace, and attunement with others. Surrendering opens hidden channels of energy in the total self, requiring little more than an openness towards Being, and releases energies of the heart-mind-soul or what exists as the unity of who we are.

Tolle wrote about surrender in terms of the 'flow of life':

"Surrender is the simple but profound wisdom of yielding to rather than opposing the flow of life. The only place where you can experience the flow of life is the Now, so to surrender is to accept the present moment unconditionally and without reservation. It is to relinquish inner resistance to what is. Inner resistance is to say 'no' to what is, through mental judgment and emotional negativity. It becomes particularly pronounced when things 'go wrong', which means that there is a gap between the demands or rigid expectations of your mind and what is. That is the pain gap. If you have lived long enough, you will know that things 'go wrong' quite often. It is precisely at those times that surrender needs to be practiced if you want to eliminate pain and sorrow in your life. Acceptance of what is immediately present frees you from mind identification and thus reconnects you with Being...." (3)

As Tolle says, surrender does not mean doing nothing in the real world. In fact, if you are aligned positively with the Life-force within, the outward effect reflects this inner condition: you will feel uplifted, motivated, and called to act in the creative energy of Now. On the other hand, not choosing to act is a form of choosing when the alternatives are clearly present in awareness. The 'flow of energy' that our Being is immersed in, through the Nowness of this life-form, requires, to some degree, a constant need to accept and surrender to reality. And this is what, in other contexts, Tolle speaks about as the potential 'alignment' of one's inner sense of Being with the meaning and purpose of existence.

In these important senses, acceptance and surrender mark the true discovery of Goodness, the essence of Being or what-is. The journey of the soul, mind, and heart is a long and often circuitous one, with many twists and turns on a rough road that may or may not take us to our desired destination. But accepting the real circumstance of Now and surrendering to them may be all that you need to reach your destination.

Intuitions of Essence and Self

2500 years ago, the Greek philosopher, Aristotle, thought that 'infinitely perfect Being' is the One God whose creative intelligence draws us to it owing to the sacred underlying purpose that exists in all life-forms and species of the Earth. Whether the essence or meaning that we can experience and know in our earthly existence can be found throughout the universe is part of the mystery of Being and the great adventure that awaits the human species in its explorations of the universe.

Overcoming the 'gap' that exists between mind and Being or thought and reality is crucial in the experience of real Being. The discovery of 'essence' occurs when a small aspect or quality of Being is intuitively seen by the intellect beyond the forms or concepts of mind. The intuitive 'seeing' of essence takes consciousness into the unmanifested realm of Being. It is an experience like diving into a great ocean and being able to see clearly to the bottom. In seeing essences in experience we are able to gain insight or an internal view of an object in time-space.

For example, Yoga philosophy assumes that 'self' is a multi-layered object, being composed of a *physical body* (the gross or outermost aspect), an *astral body* (enclosed and subtle), and a *causal body* (inner and more subtle); and these bodies or layers of energy contain the potentialities of the senses, the emotions and thoughts of knowing. When we really see or intuit who we are, the various layers of the self—collapse or dissolve—into the spiritual or universal Self to which we are necessarily connected. Thus our real being or existence as a physical body encloses hidden bodies or subtle layers that disclose a spiritual Self. (4)

Our intuitions of essence come from a deeper region of Being, i.e. the soul or a deeper Unconsciousness where visionary processes occur and are more dynamic than conceptual ones. In reality, conceptual and visionary processes are not entirely separated in experience even though thinking ordinarily occurs at a higher, manifested and conscious level of Being while the soul resides in a deeper, unmanifested level accessible through intuition processes. However, both thinking and intuiting have an entirely complementary relationship to free us from the ignorance, corruption, and violence of self and world, through the higher Consciousness.

The best that we can know of Being or an *infinitely perfect God* is a *vague, ambiguous and partial understanding*, and at best, it is more of a feeling than it is an understanding. It is like gazing upon the vast universe on a starry night through a pinhole. We must imagine that Being is infinitely greater than our awareness although there is no reason to believe that we need to fear an 'infinitely perfect Being' if we are aligned with and centered upon what-is, in the open attitude of *surrender*.

Any feeling of being overwhelmed can be checked by realizing that an unbridgeable gap exists between our finite knowledge and infinite Being; however the 'gap' in our experience of Being, can be narrowed by infinitesimal degrees with a faith in universal Goodness, Truth and Mystery. For example, the lives and teachings of the most perfect, noble and enlightened ones of ancient civilization, i.e. Abraham, Moses, Jesus, Mohammad, Mahavira, Buddha, Socrates, Plato, Aristotle, Laozi, Chuangzi, Confucius, Mencius, et al, can convey the One Truth of the Perennial Wisdom to us today, from different times and places since each of these individuals transcends time and place through their uses of intellectual and intuitive powers, in their experience of unitary Being.

Meditation, Being and Phenomenology

Our 'glimpses' or insights of Being can be concentrated through meditation. In meditation, we still our body and turn inwards towards the pure center of consciousness. The immediate experience of pure consciousness is the awareness of the formless depths of Being brought intuitively to full consciousness through essential knowing; and it is meditative absorption that provides us with the means for experiencing the depths of Being in everyday situations.

There are innumerable means or methods of focusing and deepening awareness beyond the ego level of mere role-playing. The established religions of the world are sources for meditating upon and contemplating the depths of universal Being. In fact, within the spectrum of human knowledge like the arts, sciences, and humanities, there are innumerable intuitions of essence and universal Being that have given us the most profound depths of existence. Furthermore, the awareness of each contingently existing human being cannot be separated from eternal Being.

Meister Eckhart— the 13th century Christian mystic—wrote from an intuition of essence that "time is what keeps the light [of Being or God] from reaching us. There is no greater obstacle to God than time." The implication is clear: you must step out of time into the Now and feel a transmutation of ordinary consciousness into higher Consciousness. There you can glimpse 'God' or the image of eternal Being embodied in Jesus Christ or everyman, woman, and child of the Earth. And from a perennialist viewpoint, similar moral, aesthetic and spiritual depths of Being can be seen in the mystical depths of the world religions. (4)

The unitary relation between essence and existence is a Perennial one in the world religions and the universe. According to Jean-Paul Sartre, the atheistic existentialist, 'existence precedes essence'. Religious or theistic philosophies reverse this relation and assume that essence or the soul is innate or prior to the existence of a person. Existentialists also equate essence with the lived meaning of Life and assume that we continuously create who we are, through our actions and choices. Perennialists assume that the meaning and purpose of Life is intrinsic to the Divine Ground of Being and that we can know it through intuitive insight—which is superior to discursive reason. (5)

The phenomenological approach to consciousness assumes an attitude of realism: the world exists independently of subjectivity. However, this independence is only relative, approximate and changing while Being is absolute, univocal and permanently situated in Now. These are high-sounding abstractions but it is really about the human immediacy of experience, life-situations, and relations with others. It assumes that consciousness is absolutely unified through subjective being, the natural and social world.

Consciousness is dynamic, intentional, and absolutely free-in-the-world. It is inseparably connected or constituted through subjective Being, nature, and the real world. Furthermore, 'consciousness is always a consciousness of something' yet it is translucent and transcendent of the contingent conditions of existence. Its essence is identical with human freedom yet it is inherently a nothingness or emptiness within experience and knowledge. Consciousness is, in this sense, paradoxical and contradictory, since its unity is the basis for the meaning and purpose of existence.

Existential phenomenology assumes the presence of subjective freedom within the field of consciousness. We live in the Now of existence, conditioned by temporality, nature, society, and the cosmos; yet we are inherently and absolutely free beings before absurd existence. The meaning of Life is inseparable from the meaning of aging, dying and death; and the reality of a free will, human relationships, and the situations of existence, makes choosing unavoidable and universally binding upon all. The paradoxical, absurd nature of existence is resolved in the totality of a life-world and the ever-present possibility of death and transcendence.

On a more mundane level of existence, the awareness of consciousness and its essential freedom, can enable you to get rid of any negativity, pain, and identifications that you may carry with you, in the form of negative energy of *the pain-body*, by 'bracketing' or setting aside the judging self in experience. Just learn *how to just be in every situation* and accept the continual challenge from others, to remain authentic, egoless, and free from identifications. Formless and without a worldly identity, Consciousness is the great mystery of personal existence, linked at every point with reality through the forms, desires, and conditions of real Being.

Ethics and the Violence of the Pain-body

Your essence or who you really are is a natural form of divine Goodness. Natural Goodness arises from the immediate

Presence of the Life-force in the present moment of time-eternity. Goodness exists at a trans-subjectively, objectively and universally in the world and it is the most essential Truth about who you are—no matter what horror, violence and wrong you have committed in your life. Furthermore, universal Goodness—even if it is unknowable in its totality—is a fundamental premise of any ethics that aims at the *liberation of sentient beings* from dissatisfaction, violence and suffering.

To kill any living or sentient being is absolutely and unconditionally wrong from a *perennialist or mystical* point of view. From the viewpoint of a *skeptic or materialist,* every moral act is in question from the beginning since it is doubtful that there can be any totally reliable moral knowledge; hence we live fully and completely in a world that is in question. And to this, the *agnostic* only replies that this premise or assumption too is in question for we cannot know with absolute certainty what the Truth is about questions of morality, epistemology or theology.

Perhaps the more wise, measured and relativist position in ethics is found in Pragmatism which is: a moral problem is much like any other problem in human life only its solution is not so abstract as it is in the sciences and mathematics nor is it just a solution that the hedonist or absolute materialist would offer; rather the pragmatic view of ethics gives equal consideration to the psychological, social and intellectual aspects of human action and looks to the *satisfaction of individuals in the overall improvement of society* as criteria for moral problem-solving.

When negativity and violence appear to dominate the situations of your life-world, it is a sign that the pain-bodies of your own self and others are becoming more powerful. Murder, war, and genocide are the most extreme evidence of pain-bodies since they thrive on forms of negative, violent, and pathological energy. If we realized the futility, stupidity, and brutality of war, no moral leader could ever lead his or her people into a war.

To claim that the deliberate, conscious destruction of life-forms can be justified by the circumstances of existence is pathological, ignorant, and insane. The major obstacle to realizing universal Goodness is to believe that violence is ever necessary or justified. This belief merely perpetuates ancient, inherited, pathological tendencies that block the positive, creative, and healthy consequences of realizing universal Goodness.

Paradoxically, wars and genocides are times when pain-bodies thrive and people enjoy themselves since the inner-pain body of otherwise good people, grow and are being nurtured by new pain, suffering, and violence. A pain-body also explains why many soldiers who are fighting in a war and having the choice to leave or remain in fighting roles, often choose to remain at the battle front. Indeed, there is an extremely addictive, erotic, and visceral attraction to the danger and violence of war or similar murderous patterns of ordinary human life, in the primitive or hunter brain stem of human beings (especially men).

The phenomenology of war-related experience has been described by soldiers, war correspondents, war-historians and literary writers alike, and this visceral attraction to violence combined with the comradeship of soldiers, perpetuates war and other pain-body actions.

Of course, the same tendencies can be seen in competitive professional sports, such as football, hockey, boxing, and even basketball and baseball, where winning is everything and military metaphors are often used in describing the tactics, strategies, and outcomes of such games. The Capitalistic economic system is a clear symptom of the wide-spread prevalence of the pain-body in the general population, where selfishness, greed, and the exploitation of natural and human resources are the dominant practices. While Capitalism periodically collapses from its greed-driven system of corruption and manipulation of market forces, it will not essentially change until we see its inherent injustice, pathology, and destruction of persons and the Earth.

War gives meaning, energy, and purpose to pain-bodies, feeding their power, influence, and control over us. War is about fighting, slaughtering and inflicting the maximum degree of injury and pain upon others. Although 'soldiering' may be about saving or protecting others from harm or injury, war is not.

War is about killing and destroying the 'enemy' who is usually a group of combat-ready soldiers who represent a nation-state and its material, financial and political self-interests. And typically, the 'enemy' in every war is portrayed as gorillas, terrorists, and godless beasts that have no regard for human life and must be destroyed!

The usual practices and consequences of war involve terrorist practices of all kinds, like indiscriminate bombing of cities, raping of women, theft of valuable property, the destruction of natural resources and infrastructure, the killing of non-human animals, the complete disruption of normal human life in society, etc. The most positive thing about wars is that they all eventually end, but leave the survivors with severe post-traumatic or physical injuries for a life-time. Unless we get rid of the pain-body which is both the cause and the result of injustice, corruption and warfare, the future of humanity will remain uncertain and problematic; and even if we find the cure of the pain-body virus and remove it from our species, human existence will remain uncertain but more peaceful, just and nonviolent.

Dissolving the Pain-body

Negative and positive experiences like loss and gain, failure and success, pain and pleasure, etc., are primary experiences for nearly everyone. Eliminating painful or sorrowful experiences is easier said than done; and Tolle is a psychological realist in this respect. For much if not all experience occurs through paired, dialectical and complementary oppositions.

How can we dissolve or get rid of the pain-body that interferes with healthy, sane, and creative functioning?

1. Become fully conscious. We carry with us wherever we go a penumbra or shadow entity of pain, sorrow, and negativity. If you bring the light of ordinary awareness to the pain-body— whenever it shows itself in relationships and life-situations—you can begin to dissolve the pain-body that is living within your greater, healthy self.

2. Meditating upon breathing. When you breathe, watch your breath moving in and out of your body, from the surrounding air and sustaining life-force. Count your incoming breath as *one* and outgoing breath as *two* and continue counting breaths until you reach *ten*. Just carefully follow your breath the whole time in and out of your lungs.

Watching your breath consciously can help you to become more integrated, healthy, and fully functioning. When we breathe out, we breathe toxins and carbon dioxide from our blood and replenish it with each in-breath of fresh oxygen. The effect reduces the influence of the pain-body in your breathing and body functioning.

3. Continue meditating. Sit upright, still the body and gently close your eyes. Focus your consciousness upon the breath. Do not attach your consciousness to the breath or anything else. Just follow the natural movements of the in-breath and out-breath. *Just observe any form in awareness through the witnessing or higher Consciousness at the crown of the head.*

Sitting quietly and in stillness with your body enables or empowers you to take another step to eliminate the pain-body. Quiet the mind by watching without judging or analyzing each sensation, emotion, and thought rising in the energy field of the brain-mind-body. Observe without attachment to any form in the present moment and let them disappear from awareness

Purging or cleaning the mind, body and soul of pain-body garbage is the essential work of meditation—in its first stage. The second stage of meditating involves awakening each chakra or energy center in the inner, subtle body that exists along the axis of the entire spine and brain. The third stage of meditating involves actualizing the released energy for your life-world or total existence. A continuous meditation upon the enjoyment-body enables you to realize an attunement with natural being.

4. Witness your everyday self and the real world. Watch or witness the experiences of your everyday or total self through higher Consciousness. Watch but do not activate negative emotions, thoughts, and judgments coming from the pain-body.

Watch with the energy of your higher Consciousness and the Light of nonviolence, non-attachment and non-absolutism.

Be a witness to the conditions, changes, and events of the real or social world. Become aware of the outstanding moral, political, and economic issues of the times, without absolutist answers. See all knowledge and viewpoints as relative, perspectival and changing.

Learn not to be attached to any conflict, problem, or condition of violence that feed the pain-body. Meditate upon equanimity to overcome any imbalance or disturbance of the self.

5. Change undesirable behavior. Do not judge, comment upon, and get involved in the dialogue that the pain-body may want. Just watch the pain-body as if it is another person. Watch any negative emotions rising from the pain-body like anger, sadness or self-pity. Let them go and forgive whoever hurt you and be sure to forgive yourself. Feel a weight lifting from your inner body, soul and Being.

Do not aggressively seek to change yourself. Just decide to change, at an intellectual level, any undesirable habit or tendency of your character. Watch with equanimity any negative, disturbing, or violent emotion, thought, or memory, and let-it-go into the Void. Experience the satisfaction from overcoming negativity or violent tendencies of the mind- body-soul.

6. Become more empathic. Listen without speaking or thinking. Watch but do not judge what you pereceive. When you become aware of the pain-body without any attachment or identification as 'me' or 'mine', you will begin to see the difference in how you feel and relate to others. You will notice a difference in the feeling of your inner body and life-situations.

7. Develop a conscious energy field. When you develop an energy field of higher Consciousness, the awareness will spread to your relations with other people, your roles in society, and your reasoning process about the world. Within a higher sense of Consciousness, you will become aware of the many levels of being that you experience in everyday life. This awareness creates a more realistic and accepting awareness of the self and world.

8. Experience the translucence and freedom of consciousness. Become conscious of the gap that naturally appears between the past and the future in the Now of experience. Be in the Now and experience the Presence of infinite Being. Realize the finitude of mind, ego and body, and the infinity of the present moment. See birth, life, death and rebirth as the circular route along which you journey as an embodied soul; realize that *moksa* is the final liberation of the soul from re-birth or cyclic existence.

9. Feel attunement with the soul or the essence of real Being. Become aware of the appearing and disappearing of feelings, thoughts and sensations within ordinary consciousness. See the atoms, molecules, glands and systems of your body as real structures and functions of the soul. Realize that the soul is the meta-level for the human genome unfolding in time and the experiences of the body-mind. Imagine that your total being is evolving towards perfect self-realization, liberation and enlightenment; and then see how little you may now really understand about ordinary existence and the infinite universe.

There can be no doubt that everyone has developed a pain-body from living in society and existence. It grows imperceptibly from the accumulation of negative experiences such as identifications and attachments, melodramas, emotional traumas, pain and suffering, and perceived violence of all kinds.

The pain-body grows at unconscious levels of the total self even when we think that we are having a good time; but it constantly diminishes our capacity to be fully in the here-and-now, and be truly happy. When we learn to love just being where we are, no matter where we are, we are making real progress towards liberation and the freedom from pain, suffering and the negativity that caused the pain-body to develop in the first place.

If you remain open, conscious, and positively oriented in everyday experience, the pain-body can be destroyed. Its energy field of negativity, doubt, fear, anxiety, and uncertainty cannot survive in the Presence of higher Consciousness. The intensity, energy and power of Consciousness can destroy all traces of a pain-body, just by observing and being aware of its insane tendencies. By being open, positive, and optimistic about living in the present moment, you can get rid of or dissolve the pain-body, forever.

Once you get rid of your pain-body, you become happier, more joyful, loving, and alive. All this may sound like a fantasy or a dream, but it is really a possibility of existence and a potentiality of your own natural and infinite Being.

Goodness or the Essence of Who You Are

Noticing things that are violent, negative, and evil in your own thoughts is a challenge to realizing universal Goodness. Affirming the natural Goodness of Life does not mean that you are a Pollyanna or being naïve about Life in society and existence. Focusing upon universal Goodness is a great corrective to the corrosive presence of the pain-bodies that populate the social institutions of culture, on local, national, and international levels.

Natural Goodness is like a great, invisible sun within this and every other universe—that is within the dark energy and dark matter of the Great Unconsciousness. When you focus awareness upon the pain-body in meditation you dissolve its negative energy and reveal the natural Goodness within the body, mind, and soul of inner being. The effect is a natural healing process that comes from your own inner guru or source of wisdom, compassion and courage.

Refusing to fight or give into the hate, misery, and violence of the pain-body is crucial to the success of your meditations, ordinary decisions and actions in Life. You will experience a great release of tension from your physical, psychological, and interpersonal sense of Being when you give up fighting and resisting what you may judge as evil; for there is a creative goodness, intelligence and sacred Life-force that exists deeply within all sentient beings.

When you find yourself in situations that are intolerable or painful and yet you are not able to make any significant changes, there may be only one course of action: surrender deeply and completely to the situation by giving up fighting or resisting the opposing current of energy. As you accept and cease resisting what is painful, with full awareness, the pain lessens and instead of suffering you begin to experience the healing Goodness of your inner being.

At first the effect from surrendering to a painful situation will only be subjectively or individually liberating. But after a brief time, a deeper, ontological level is experienced and your sense of liberation spreads to the higher Consciousness of Being. Now, in the sun of Eternity and universal Goodness, everything suddenly looks brighter, more promising than you ever thought possible!

Tolle wrote in this connection, "It is the quality of your consciousness at this moment that is the main determinant of what kind of future you will experience, so to surrender is the most important thing you can do to bring about positive change. Any action you take is secondary. No truly positive action can arise out of an unsurrendered state of consciousness." (6)

Fighting, resisting and opposing are futile and self-defeating in the end. Learning to live and make peace with opposing forces, persons, and realities is an essential part of learning, maturing and living, in ordinary existence. If you learn that Goodness is the universal, dominant and most powerful Force in this world, then every life-form has the potentiality of Goodness in nature, society and existence.

Tolle quotes from the *New Testament* and one of his favorite passages from Christian Scripture: "Look at the lilies of the field, how they grow, they neither toil nor spin."—A new sense of Life, learning and living can occur from just imitating the 'lilies of the field' and remembering your sacred Being. (7)

In sum, seeing your natural Goodness is vital in getting rid of the pain-body. A great opening and clearing within awareness occurs when you experience universal Goodness. The most vital connections between nature, humankind and the universe are formed by the eternal energy of Goodness. Seeing and understanding who you really are, in actuality and potentiality, can make the greatest difference in the world.

Realizing essential Goodness is realizing who you really are, in terms of the body, mind and soul; and this Self-realization is the basis for the wisdom that brings liberation and happiness.

Story from Chuangzi: the Useless Tree

This story is attributed to the enigmatic Taoist philosopher of the fourth century BCE, Chuangzi. What follows is my version of it, based upon several English translations.

One day Huizi, a courtly friend of Chuangzi, sought out Chuangzi's advice about a tree on his land. He said: "I have a large tree that has such a fetid odor from its spring time leaves that everyone avoids it. Its trunk is so gnarled that it cannot be measured by a chalk line, and its branches are so twisted that a carpenter's square cannot be used on them. It stands close by the road but it is so ugly that builders hardly notice it. Actually, your talk reminds me of my tree—your words are big but useless—and people just turn away from it."

Chuangzi was not offended by his dear friend but sought to draw a moral truth from his words. He said: "Huizi, have you ever seen a wildcat or a weasel? It crouches down and waits until a wandering prey approaches. It jumps this way and that, and does not worry about distances, heights or depths. It may land in a trap or a net and there it dies. Similarly there is the yak, and it is so big that it looks like a cloud hanging in the sky. But he cannot even catch a mouse. Now you have a large tree and you are upset because it is useless.

"Huizi, why don't you plant the tree in the *Village of Nothingness* or in a wild and barren land where no one ever goes? There you could rest at ease beside it, sleep for a while or dilly-dally as you please. You need never fear that the ax of a wood's man will bring harm to it. Since you know that the tree is useless, how could it not outlive all the beautiful trees in the world?" (8)

Does this not set the useless tree apart from all others—that it will outlive them? And is not the awareness that something can be useless and yet possess superior value a most important form of knowledge?

Chapter 24

TRUTH, EXISTENCE AND WISDOM

What is Truth in relation to experience, information and knowledge? How is Truth related to understanding, wisdom and enlightenment? And why do many deny their original state of Goodness, Wisdom and Enlightenment?

"Grant an idea or belief to be true, what concrete difference will its being true make in any one's actual life? How will the truth be realized? What experiences would be different from those which would obtain if the belief were false?" William James

"Wisdom without action has its seat in the mouth; but by means of action, it becomes fixed in the heart." Shekel Hadodesh

"There is no other means than knowledge for obtaining complete and final Deliverance. Knowledge alone loosens the bonds of the passions; without knowledge, Bliss (Ananda) cannot be obtained." Shri Sankaracharya

"St. Augustine says 'The soul has a private door into divinity where for her all things amount to naught.' There she is ignorant with knowing, will-less with willing, dark with enlightenment." Meister Eckhart

"Thus, Ananda, on name and form depends consciousness; on consciousness depends name and form; on name and form depends contact; on contact depends sensation; on sensation depends desire; on desire depends attachment; on attachment depends existence; on existence depends birth; on birth depends old age and death, sorrow, lamentation, misery, grief, and despair. Thus does this entire aggregation of misery arise." Digha-Nikaya

451

In the *Digha-Nikaya,* a seminal text of Buddhist philosophy, there is the doctrine of *Dependent Origination* within the second of the Four Truths of existence. The above quotation is a summary of its twelve parts or links of Origination for all sentient life-forms. This doctrine among others is seen as skeptical, agnostic and materialist by some, especially in relation to the One Truth of the mystics; but for others who are mystical, gnostic and spiritual, this doctrine describing *samsara* or the wheel of existence is only the problem to be solved or acted upon through the free will of the *Middle Way* (the fourth of the Four Truths). (1)

The New Crisis of Faith

The Chinese Taoists use the terms Heaven (*T'ien*) and Earth (*K'un*) to indicate that there are different realms of the universal Way (*Tao*). These realms show up in a great variety of ways in ordinary experience and knowledge. For example, we think of ourselves as having a mind and a body which enable us to experience and know the world. But we do not ordinarily conceive of the mind or body as enabling us to experience a heavenly realm of bliss, perfection, and eternity, as many mystics do.

The difference between the natural world of the body and the symbolic world of the mind is one of the greatest sources of confusion and tension in the world. But a third term exists that can resolve the contradiction between heavenly and earthly elements, i.e. *something* absolute and transcendent. However, there is no timeless or infinite absolute that can persuade the disbelieving skeptic about the ultimate purpose and meaning of Life. In short, we are at another proverbial crossroads in the history of civilization that is a crisis of faith, reason, and vision.

The Perennial crisis of faith is at a new crossroads in the history of the world, this one occasioned by the growing realization that no individual, group, or nation can exist separately or in isolation from others, and hope to survive and flourish. This realization shows up in a number of differing ways: first in education that 'all children are God's children' and none should be taught and treated unequally in terms of the resources for learning and opportunities of growth and development. In politics, the new realization is that a government which ignores the Will of 'The People' will not survive for very long or be respected throughout the world. In economics, the new realization that a monetary system based upon greed, exploitation, and selfishness is not moral and sustainable in society, no matter what the system of government is called. And in ethics, science and religion, it is the realization that knowledge and culture are dynamically evolving and changing, in ways that are more complex, unpredictable and unknowable than we ever previously thought.

The upshot of this crisis is the realization that no one can absolutely know or control what happens and we are all equally ignorant before ultimate ends or purposes of the universe. We can only know the present moment with something like absolute certainty; and through the *gap* between the past and the future or Now, we can intuit and experience the Truth of what-is even if it only through a glass darkly. And the new realization is that faith is necessary but not enough to transcend every crisis in living; reason, informed intelligence and action are required to realize the vision of a better tomorrow, Now.

The Mystical Viewpoint: Eliot and the *Upanishads*

To paraphrase the poet T. S. Eliot in "Four Quartets" we are back at the beginning in the journey towards wisdom; only now we realize it for the very first time. He wrote:
"Do not let me hear
Of the wisdom of old men, but rather of their folly,
Their fear of fear and frenzy, their fear of possession,
Of belonging to another, or to others, or to God.
The only wisdom we can hope to acquire
Is the wisdom of humility: humility is endless."
And there is this stanza:
"We shall not cease from exploration
And the end of all our exploring

453

Will be to arrive where we started

And know the place for the first time" (2)

In the real world, problems, conflicts and tensions are said to exist at every turn in the road. According to the pragmatic model of reality, human experience is an unending story of conflicting forces showing up in ever new forms, requiring new solutions, resolutions, and prudence. In this sense, material change, in a pragmatic and existential sense, is the great leveler and decider in human existence, as various histories and stories have repeatedly shown.

For example, in Samuel Butler's novel, *The Way of All Flesh* it is just the death of human beings, that is the unspoken tragedy of existence. But in the greater world of nature, non-human animals, rocks, stars and galaxies in the cosmos, dying, destruction and oblivion, of all forms of living and non-living beings, that inevitably go the same Way to eternity—as human beings.

Or as many philosophers have thought since the time of Socrates and Plato, "Death is the true inspiring genius or the muse of philosophy....Indeed, without death men could scarcely find reason to philosophize" wrote the pessimistic and grim existentialist, Arthur Schopenhauer. On a similar side of the fence, there is the more upbeat insight of Ernst Cassirer, the expert on language and myth: "In a certain sense, the whole of mythical thought may be interpreted as a constant and obstinate negation of the phenomenon of death." (3)

In short, Nature teaches us—whether we conceive of Life as sacred or not— that *time* erodes, degrades and destroys all natural and human forms. Divine Nature or the Earth is the matrix or womb of all life-forms; but without the eternal Life-force, *Purusha* or the Person, the miraculous and universal energy that seeds the potentiality of material *Prakriti* or Nature, the atomic elements and Forces of the universe—there would be no natural or life-forms anywhere in the known universe.

The metaphysical assumption of a *Divine Unity* between Spirit and Matter or the invisible and visible realms of existence is a basic premise of the *Perennial Philosophy*; and it is also a basic premise, in one language or another, of every religious tradition of the world. Among the first narrative expressions of one of the oldest forms of the Perennial philosophy is the *Chandogya Upanishad* of the sacred *Vedas* of the Hindus, in northern India.

The story begins with a father sending his son away to study with teachers for twelve years and the first scene is the son's return home at the age of twenty- four. Detecting arrogance in his son, Svetaketu, the father begins to question him on the basis of his knowledge—whether his son possesses "knowledge by which we hear the unhearable, by which we perceive what cannot be perceived and know what cannot be known." But the father is not satisfied by his son's answers; and then the father says to his son that he will impart the eternal Truth to him, the possession of which is the basis for all that we know. And the son is not pleased to hear the criticism of his former teachers; until he reflects upon what he has actually learned from them.

The son then realizes that his teachers had not possessed the kind of knowledge his father describes; otherwise they would have transmitted it to him. The son is then ready to receive the sacred teaching of the *Vedas* from his father, desiring to know *"That by which* all this world is pervaded." And it is a crucial moment in the relationship of father and son.

The father said, "Bring me a fruit of the nyagrodha tree." "Here is one, sir," his son said. "Break it." "It is broken, sir." "What do you see there?" "Some seeds, sir, exceedingly small." "Break one of these." "It is broken, sir." "What do you see there?" "Nothing at all."

"The father says, 'My son, that subtle essence which you do not perceive there—in that very essence stands the being of the huge nyagrodha tree. In that which is subtle essence all that exists has its self-identity. That is the True, that is the Self, and *thou*, Svetaketu, *art That.*'" (4)

On the basis of simple parables such as this of the nyagrodha tree, the sacred teachings of the Hindu, Buddhist, and Jain philosophies of India can be seen. Similarly, the Unity of the world religions, East and West, can be seen in the mystical viewpoint, summed up in the Hindu aphorism, "Thou art That" pointing to the same unitary or One Truth that pervades the real world of forms, qualities, and differences.—And it is where idealism and realism, ideas and things, spirit and matter, meet and fuse together as the eternal *One*.

Perennialists assume or believe that Life is a universal and sacred force that interpenetrates the basic elements and Forces of nature with its creative energy or *chi*—in the here-and-now of Being. Skeptics, materialists, and atheists, on the other hand, believe that physical, organic and evolutionary nature is alone sufficient to explain the appearance of life-forms, in their vast diversity, without introducing any external agency like 'Life', 'God' or any other metaphysical Absolute. And this philosophical debate has continued without universal agreement or resolution for centuries; but for a significant number—whether philosophically inclined or not—the debate, the tennis game between mystics and skeptics, mystics and pragmatists, is over and it has been resolved on the intuitively elegant basis of the Perennial Wisdom of philosophy.

Conversation about Philosophy

There are innumerable perspectives and interpretations about what Life means in terms of everyday experience. Philosophy is a conversational record or history of the agreements and disagreements among thinking persons. It is thousands of years in the making, from all over the world, and it is likely to continue for as long as human beings do. Alfred North Whitehead, the American pragmatist, once described a philosopher as 'someone who confessions his ignorance in public places'; and it is the attitude of not-knowing or agnosticism that is most sensible in many if not most philosophical discussions—especially the metaphysical kind.

Tolle's philosophy has been informed by a unique vision of Being and an integrative intelligence that draws from the great wisdom traditions of the world. It is also the work of a creative genius who has brought humanity closer to the ultimate truth about reality; but it is not possible for one individual, no matter how brilliant or informed, to end the conversation of philosophy. Philosophy or some form of it will continue for as long as human beings continue to survive and flourish in the world. Tolle, for one, makes no claims about having the final, complete, or ultimate truth and expresses the same humility as Whitehead, Siddhartha, Socrates or Lao tzu.

The meaning and purpose of philosophy has gone through many changes in the last twenty-six hundred years, in Asia and the West. The ancient Greek philosopher's love of knowledge and wisdom is primarily based upon observation, reason, and speculation. Medieval European philosophy and theology moved away from the human reason and wisdom of the ancient Greeks, to an emphasis upon individual faith and God's grace and wisdom, as its essential basis. In the early modern European and American periods of Western philosophy, doubt, experience and analysis became the primary means or way of philosophy. Now, in the twenty-first century, professional academic philosophy has become fragmented and highly specialized by its emphasis upon issues in the sciences, theory of knowledge, logic, ethics and politics.

In other words, the goal of *Perennial Wisdom* has been largely given up by postmodern teachers of philosophy, due to the secularization of knowledge, the pragmatic *Zeitgeist* of American culture, and psychological *nerve*. The disinterest of modern philosophy about metaphysical or even ontological Truth is only a symptom of a larger societal indifference to religion and spirituality; and it also based upon a denial of death, impermanence and non-being in average, everyday life of ordinary existence.

Meanwhile, the emphasis upon questioning, doubt and skepticism in philosophy and higher education has led to generations of credentialed professions and others who believe in nothing, lack all conviction, and consider these qualities virtuous. In the cultivation of a balanced, integrated and holistic sense of the world, constitutive of *Perennial Wisdom*, the skeptical tendency is a major obstacle or block if carried to its extreme end; in such cases, skepticism denotes a shut-down, closed-off self that has disengaged from human experience and is often alienated from any suggestion of human fulfillment or happiness.

While *reason, revelation, doubt and experience* are four rather traditional bases of philosophy—faith and revelation is more subjective, experiential and heart-centered. At the same time, reason and doubt cannot exist independently of emotion or faith in their efficacy to realize its relativistic forms of truth. The fact that we exist as total beings or in terms of the body, mind and soul means that our cognitive thinking processes are inseparably connected with the perceptual, proprioceptual, intuitive, intellectual and spiritual aspects of Being. In fact, no listing of levels, dimensions and functions of individual being can really exhaust its totality.

The human mind is essentially about symbol-using and abstract ideational processes. Its chief means of persuasion is argument, particularly arguments that are thought to be logical, consistent or non-contradictory. Logical arguments come in at least three modes, i.e. arguments of *coherence, correspondence, and dialectics.* The first concerns the consistency or non-contradiction of ideas with one another and the second is based upon the agreement of statements with our observations of reality, and the third assumes that 'A' can be 'A' and 'B' and 'C'. Dialectical arguments close the gap between coherence and correspondence arguments in asserting that a higher principle exists that synthesizes 'A' and 'B' or what are conflicting logical tendencies.

In general, common logic—whatever else may be its symbolic form—follows a familiar pattern of distinctions: 1, 'claims' or assertions about truth or falsity, good or bad, value or disvalue, etc.; 2, 'evidence' or data of some kind that support the claims made in a line of reasoning or argument; 3, 'symbols' or the signs of meaning and truth that are expressed in a coherent, persuasive and consistent way; 4, 'backing' or an ultimate and final basis for an argument that is expressed; 5, conclusions that are based upon evidence that confirm or disconfirm the assumptions or hypothesis that the claims express about the question or problem at hand.

There are five major realms or regions of epistemology or theory of knowledge and truth: *1 information, 2 knowledge, 3 understanding, 4 wisdom and 5 enlightenment.* When one climbs the ladder of philosophy and has reached the summit, there may be no need for formal philosophy. The ladder that enables us to gain a vision of the whole of reality has served its purpose. We must lighten our burden and free ourselves of unnecessary cargo. Philosophy is a history of ideas and thought that is only useful or meaningful if it serves our needs and interests of the present moment. (5)

The history of intellectual agreements and disagreements is the sum and substance of philosophy. As *only* an intellectual discipline, philosophy cannot direct us to the best or truest vision of reality, knowledge, and values—the three major areas of study. To realize the vision of Perennial Wisdom and Truth, we must abandon any dogmatic or doctrinaire mission of argument and reason from the history of philosophy and theology. *Existence, Being, and Consciousness* are deeper, broader, and more inclusive than the conventional and historical biases of philosophy.

The greatest depths and heights of the *Perennial Wisdom* cannot be reached by merely intellectual or rational means. They require a daring and risk-taking in human thought that is unmet with in the halls of academia. Wisdom and its fulfillment in the enlightenment experience can only be experienced and known in moments of intuitive and meditative stillness and silence far from the mad rush to education, careers and money. And it can only be fully realized beyond these and all other symbols that merely suggest, provoke and inspire one to the greatest of adventures: the experience of Being—or whatever symbol that best fits.

The conventional basis of philosophy as reason, knowledge and intellectual development has little to nothing to do with the moral, psychological, aesthetic and spiritual values of liberation, wisdom and enlightenment. Even philosophy's noble goal of wisdom has been largely ignored if not altogether lost in the contemporary obsession with the theory of knowledge that is based upon logic, reason and science. As Shakespeare wrote, 'There are more philosophies under Heaven and on Earth than are dreamed of in your philosophy'. And many similar sentiments have been expressed in criticism of formal or academic philosophy.

That said, there is not a more inclusive or integrative discipline for pursuing Wisdom than philosophy. However, the chief weakness of philosophy is its obsession with old texts, dead ideas, and intellectual history. An obsession with old texts, technical distinctions and language, and philosophies of ancient origin, foster an attachment to and identification with ideas and knowledge for their own sake. The historical habit of mind creates alienation from change, newness and the Nowness of experience. We can only step into the past through the abstractions of memory and the intellect, at the risk of neglecting immediate perception and intuition, psychological feelings and attitudes, and the existing, ongoing, present moment or the Eternal Now of personal experience.

Until philosophy returns to the primordial, natural Goodness of Life, its knowledge will remain unbalanced, alienating, and lacking the spiritual Center that it everywhere. Tolle's critique of the intellectual sphere of consciousness is a healthy correction to philosophy's emphasis upon conceptual, analytical and historical knowledge. Perennial Wisdom can awaken us to the infinite levels, dimensions, and possibilities of Now— if and only if we are willing and ready to receive it.

Social Masks and Authentic Being

It is perfectly obvious that the major social, economic, and political problems of the world cannot be solved through the present world consciousness. We need a transformed consciousness, one that exists fully in the Now and realizes its essential divinity; and this can begin individually or through small, intimate groups. Looking outside ourselves for answers—to governments, corporation, and universities— has given us more of the same: an abyss between the rich and the poor, social class divisions, gender and racial discrimination, and other cultural conflicts that seem unsolvable. The vision for a new Earth must begin within the awakened Consciousness of each individual, where we can find the essence of Being or the soul of an authentically existing person.

To the political realist, the materialist, and the skeptic of human possibilities, the perennialist recipe for Wisdom may seem like 'pie in the sky' or something more ridiculous. Indeed, one must be *tender-hearted and tough-minded,* as the American Pragmatist, William James implied, in approaching any new proposal for change or transformation among individuals and in society at large. One does not have to go very far in search of *home* to see what must be done to transform the *house* that we live in.

The decision to stop fighting and begin affirming Goodness in our life-situations is one that brings peace, tranquility, and new light into the world. The history of persons, religions, and moral perspectives favoring nonviolence, universal justice, and natural Goodness is ancient in origin and continuously growing. The awareness that something must be done to stop the wanton killing and slaughter of innocent people and animals in wars and genocides is also growing. The consciousness of growth or the creative evolution of persons to a higher Consciousness is the new narrative of our times and not the old narratives based upon negativity, pessimism, and doubt. *Goodness, Beauty and Justice* are the deeper, more creative energies of Life and far stronger than the evil, destruction and horror of world history.

Too often, we allow a mundane life-situation that we are caught up in, to determine our attitude towards Life and the possibilities of the present moment. We must begin to live fully in our particular life-world situations beyond negativity, time, and contingent conditions. We must surrender to the deeper, hidden level of reality beyond surface conditions and mere appearances. When we do this, the power of Nature illuminates consciousness with its creative energy, original Goodness, and the inner, embodied spirit of Being.

When we *feel the energy of original Nature,* we perceive the beauty, design and miracle of the present moment. If God exists in a knowable form, then God exists as Nature, through all its atomic elements, physical laws, and universal Forces. The concreteness of God can be known through the perceptions, emotions and thoughts of mind, body and soul. The wholeness of our own Being is sacred in origin and that is why all parts of identity can awaken us to our divine origin, Presence and destiny.

For sure, people, animals, and life-situations are challenging to the attitude of non-resistance, non-violence, and non-aggression. The *pain-body* thrives on tensions, problems, and conflicts of all kinds. Stress, aggression, and restless activity keep it going and alive; but as the pain-body begins to die, tranquility, equanimity, and peace are experienced and become habitual; and we begin to see with new eyes, ears and a total sense of self that is informed by the higher Consciousness of our innate essence, the soul.

There is often an unavoidable suffering that the ego nurtures—often at unconscious levels even when one appears to be happy and peaceful. However, once awakened to higher Consciousness, *the soul intuitively knows the Truth* of who you are beneath the role-playing, ego-posturing and social masks that society conditions you to put on and wear in your interactions with others; and this awareness is the opportunity for liberation or authentic being. Your awakening to authentic Being is realizing the inertia of Unconsciousness, mindless conditioning, and the fear that inhibits your unmasking; for the greatest of fears is the fear of freedom.

The socially conditioned, ego-based, role-playing self of inauthenticity is the greatest obstacle to the goal of perennial wisdom: awakening to the Truth of existence. For sure, there are persons who can be truly honest, happy, and authentic while just role-playing in society. If you merely think that you are, you may be living in delusion, unconsciousness, and ignorance of your authentic self; but if you can genuinely experience the purity of your own soul, your authentic self or real being will show itself to others.

In sum, what is the basis for the difference between the authentic and inauthentic self-Being? The former sense of self is based upon the soul or the essence of who you are, while the latter is derived from our social belonging, egoic identification and role-playing. This moral and ontological split in our identity is reflected in the private and public roles of the typical person, living and working in society. The vast majority of persons may be so caught up in their working roles in society that they are unable to wake up to the truth about their life-situations and the universal or existential Truth about Life.

Real Education and the American Dream

Awakening from the sleep-walk of normal everyday existence should be the main purpose of education. Instead education as well as the popular culture to which it is intimately linked, is a conspiracy against real consciousness or individual awakening of any kind—especially to the truth about living in the material, economic and social world. Instead, it merely sends out the message of consumerism, buy, buy now and pay later; and if you go to school, and belong to the middle class of slaves to the Plutocracy, you can buy and become indebted to the God of materialism forever and go to a Heaven of stuff after death!

If you can really wake up, through only one moment of intuitively or deeply glimpsing the truth about your life-world, you will become aware of your inner body and its moral, aesthetic and spiritual essence. The profound insight and intellectual feeling that follows upon the awakened soul frees it from the moral corruption and causal conditioning of the real, social world. Authentic education or learning begins when you wake up to who you are and gain real self-knowledge which is knowledge of your divine soul, the energy or *chi* of the universal Spirit in all forms; and by comparison, the *American Dream* is a pathetic thing since it is only about material and financial success and learning how to play the established social roles, successfully or competitively.

In this context, real education is about awakening to the Truth and not about just learning how to play the social and intellectual game competitively. There is much more to Life than working and making a living; it is about *really living* and experiencing the freedom of the awakened soul and its potentials of wonder, ecstasy and joy in just being who you are, in the present moment. In the mad dash to prepare for the world of work, too many young and older people have forgotten how to play, live and be in the Now where everything is always new and alive with sacred Presence.

The Utopian or Perennial vision of education is nothing new in the history of civilization. It is as old as Parmenides, Socrates and Plato in ancient Greece, the *Upanishads* of the Hindus, the *Sutras* of Siddhartha and Mahavira in India; Laozi, Confucius and Chuangzi in China. Its Middle Eastern roots are visible in the visions of Zarathustra, the Jewish Prophets, the *Beatitudes* of Jesus, and the *Koran* of the Moslems. Education, especially when it is conceived in terms of the Perennial Wisdom, is a timeless, mystical, and ineffable experience that allows us to see the moral law within and the cosmic law without, and declares it to be one and the same.

Most parents, understandably, want the best for their children and make great sacrifices to that end. This fact should be a given in school planning, teacher training, and curriculum building. The problem is that the institutions of mass education have, too often, failed to awaken children and young adults to 'who they are' or the self-knowledge of real being. Schools and colleges have too often failed to awaken students to their infinite potentiality for self-actualization and personal fulfillment. And this does not mean buying into the American dream or any other nationalistic illusion; instead it means waking up to the inner meaning and purpose of Life as it relates to self-awareness and the real world.

The American Dream has become a nightmare for many if not most citizens. Intense levels of stress, fragmentation, and alienation from self and others are obvious to everyone except the blind; and judging by the number of people seeking psychological help, the addictions to alcohol, sex, nicotine, and illegal drugs—things are only growing worse. Instead of facing the truth about ordinary life in the real world, the majority seek the continuous distraction of television, movies, and spectator sports. If the American Dream is ever to mean anything vital, moral and spiritual, it will have to be based on a new standard for success, one that does not promise learning for wealth and security but one that presents the possibility of liberation, adventure and self-knowledge.

American society has always been a bakery for dreams and dreamers, schemers and schemes for adventures and riches. We are a society where money is more important than people; and the value of a person's life is determined by the size of his portfolio and the frivolous and wasteful toys that he dies with. Money, material wealth, and consumption have now become the dream of almost everyone in the developing world. *Getting rich* has become the central purpose or reason for living—not just in China but all over the world—but for the majority of poor, working class, and middle class people even if they have no understanding of how to get rich or what *qualitative difference* it would make in their lives. And it is mostly a pathetic if not tragic story from the beginning to the end.

Illusion, Global Change and Catastrophe

Enlightenment is one of those symbols especially apt to delude or mislead those using the term as to what the word really means. We are constantly more or less bewitched by the words that we use so much so that they use us. For language creates its own universe of meaning which we unwittingly identify with and it too often becomes our undoing.

The reality is that disaster, catastrophe, and collapse are constant possibilities in the most idyllic or peaceful of circumstances, for the enlightened and un-enlightened alike. We are more or less constantly seduced by our particular, limited, and local situations into thinking that 'everything is just fine' or O.K; while all the time the universe and all forms within it, is *on fire*—as the ancient Greek philosopher, Heraclitus wrote; while Siddhartha, the Buddha, was inspired to give his famous *Sermon on Fire*. (6)

In a similar and related sense, *greed, hatred, delusion and fear* are among the leading toxic emotions and poisonous states of psychological being in almost anyone's philosophy—especially that of popular Buddhism. If you identify through your speech, thoughts and actions with any of these deadly phenomena, you will find yourself living in a hell of fire from which you will have a most difficult time extricating yourself, psychologically.— De-constructing, reflecting upon and working on these *fires* cools their disturbing influence, with patience and vigilance.

In the present world, national security is an obsession and an illusion since humanity is Now and will forever totter on the edge of a great precipice; and it would take only the slightest miscalculation on the part of world leaders, to end civilization in a thermonuclear conflagration. Of course, few people ever worry about such possibilities anymore, since there are so many 'safeguards', surveillance systems, and career bureaucrats that worry about such contingencies. The world that humans have constructed is so profoundly unjust, dangerous, and non-conducive to anything resembling 'life, liberty, and justice for all' that such ideals have become practically empty of meaning, platitudinous and ridiculous *in extremis.*

From the earliest of years, we are taught to 'fight' with others and be aggressive, to get our way— the ego's way, the way of vanity, greed, and control of others. Because most people conform to such conditioning and rise to the top levels of society, economically, and exercise great control over others, present society has become sick, corrupt, and absent of anything remotely spiritual. At the same time, the precious metaphysical touchstone called the *soul* or the essence of total being is all but lost in the techno-babble and mindless consumerism of our times.

Compounding these conditions and making it easier for the rich or highly successful few, is a world society divided sharply between the haves and have-nots or the rich and the poor; and to almost no one's surprise, the poor and the very poor are in the majority. Meanwhile, the very rich amass billions of dollars and number in the thousands; and the very poor make about one to five dollars per day and number in the billions. And the reasons for this great economic injustice and human divide in the world are not very hard to find.

Not only is there systemic world poverty or a *de facto* slave system for the benefit of international Corporations and their stock holders, but the economic class system is deeply racist, sexist and speciesist. The egregious success of the few in the Capitalist system guarantees that there is a corresponding enslavement of the many. At the same time, the banking, financial and credit system is controlled by the few and ensures that the many will be beholden to it all their lives. And for the middle or working class professional workers, entrepreneurs, and tradesmen, there is no such thing as the absolute freedom from economic catastrophe.

International Corporations, financial systems, and technocratic entrepreneurs are rapidly becoming more powerful and important than military institutions, political ideologies or parties. National security is pegged to the state of the economy as much as a military campaign, a nuclear arsenal, or new surveillance system. All this and more is due the fact that we live in a globalized *web* of relations where there is no one weaver and where the slightest movement in one cell, organism, or weaver can vitally or directly affect all other parts, as never before.

When the world population mushrooms to over 10 billion in the middle of the twenty-first century, the former struggle over natural resources like the oil wars of the early twenty-first century, will give way to wars over clean water for drinking, clean air for breathing, and arable land for growing food. Global climate change, in the form of rising sea-levels and the flooding of large areas of the inhabited world, will likely require massive population re-location sites or new cities before the mid-century point, even if all preventive and ecological measures are taken.

Catastrophic global change seems inevitable in the short, middle, and long view of human beings. In the short view, we will all suffer or undergo the dying process of social change, in one form or another; and in the long view, the planet that we inhabit, will—with astronomical certainty—be utterly destroyed by a dying sun, a few billion years from now. In the present early period of dramatic global change, humankind and the tens of billions who will inhabit the Earth, will likely succumb to any number of global catastrophes—from a microbial plague to the consequences of environmental exhaustion and resource depletion, to a holocaustic war that ends with a 'bang *and* a whimper', sending cyborg humans and their offspring back to the new Stone Age.

To think that humanity can prevent globalized social and existential catastrophes from happening is only a pathetic illusion. The other and parallel illusion is that we will develop enough scientific knowledge and technology to 'fix' whatever material or social problem arises. Since deluded reason, insatiable desire and the competitive ego are the sources of the very problems that presently haunt humanity, it is unrealistic to think that there will be available moral or existential solutions to them. The way out of *the insanity of the world* and the ignorance, injustice and violence that causes so much human suffering and unhappiness, will not be easy nor will it come without sacrifice, prudence, and serious alternatives to the present global mess.

In sum, enlightenment means waking up to the illusions that we have about ourselves and the world we live in. There is no substitute for the experience and knowledge of what is real, true and good. Absolute Being or Goodness may seem remote and abstract to the many and the luxury of the few, but it is most essentially *who we are,* rich or poor, male or female, black or white. When we experience the inner body or soul, then we will realize that we are already, always saved from the madness of the world. And it is this self-realization—not worldly success—that is the primary condition for the Light of Being pouring in upon the Earth from the farthest regions of the vast and mysterious universe.

Chapter 25

NOW, WISDOM AND ENLIGHTENMENT

What are Wisdom and Enlightenment and how are they related to the present moment and the total being of a person? How can we be consciously and authentically present in the Now of experience? Why are the present moment and self-knowledge important to the experience and knowledge of Wisdom and Enlightenment?

"Our original Buddha-Nature is, in highest truth, devoid of any atom of objectivity. It is void, omnipresent, silent, pure; it is glorious and mysterious peaceful joy—and that is all." Huang Po

"Reason is the substance of the universe....The design is absolutely rational." George W.F. Hegel

"Politics and religion are obsolete; the time has come for science and spirituality." Vinobe Bhave

"Form is emptiness and Emptiness is form...." Zen aphorism

"It both is and is not; it neither is nor is not." The Buddha

"The most beautiful and most profound emotion we can experience is the sensation of the mystical. It is the sower of all true science. He to whom this emotion is a stranger, who can no longer stand rapt in awe, is as good as dead. That deeply emotional conviction of the presence of a superior reasoning power, which is revealed in the incomprehensible universe, forms my idea of God." Albert Einstein

The Present Moment: the Gap in the Past-Future Continuum

Tolle asserts that the present moment "creates a gap not only in the stream of mind but also in the past-future continuum."

471

Furthermore, *"Nothing truly new and creative can come into this world except through that gap, that clear space of infinite possibility."* And when we cease identifying with the mind—no matter how 'educated', 'intelligent', or informed you may be—we are then able to make genuine, free choices—choices that come from the translucence of Being, its unconditional free will and the pure, eternal soul—the essence of Being. (1)

This may be an unfamiliar even complex idea but it is one that can make a profound difference in your everyday life; if you really understand the truth about your identity as a human being, then you can live in a more authentic way without illusion or confusion. Whatever situation that you are presently facing in your life is necessarily related to inner Being or the eternal Life-force; and the possibility of peace, joy and happiness in the Now is one that only requires surrendering the ego to the divine energy of Being, the essence of which is the eternal soul.

The 'gap' in the Now of time is the inner freedom of humanity existing as the *will*. If you are not addicted to some substance, role or relationship and thus suffering from the pain-body, you are able to choose and choose from real self-knowledge. Choosing to be in the Now is *the most important step* that we must take to realize who we are and enter the path of enlightenment: *Be in the Now of existence.* The present moment or the Eternal Now is the 'gap' through which we can see, feel, and experience the Light of supreme Being.

Enlightenment: the Radiance of Being

The experience of Enlightenment or breakthrough to higher Consciousness is the innermost radiance of Being within the unique soul of each individual that connects the body with the universal Self. You should think about the ordinary or everyday self of society as hiding a big secret, an undisclosed treasure of priceless value, more valuable than all the gold, silver, and money of the world. And the secret is the infinite possibilities of Being existing in the present moment.

This treasure has been unconsciously covered over by a person's mind, ego, and social roles. The process takes place over your entire life-time, nurtured by your family, the schools that you have attended, your exposure to the mass media, your friends and enemies, whoever you have known and whatever you have done. Society is a conspiracy against you discovering who you really are and what lies deeply within your self-Being: a divine soul, intellect and body that it has freely chosen to live authentically for spiritual liberation. And you are here to create and discover the potentialities within your total self, thereby contributing ever so imperceptibly, to the moral, intellectual and spiritual transformation of humankind.

The layers of distraction, entertainment, desire, and material goals that have weighed down the great majority of persons in society: the regrets and guilt of the remembered past, the worry and anxiety of an imagined future, and the stress and conflicts of existence—are real in the pain-body of global culture. The unconscious self is a great ocean of desires, wants, and lacks that are conditioned and implanted by others and the *karma* of unknown lives and generations. If you enter into the Now of liberation—where the will-to-Being or Consciousness exist—and accept the Presence of what-is without fighting or resisting, then you can penetrate through the conditioning of the mind, language, and its ego constructions, to the sanity, peace, and natural Goodness of Being where there is a pure radiance and illumination of the soul.

Path of the Soul: Enlightenment

When you decide to take the first steps on the Path of enlightenment, you make a life-changing decision that will always have unforeseeable consequences. For example, when you realize that the pain-body is the biggest obstacle on the path of enlightenment, you experience a breakthrough to higher, ineffable Consciousness—this is the first step; and when you become aware of the infinite potentiality of the soul for true happiness,

Now and which began at the first moment of conception or your Presence in existence—this is the second step in awakening to Wisdom.

Until you are ready to know or really experience who you are, enlightenment is just as idea, an abstraction of the mind, reinforced by language and meaning. Once on the Path, the way to your destination is clear and you cannot turn back. At this point, you realize that you have made a commitment to a life-world with greater certainty and unlimited possibilities. In this respect, Tolle has written:

"Enlightenment consciously chosen means to relinquish your attachment to past and future and to make the Now the main focus of your life. It means choosing to dwell in the state of presence rather than in time. It means saying yes to what is." (2)

Saying 'yes' to Being and existence, to the totality of what-is, means freely choosing from your innermost Being or the eternal, pure soul and not from the conditioned, societal self that exists unconsciously and irrationally. A single moment of fully conscious decision-making can make the most profound difference in the quality of your life-world. And until you choose with clear awareness, you cannot choose from the soul or the essence of who you are—which is the most important step on the Path of Wisdom.

Moments of experienced Radiance may be rare but they are unforgettable in the existence of everyone. Freely and authentically made decisions are breakthrough moments—breakthroughs to Being—moments of genuine self-awareness where you suddenly see with a new clarity, depth, and sense of detachment that is ineffable—since words cannot describe the experience. When you make a decision on the basis of your soul, you choose to really live and not just exist since you are now walking on the essential path—the Path towards Enlightenment.

This is the fourth step on the Path of Wisdom and Enlightenment or the step where you renounce pain, negativity and violence and freely choose the path of the soul where true joy, hope and peace can be experienced. It is the inner path of freedom where true self-knowledge is found and not the false self-knowledge of roles, ego and material relations; and it is the means whereby we can realize harmony with others, peace of mind and soul, and the experiences of wonder, mystery and possibility.

Perspectives of Truth

Words alone cannot describe or explain the fullness of enlightenment; and that is why it is sometimes termed 'ineffable' or a wordless experience. The depth, radiant, and translucent clarity of the experience is all that you need to know, to recognize the Presence of Being through inner being or the soul. It is through the inner sense of self, that we can find salvation, redemption and divinity.

The Zen Buddhists refer to enlightenment as 'satori' or an intense absorption of self when we ascend through the energy levels of Consciousness to formlessness and beyond. The Indian Jains use a fourteen level yogic model of experience to aid their monks in purifying the karmic corruption of the soul. And the Chinese Taoists speak of *wu-wei* or 'action-less doing' as a going-with and yielding to the cosmic *chi* or energy of *yin—yang* that align the soul with the *Tao* or the invisible Unity of every form in nature, society and the cosmos.

There are in the history of religion, philosophy, and psychology, many different models or intellectual constructions for working towards the sense of liberation that brings enlightenment. But none of them may be as easy and brilliant in insight as the Perennial model that Tolle advocates: simply be consciously and fully present in the Now where you can find the answers to the most basic questions of existence. Learn to meditate or focus your higher Consciousness upon the experiences of the body, heart-mind and soul with a completely open and non-attached awareness. Experience the profound peace, love, and joy that exist within your sense of Being-present in the here-and-now.

You can choose an established model for enlightenment—perhaps a path that has been taken by millions of persons before you—or one that needs new use. The most important thing is to go the whole way and not half-heartedly.

For example, the Buddha's Eightfold Path or the Middle Way for spiritual or personal liberation; or if you decide to become a renunciant, you should consider the fourteen steps in the *Ladder of Liberation* that Jain monks and nuns follow. The Jain Path to *moksa* or freedom is one that is based upon an eternal soul with infinite possibilities for knowledge and wisdom; and the Buddhist Path assumes that an infinitely subtle consciousness enables you to realize the Way from Here-and-Now to complete Liberation from cyclic existence. Both Paths are equivalent in power and can take you to the same goal: the freedom of real Being.

If you access the Perennial Wisdom, as Tolle has done, you can develop your own synthesis and vision of the Truth; and although there are many pathways in existence, none is more important than the one that is right for you, owing to your existential uniqueness and relation to universal Being. Finally, although the perennial vision of Truth is absolute and universal, our own knowledge of it is limited, conditional and ever-changing.

Immeasurable Goodness

What is Immeasurable Goodness? Is it the Holy Grail or Absolute Truth? Or is it 'the peace of Being which surpasses all understanding'?

Tolle writes that the experience of ordinary happiness is a quite shallow thing compared to the enlightenment experience. "With radiant peace comes the realization—not on the level of mind but within the depth of your Being—that you are indestructible, immortal. This is not a belief. It is absolute certainty that needs no external evidence or proof from some secondary source." (3)

The *absolute certainty* of universal and immeasurable Goodness is deeply personal and emanates from the essence of Being.

Goodness is the Unconditional Truth of real existence; and it is the Source of your unique, indestructible and eternal soul since Goodness is the means whereby your soul has real existence. While everything else is constantly changing and impermanent, the soul is the basis of the will-to-live, create and power. In this sense, the soul is the locus, the gravitational center without limits that anchors you to the universe for eternity. It is the path to the infinite possibilities that Truth, Goodness and Enlightenment symbolize in existence.

The Path of the soul is the inner body, where experience begins and ends, in real existence. However, the inner body is the region of higher Consciousness along the spine beginning at its lowest point to the crown of the head. The energy centers of the inner body are oriented towards: *survival, enjoyment, success, compassion, creativity, understanding and vision.* These are the dynamic centers of the will-to-self-realization that transform ordinary consciousness to higher Consciousness, through the experiences of enlightenment. They function at the core of inner body, continuously in experience, in *the Now of real time and eternity.* They enable us to experience the Omniscience that is necessary for survival, self-realization and final liberation.

The divine Unity of the body-mind -soul is an immeasurable Goodness. It is the Presence of something sacred, imperceptibly, subtly changing and transforming each of us, within and beyond awareness. It is the perfection of each moment, as *Prakriti* (Nature) the manifestation of each blade of grass, star, and tree, and the simultaneous Presence of *Purusha* (Spirit). And it is the perfection of each soul struggling to free itself from the entanglements of the world.

The Ladder of Liberation

The following analysis of the experience of liberation is taken from an ancient Jain theory of liberation which I have taken the liberty to call the *Ladder of Liberation*. The much fuller discussion of this ascetic theory is contained in the *Tattvartha Sutra* of the Jains although there are numerous other discussions of this important doctrine elsewhere in Jain literature. I have culled a few of these other sources and my own experience for this interpretation.

In the Jain theory of spirituality, known as the *Ladder of Liberation*, there are fourteen stages of enlightenment:

1, *embodiment* (of the soul (*jiva*) within the body-mind (*ajiva-chitta*); this stage of enlightenment is known as that of wrong faith where a person identifies with the body, is impulsive, non-reflective and acts mainly for that sake of pleasure and sensation; yet it is a necessary and important beginning of the human organism.

2, *presence* (or awakening to the inner struggles of body, mind and soul); this stage of enlightenment is known as that of right perception where questions of right and wrong, true and false, faith and doubt, arise in the mind. Only right perception can sort them out although the higher stages can only complete the process.

3, *awareness* (of conflicting desires, emotions, and goals); this stage of the enlightenment process is that of developing intellectual discernment for overcoming confusion brought on by the crazy mixing of alternatives that have no purpose or meaning. A clear mind, warm heart and deep soul are needed here.

4, *conflict* (between free-will and lack of restraint); this stage of enlightenment occurs when a person realizes how ephemeral all experiences are in comparison to the soul. A glimpse of the pure soul is sufficient to clarify many earlier stage conflicts; but many attachments remain in spite of a new freedom from *karma*.

5, *self-restraint* (frugality, asceticism, simplicity); this stage of enlightenment occurs when a person achieves right perception which is based upon faith in the soul's existence and the potentialities of the seven truths: the soul, lifeless matter, incoming karma, bondage, prevention, eradication and liberation.

6, *control over* (negative emotional processes like fear, hatred, greed and delusion); this stage of enlightenment enables the spiritual seeker to give up worldly life and even renounce it to remain free from incoming karma. It marks real control over negative emotions, sensations, thoughts of the inner body.

8, *acceptance* (of change like loss, aging, disease, dying, and endings); this stage of enlightenment involves acceptance of change in its many universal forms especially as personally experienced and understood. Right action is the last challenge to the path of liberation, following right perception and knowledge.

9, *control over* (over sexual urges and emotions associated); this stage of enlightenment involves control over the gross, physical instinct of sexuality. The sexual ego and the forms of Maya may attract the soul in subtle and gross ways as greed and desire; but attachment to other forms is still strong at this stage.

10, *loss and gain of interest* (loss in outer or real world affairs and gain of inner world as unity of being); at this stage of enlightenment the seeker realizes a very subtle level of consciousness having overcome gross instincts and subtle defilements to the soul; it marks the true beginning of an inner life and being.

11, *awakening to transcendence* (withdrawal of consciousness from the world); this stage of enlightenment is fraught with danger since the control, restraint and transcendence of earlier stages can be lost in a moment of defilement through the lack of vigilance and concentration; but quickly regaining this stage is possible.

12, *overcoming* (of the influence of ego, karma and body and awakening to perfection, bliss and omniscience); this stage of enlightenment involves a powerful effort to overcome delusions that remain in the soul from past defilements, obscuring perceptions of the soul, and obstructing categories of the mind.

13, *active form of enlightenment;* first stage of passing beyond death as a transcender (*kevalin*), a hero (*jina*), or worthy one (*arhat*); at this stage one attains full enlightenment as an omniscient transcender of death. The *kevalin* is endowed with *infinite* perception, bliss, and energy and thus *enlightened as embodied souls.*

14, *passive transcendence* (*ayoga-kevati*); This is the second and shorter stage of transcendence. One becomes a fully liberated or perfect being (*siddha*-yogi). This condition occurs just prior to the death of the physical body. Beyond this stage is a perfectly luminous condition known only to a *siddha-yogi* whose soul is free from embodiment, karma, and reincarnation. (4)

Dying, Death and Enlightenment

It may be consoling to think that we will live forever in our present bodily form—as believers in the *rapture* apparently do. But common sense is completely at odds with this belief as it is with any belief that denies the reality of 'death and dying'. The certainty of the death of the body is beyond all doubting; but the greatest question of all concerns *the possible existence of an eternal soul* or the real means by which we may realize metaphysical immortality and not just social immortality.

A small consolation of skeptical and naturalistic origin is that we never really experience or know death. As Ludwig Wittgenstein, the logician, skeptic and atheist has said, "Death is not an event in life. Death is not lived through"— by one who is dying. *Death is a non-experience*—an insight about the importance of living in the here-and-now, rather than worrying about the future. (5)

Soren Kierkegaard, the Existentialist, wrote that there is an *objectivity uncertainty* about the existence of God; and in a parallel or dialectical assertion, Kierkegaard also declared the *Truth is subjectivity and Subjectivity is truth*. Similar assertions can also be made about an immortal or eternal soul, higher Consciousness or even the human link to the Universal Mind.

In the terms of what could be called the *enlightenment experience,* there is the dialectical perspective of impermanence and Eternity, change and Being, manifestation and Un-manifestation. In other words, everything in space, time and materiality, is subject to constant change, known only approximately, and contingently related to everything else. We can only intuitively sense or inwardly experience Being or the eternity of Now, while external becoming and material relations can be seen and understood through the objective forms of knowledge and Consciousness.

It is something like a consoling assumption that everything is unified and one or necessarily and lawfully linked with Eternal Being. We assume and say that the body and mind are interrelated, but how much do we really understand those relations, links and mechanisms? For sure, there is as much weight on the *skeptical* side of the scales of knowledge as there is the *mystical* one. And yet our lowly *pragmatist* may win the day and argument after all: it is not what you think or believe that so much matters, but what are you going to do that really matters; and how does what you believe make a difference or not, in your personal experience?

It is the enlightenment experience that brings the necessary *evidence (or not)* that is needed for some to really *know* that an immortal soul exists within each of us. This evidence is internal, absolute, and trans-subjective in that it raises ordinary consciousness to the highest level of awareness. Anyone who has experienced the light of Being knows with a certainty that exceeds all the horror, terror, and fear of death and dying, that eternal Life and not death and oblivion is the real destiny of the soul.

You will *not* find such assertions in biology, psychology, or even most philosophy books since these disciplines are empirically biased. Tolle and other Perennialists urge us to go beyond the mind, body, and egoic levels of Life to assumptions, concepts and beliefs that support the survival of death. Can we survive death as liberated *and* conscious beings? The liberation from cyclic existence seems quite meaningless without the possibility of a surviving Consciousness since its total absence would be equivalent to *oblivion* forever—following death.

If the enlightenment experience means anything at all, it frees us from ignorance while we are alive in the here-and-now. Furthermore, the enlightenment experience or *education* in the most noble, multi-dimensional and ideal of senses, frees us from ignorance, suffering and delusion, here-and-now. The sense of liberation that attends the enlightenment experience (*read*

481

educational), occurs in terms of the means-ends continuum, in far greater intensity, depth and the elevation of consciousness than is realized in ordinary states of experience or even happiness.

So what, if anything, is there to lose in seeking enlightenment or the liberation from ignorance, suffering and delusion? Would not personal and social existence be infinitely better if all *pain, suffering and violence were minimized* and the opposing conditions—*well-being, self-fulfillment and non-violence, maximized?* What do we have to lose by investing our energy and effort, natural and human resources, time and intelligence, in the development of a more just, compassionate and caring society that includes all people in full equality regardless of class, race, gender, and age?

I propose that we have everything to gain and nothing to lose. In spite of all the present problems, real and imagined, of human existence, we cannot console ourselves with beliefs, hopes and dreams that tomorrow will somehow be better than Now. The real solving of any problem like ignorance, injustice and violence, must begin, go forward and be solved in the present moment; and although Being is forever, human beings are dependently related to the Source. In other words, it is the pure soul of each of us that has the power, potentiality and creativity to participate in the unlimited possibilities of the Eternal Now.

CONCLUSIONS: REFLECTIONS UPON THE

PERENNIAL WISDOM

"May you find your path and follow it." The Buddha
"I have found my way; don't follow me. What is your way?" Friedrich
Nietzsche

Wisdom is the perennial or universal goal of philosophy and
one could argue human existence. No single individual, philosophy or religion can have a monopoly or totally inclusive perspective of wisdom; all views of wisdom are relative, approximate, and
subject to re-vision. And although all knowledge is situated, con-
textual, and historical, there remains the possibility that there
are universal truths that transcend time, place, and individual
perspective and which provide us with the most fundamental
insights about our place in the universe.

This book has assumed that universal truths or essences do,
in fact, exist. Otherwise, much of what we daily think and feel,
choose and act upon, would surely make far less sense than they
commonly do. Contrary to Plato and other dualistic idealists
of philosophy, essences or universal Truths are not located in
another world or some timeless, perfect, and unchanging realm
of Being. The intuitive fact appears that essences are found in
human existence or the transcendental subjectivity of higher
Consciousness. Asserting this, of course, does not make an
essence any easier to understand or comprehend, for the student of philosophy and wisdom.

483

Let us approach the subject of wisdom and its philosophic essence, from another angle. In education and elsewhere, we hear much about knowledge or belief that is supported by empirical evidence, logical reason and fact. But we do not hear uttered the dialectical counterpoint to such knowledge, namely *experience* or the subjective connection that we naturally form through the body, mind and soul in the evolution of existence. Knowledge and experience cannot be separated from one another anymore readily than ordinary consciousness can be separated from subjective being, nature, society, and the universe.

We are, at present, faced with a great revolution in the consciousness of individuals nearly everywhere in the world, caused by forces released from pre-historic, ancient and modern times. The Now of human experience, knowledge and Consciousness has always been a confluence of universal and contingent forces, far greater than the power of single individuals or even humanity itself. A considerable and perhaps immeasurable degree of these global forces is of human origin, especially the global climate change that threatens to undo the secure habitats of cities and nation-states around the world. The debate is now fueled by the science of global change and the entrenched economic self-interests of the *status quo.*

It is no accident that an emergency presently exists among the developing and developed countries of the world with respect to energy-resources and the depletion of fossil fuels. Greed, violence, and the lack of prudence seem to go historically together in the make-up of most human beings and their cultures. Evidence of this extends from the extinct Indus Valley civilization of India to the Aztec ruins of Central America. The moral path of frugality, nonviolence, and simplicity in living seems to have always been the way of the few and not the many. Much that is stupid, unwise, and imprudent in living seems more a function of the lack of information, education or awareness than it is of native intelligence or a capacity for acting otherwise.

In acquiring wisdom about one's self, the real world, and existence, there are no magic bullets or instant recipes. However, my own view is that there is no substitute for information, knowledge, and understanding that is based upon evidence in the most inclusive sense of the word. This means that mythology, religion, and science can give us real evidence through belief, experience, reason, and experiment that produce differing forms of knowledge, understanding and wisdom. However, it is at least debatable whether the theoretical and empirical sciences (and scientists) can ever give us the wisdom and insight of sages, saints, and mystics without faith in the Divine Ground of Being.

The so-called ontological argument for the existence of God is based upon the priority of mind in the world: if an *infinitely perfect Being* can be conceived within the mind, then that Being must exist in an extra-mental sense. It is at least questionable whether finite human beings can conceive of absolute or infinite perfection. Perhaps the best we can do is to imagine perfect Being; and if we can imagine perfect Being or what-is, then, in spite of our limitations, it *could* (not must) exist independently of our imagination. –Thus much depends upon *possibility* in our arguments about God and related metaphysical matters.

Being or what-is-real is more perfect than what we can know through our perceptions, conceptions, and imaginings of reality. We know this by a transcendental sense of the soul that has been known through intuition, insight and even revelation. Ordinary knowledge or the intellectual forms through which we claim to know reality come to us through the interactive mechanisms of the nervous system, symbolic language and the mind. Furthermore, there is clear evidence of an extraordinary potentiality within human nature, which once awakened, can lead us to essential discoveries and insights.

What, though, is the origin of knowledge that we may daily take-for-granted? First, there are the experiences based upon the senses, emotions, and thoughts of a person, which form the impressions of intellectual reflection and understanding. This is the most immediate, organic, and subjective basis of experience that forms the neural layers and connections of higher cognitive processes. Just as the skin of a person is formed by several layers of tissue beneath the visible surface, our higher reasoning processes, emotions and perceptions are constituted by an invisible network of nerve cell bodies, electro-chemical processes, blood tissue, and synaptic connections of the brain and the central nervous system of the body.

Indeed, what is deemed abstract in one context of thought and reasoning is, in terms of immediate experience, entirely organic, affective, and subjective in nature. Oftentimes, our judging a form of thought or reasoning to be 'abstract' rather than 'concrete' is merely conditioned by the conventions of language and what may be an empty or meaningless use of words. The fact is that speech is a metaphorical abstraction of how we feel, what we know, and intend to communicate. The written word is even more abstract than speech since it lacks the nonverbal embodiment of the speaker.

The rather common opinion that philosophy is too abstract to be of practical value to humankind comes mainly from those who do not know the vocabulary whereby philosophy's treasures can be found. In this respect, philosophy does not differ from any other intellectual discipline of knowledge; and it is foreign only to those who do not take the time to learn its language. Indeed, we have only to realize the gaps and weak connections between words and things, or reason and the body's systems and functions, to appreciate how virtually abstract and metaphorical all language is, regardless of its 'concreteness' in naming and describing the world of immediate experience. All of which brings us to the metaphorical basis for *evidence* or what we mean by *reason, experience and knowledge*—in the first place.

The history of Western and to a lesser extent Asian philosophies can be mapped to the discovery of reason, in contrast to 'mere belief' and mythology—as is often repeated in the studies of logic. The renewed discovery of reason, ideas and the universe from the 15th century and the European Renaissance to the 18th century and the Enlightenment period led to the idea of Progress in human knowledge, science, and especially the more pragmatic ways of thinking and acting about the world. In strong support of multi-leveled progress was the ideology and science of Evolution in the 19th century which elevates organic nature to a dominating role (over God) in the struggle for species survival and the resulting, assumed superiority of *Homo sapiens.*

One does not have to be a follower of Plato or Aristotle or even Western philosophy, to believe in the value of reason, logic and the human mind. Without the discovery, cultivation, and habits of mind that have come from the rational use of language and thought, it is extremely doubtful that humanity would have come as far as it has, in terms of its material, technological, and scientific progress. However, to many educated or informed persons, humanity has not come nearly far enough on the road to genuine progress in its *moral and ethical* development, to be thought of as a superior species.

It is only a matter of time before we must face the great *pain-body of existence* itself that is reflected in the insanity, injustice and sickness of civilization—as so many social critics have said—and 'pay the piper' his due. This means—if we wish to rid ourselves of the pain-body—then we must make radical changes in our habits of reasoning, feeling and acting or the everyday ways that we live, interact with each other, and the world around us. This will require a re-discovery of the human will and the power to make different choices about how we spend our time, and the moral, psychological and intellectual content of those different choices. And among those new choices must be making the world a better place for all sentient beings, regardless of social class, ethnicity, gender, religion, etc.

Before that fateful and happy time, humankind may well destroy itself from the uncontrolled development and proliferation of thermonuclear weapons that threatens humanity and other species with extinction. Well-over one hundred million people were slaughtered in the last century, largely without the use of such weapons; and if a Third World War were to occur, the use of such weapons would certainly result in many more casualties. The anti-war anthem comes readily to mind: *When will they ever learn?*

Add to the list of humanly created horrors is our profligate and irresponsible use of fossil fuels and carbon-polluting products. Sea-level rising and dramatic climate change, caused by extreme temperature changes, droughts, glaciation, floods, etc. on a global scale, is another consequence of Capitalistic plunder and the exhaustion of natural resources, rooted in the mania of material consumption, Corporate power, greed, and profit-taking. The extreme ideology of global Capitalism that supports the greed, selfishness, and the arrogance of governments, mass media, and Corporations, fuels our present crisis at intellectual and cultural levels. And add to this unsavory mix, the extent to which education, at all levels of development, is uncritically linked to the Corporatocracy or industry, government, and mass communications.

Unless we begin to put people and human life-forms before profit and the abstractions of Capitalism, extremist politics, and material progress, we are doomed as a species by our own hands, habits, and imprudence. Furthermore, we cannot begin to solve the problems of civilization until we understand who we are, individually and in relation to nature, existence and the cosmos, and what is seen, believed or felt to be ultimately important in Life.

Science and technology is at least a two-edged sword since its use has brought us both nuclear weapons and the peaceful use of nuclear energy—although the development of peaceful nuclear energy has many unsolved issues, beginning with radioactive waste products and the relative ease with which nuclear weapons can be developed from peaceful forms of energy. Underlying the development of nuclear weapons and the war-making industry is the deeper habit of violence and the use of brute, physical force in solving issues of human need and conflict. Unless we learn to use our 'higher cognitive powers' in peaceful, nonviolent, and compassionate ways, we may not survive much longer as a species—so lethal, multifarious, and accessible have the weapons of mass destruction become to nation-states and the terrorist groups of the world.

In this context, one wonders how much more evidence we need to persuade the leaders of nations that no greater priority exists than getting rid of the inner pain-body—its violent habits of thought, emotion, and action—that are manifested on personal, interpersonal, and international levels? It is obvious to even the most casual observer that we are rapidly destroying the planet Earth—all in the name of progress, development, and an increase in material and financial wealth. Space exploration and the colonization of other planets may well be the next bold frontier in science and technology, but it is of marginal or perhaps negative value to humankind if we merely bring our internalized pain-bodies with us to these new environments and act from the same sick melodramas of the ego's mental and emotional habits, in nationalized outer-space.

Abstract reason, science and sinister calculation have brought us this far in our development as a species and planetary civilization. Nietzsche and other existentialists have asked—since Socrates and the ancient Greek obsession with Reason—whether a civilization or species can long endure that ignores its greater or higher potentialities?

Meanwhile, the pragmatic testing and verification of ideas is practically synonymous with all real world philosophies in the modern age—an attitude that counterbalances that of speculative reason, intellectual imagination, and metaphysical certitude. Both tendencies of mind have accompanied the long and winding road of philosophy and civilization, to the present day.

It was realized in ancient times among the skeptics, materialists, and naturalists of the East and West—minorities though they were—that reason, logic, and theory can go easily and terribly wrong, distorting the way things really are, rather than as we merely intend them to be, in the real world of *unintended consequences.* Thus, sensory, emotional, and psychological perception was seen by the Buddhists, Jains and Carvakans of ancient India as well as the Atomists, Epicureans and Stoics of ancient Greece, as necessarily connected with the intellectual, logical, and symbolic processes of mind or consciousness, in virtually every act of human experience. And we have inherited the non-dualistic attitude in knowledge and experience that if *something* spiritual or metaphysical does, in fact, exist, then it can and must be experienced and understood in the great here-and-now to be considered real and not just imagined.

For we exist first and foremost as whole beings on a natural and existential level of Being; and we enjoy an individual life-form due to Nature which is the designer of our origin as functioning organisms. What of course too few postmodern thinkers are willing to concede is the necessity to posit a supreme Architect of creation, one whose intelligence, perfection, and qualities exceed all human imagining or conceiving. With or without such a belief, our integrated and holistic nature points to dimensions of Being that we often do not fully appreciate much less comprehend.

Language and its role in human thought processes cannot be ignored in the philosophical and theological constructions of culture. Words condition the brain by wiring neurons together like the cars of a long freight train and create linguistic pathways along which the goods of the mind are carried. We have deluded ourselves into believing through the bewitchment of language that just because a speaker or writer uses beautiful language or seductive phrases and metaphors that he or she really knows or understands what they are saying!

The most that great writers, speakers or thinkers can ever do is to inspire or evoke a significant response from others and lead the listener or reader to the timeless music, sounds and meanings of Eternal Being. We love others most intensely when we are attracted to traits or qualities that we see in ourselves; for all love begins in self-love; yet self-love can only thrive when there are others who may be like or unlike ourselves and who we are attracted to. And we rise above self-love and grow stronger through the love of others and feelings of compassion, altruism and selflessness.

All real inner work begins in the outer world of experience. This fact leads us to the third and most inclusive basis for evidence: the intuitive processes of consciousness, the intellect and the soul. All real understanding begins in the profound silence and stillness of the soul and returns to it at last—after all is said and done. The greatest discoveries, insights, and visions of reality in the sciences, religions, arts and humanities, begin in a great passion or yearning of the soul that cannot be easily quelled by outer adversity or discouragement. One secret to the search for wisdom or true understanding about Life, death, and re-birth, if there is a *secret* at all, is to *never give up*. We hear this phrase invoked in the most unlikely of places, like the campaign trails of politicians, or from those who are struggling to survive another day without enough money, good health, or friends—and we instinctively realize the pragmatic sense of such sayings.

Wisdom is realizing the truth of nonviolence, peace, and justice; and as Mahatma Gandhi believed and acted upon *Satyagraha* or the power of Truth, power which comes from *staying nonviolent* in the face of injustice. Until we get rid of the violence in our inner lives that may reflect the violence of an entertainment industry, the violence of a militarized government, and the violence of the competitive Capitalistic system—our speech, emotions, and actions will only perpetuate the madness and sickness of the wider world. Riding ourselves of inner violence or the pain-body must be done mindfully, compassionately and non-violently.

There is something fundamentally wrong with a government that spends over half of its annual budget on building up and maintaining the armies and Weapons of Mass Destruction—whether that government is called democratic or not. We are presently living in a world that is out-of-control of its own destiny, one that has identified itself with the Furies of Unconsciousness—fear, violence, negativity, and a darkness of the soul.

For what is not sufficiently seen and seriously discussed among the educated and uneducated alike, is the irrationality of everyday life in society—its egregious contradictions, injustice, and violence. The irrational, blind, and driven nature of social existence has permeated the unconscious mind in human beings and throughout nature; and until we acquire real consciousness or awareness, we cannot expect to really change our lives for the better. However, once we awaken to the possible wisdom and redemption of higher Consciousness and the creative light that it brings to the world, there is no limit to who we can become and the increase in the quality and meaning of our lives.

The potentiality of higher Consciousness is the supreme potential in our lives—not money, materialism, or even the knowledge that only brings more power, injustice and ego-development in the world. In other words, when we learn to appreciate who we really are, a person endowed with the potentialities of Consciousness or sacred Presence, then the power-trips, money and stuff of worldly existence cease to matter. Existence remains the inescapable condition of universal Life; and this means fully realizing that we cannot experience what is sublime, perfected and eternal in this life-form apart from nature, society, and the universe.

From birth, we carry the burden of a pain-body, a suffering mind and a karmic soul with us. Although spiritual liberation is the goal of many religious traditions, there are no absolute certainties in individual existence. Hence, no matter what we do or become in this life-time, we remain finite, mortal and contingent beings; and the sole basis for hope, courage and love among the faithful and the faithless may be the quest for the liberating Peace of the soul, heart and mind.

Joy, love, and peace are among the most essential experiences of an enlightened Consciousness since they are the experiences that transform the self and its life-world and join us with the Source of everything. There is only one supreme Truth of Being and it is this knowledge that can save us from the violence and destruction of *Homo sapiens* and a world that is unbalanced, insane and de-humanizing. The more individuals see, experience, and realize the absoluteness of divine Presence, the more readily their lives can be improved and the world can be changed for the better.

Emile Pascal, the brilliant French scientist and writer of *Pensees* (*Thoughts*) lived at the beginning of the modern era in the 17th century. Pascal is embraced by mystics, skeptics and existentialists for the insight, depth and passion of his writings; he argued that that knowledge of God cannot be rationally established since nature does not give us such knowledge that overturns doubt; instead, *faith,* the 'ways of the heart', are greater than those of the mind or reason; and in the end Pascal claimed to undergo a *revelation* of mystic fire that left him transformed and speechless for days. Pascal's faith in the divinity of Christ was a sufficient basis for his mystical spirituality; and it is one that can unify rather than divide the religions, peoples, and cultures of the world—if it is experienced through higher Consciousness.

With or without the religions of the world, natural Goodness is the manifestation of invisible, sacred, and mysterious Unity or the universal Source of everything, excluding no one in the perfect equality, love and mystery of existence. Pascal's own *wager* held that one has nothing to lose by *believing* in the divinity of Christ since it is sufficient to enable one to enter the kingdom of Heaven. By analogy one has nothing to lose and everything to gain by believing in natural, social and metaphysical Goodness since human nature and existence is integrative of all differences.

If we intuitively and deeply awaken to the natural Goodness of all life-forms as the manifestation of the unmanifested realm, then an infinitely greater wisdom will flow into the world. Unblocking the pathways of *chi* or universal energy within the body, mind, and soul is not just good Yoga practice, but it is also good psychotherapy, philosophy, and religious spirituality. We need only actualize our infinite potentiality for awakening to Consciousness through meditation, thought and action to see the Radiance of infinite Being that shines within universal Life. The consequences are logical and psychological, intellectual and organic, personal and interpersonal, bringing greater wholeness, peace, and wisdom to the self, others, and the world.

Finally, there are a few further conclusions by way of some *Principles of Perennial Philosophy* that I wish to end upon, and which were submerged at times in the Text:

1. *Change* is the universal law of life-forms and the universe; and it is the source of *wonder, experience* and *knowledge.*

2. *Uncertainty* exists owing to the lack of complete or final knowledge of Being; uncertainty is the source of the mystery, adventure and ambiguity of Being.

3. *Something eternal* and ultimate exists but it is vague, ambiguous and variously named: *soul, Self, Consciousness, Being, God,* etc. These and numerous other terms from the spiritual traditions or religions of the world are important metaphors in the higher Consciousness of humanity.

4. The *unity* of everything is of divine origin and it exists due to the *original Goodness* of Creation, human nature and the real world; and original goodness gives rise to the sense of *beauty, justice and virtue.* The perception of *perfect or infinite* Beauty, Truth and Goodness are intuitive, non-conceptual and pre-cognitive experiences.

5. Human beings are *sacred life-forms;* they exist in seven dimensions: *physical, biological, social, ethical, aesthetic, intellectual and spiritual;* and these *dimensions* constitute the seven potentialities of the chakra system and the inner body.

6. Human *knowledge* is grounded in the common experiences of nature, self, society and the universe and it is reflected in the arts, sciences, and humanities of personal and social existence. Human creativity and the authentic free-will are the sources of moral, intellectual and technological progress.

7. Being (what-is) exists on organic, social, and transcendental levels of the body, mind and soul and can be uniquely experienced and *approximately* known through the first person singular perspectives of subjective beings and their symbolic discourse.

8. The religions of the world are essentially identical at an *esoteric or mystical* depth of experience and they only have different words, concepts and symbols that refer to the *same spiritual or metaphysical reality*; and although religion and science differ in their means and ends, they are embedded in the same sacred ground of Being.

9. Although something *Absolute* exists, we can only approximately, aesthetically and intuitively know *It* owing to the limits of human reason, perspectival awareness, and conditional existence. Claims of absolute or metaphysical certainty cannot be confirmed beyond subjectivity whether of theistic, atheistic or agnostic origin.

10. The purpose of Life is to awaken to the unity, Goodness and transcendence of ordinary existence and the sacredness of all life-forms on Earth and throughout the universe.

11. Although the *meaning of life* is important, intellectually, the more important purpose of Life is to live intensely, creatively, and authentically in the present moment, and to realize that you are a unique witness to social change and Eternal Being.

12. The aim of existence is to awaken to the divine Source in nature, awareness, and the universe; and your purpose is to participate in the progressive unfolding, goodness and mystery of everything.

The mythic owl of Minerva, the symbol of wisdom, intuition and mystery, flies at evening time and sees into the darkness of approaching night, dreaming that he is awake. In the 'crazy wisdom' of the Taoist philosopher, Chuangzi, 'dreaming we may think that we are awake, only upon waking we may then believe that we are only dreaming' is an apt metaphor for the philosophy of Being, Now and Consciousness.

The *Perennial Wisdom* turns most conventional assumptions and values upside-down and inside-out and challenges us to think in deeper, more positive and hopeful ways. The *perennial* assumptions, concepts and values of philosophy, religion and psychology are truly essential since they ask us to open ourselves to the immensity of the universe and eternal Being and awaken to the one, unifying Truth. It is only our attachment to fear, egocentric thinking, and the negativity of the 'pain-body' that enslaves us, sickens the soul, and dims the light of higher Consciousness.

Finally, *The Perennial Wisdom* is intended to inspire interest in the study and meditation upon humanity and universal Being. Ultimately, the experience of real *awakening* is the means of transformation from fragmentation and brokenness to the wholeness of Being. Wisdom is the inner joy, peace, and love of eternal Being in all its human, social and existential manifestations.

Om Shanti Om

APPENDIX

i. *Chapter Notes*

Introduction

1. The *Bhagavad-Gita* "Introduction," Aldous Huxley, translated by Swami Prabhavananda and Christopher Isherwood (Mentor, New York, 1960), p13.

2. *The Encyclopedia of Eastern Philosophy and Religion, Maya (Shambhala, Boston, 1996) p.223.*

3. *A New Earth,* Eckhart Tolle *(A Plume Book, New York, 2005) p. 71.*

4. *The Power of Now,* Eckhart Tolle (New World Library and Namaste Publishing, Novato, CA, 2004) pp. 3-32.

5. *Ibid. p. 3.*

6. Joseph Campbell, *The Power of Myth with Bill Moyers* (Doubleday, New York, 1988) p. 123. See Joseph Campbell's many other books, including *The Power of Myth* which was made into a series of interviews and videos with Bill Moyers of PBS.

7. *Ibid.*

8. *The Collected Dialogues of Plato,* edited by Edith Hamilton and Huntington Cairns, *Laws,* translated by A.E. Taylor (Pantheon Books, 1966).

9. *A Treasury of Traditional Wisdom,* edited and compiled by Whitall N. Perry, *Preface* by Huston Smith (Harper and Row Publishers, San Francisco, 1986) p. 861.

Chapter One

1. *The Pre-Socratic Philosophers,* "Heraclitus of Ephesus" C.S. Kirk and J.E. Raven (Cambridge University Press, New York, 1966) pp. 182-215

2. *The Cambridge Dictionary of Philosophy, "Empiricism"* Robert Audi, general editor. (Cambridge University Press, Cambridge, UK) *p.224-5*

3. *A New Earth,* Tolle, *p. 128.*

4. See Paul Davies, *God and the New Physics and The Cosmic Blueprint.* Paul Davies is among a growing number of astro-physicists who have seen the patent inadequacy of the standard model of explanation for the universe. He assumes that: God or an infinitely perfect Being created the universe; 2, human beings are merely one among innumerable other planetary beings in the universe; 3, the ultimate meaning and purpose of human existence is to realize our origin, identity and destiny; 4, human consciousness is *prime fascia* evidence or proof that God exists in the heart, soul and mind of the human organism. And so forth.

5. *The Power of Now, Tolle, p. 115.*

6. *The Bhagavad-Gita, "Introduction"* by Aldous Huxley, translated by Swami Prabhavananda and Christopher Isherwood (Mentor Books & Vedanta Press, New York, 1951).

7. *Readings in Classical Chinese Philosophy,* edited by Philip J. Ivanhoe and Bryan W. Van Norden (Seven Bridges Press, New York, 2001) p. 214.

Chapter Two

1. This felicitous phrase—*undifferentiated aesthetic continuum*—is from Alfred North Whitehead's *magnum opus, Process and Reality,* a speculative book that put him on good terms with both Buddhists and Essentialists.

2. *The Power of Now, op. cit., p. 71-2.*

3. Or an absolutist view of the karma or causal determinism closes off the possibility of real freedom in existence. It is the logical fallacy of many social scientists and atheists.

4. This distinction between the spiritual and the material dimensions runs through many differing ways of thinking in the perennialist library of great works. One can become so identified with one

dimension or the other as to lose sight of the other, creating a dualism in the conception of who we are (matter and spirit).

5. *The Power of Now, Tolle (Penguin Books, New York, 2005) pp. 12-13*

6. The Existential questions about the meaning of life, origin and destiny, a personal purpose in the universe as related to Being or something universal and eternal show up the literature of Perennialism as well. Hence the strong case can be made that Existential philosophy is another instance of the more ancient Perennialism—in updated language.

7. *The Power of Now, Tolle, from the dedication page (Penguin Books, New York, 2005).*

8. *Chuang Tzu, translated by Burton Watson (Columbia University, New York, 1996).*

Chapter Three

1. *The Encyclopedia of Eastern Philosophy and Religion, (Shambhala, Boston, Massachusetts, 1994)* p. 114.

2. *The Matrix: the Quest for Understanding, Wisdom, and Enlightenment, Book II, Chapter 12, "Christianity," Section 11: "The Theologians: St. Augustine"* with Readings, by Courtney D. Schlosser (CD-ROM, Privately Produced by the Philosopher's Club, octobernight.com, 2013). 3. The Encyclopedia..., p. 325.

3. *See Andrew Weil's many books on restoring and maintaining health the natural Way; especially Natural Health, Natural Medicine and Eating Well for Optimal Health.* The later book contains an essay on "The Possibility of Surviving without Eating" in the Appendix and inspired by his reading of Yogananda's *Autobiography of a Yogi.* This 'possibility', called *bigu,* involves *chi* or Life-giving energy and Chinese *Qigong* practices. If nothing else this is a clear alternative to the industrial food system and its advertising!

4. See *The Light of Nonviolence in the Jain Tradition,* by Courtney D. Schlosser "Introduction to Jain Philosophy" in the *Appendix* (CreateSpace, Amazon.com, *20130.*

5. *The Power of Now, op. cit. Tolle, p. 115.*

6. *A Treasury of Traditional Wisdom, Huang-po, p. 867.*

Chapter Four

1. *The Power of Now, p. 135-6.*

2. *The Matrix, Book I, Chapter Two, Section 10: "The Allegory of the Cave"*

3. Recently, astronomers hypothesized that we can only 'see' about 3% of the total mass of the universe. The rest they call "Dark Matter" which is controlled by black holes or great maelstroms of energy that exist at the center of every galaxy. Similarly, we can think of the unmanifested realm surrounding us in everyday awareness (the manifested realm of existence); and it is the Unmanifested realm—and by analogy 'Dark Matter'—that is the greater Unconsciousness within the self of everyday experience.

4. *The Power of Now, p. 130.*

5. *The Encyclopedia of Eastern Philosophy and Religion, "Zen"* (Shambhala, Boston, Massachusetts, 1994) p.442.

Chapter Five

1. *The Cambridge Dictionary of Philosophy,* Robert Audi, general editor. (Cambridge University Press, Cambridge, UK) p. 768-69.

2. See Aldous Huxley's *The Perennial Philosophy* (Harper Colophon Books, CN, 1970). This is a ground breaking anthology of readings from the world religions, illustrating their agreement at the mystical level of reality. He develops a *perennialist* concept of human nature or its empirical and Transcendental aspects, the essential assumptions of which has gone unchanged since the earliest of times in every known culture of the world.

3. *The Person in Education: a Humanistic Approach, edited by Courtney Schlosser, "Existentialism is a Humanism" by Jean-Paul Sartre (Macmillan Publishing Company, New York, 1976) p. 57-8. See Sartre's discussion of the priority of existence* (temporality) over *essence* (eternity) in this important essay. The distinction between essence and existence makes the difference between Essentialists like mystics, theists and other eternalists *and* the Existentialists who were influenced by a crazy mix of philosophical naturalists, Stoics and atheistic ontologists (like Sartre)—as clear as anywhere.

4. *Basic Teaching of the Buddha, Glenn Wallis (Modern Library, New York, 2007) p. 63.*

5. *The Power of Now, p. 141-2*

6. *Ibid., p. 142.*

7. *See The Tibetan Book of the Great Liberation, or the method of realizing Nirvana through knowing the Mind*, edited by W.Y. Evans-Wentz, Commentary by C.G. Jung (Oxford University Press, 1981).

8. *See* Professor E. research at the University of Virginia on reincarnation and afterlife cases. Although his efforts to verify many reported cases of reincarnation were inconclusive, his faith in Buddhist philosophy was unshaken as was his faith in reincarnation.

9. *The Encyclopedia of Eastern Philosophy and Religion*, Shambhala, Boston, Massachusetts, 1994) p. 229-230.

10. *Readings in Classical Chinese Philosophy*, edited by Philip J. Ivanhoe and Bryan W. Van Norden (Seven Bridges Press, New York, 2001) p. 236.

Chapter Six

1. *The Encyclopedia of Eastern Philosophy and Religion* (Shambhala, Boston, Massachusetts, 1994) p. 143.

2. *See The Matrix, Book III, Chapter 24, "20ᵗʰ C. "Existential Phenomenology" work cited.*

3. *The Power of Now, p.147.*

4. *Ibid., p. 146-7.*

5. *The Power of Now, p. 146.*

6. *A New Earth, p.137-8.*

Chapter Seven

1. *Three Thousand Years of Educational Wisdom*, edited by Robert Ulich "Comenius" (Harvard University Press, Cambridge, 1947) p. 339—346.

2. *A New Earth, p. 25.*

3. *Ibid., p. 29-30.*

4. *Ibid., p. 35.*

5. *See Lack and Transcendence, by David Loy (Humanity Press, New York, 1996) for an excellent analysis of the relations between psychotherapy, existentialism and Buddhism with reference to their views of life and death.*

6. *Ibid., p. 54-6.*

7. *Ibid.*

8. *The Matrix, work cited, Book II, Chapter 14, sections 2-6, "Rene Descartes."*

Chapter Eight

1. *The Matrix, work cited, Book III, chapter 29, section 3 "Ludwig Wittgenstein."*

2. See Alfred Korzybski's *Science and Sanity* for his theory of General Semantics in this connection. Korzybski, the skeptic and scientific positivist, believed that we could solve the problem of war—among other human ills—if humans were taught to use language *sanely* or according to the Empirical Gospel. He invented something called the 'Semantic Differential' to teach sane language usage!

3. Ibid.

4. *The Matrix, work cited, Book III, Chapter 23, section 11 "Friedrich Nietzsche.'*

5. See the collected writings of Martin Luther King as an example of someone who used language creatively to awaken the masses about the interrelated evils of race, class, and gender.

6. *See Gopi Krishna's, Awakening to Evolutionary Energy.*

7. I will discuss the chakra system more completely in Chapter 13.

8. *A New Earth, work cited, p.71.*

9. *Ibid., p. 72.*

10. *Ibid., p. 72.*

11. *Chuang Tzu: "Metaphorical Language" from The Sacred Books of the East, edited by F. Max Müller, Vol. XL: The Texts of Taoism.* Translated. by James Legge.

Chapter Nine

1. *The Nag Hammadi Library in English, gnostic scriptures in one volume "The Gospel of Thomas"* (Harper Collins, New York, 1978) pp. 124-139.

2. *The Journey of Man, by* Spencer Wells (Princeton University Press, Princeton N.J., 2002).

3. *See Noam Chomsky's Profit over People* and numerous other books which are mostly in an interview format. Chomsky remains the reigning

Left-thinking social and political critic of our times especially his dev-
astation of American Foreign Policy which is the underbelly of the
American Dream machine.

4. Carl Sandburg, Collected Poems, from "The People, Yes" (Harcourt,
   Brace and Company, New York, 1950) p. 615-17.

5. Ibid, p. 453 and 617.

6. *A New Earth, op. cit., p. 85.*

7. *Ibid., p. 86.*

8. *See Gwynne Dyer's On War.*

9. *Ibid., p. 89.*

Chapter Ten

1. See Plato's *Meno* for his view of knowledge as only recovered knowledge from the soul's journey through the universe of heavenly eternal, perfect *Ideas.* For all of his explorations in dialogue form with
   others, Socrates was ambiguous if not doubtful about real ethical
   knowledge; his student, Plato, apparently believed that metaphysics must accompany ethics and every other branch of knowledge, to
   adequately answer problems and questions about human existence
   and beyond.

2. Ram Dass, *The Only Dance There Is.*

3. *No death, No fear,* Thich Nhat Hann *(Riverhead Books, New York) p. 5*

4. *See The Person in Education: a Humanistic Approach* (Macmillan
   Publishing Company, New York, 1976). *Some of the readings may be a
   little dated but the ideals of a humanistic education are not.*

5. Tolle, *Power of Now, op. cit., p. 155.*

6. *A New Earth, p. 42-5.*

7. *Ibid., p. 45-6.*

8. *The Heart of Jainism, Sinclair Stevenson (Munshiram Manoharial Publishers,
   New Delhi, India) p. 163-9.*

Chapter Eleven

1. See the many hours of excellent videos created for PBS by Bill Moyers
   and Joseph Campbell; and of course, the many gorgeously illustrated,
   researched and written books by Campbell, much material of which is
   interspersed in the videos.

2.   *The Power of Now, p. 13.*

3.   *The Encyclopedia of Eastern Philosophy and Religion, (Shambhala, Boston, 1996) p.130-1.*

4.   C. G. Jung, Foreword to D.T. Suzuki, *An Introduction to Zen Buddhism* (New York: The Philosophical Library, 1949), p.26.

5.   *Power of Now, Ibid. p. 13-14.*

6.   See the *I Ching or the Book of Changes* for the seminal source for understanding the relationships of *Yin and Yang* or Earth and Heaven in the sixty-four patterns or *hexagrams* of human experience and the universe. A hexagram is composed of six horizontal lines, some or all of which are broken or solid and conveying a unique meaning found in the experience of every situational Now or the universal change of eternal Being.

7.   On this topic (Shiva-Shakti) and related ones of Yoga philosophy in Indian traditions, Georg Feurerstein has written perhaps the most definitive single book: *Yoga tradition, Its History, Literature, Philosophy and Practice (Hohm Press, Prescott Arizona, 1998).* Among other virtues, the *Yoga tradition* explores the theory and practice of Yoga in its Hindu, Jain and Buddhist contexts.

Chapter Twelve

1.   *A New Earth, pp. 129-160*

2.   *Ibid., p.141.*

3.   *Ibid., p. 140*

4.   *Ibid., p. 129-160.*

5.   From *Selected Writings of Sigmund Freud, Introduction.*

6.   *A New Earth, p. 141*

7.   *Ibid, p. 160.*

8.   *Dancing with Siva, Hinduism's Contemporary Catechism,* Satguru Sivaya Subramuniyaswami (Himalayan Academy, USA) p. 701.

9.   See Gwynne Dyer, *On War.*

10. *A New Earth, p. 181-2.*

11. *Ibid., p. 183-4.*

Chapter Thirteen

1.   Georg Feurerstein, *Yoga tradition, Its History, Literature, Philosophy and Practice* (Hohm Press, Prescott Arizona, 1998) p. 193.

2. *The Power of Now, op. cit., p. 115.*

3. *The Bagavad-Gita, Chapter 3 "Krishna to Arjuna" The Encyclopedia of Eastern Philosophy and Religion.*

4. *See The Matrix* and Part II of Book I for a more detailed discussion of Hinduism, Buddhism, and Jainism of Indian origin.

5. *The Encyclopedia of Eastern Philosophy and Religion, Shambhala,* Boston, p. 121.

6. *The Matrix "Readings" Part X Science, Ethics, and the New Spirituality, Schlosser, C.D. "The Chakras: Scientific, Philosophical and Mystical Dimensions of Consciousness" Introduction: 1, An Integrative Model" The Chakras: Scientific, Philosophical, and Mystical Dimensions of Consciousness*

7. *See Francis Collins, The Language of God.*

8. *See The Chakras, Schlosser, Readings Part X, Integrative Model, Chart # 3, "Correlations of the Seven Chakras (Subtle Body) with the Twelve Anatomical & Physiological Systems at Anatomical Sites"*

9. *Anatomy and Physiology, The Unity of Form and Function,* Kenneth S. Saladin *(McGraw Hill, 2001).*

10. See William James' classic essay, "The Will-to-Believe" and other great writings. Also refer to The Matrix, Book III, Chapter 30, "William James: Pragmatic Philosopher of Psychology and Religion" for writing on his life and thought (CDROM)

11. See The Matrix, Book III, A Background to Existential Philosophy, Section 16, "Blaise Pascal" for writing on his life and thought (CD–Rom)

12. See A New Earth, by Eckhart Tolle, Chapter Five, "The Pain-Body" p. 131-159, for further insights about this most important concept.

13. Dialogues, recorded by Lucien Price "Alfred North Whitehead" (New American Library, New York, 1954) p. 12.

14. *A New Earth, p. 122.*

Chapter Fourteen

1. *The Matrix: the Quest for Understanding, Wisdom, and Nonviolence,* written and compiled by Courtney Schlosser, Chapter One, "The Pre-Socratics: Parmenides" (CDROM, privately published).

2. *What is Metaphysics,* Martin Heidegger, translated by Ralph Manheim (Anchor Books, New York, 1961 p. 31.

3. *Being and Time,* Martin Heidegger, translated by John Macquarie and Edward Robinson (Harper and Row, New York, 1962) p. 306-7.

4. *The Matrix,* Book I, Part 1, Chapter Three for "Atomism." (Quotation from Democritus)

5. Lucretius, *On the Nature of Things,* Book I, "Eternal Substance"

6. *Ibid., "The Void"*

7. *The Matrix:* Chapter 19, Sections 7 "Charles Sanders Peirce" 8 "William James" 9 "John Dewey;" Chapter 29 Section 02 "Alfred North Whitehead;" Chapter 30 "William James: Charles Renouvier, Josiah Royce, John Dewey, Henri Bergson."

8. *A New Earth, op. cit., p. 49-50.*

9. *Ibid, pp. 53-4.*

10. *Ibid, p. 251.*

11. Many of these questions and speculations come from my decades of teaching about the spectrum of views relating to the Perennial Philosophy. Thus in this text I am *not* inquiring about just one viewpoint but many in relation to one another. (See my notes on Comparative Philosophies of Perennial Wisdom in the *Appendix*)

12. *A New Earth, p. 254.*

Chapter Fifteen

1. *The Power of Now, op. cit, p. 28*

2. *Ibid, p. 29.*

3. *Ibid, p. 29-30.*

4. *Ibid, p. 31.*

5. *Ibid.*

6. *Pascal's Pensees, translated by Honor Levi with Introduction and Notes by Anthony Levi (from "Knowledge" #230) (Oxford University Press, New York, 1995), p 55. The various excerpts are numbered and indicated by sub-section titles as indicated in the original text.*

7. *Ibid.*

8. *The Encyclopedia of Eastern Philosophy and Religion, Shambhala, Boston, p.372-74.*

9. *Ibid., p. 228*

10. *Ibid., 402*

11. *Chuang tzu: "Metaphorical Language" from The Sacred Books of the East, edited by F. Max Müller, Vol. XL: The Texts of Taoism,* translated by James Legge.

Chapter Sixteen

1. *The Bible, Revised Standard Version, "Ecclesiastes or the Preacher" Thomas Nelson Inc., New York, 1972) pp. 485-92.*

2. See Alfred Korzybski's, *Science and Sanity.* This book laid the foundation for *General Semantics,* a rather cultish theory of language and communication that many people were persuaded by, in the 1930's through the 1960's. Korzybski and his faithful followers believed that if people had a more critical sense of language usage, based upon an empirical understanding of reality and the difference between words and things, they would act more sanely. He and his followers believed that most wars would never be waged if humanity understood to what extent language controls their thought, emotion and action.

3. *A New Earth, op. cit., p. 38-42.*

4. *Ibid, p. 43.*

5. *Ibid., p. 42-6.*

6. See St. Thomas Aquinas' for the "Five Proofs for the Existence of God." It is a curious doctrine in that it assumes, like much else of the Good Doctor's theology, that it is inconceivable that God would create a universe in which faith contradicts reason. On an ontological level, this is acceptable but on an empirical level I do not see how the argument can be sustained—given the fallibility of belief and reason.

7. *A New Earth, p. 246-8.*

8. *Ibid., p. 53-4.*

9. *Ibid, p. 104-5.*

10. *Ibid, p.108-9.*

11. See Martin Buber's *I and Thou* in this context. Buber's philosophy of I—Thou (as opposed to I—it) influenced a more humanistic theology and inspired many believers and non-believers alike to experience a depth of existence that redeems and heals any alienation from objectivity and the real world.

12. *A New Earth, p. 109.*

Chapter Seventeen

1. *Philosophy in the Middle Ages, The Christian, Islamic, and Jewish Traditions,* edited by Arthur Hyman and James J. Walsh, "Al -Ghazali" (Hackett Publishing Company, Indianapolis, 1974) p. 263-281.
2. *A New Earth, op. cit., p. 106.*
3. *Ibid, p. 96.*
4. *A Treasury of Traditional Wisdom,* Whitall N. Perry, Preface by Huston Smith (Harper and Row, Publishers, San Francisco, 1986) p. 753.
5. *The Making of a Yoga Master,* Suhas Tambe *(Hohm Press, Chino Valley, Arizona) p. 267-72.* This is a superb new translation of Patanjali's *Yoga Sutras* and Tambe's unique and penetrating interpretation of its aphorisms.

Chapter Eighteen

1. *The Encyclopedia of Eastern Philosophy and Religion, work cited, "chakra" pp.58-61.*
2. *The Cambridge Dictionary of Philosophy (see 'Desire').*
2. *Noam Chomsky's Profit Over People (South Boston Press).*
3. *A New Earth, op. cit, p. 291.*
4. *Ibid, p. 295-305.*
5. *Ibid, p. 296.*
6. *Ibid, p. 297*
7. *Ibid, p. 298)*
8. *Ibid, p. 299-300*
9. *Ibid, p. 301-2*
10. *Ibid, p. 302*
11. *Ibid, p. 303*
12. *Ibid, p. 304*

Chapter Nineteen

1. *The Matrix,* work cited, Book III, Chapter 30, "William James: Pragmatist."
2. *The Power of Now, op. cit., p. 188*
2. *Ibid, p. 188-9.*
3. *Ibid, p. 254*
4. *The Power of Now, p. 137. 189-90.*

5. *Ibid, p. 192.*
6. *Ibid, p. 137.*
7. *Ibid., p. 47-8.*
8. *The Power of Now, p. 155.*
9. *Ibid, p.100.*

Chapter Twenty

1. *Philosophy in the Middle Ages, The Christian, Islamic, and Jewish Traditions,* edited by Arthur Hyman and James J. Walsh, "Islam" (Hackett Publishing Company, Indianapolis, 1974).
2. *The Power of Now, op. cit., p. 147.*
3. *Ibid, p. 149.*
4. *Ibid, p. 150-3*
5. *Ibid, p. 154*
6. *Ibid, p. 174*
7. *The Matrix, see Readings: "Universal Declaration of Human Rights."*

Chapter Twenty-One

1. *The Encyclopedia of Eastern Philosophy and Religion, work cit., p 63-4.*
2. *The Power of Now, op. cit., p. 215.*
3. *The Fabric of Existentialism edited by Richard Gill and Ernest Sherman (Prentice-Hall, Englewood NJ., 1973) p. 633.*
4. *Ibid., p. 635.*
5. *Ibid, p. 296.*
6. *A Source Book in Chinese Philosophy*, translated and compiled by Wing-Tsit Chan (Princeton University Press, Princeton, New Jersey, 1963) V. 1, p. 483.
7. *The Matrix, Book I, Chapter 10, "The Changing Face of the Dragon" sections 11 through 16. .*

Chapter Twenty-Two

1. See D.T. Suzuki's *Mysticism, Christian and Buddhist (The Eastern and Western Way)* Chapter One "Meister Eckhart and Buddhism" (Collier Books, New York, 1962) pp. 11-33.
2. Ibid, p. 82.
3. Ibid, p. 13-4.

4. Ibid, p. 17-9.

5. *A New Earth, op. cit., p. 290.*

6. *The Encyclopedia of Eastern Philosophy and Religion, p. 37-8.*

7. *Ibid, p. 291.*

8. *The Power of Now, op. cit., p. 276.*

9. *See Emile Pascal's Confessions.*

10. *Chuang tzu, Basic Writings, translated by Burton Watson (Columbia University Press, New York, 1996) p. 77.*

Part VII Introduction

1. *The Making of a Yoga Master, Suhas Tambe (Hohm Press, Chino Valley, Arizona) p. 228.*

Chapter Twenty-Three

1. *The Cambridge Dictionary of Philosophy, work cited, "Plato" p.620-2.*

2. *The Power of Now, op. cit., p. 205-*

3. *The Making of a Yoga Master,* Suhas Tambe *(Hohm Press, Chino Valley, Arizona, 2012) p.109-11.*

4. *Matrix, Book II, Chapter 12, section 11 "Meister Eckhart" work cited.*

5. *The Power of Now, p. 208-9*

6. *See Aldous Huxley, The Four Doctrines of Perennialism, op. cited.*

7. *Ibid.*

8. *See Burton Watson's Chuang tzu, Basic Writings, in this early translation before the change-over from Wade-Giles to Pinyin forms. It is still the most readable of many translations. The story appears at the end of Chapter One, "Free and Easy Wandering" here and in most other translations (pages 29-30).*

Chapter Twenty-Four

1. See the numerous secondary writings on the "Four Truths" of Buddhist philosophy composed and published in response to the great popularity of its teachings and practices. Among the many writings is the beautifully composed *Dhammapada* or 426 verses on the basic assumptions and precepts of the oldest branch of Buddhism, *Theravada.* The primary source of Buddhist philosophy is contained

in the five baskets or *Nikayas,* in the Pali language, and in many translations.

2. T. S. Eliot, *"Four Quartets: East Coker, II"*

3. *Philosophy: An Introduction to the Art of Wondering, James L. Christian (Holt, Rinehart and Winston, Fort Worth, 1990) p. 554-5.*

4. *See The Perennial Philosophy, by Aldous Huxley (Harper and Row New York, 1944)* an anthology of famous writings from the world's spiritual literature and Huxley's interpretations of them in light of the One Truth or core, mystical Unity of world religions. This particular story appears on pages 3-4 in greater length, taken from the *Chandogya Upanishad.*

5. *Philosophy,* work cited, James Christian This progressive array of concepts—*1 information, 2 knowledge, 3 understanding, 4 wisdom and 5 enlightenment*—first came to me through my reading and use of James Christian's excellent book on general philosophy.

6. Heraclitus of Greece bears a striking resemblance to Siddhartha, the first Buddha, in their view of *fire* as the most potent symbol of universal change. Everything is on fire, Heraclitus wrote, an insight that also moved Siddhartha to give his famous *Sermon on Fire.*

Chapter Twenty-Five

1. *The Power of Now,* Eckhart Tolle, *work cited, p. 227.*

2. *Ibid, p. 226.*

3. *The Person in Education: a Humanistic Approach, edited by Courtney Schlosser, from "Existentialism is a Humanism" by Jean-Paul Sartre (Macmillan Publishing Company, New York, 1976) p. 57-8.*

4. *Ibid., p.*

5. *Power of Now, p. 220.*

6. *Tattvartha Sutra,* Translated and Commentary by Manu Doshi (Jaina and Shrut Ratnakar, New York, 1981) p. 223-229; although the theory of liberation is summarized in the Appendix, there are numerous insights about key aspects of the theory throughout this seminal text of Jain philosophy.

7. George Feuerstein, *The Yoga Tradition* (Hohm Press, Prescott, Arizona, 1998) pp. 196-198. Feuerstein's classic on Yoga theory in several

Indian philosophies contains a sound comparative analysis of Jainism and its theory of liberation.

8. The insight that although death may be in the view of the *skeptic* and naturalist as ultimate, it is nothing or a non-experience. Yet, we the survivors still of life, know that existence has an ending that seems absolute, final, complete. The *mystic,* on the other hand, simply negates the absoluteness of death by believing in what appears to be an impossibility to the *pragmatist* or those with their feet firmly on the ground—while they are still able to experience it. But the mystery, the question and myth remain, for the living.

ii. Glossary of Terms:

Ahimsa: the ideal of non-violence emphasized in Jainist, Buddhist, and other religious philosophies; the essential nature of the soul or *jiva* in Yoga and Jain philosophy; the ideal for personal and social ethics; in contrast to 'himsa' or the use of violence and force to reach human ends; also in contrast to our animal nature and the physical universe

Atman: the Sanskrit term for the impersonal, eternal Self universally and energetically linked with *Brahman,* the Absolute Oneness of everything; a common Hindu belief about the inner divine nature of the mundane or worldly self; contrasted with the physical body and empirical ego of the self; experienced inwardly as the inner body in Yoga philosophy

Avidya: Sanskrit term for spiritual or metaphysical ignorance; ignorance is also the first and most important of the 12 links of interdependent origination in Buddhist philosophy; the most basic condition of human awareness without the experience of liberation; the conclusion of Agnosticism concerning ultimate or final answers

Awakening: the active, initial experience of the truth about human existence and our place in the universe; an open, alert, and fully aware process that leads to the discovery of who you are, the meaning and purpose of existence, and how to live a moral or nonviolent life; an experience that leads to the knowledge of liberation and enlightenment

Awareness: the waking mode of Being having the potentialities of Higher Consciousness or the awareness of the Life-force and the soul; the most basic condition for human change, learning, and transformation; consciousness in its everyday mode of perceiving and experiencing reality

512

Being: in its capitalized form, what-is or the totality of known, unknown or unmanifested existence; a seamless continuity that runs through all change, forms and events; 'God' or the infinite, eternal, and formless Source, Presence, and Destiny of life-forms and cosmos; experienced as a Radiance, Light, and Effulgence within visions, or through feeling-states, intuitive insight, and integrative cognition

Body: the organic and energetic matrix of the total self; the karmic Presence of the Life-force in terms of Prakriti (Sanskrit) or Nature; the biological systems of modern biology and the chakra system of ancient Yoga philosophy best represent the physical and spiritual or outer and inner dimensions of the body; it is the individual life-form and living Presence of Life-force; the most immediate form of impermanence

Chakra: an energy center along the spine from its lowest point to the crown of the head and traditionally numbering seven; it is believed that by activating, circulating and awakening the energies associated with these centers, the yogi can fully awaken to the inner body that is astral and causal, actualizing the highest states of Consciousness for liberation.

Consciousness: a necessary condition for a human life-form which has the potentiality of higher or enlightened Consciousness (in its capitalized form); a universal that reveals the Mystery; the Presence of God or Absoluteness in its everyday form; awareness or everyday consciousness in its ordinariness as existing in nature and humans; the potentiality for reflection, meditation, and liberation

Corruption: the fallen or darkened state of a soul, self or consciousness in the material, psychological and social world; actions and habits associated with the pain-body, violence, attachment, and greed; the moral argument against personal and social materialism that reduces the meaning of life is physical matter; vices, evil, ill-will and habits associated with them

Darshana: a 'view' or 'system' of thought in Sanskrit language; six such schools exist in Hindu philosophy; the term posits the same goal for all views, i.e. the liberation of soul, Self, or Consciousness from samsara or the endless round of births and deaths, and the union with ultimate Being or Absoluteness; the relativity of knowledge and the pluralism of systems is implied

Desire: the primary reason for existence from a karmic perspective since we desired to exist, prior to conception, to free the pure soul from the corruption acquired in previous lives; otherwise ordinary life is absurd, unnecessary and meaningless; the control of desire if not the total elimination of it is the goal of Yoga or philosophies influenced by it

Dharma: the moral or ethical basis of one's existence that is necessary for final liberation from existence (see *moksa*); the objective moral order of the universe in several philosophical traditions of the world; living one's dharma is knowing the right or true path that places one in alignment or attunement with nature, society and the cosmos.

Education: the formal and informal process of the transmission of knowledge and culture; the Transformation and evolution of consciousness through awakened states of Being; the relationships of experience and knowledge, theory and practice, teaching and learning, school and society, in professional contexts; the philosophy of Life as related to stages of learning and growth; a life-long process connecting generations and believed to improve the character of the individual, the quality of social life, and the evolution of Consciousness

Ego: the separate sense of self that develops from the greater illusion of separateness; conditioned to play roles, the ego put on masks to play the separate roles, hiding the real self or soul beyond the layers of ego, mind and self; only an uncorrupted or pure soul which the ego and its roles have no way of knowing much experiencing. Thus persons quite typically lives in ignorance of 'who they really are' in society or ordinary existence

Emotions: inner forms of the body's neuro-physiological systems that are felt and influence desires, actions and thoughts; the dynamic, often unconscious energies of the body in relation to internal experience and external circumstances; action-reaction patterns of the body, mind and ego in relation to external stimuli; the range of body feelings from negativity to euphoria; internal conditions of the pain-body and pleasure-body that cause neurotic responses when not controlled by awareness

Emptiness: the experience deriving from the sense of lack, voidness or insufficiency; understood in the dialectic or co-arising of something and nothing (Nagarjuna); the belief in the lack of intrinsic or permanent essence like the self as in certain sects of Buddhism; the general view of the emptiness (or lack of substance) of appearances, forms and knowledge in relation to the formlessness of the Absolute; the mystic's experience of what is Ultimate

Enlightenment: the personal experience of something ultimate in the Now through higher Consciousness; denotes an absolute experience of awakening in relation to Being (Absoluteness) in a more approximate, finite, and conditional sense; the Pragmatic meaning of the term is understanding in experience; the Existential view is a subjective experience that is the basis for Truth; awakening to who you are or self-knowledge

Essence: the soul of a sentient being believed to be the basis for the survival of death and re-birth in many other life-forms (Jainism, et al.); the Platonic and general theistic belief in a separate and autonomous entity that is the basis for survival following the death of the body; a meaning of Being (eternal Substance) that exists within existence as the basis for meaning, etc; the inner quality, meaning, and experience of existential freedom

Existence: the total matrix of human life in a Perennialist perspective; birth, Life, and death in contingent, conditional, and situational freedom; the totality of Being-in-the-world, as here-and-now; temporal Being as the intersecting experience of Eternity and temporality; Life understood as essentially subjective, contingent and uncertain

Form: the internal and external phenomena or appearances of reality; physical, emotional, intellectual, and spiritual energies that give content and meaning to the mind; the manifested or visible realm of unmanifested or invisible reality; in Platonic philosophy, a perfect, timeless, and pure realm of Ideas existing in a Heavenly region and creating the imperfect, changing, and corrupted forms of the known or 'lower' world of perception, thought, imagination, etc.; the complement or completion of 'content'

Formlessness: the unmanifested, invisible, and spiritual realm of reality; the Source from which all forms arise and return; indicating what is invisible, underlying or eternal in the material world; one of the three realms of Mahayana Buddhism, besides Form and Desire; the nothingness or voidness of Consciousness prior to the experience or knowledge of particular forms

Goodness: a metaphysical, emanative and pervasive condition of all life-forms, structures and possibilities of the universe; the ultimate Source or God of everything that is essentially unknown yet experienced in existence; the eternal Idea that controls all other ideas and forms of the world and does not change although everything else does (Plato, Mencius, Plotinus and the Idealists)

Illusion: a necessary condition for the experience and knowledge of reality; the supposition of Hindus, Platonists and other absolute idealists that this world is an illusion compared to the realm of Absoluteness or Heavenly Ideas; the sense of reality and the experience thereof that represents or dramatizes the real life situations; delusion or not aware of the spell of illusion created by mind, ego and symbols

Inner Body: yogic concept referring to the field of subtle energy unifying the physical, astral and causal bodies surrounding the soul; when differing degrees of self-realization or actualization occur the inner body motivates and creates thought, feeling and action of various kinds; the real body where experience of the physical body is known

Karma: the universal, causal force that controls each life-form in material existence; a fallen, corrupted condition of each embodied soul that struggles in worldly existence to free itself from karma; it is the accumulated effect or consequence of all past actions in the energy field of Now; in re-incarnation or re-birth doctrines, karma denotes the continuous survival of an eternal soul that links us to the future and past; mechanical causation

Jiva: the soul in Jain philosophy; the essence of the body (*a-jiva*) or materiality; a spiritual energy atomic in structure and function in the real world; believed to be eternal, pure and unique in each person; we are here to purify the karmic soul of its corruption from ordinary experience and violence of all kinds

Kundalini: meaning 'serpent power'; form of yogic practice and theory based on the chakra system; the aim is to fully awaken consciousness and raise its energy to states of experience that activate the seven chakras of the inner body; in most yoga systems, these chakra centers represent (from lowest to the highest), the potentialities for *survival, pleasure, power, compassion, creativity, understanding and liberation.*

Language: articulate sounds and meanings in a system of thought; the oral and written forms of thought, emotion, and experience forming knowledge; the rational expressions of Consciousness in limited and symbolic forms; shapes the forms of thought through reason and experience; a symbolic essence of Being that enables sentient beings to express, create, and discover meaning; a gift of Being and potentiality that separates humans from other sentient beings; the bewitchment of thought

Life: capitalized means a universal, eternal and impersonal energy within nature, life-forms and the universe; although Life is eternal, infinite and the creative energy of every life-form, material form and structure of the universe—all life-forms are impermanent, finite and constantly changing into other forms; the ultimate, sacred or divine basis for all contingent or mortal life-forms; the metaphysical Source that sustains biological life-forms; the invisible, necessary, unconditional manifestation of Divinity; the Mystery

Life-force: the active, creative energy of Life that is necessarily present in each life-form; the Will in its cosmic form and essential in the free will of ordinary consciousness; the energetic, dynamic and experienced Presence of what is ultimate and eternal in personal existence; the eternal essence in the flux

Life-form: a living organism endowed with a soul but vulnerable to changes of all kinds that condition its ego or separate sense of self; a contingently existing being caught in the web of samsara or birth, life, death and rebirth unless it gains full realization of its essence and realizes nirvana (release) or freedom from samsara; a karmicly tainted being, due to embodiment

Love: the universal or non-attached mode of intense feeling or empathy; a felt inclusion rather than the exclusion towards self and others; the sublime, unconditional feeling of Unity or Oneness; the unqualified, unlimited experience of perfect 'Being, Consciousness and Bliss' in relation to what-is; the creative principle of Life, Being, and ordinary existence

Mind: the phenomenal basis for thought, language, and meaning; it differs from the brain but exists in quasi- dependence upon it; the creative basis of thinking, ideas, and meanings in experience; a limited form of Consciousness or higher Awareness, subject to social conditioning and miseducation; a means by which knowledge and culture is transmitted; being without the vision of Consciousness, the mind is passive, vulnerable and subject to indoctrination; the yogic Universal Mind greatly transcends the ordinary or personal mind

Moksa: absolute freedom or the goal of existence in Hindu thought; the absolute end of physical existence with no possibility of re-birth or return; the beginning of true freedom; the merging of personal awareness with the formless, eternal, and infinite Self that is the same in all life-forms; the after-life in 'perfect Consciousness, Being, and Bliss' and the freedom from cyclic existence

Nirvana: the Indic belief that the extinction of craving, attachment and violence leads to a heavenly bliss or freedom-in-samsara; non-attachment or the complete acceptance of change or impermanence; the dialectical opposite and complement of *samsara* or karmic causality and cyclic existence; the necessary pre-condition leading to *moksa* or freedom from *samsara*; the possibility of transcendence or absolute freedom from pain, suffering and misery

Now: the intersecting of time and Eternity in the present moment; the Presence of all past and future moments; the totality of what-is or Being; the undifferentiated aesthetic continuum of experience and reality; the mystical experience of the universe; beyond words, concepts and theories and without limits or boundaries; the power of will and liberation associated with it

Pain-body: a subtle, negative field of energy within the body and corrupting the soul, mind, and personality; it is identified strongly with hatred, despair, aggression, greed, and violence; its actions are blind, ignorant and irrational; its ultimate origin is karmic or from past lives and it develops quite unconsciously through violence, desire and negative emotional states associated with speech, thought and action; desires, attachments and identifications feed the pain-body; anti-dotes are non-violence, compassion and understanding in speech, thought and action and practicing the principles of dis-identification, non-attachment, and non-absolutism; pain-bodies attract each other and ultimately control and destroy relationships unless they are undetected and untreated.

Patterns: forms and relationships based upon laws or principles of natural, culture, and the universe; movements of phenomena over extended periods of time and space; life-forms that express or are embedded in observed or predictable actions; the opposite of chaos or randomness and expressing rationality in some way; a pain-body or pleasure-body that expresses habit formations and repetitive actions of some kind

Perennial: re-appearing year after year, continuously, as is said of certain plants; in Perennial philosophy, the view that there are certain assumptions, questions, Truths that appear generation after generation, in human thought and Consciousness; also, the unitary view or consensus of truths found in religions, philosophies, or knowledge in general; an essentially mystical viewpoint among competing ones found in scientific, pragmatic and analytic views; the primordial Truth of Oneness, Unity, and Identity present in civilization and knowable through Love, Beauty, Justice, Goodness and other universals that makes real knowledge and Transformation possible; the visionary sense of Being that is integrative of science, religion, philosophy, and all knowledge and experience

Person: the organic, conditional and finite unity of body, mind and soul in everyday social functioning and the potential states of higher Consciousness and self-realization; the total self in nature, society, existence and the cosmos; the opposite of a mechanistic concept of human nature that only deconstructs the parts

Philosophy: the conscious involvement and participation of persons in the meanings, purposes, and essences of Life; the pragmatic, existential and universal quest for truth, being and meaning; education or the formal study of reality, knowledge, and human values; the historical record of all human viewpoints concerning the major questions, problems, and meanings of birth, Life, death, and re-birth; experience, knowledge, understanding, wisdom, and enlightenment are the major sources of knowledge relating to its essence and existence

Relationships: self and other or any other dialectic of paired relationships naturally occurring in existence and constituting human nature; subject and object, truth and falsity, right and wrong, inner and outer, etc. as necessary or universal relationships; others are merely contingent, accidental, and external in nature and experience; relationships cannot be separated from the constituent phenomena that form them; relationships exist at all levels of Being and are subject to alienation or dis-union; the most supreme relationship is that which transforms the self through a visionary Consciousness or the love of universal Being

Role-playing: a societal and karmic mode of experience specific to vocational and social activity; a mask of the ego, condition of mind, and mode of mundane or worldly experience; a social construct or artifice thought to be necessary; when Consciousness is present in role-playing, a creative space can develop between self and others, nurturing the expressions of love, joy, and peace; otherwise, the effect is sickening, distorting and corrupting to the soul

Samadhi: in Sanskrit, literally 'to make firm' or established beyond the usual states of experience, i.e. waking, sleeping, dreaming; in *samadhi*, awareness is totally absorbed and conventional mental activity ceases; a deeply absorbed state (s) in which a profound experience of unity with the object (or no-object) of consciousness results; meditation as such in its most essential union of self with Being or the awakening to higher Consciousness and the Truth of existence as often seen in the mystical experience.

Self: the inner Presence of the Life-force or higher Consciousness in the immediate experience or Now; the universal and inclusive experience of the Unity and equality of life-forms; the eternal, infinite, and impersonal Presence of 'God' or 'Brahman' in the Hindu religion; universal or higher Consciousness in personal experience; in its mundane form, the self exists in theories of psychology, sociology and ethics; the concept of self in Buddhism is a unitary combining a metaphysics of profound emptiness and the ordinary phenomena of the body and mind; the self implies at least three essential levels of analysis in most traditions: 1, empirical or organic presence of the living body (unconsciousness) 2, the phenomenal or intellectual presence of the conventional mind (consciousness) and 3, the metaphysical presence of extraordinary awareness (higher Consciousness)

Senses: external and internal means for knowing what is real, true and good, in limited and symbolic forms; sight, hearing, tasting, touching, smelling (external senses of perception); internal sensing of sensations and conditions in the body (internal sense or proprioception); each sense of reality, whether internal or external, must be seen as unified and interpenetrated by consciousness, in the constitution of their objects in experience

Sentience: awareness that is based upon sensory impressions, emotional and intellectual being; a compassionate sensitivity to all life-forms and a capacity for experiencing pain and suffering, gain and loss, joy, love, and peace; each and every life-form is a sentient-being, to some degree, depending upon the species and capacities of awareness

Silence: the primordial vibration of nature from which movement, form, and language arise and to which it returns; silence and sound co-exist as potentialities in primordial nature and thus are complementary; silence also accompanies stillness although both exist relative to an observer or receiver; silence is a crucial experience and value in many fields of contemplative and intellectual endeavor

Society: the collective experience of persons living in and through relationships, roles and institutions that they learn to play through a process largely unconscious and alienating of the existential sense of Life or Being; the totality of ideas and knowledge that are transmitted through socialization, education, and the mass media and which shape the values, goals, and personalities of individuals according to conventional or mainstream morality; self-interested, hierarchical, class-based, racist, sexist, speciesist structures, functions, and processes that resist significant change or Transformation to a higher or liberated form of Consciousness; the possibility exists that—through visionary leaders, perspectives, and institutions—a radical Transformation to justice, nonviolence, equality, and enlightenment could occur on a widespread or revolutionary basis

Soul: usually not capitalized because it exists in an entirely individuated form; yet it is eternal, perfect and uncorrupted in its original form, prior to any embodiment; the essence of Being or who you really are; the underlying essence of Being, Consciousness, and Bliss or the three unconditional absolutes in Hindu Vedanta religious philosophy; the unique, eternal and pure essence of each individual person in the Jain religion; the well-being of the soul is also the primary value of Life (not money or worldly things) as affirmed by Socrates in the *Phaedo*; the soul is the chief basis for believing in immortality or an afterlife in heavenly realm as in theistic religions; for skeptics, the soul is a fiction of religious faith invented to console and delude its followers and lacking in 'proof' of an empirical kind; meanwhile the belief in consciousness (Buddhists) Self (Hindus) and the soul (Jain) are equivalent in meaning since some sense of Transcendence is a metaphysical possibility in all three traditions

Stillness: the experienced absence of movement or a relative state of Being; the initial condition of all beginnings, endings, prior and subsequent to the existence of individual life-forms; stillness is one of the inner conditions necessary for the deep absorptions of meditation that lead to *satori* or the awakening to higher forms of Consciousness; stillness can trigger equanimity or the realization that 'form is emptiness and emptiness form' as in Zen tradition; in stillness, the insight leading to the realization of the inseparability of subject and object, absoluteness and relativity, one and many and other unities, in awareness

System: any structure designed to function as a living matrix of relations and interactions; the body's organic structures and functions that sustain life as we ordinarily know it; a matrix of relations sustaining higher potentialities of self and Consciousness in ordinary existence; physical, organic, and conscious systems are related through their material structures but occupy different levels of complexity and awareness; any system of knowledge is necessarily limited in comprehending the totality of phenomena and is subject to the same limits of finite, sentient beings; 'only God understand the system of reality' (Soren Kierkegaard)

Tao: in Chinese Taoism, the universal principle or Way of everything; the *Tao* through *chi* (universal energy) gives rise to *Yin* (Earth) and *Yang* (Heaven) or the dual, completely interrelated forces of the five elements or movers of nature (earth, wood, fire, water and metal) and the ten thousands things or forms of the world (of which humans are most important); a cyclic view of reality in which everything is seen coming into being and passing away, endlessly; upon reaching an extreme state or stage, each basic pattern (there are sixty four) is transformed through universal change; thus opposites are complementary, interactive, and transforming each other continuously at all levels due to the unifying actions of *Tao* (cosmic force) and *Te* (the objective moral force of the universe); together forming the mystery, uncertainty and wonder of ordinary existence

Thought: a form, concept, or principle created by the mind; a limited form of awareness and understanding largely unconscious or social in origin; a necessary but not sufficient condition for awakening to the presence of Being in the Now; an obstacle to full awakening when attached to and believed to be the basis for enlightenment; a relative condition of understanding reality leading to approximate truths; an object of typical attachment through language or verbal consciousness and blocking the awakening to primordial or Perennial Wisdom; it is intuitive awareness or deep insight (not thought) that leads to enlightenment or the liberation from mind and other egoic states of awareness (Eckhart Tolle)

Unmanifested Realm: the hidden, invisible dimension of reality that is the ground or basis for the manifested or visible world of appearances; in humans, the unmanifested realm is present in the form of the unconsciousness or those forces that play beneath conscious thought and action but which have not risen to full or higher Consciousness; it also represents the infinite realm of potential awareness in humans, feeding all levels of manifestation, in the Now of experience and knowledge; it is the greater reality of ordinary experience and knowledge, what is infinite, eternal, and spiritual in essence; seeing what is unmanifested is the beginning of awakening to the Truth about reality in its manifested forms of impermanence, limits, and understanding; what is unknown and mysterious

Wisdom: a humility based upon intuition, knowledge and insight into the right or moral way to live in tranquility, equanimity and liberation; the traditional end or goal of philosophy, denoting an ethical way of living, in freedom from the fear of death and dying; a deep understanding about one's meaning in life, human nature, and worldly affairs; wisdom makes connections between abstract ideas and human experience in numerous ways; in certain religions, wisdom is considered less than a fully 'enlightened' state of being; the awakening to the truth about existence or birth, life, death and re-birth as it relates to the here-and-now of personal experience

Wu-Wei: the easy, spontaneous or natural way of nature (Chinese Taoism); action without intention or deliberation, termed 'non-doing'; 'without form there is no desire, and without desire that is tranquility' (the *Tao-te-ching*); in common language, 'going with the flow' or the natural energy of everything; not resisting or fighting what is inevitable and infinitely greater than self; awareness of natural energy that enables one to take an easier or more powerful way through the connections as found; surrendering to universal and pervasive change, transformation, and what is ordinary and ultimate in nature

Yoga: literally a real 'union' with the body, mind and soul; a physical, psychological, intellectual and metaphysical discipline that trains the body and mind to realize states of Consciousness leading to enlightenment or the liberation from karmic influences; hence, yoga teaches the possibility of transcendence or going beyond existence, causality and extinction; different traditions of India—Hindu, Jain, Buddhist—emphasize different yogic paths; the path of union with what is divine or sacred as seen in the synthesis of Patanjali's *Yoga Sutras.*

iii. Recommended Readings
Introduction: Framing the Perennial Philosophy of Wisdom
Aldous Huxley: *The Perennial Philosophy / Four Doctrines of Perennialism*
Eckhart Tolle, *The New Earth*
Nagarjuna: *The Tree of Wisdom*
Plato: *The Allegory of the Cave* (from *The Republic*)
William James: *On Mysticism* (from *Varieties of Religious Experience*)
United Nations: *Universal Declaration of Human Rights*

CHAPTERS

1. AWARENESS: THE PRESENCE OF BEING
   Paul Tillich: *The Eternal Now*
   Friedrich Nietzsche: The Birth of Tragedy
   avid Hume: An Inquiry Concerning the Human Understanding

2. NOW: THE EXPERIENCE OF ETERNITY
   Eckhart: *The Power of Now*
   Bertrand Russell: *A Free Man's Worship*
   Josiah Royce: *The Reality of the Temporal*

3. STILLNESS: AWAKENING TO LOVE AND ONENESS
   Lao tzu: *Tao Te Ching*
   Ralph Waldo Emerson: *On Love* (from *Essays*)
   Leo Tolstoy: *Esarhaddon, King of Assyria*

4. SILENCE: THE FULFILLMENT OF STILLNESS
   Chuang tzu: Selected Writings
   Ralph Waldo Emerson: *Friendship*
   Shubun: *Ten Oxherding Pictures*

5. AWAKENING: ESSENCE OR WHO YOU ARE
   Dali Lama: *From Here to Enlightenment*
   Mencius: *Selections*
   Thomas Merton: *Mystics and Zen Masters*

6. CONSCIOUSNESS: AWARENESS OF SELF, WORLD, AND LIFE
   William James: *What Pragmatism Means*
   Ralph W. Emerson: *Circles*
   T. S. Eliot: *Burnt Norton*

7. EGO: UNCONSCIOUS LEARNING OF ROLES
   Meister Eckhart: *Inward and Outward Morality* (*from Sermons*)
   Jean-Paul Sartre: *Existentialism is a Humanism*
   Soren Kierkegaard: *Philosophical Fragments*

15. MIND: MEANING, PURPOSE, AND KNOWLEDGE
   The Buddha: *Dhammapada (Khuddaka-nikaya)*
   Charles S. Peirce: *The Fixation of Belief*
   Bertrand Russell: *The Problems of Philosophy*

16. THOUGHTS: FORMS AND MEANINGS OF THE MIND
   Marcus Aurelius: *Meditations*
   Averroes: *On the Harmony of Religions and Philosophy*
   Mohammad: *The Koran*

17. SOUL: THE ESSENCE OF BEING, CONSCIOUSNESS, AND BLISS
   Aristotle: *On the Soul*
   Vedas: Bhagavad-Gita / Upanishads
   Gary Zukov: *The Seat of the Soul*

18. DESIRE: THE WILL, NATURE, AND SOCIETY
   Arthur Schopenhauer: *Love, Sex, and the Will*
   Henry David Thoreau*: On the Duty of Civil Disobedience*
   Mahatma Gandhi: *Satyagraha and Ahimsa* (from *Autobiography)*

19. EMOTIONS: PSYCHOLOGICAL EXPERIENCES OF THE BODY AND MIND
   William James: *On a Certain Blindness in Human Beings*
   William James: *What Makes a Life Significant?*
   William James*: Habit (from Principles of Psychology)*

20. RELATIONSHIPS: SELF, OTHERS, AND WORLD
   Confucius: *Great Learning / Doctrine of the Man / The Analects*
   Friedrich Nietzsche: *Free Spirits* (from *Twilight of the Idols)*
   Martin Buber: *I and Thou*

21. FORMS: AWARENESS OF CHANGE, *TRUTH,* AND MORALITY
   Charles Darwin: *The Descent of Man / In Relation to Sex*
   William James: *The Moral Philosopher and the Moral Life*
   Carl Gustav Jung: *Forward to the I Ching*

22. FORMLESSNESS: THE WISDOM OF ETERNAL BEING

Buddha: *The Diamond Sutra/ The Lotus Sutra*

Sixth Zen Patriarch: *Dhyana, Samadhi and Final Teachings*

Meister Eckhart: the *Mystical View of God (from Sermons)*

23. ESSENCE: ATUNEMENT WITH INFINITE GOODNESS

Aristotle: *On Happiness (from Ethics)*

Empedocles: *Unity of Soul, Love, and Strife*

Gospel of John: The New Testament

24. ENLIGHTENMENT: WAKING UP TO REALITY

The Yellow Emperor: *I Ching (the Book of Changes)*

Fritjof Capra: *Uncommon Wisdom*

Alan W. Watts, *The Wisdom of Insecurity*

25. NOW, WISDOM AND ENLIGHTENMENT

Earnest Becker, *The Denial of Death*

Friedrich Schiller: *On the Sublime*

Walt Whitman: The Song of Myself

Concluding Reflections

Mencius: *Collected Writings*

Karl Marx: *Communist Manifesto*

Buddha: *The Foundations of Mindfulness (Mahasatipatthana Sutta)*

Edmund Burke: *A Philosophical Inquiry of the Sublime and Beautiful*

T. S. Eliot, *The Four Quartets*

Kurt Godel: *Mathematics in the Light of Philosophy*

Courtney Schlosser, *The Matrix, Philosophy Text and Readings. Available through: octobernight.com/matrix*

iv. Comparative Philosophies of the Perennial Wisdom

In the effort to suggest that volumes of material have been generously left out of *The Perennial Wisdom*, I have included some notes on several philosophies, religious and non-religious, Asian, Middle Eastern and Western, that have relevance to the present effort. Further volumes are needed for the details and the deepening of understanding.

527

Western Philosophies: Naturalism, Rationalism, Empiricism, Pragmatism and Existentialism

Ancient Western Philosophy began with the discovery of human *reason* in relation to physical nature in its individualized, observational and speculative forms in Greece during the Axial Age (6th—2nd centuries BCE); *faith* became more important than reason in the institutional and theological development of the major religions of the Middle East in the Common Era (following the birth, death and resurrection of Christ) until the European Renaissance of the 14th century. Although the first philosophers—Thales, Anaximander and Anaximenes—of ancient Greece were an odd mixture of philosophical *Naturalism and Rationalism,* it was Rationalism that became the dominating perspective of ancient Greece. The early naturalists were united in their search for the *basic stuff* (*Arche*) of everything or that which never changes and yet is the basis for the universal change observed in all forms; and they found the answer in the elements of Nature: *water* for Thales which is plentifully found in nature in differing states of being yet remaining constant; the *Boundless* (the *Apeiron*) for Anaximander which is not found in the elements of nature but is the basis for its diversity; and Anaximenes returned to the four root elements (earth, air, fire and water) of nature and believed that the more abstract *element of air* is the basic stuff of the universe.

Rationalism is the belief that the knowledge and truth of reality can be gained through the ideas of reason and the human mind and this way of thinking dominated Western philosophy in one form or another for over two-thousand years; and there is little to suggest that the belief in the power of reason to effect social change in society or actualize the potentialities of individuals is about to pass from the world scene, anytime soon—Tolle's critique of ideas and the mind notwithstanding.

Even though rationalism enjoyed a philosophical dominance in ancient Greece through the thought of the pre-Socratics, Socrates, Plato and Aristotle of the Axial Age, there were other streams of reflective or conscious thought and action that started during the same period and continued into Roman times. Among these other currents of thought were: Skepticism, Atomism, Epicureanism, Stoicism, Sophism, Cynicism and Neo-Platonism. The ancient skeptics, Pyrrho and his student Timon, set the tone of the Hellenistic age in satirizing Homer (see *Lampoons)* and a radical questioning of all knowledge:

Pyrrho, the famous Greek skeptic, taught that the all forms of *knowledge cannot be trusted.* And this included those based upon reason and logic, the five senses, and the emotions. And this attack upon human knowledge, put in doubt what was then the three sacrosanct categories of philosophy—physics, logic, and ethics. Prryho's purification of the mind and its illusions did not leave much that was worth knowing beyond immediate appearances towards which he expressed a stoic indifference. Pyrrho's eccentric ways were probably the result of his travels with Alexander the Great to India and his meeting with the naked Jain monks there. Their asceticism, radical skepticism (save their belief in a *pure soul*) and stoicism left a lasting impression upon Prryho and Greek philosophy.—By disregarding all perceptions and values, Pyrrho sought to realize the intellectual tranquility that he found in the Jain monks. (See Prryho's student and publicist, Timon)

The earlier Greek atomists, Leucippus and Democritus, believed that everything is made from tiny, eternal and indestructible atoms that come together and separate in time causing the changes that we can directly perceive. Epicurus (founder of epicureanism) wrote that "of all the things which *wisdom* strives to produce in the blessedness of the complete life, the greatest is the possession of friendship"; and the philosophical poet and Roman naturalist, Lucretius wrote in *The Nature of Things*: "Whence Nature all creates, and multiplies / And fosters all, and whither she resolves / Each in the end when each is overthrown. / This ultimate stock we have devised to name / Procreant atoms, matter seeds of things, / Or primal bodies, as primal to the world."

Stoics like the Romans Seneca and Marcus Aurelius aspired to realize the ideal of the *sage*. The sage is one who is in tune with a universal sense of justice and whose actions are virtuous and rational. But this ideal is one that no human being can perfectly or completely realize; and Socrates—and other mystics—have come to the same conclusion in their quest for eternal Truth.

The Greek sophists like Protagoras, Gorgias and Isocrates continued their critique of the establishment philosophers especially Plato and Aristotle, with their emphasis upon the importance of humanity, nature, and useful knowledge; the cynics like Diogenes, Crates and Hipparchus were inspired by the life of Socrates who lived a life of poverty, simplicity and indifference to wealth and the material goods of society; Diogenes, as Plato once remarked, took the frugal example of Socrates to the extreme limit, going mad from it; in modern times, we have the example of Henry David Thoreau who lived in the woods of Walden Pond for two years so that he could confront the essential facts of life before he died; and there were the ancient cyrenaics who advocated hedonism or pleasure-only as the way to happiness; and among them Hegesius argued that suicide is recommended if life proves to be unbearable—so successfully that he was banished from Athens. Last but not least was Alexander the Great who put into ruthless, bloody practice the cosmopolitan philosophy of his early mentor, Aristotle. In all fairness to Aristotle, it was the military heroism that Homer described in the *Iliad and the Odyssey* that inspired his late night reading and epic exploits from North Africa to Eastern India in his effort to expand the influence of the Greek Empire.

All this and much more vividly occurred in the short span of three hundred years or so, leaving a legacy of conflicting values and attitudes towards life, its metaphysical and moral basis. Gone was the metaphysical speculation of the earlier period from the pre-Socrates through Socrates, Plato and Aristotle; and when Christianity arose and became the State religion of the Roman Empire, the philosophies and philosophers of ancient Greece were replaced by a religious faith that promised eternal salvation for the identification with Christ, the World Redeemer and Son of God.

The story of Greek philosophy went largely underground and then morphed into the Jewish, Christian and Islamic theologies of the middle ages of eastern Asia. At first, a purified strain of Platonic philosophy appeared in the 3rd century with the mysticism of Philo of Alexander. Gradually the theologians of Judaism, Christianity and Islam from the 4th century to the 12th centuries discovered and translated Plato, Aristotle and other Greek metaphysicians into their native languages and the renewal of ancient knowledge. However, this discovery and rebirth of ancient Greek culture contributed to more naturalistic, humanistic and skeptical ways of thinking in the sciences, arts and humanities, giving rise to the European Renaissance of the 12th through the15th centuries.

The Renaissance was a period of European philosophy and culture that brought many changes due to the evolution of consciousness in society through the physical sciences and mathematics, philosophical naturalism and skepticism, the Protestant Reformation in religion, international trade and exploration, realism in the arts and humanities, and new, humanistic conceptions of ethics, politics and psychology. Outstanding was the Copernican theory of the solar system which overturned the Earth-centered view of the universe for a sun-centered or heliocentric solar system; and linked with this was criticism of Aristotle's cosmology and the medieval Catholic hegemony in society and religion. In all, the European Renaissance brought forward many new ways of being, thinking and acting in the established and newer fields of knowledge; and it ushered in the Modern era in the sciences, the arts and the humanities.

With the modern period in philosophy came *Rationalism and Empiricism* or philosophies that were based upon *reason* and *experience*, respectively. First, the major rationalists or Rene Descartes, Benedict Spinoza and Wilhelm Leibniz were deeply religious philosophers in spite of their knowledge and genius in the physical sciences and mathematics. Descartes wrote the *Meditations* claiming to have found absolute certainty for the truths of philosophy and religion through the method of systematic doubting and meditative consciousness, where clear and distinct ideas could be found especially the 'One Innate Idea' planted by God within the mind of humans during the act of Creation. Spinoza was similarly persuaded and inspired by the existence of God, an eternal, underlying *substance* that pervades extended nature, human reason and the vast cosmos. Spinoza's so-called method of thinking about eternal *substance* was the language and assumptions of geometry applied to ethics and politics, the mind and body, the psychology of the emotions, and the necessary existence of God in Nature. Leibniz was a more complex philosopher and mathematical genius for inventing the calculus with Newton; Leibniz' more esoteric side moved him to speculate upon the 'absolutely perfect Being" or God who brought us the paradoxes of human freedom and pre-determination. In many ways, the rationalists were strongly influenced by the theology of the middle ages and the philosophical naturalism of the ancient Greeks.

Empiricism first appeared as a philosophical school of thought in Europe in the 17th and 18th centuries mainly through the life, teachings and writings of John Locke, Bishop Berkeley and David Hume. In many ways, empiricism characterized the new or modern age of culture in Europe more than the more traditional beliefs and values of the rationalists. For one thing, there was a new skepticism about religious truth that was atheistic and agnostic; and for another, empiricism valued and affirmed the primacy of *experience* in the creativity of human knowledge as never before. For example, Locke

531

affirmed that the five senses of seeing, hearing, touching, smelling and tasting are the chief means for gaining *sensations* from experience and forming the most 'simple ideas' of our understanding. Second, there are the operations of the mind like perceiving, remembering, imagining, doubting, believing, etc. that are the basis for *reflection* and the 'complex ideas' of knowledge deriving from it. David Hume is, arguably, the most important early modern skeptic. He most famously said that the human self is nothing but "a bundle or collection of different perceptions which succeed each other with inconceivable rapidity and are in perpetual flux and movement." This statement appeals to both pragmatists and Buddhists for its assertion of change, perception, and the tenuous or conditional reality of a 'self' that has no permanence. Bishop Berkeley, like other empiricists, first affirmed the primacy of perception or sense-based knowledge in our understanding of 'self' or 'world'. However, unlike Hume and to some extent Locke, he defended an idealist metaphysics which affirmed the existence of God as the ultimate perceiver of everything that we count as real whether we perceive the things of the world or not.

Pragmatism is a uniquely American philosophy which slowly developed from an action-based, adventure-seeking and inquiring mentality among the early American settlers. Of course the dark side of European Colonialism and the resulting genocide of the indigenous people of the entire Continent often only received a passing mention in history books. Albeit, the European Colonists and Conquistadors seized the land and destroyed the culture of the indigenous people of the 'Americas'; and it is a dark tale of murder, rape and pillage of the lands' 'godless' inhabitants. The pragmatic philosophy of the United States grew partly from a soil of historic denial and the affirmation of the new method of knowing popularized by the English philosopher Francis Bacon's *Novum Organum* in 1620. Bacon's theory of 'idols' or hindrances bear a striking resemblance to the doctrine of hindrances among the Buddhists at a much earlier period (see the doctrine of the Four Truths or Facts). Among the *idols* are those of: 1, the *tribe* whereby we collectively project our desires, needs and feelings upon nature and others; 2, the *cave* which is the individual form of tribal tendencies having the effect of fixing opinion rather than making discovery of nature possible; 3, the *marketplace* or the public world of verbal discourse where language often creates a world separate from actual or real things and creates confusion, obfuscation and empty abstractions; 4, the *theater* or ideas and theories from the past that prevent one from making genuine discoveries, new technologies, and expanding understanding about nature, the real world and cosmos.

Pragmatism only became a self-consciously held philosophy in the late 19th century through Charles S. Peirce, William James and John Dewey, the most important early pragmatists. It was an exciting philosophy because it embodied the new methods of science and the modern world. And even though it offered a strong critique of the *status quo* and the world of ideas, its liberal approach to knowledge left the door open to the more metaphysical and traditional ways of thinking in philosophy; and respecting human differences was its moral strength. Peirce affirmed that there is no knowledge beyond doubting or questioning, a doctrine he called *fallibilism*. He thought that conflicting opinions are ultimately settled through a sophisticated analysis of the consequences of acted-upon belief, a rather loosely defined doctrine that James and Dewey accepted and developed in their own ways. Language was early seen among pragmatists as crucial in understanding logic and the thinking process which was conceived of in terms of the method of thinking found in the physical or natural sciences. In fact, Dewey developed a general theory of scientific intelligence based upon the natural sciences and applied this to his views on education, society and human nature. Peirce developed a theory of signs, called semiotics, and affirmed a triadic relation between sign or symbol, the thing symbols stand for or represent, and an interpreting subject or real user of symbols. Ultimately if signs or symbols have any meaning or significance they result in changes in character, habits and values. James differs from Dewey and Peirce to a lesser extent in emphasizing psychological, moral and religious tendencies in individuals as they influence knowledge and society. Perhaps the image of Prometheus, the Greek god of power, best describes the concept of self that James held and reflects the cult of the self-made person in American society. James' *Varieties of Religious Experience* in 1910 left little doubt that religion, especially in its more mystical, individual forms, played a significant role in American thought and culture. In general, James view of knowledge was an extensive as the *stream of consciousness* that he envisioned having necessary connections with the total self, nature, society, existence and universe, in the organic and personal processes of experience.

Meanwhile, other philosophers appeared in defense of pragmatism against the absolutists and scientistic approach to knowledge or those who wished to reduce philosophy to matters of *logic only*—the logical positivists, scientific analysts and traditionalists or followers of Aristotle—a tendency that James has little use for and found meaningless beyond the obvious important of language, perception and reason. Josiah Royce related the new pragmatic method to traditional Christian doctrine and won many new adherents to his side; George Santayana, a Spanish born American, married Platonic idealism or the theory of eternal Ideas (*essences* for Santayana) with the animality of human beings contingently placed in nature and evolution. In spite of (and due to it) his skepticism (see *Skepticism and Animal Faith*), Santayana believed in the spiritual realization and beauty of a life that gains intuitive enjoyment of the eternal essences which are everywhere in nature and human existence. Alfred North Whitehead, an English American philosopher, whose interest and knowledge of mathematics and the philosophy of science did not prevent him from speculating about the eternal essences and natural processes of reality in *Process and Reality*. And there have been many parallels seen between Whitehead and a Buddhist theory of reality.

Also, present in the great stir and mixing bowl of ideas and cultural ideas was Charles Darwin's theory of species evolution from the middle of the 19th century. Darwin's evolutionary doctrines like natural selection, chance variation, and species superiority through successful adaption to change, was applied in a number of ways to social institutions and human knowledge. For example, Dewey seized upon the theory of evolution to argue for justifying getting rid of old assumptions, habits of thought and ideas in philosophy that were inconsistent with new assumptions, methods and ideas found in the physical and social sciences. And many others came to Dewey's side while the traditionalists and defenders of the status quo argued against such radical and progressive change.

Added to the fuel burning within Pragmatic philosophy were theories from English Utilitarianism and its democratic ethos of progress based upon 'one person, one vote' in the pursuit of justice and the greater good of ethics. This implied equality among persons and the right of each to pursue happiness, on an equal rather than a class-based playing field. Add to this fire was older economic, ethical and political movements based upon equality of opportunity for persons of color, women, and minority groups. *Feminist philosophers* and political activists in *Civil and Human Rights theorists and activists* came forward in the free-for-all to wrest power from established special interests in government, business, education, and throughout society; and the struggle against the Corporatocracy continues.

Suddenly, a perfect global storm of forces seem to be converging everywhere: global climate change, the depletion of natural resources, and the collapse of banks, currencies, and stock markets. Environmental ethics was not up to the task of sorting it all out. Politicians, educators, scientists, economists and others were suddenly put on notice. Philosophers like everyone else in the business of educating the next generation, were swimming in unfamiliar waters. The embarrassing truth is no one really knows how to fix the mess of the human condition. We run on temporary fixes, gimmicks and inventions that seem to solve the problems of an unplanned, run-away society; but we only end up kicking them down the road, for the next generation to solve.

The struggle for 'life, liberty and the pursuit of happiness' is unending. Now, in 2014, it seems that the *Dream will never* end due to entrenched special interests, the rich and powerful one percent, and the growing gulf between the *haves and the have-nots*. Philosophy, more than ever, needs to be brought into the modern, contemporary world, Now, even if it means shifting all attention upon the present moment, in human existence, society and Life. Pragmatism has much to do with the *shift in cultural consciousness*, to present needs, interests and developments. But All has lead up to the present moment; and All remains in the moment of eternal Now.

One other Western philosophy needs an airing for its contribution to Now: existentialism. *Existentialism* is a many-storied philosophy divided between theistic, atheistic and agnostic tendencies. Its divisions are reflected in the uniqueness of individuals involved, what they stood for and what they were against. The Danish philosopher, Soren Kierkegaard, stood against the rationalist tradition which reached its culmination in George Hegel's system of philosophy. Kierkegaard believed that only God could know the system of the world since human reason is not capable of such understanding; furthermore, systems of thought such as Hegel's were not able to account for the uniqueness and subjectivity of individuals. In fact, Kierkegaard's theory of knowledge assumed that the subjectivity of the existing individual is the real basis for Truth and values and not the abstract ideas of a system. Among other things, Kierkegaard reasoned that there are three distinct stages of development for individual, beginning with the aesthetic stage where sensuality, pleasure and immediate experience dominates one's life; and this gives

535

way to the ethical stage where individuals must struggle with the dilemmas and moral conflicts of existence, which require a moral commitment lacking at the aesthetic stage of existence; and the third stage is religious which may requires 'suspension of the ethical' or societal values for the higher values of love, faith and wonder that have the power to replace the anxiety, despair and guilt experienced at the earlier stages.

Many have seen Kierkegaard as a modern Socrates in his devotion to philosophy and his unorthodox Christian theology which he thought could purify the Church of its corruption. Kierkegaard's devotion to philosophy as a life-long avocation certainly resembles Socrates and his creative use of irony, allegory and autobiography cleared new paths for living individualists to tread and *find their own way.*

Friedrich Nietzsche, the German atheist and anachronistic individualist, represents a differing branch of what, in the 20th century, became known as existentialism or a philosophy that emphasized the primacy of Being, human freedom and subjectivity. Nietzsche believed that his thought symbolized a 'philosophy of the future' when generations would better appreciate and understand his critical sense of humankind, knowledge and society. In particular, he took on the *mummified* view of knowledge coming from absolutist philosophers and their inability to deal with the Void left in society by the 'death of God'. His naturalistic view of human existence led him to nihilistic conclusions about the conventional meaning and purpose of life which pleased the Darwinians of his day. That said, he believed in the *will-to-power* within individuals, the ability to rise about the moral slavery of the masses, and realize the creative potentiality that overcomes social and existential nihilism. *God* or a metaphysical absolute no longer exist, reported Nietzsche, because He had been murdered by the ways of humankind; and furthermore, he declared that only a cyclic universe was eternal, an idea he enshrined in the doctrine of *eternal return.* However, the possibility exists among saints, geniuses and artists, Schopenhauer, an idol and mentor of Nietzsche, declared; and Nietzsche brought this elitist prejudice to new heights with his fanciful notion of the *Superman* (*ubermensch*). This ideal brought with it new difficulty with *amor fati* or the love of good and evil, alike, in the identity of the *true individual.* That said, there may be no greater pay-off, meaning or redemption in individual existence than the realization of a higher and more creative morality that rise above the mediocrity and superficiality of crowd morality; and it was through this perspective of individual willing and creating that Nietzsche sought to persuade future generations to actualize their highest and deepest potentialities for self-fulfillment.

The development of Existential philosophy became most significant after WWII in the United States and the rest of the world. Its individual viewpoints were so diverse and overlapping within ambiguous developments in art, literature, music, film, theology and psychology, that many thought that it could not be coherently described or explained since its center or basis was often seen to contain an irrational image or concept of humankind and a nihilistic view of life. William Barrett's *The Irrational Man* was a case in point. Albeit, on one side of the divide were Edmund Husserl, Martin Heidegger, Jean-Paul Sartre, Albert Camus, Simone de Beauvoir, and Maurice Merleau-Ponty, emphasizing Being, human freedom and courage, among other values; and on the other side were Martin Buber, Paul Tillich, Nicolas Berdyaev, Miguel de Unamuno, Karl Jaspers, Jose Ortega y Gasset, and Gabriel Marcel, who emphasized God, the Eternal Now and Salvation. (Alas, this philosophy has been more complex, rich and diverse in its developments than I have space to describe here.)

Middle Eastern Religious Philosophies: Zoroastrianism, Judaism, Christianity, and Islam

There are four major religious philosophies in the Middle East from the ancient, medieval and modern times; Zoroastrianism, Judaism, Christianity, and Islam. Each of them plays the onto-theological game: there is a sublime Unity or Oneness in the world and it is knowable through following the rituals, moral precepts, and Holy Scripture that is the revealed word of God called Ahura Mazda, Yahweh, Lord, and Allah, respectively. If you learn the eternal Truth that has been conveyed to the representatives and messengers of each tradition, then you can be saved from eternal damnation and the corruption of the soul.

The Perennial Truth that underlies and exists at the mystical core of each theistic tradition goes as follows: 1, there is a Divine Ground and it is the underlying, deepest truth about each transient form of existence; 2, human beings have a two-fold or dualistic nature: a Transcendental aspect or eternal Higher Self and an empirical ego or body and mind; 3, there are two ways of acquiring or learning the Truth about existence: the discursive or analytic way of knowledge and the meditative or contemplative way of experience; and the way of intellectual analysis is inferior to the way of meditative insight; and 4, the aim or purpose of life is to awaken to who you really are and thus to see that the real you and the Divine Ground of everything are one and the same reality.

Another way to think about the game of religious philosophy is to realize that you do not know really know who you are. You have spent a lifetime identified with your body, social roles, ideas and things of the world. Your worldly being is firmly established in completely impermanent stuff—since all the forms of the world and you are the illusions of eternity. And the only way that you can save yourself from the crunch of time, aging and death is to believe—believe in the God of Holy Script and Revelation, who created you and every other form of the universe.

Zoroaster: he who dreamed the Holy Idea and put it into practice with the King of Persia. He who soared to Heaven from Earth and declared Earth and all upon as evil, corrupt and false; and Zoroaster envisioned, designed and executed the institutional organization for religion. First, State or secular support, an army or a horde of true believers in the ideology of the privileged, the elite of wealth and power; and Judaism, Christianity and Islam would faithfully follow the plan having seen the spectacular growth of power and wealth in the Persian Empire of the Zoroastrians. Second, the dream turned nightmare when the fighting broke out against the ancient Greeks, the unwitting carriers of the *disease of the pain-body* or the worship and ideal of all-out-violence in the name of Truth, the One Truth of Being. Third, the architect of the myth, a cunning strategy for controlling the masses through the fiction of the social Lie that stops all resentment and discontent against the powerful; Zoroaster is the birth of mystification, illusion and spiritual irony.

Ancient Middle Eastern philosophies: the wisdom of Divine Incarnation and Salvation for the masses in the identity and mythology of the One, the only One who embodies Perfect Goodness for salvation and deliverance from evil, violence and injustice on Earth. The practice of prayer, selfless-service, sacrifice and love for another as the ethics or way of life leading to satisfaction, fulfillment and happiness—forever through a divine soul; and early evidence of the willful selfishness, meanness and hostility in the human animal in the interest of the higher principle.

The procession of Jewish Prophets or those blessed with revealed knowledge and direct communication with the Holy One, invisible and hidden

Yahweh. The culmination of the Prophetic lineage in the coming of the Christ, Jesus of Nazareth, Mary and Joseph as the recipients of the divine Blessing for the silent masses; and the unconscious, natural desire to replicate, multiply and fructify the Earth with baby Jesus. The moral and ethical immaturity of the human species to understand the real significance of the divine act of Life-embodied; and the mindless drive to protect and self-righteously fight everyone who threatened the holy land and words of the Torah.

Jesus, shrouded in mystery, ambiguity and the miracle of divine intervention; Jesus, the Christ, come down to Earth in the form of man, and incarnating the Holy Word, the One Principle, Truth and impossible Possibility. Jesus, the God-in-man, within every man, woman and child, is suddenly elevated to divinity and saved from death and sheer animality. The sacred Gospels of Jesus, the Savior of man, sacrificing himself for the sins of man, and promising resurrection and life-after-death through the divine soul or essence of Being.

What greater good could come to a man or a woman than being saved from nihilism, oblivion and the Void of eternal silence? It is the promise, hope and reward that every religion must offer to gain and hold faithful followers of the path to redemption and salvation. The certainty of death must be countered by a greater Certainty: that of the promised One, the One who embodies the Truth and the Way to eternal, infinite and perfect happiness.

Islam: a natural response to the failure and immaturity of Roman Christianity to understand the nonviolent, forgiving and loving message of Christ and the empowering of the people, every man, woman and child, through the divine Messenger: Mohammad—the updated Prophet for delivering the masses from ignorance, fear and worldly corruption and to the Perennial Promise, the certainty of Paradise for the faithful and the good. A beautifully abstract, unadorned and elegant architecture in which to worship the hidden, unknown and unknowable God beyond the crude God of the Christian masses; the most truly intellectual God beyond all human imagining and embodiment; Islam is a divinely inspired Mosque, a place of safety and security away from the brutality of human society, tooth-and-claw.

Among the earliest Jewish theologians and philosophers were Philo, Saadia, Gabirol, Haveli, and Maimonides; among the earliest Christian theologians and philosophers were: Plotinus, Origen, Mani, St. Augustine, Arius, St. Thomas Aquinas, and Meister Eckhart; and among the earliest Islamic theologians and philosophers were: Alfarabi, Alghazali, Avicenna and Averroes.

Meanwhile, each of these religions has a deep and rich mystical tradition of experience and community life. For example, the Jewish community has the Hassidics and Kabbalists; the Christian community has the Essences (although now murdered by the Romans) and Gnostics; and the Islamic community has the Sufis. Add to this is the fact that Scripture in each religion is replete with references to noteworthy Prophets, beginning of course with Abraham (who all claim), Moses of the Jews, Jesus of the Christians, and Muhammad of the Moslems.

Post-modern skepticism, atheism and materialism have all but annihilated unconditional faith in the Gods, language and rituals of Theism, wherever they appear. However, the wealth, power and titular authority of the major religions remains in place while no adequate substitute has been developed in the mass cultures of the world. In fact, with the population explosion and growth of materialism, new faiths and cults, sown out of desperation, pessimism and nihilism, have sprung up seemingly to compensate for the archaic values and attitudes of established religions. Lost is the doubt of common sense and absolute certainty in the incarnated God of history; gained is the God of mysticism, embodied as the soul, the God of living experience, wonder, mystery and the hope of eternal Life.

Indian Philosophies (*darshanas*): Hinduism, Jainism, Buddhism and Carvaka

At least three major traditions of philosophy developed in ancient India: Hinduism, Jainism and Buddhism. Hinduism is a general term that refers to six *darshanas* or schools of thought. Agreement among these differing schools is centered upon a Creator God called *Brahman,* which is present within each person as a Higher Self called *Atman.* The contraction, *Atman-Brahman,* refers to the divine connection within each person with Brahman, the eternal, infinitely perfect, and sublime God of birth, life, death and rebirth as a living Self in bodily form. Furthermore, although Brahman is impersonal, abstract and transcendent of the relative and material world, Brahman shows three faces to humanity, as *Brahma* or the birth of all new life-forms, *Vishnu* or the preservation of all life-forms, and *Shiva* or the transformation of all life-forms at death and re-birth.

Existence or birth, life, death and re-birth is cyclical, casually structured and somewhat pre-determined by the intentions of *Brahman* although

540

humans are generally ignorant of the hidden processes and consequences of the Divine Will. The limited free will that humans possess is sufficient to awaken to *karma* or causal relations, but human understanding is limited by reason and perspectival awareness or the first person singular point-of-view. Whether human beings are capable of awakening to their innermost Self or individual soul is controversial. However, the Hindus are unanimous in claiming that spiritual enlightenment comes to those who realize that their body, mind or ego are corrupted, deluded and attached to impermanent forms and illusions which they mistakenly believe are real.

In fact, upon truly awakening to the absolute Truth of *Atman-Brahman* we can see that all of creation is merely an illusion created by the worldly energy of *Maya and Brahman's* personal God of the world, *Ishvara.* The shaping energy of *Maya* continuously attracts the desires of sentient beings in the real world of the appetites, senses, emotions and thoughts of human beings. *Samsara* or the endless round of birth, life, death and re-birth is the perennial condition of sentient beings caught in seamless web of *Maya* who lures all by her powers of creativity, imagination and intelligence. *Prakriti*, the principle of matter, nature and gravitational Force, is the energy or fuel that drives *Maya*, who is the intermediary, necessary dialectic for *Brahman's* direct influence upon Earth and humanity. The aim of existence is to free oneself from *Samsara* and thus the attractions of *Maya*; in so doing, an individual can come to realize the *Dream of Moksa* which is the principle doing of *Maya.*

The promise of the varieties of Hinduism is to save or deliver humans from *samsara* or cyclic existence and the suffering created by desire. This same pattern of universal existence can be seen—with a few important differences— in the family of Buddhist and Jain sects in India and elsewhere. Furthermore, this theistic way of thinking can be seen in many of the other theistic religions of the world like Jewish, Christian and Islamic religions.

Many skeptical, atheistic and materialistic ways of being, thinking and acting also developed in ancient India. Among them were the Jainist, Buddhist and Carvakan *darshanas*. In the long history of India, the Jains date back to the 8th century BC while the Buddhists appeared in the 6th century. Both of these philosophies are atheistic, naturalistic and mystical in origin, structure and function and there are many ways that these two philosophies fit into the Perennial pattern and some ways in which they do not. For example, the Jains believe in a metaphysical or pure soul that is eternal within each unique person, while the Buddhists do not generally have a belief in a soul although karmic *consciousness* comes quite close to the same thing, in many sects of Buddhism. However, Buddhists and Jains share virtually the same view of karma, samsara, maya and moksa as the Hindus, although there are differing rituals, scripture, and public expressions of the same esoteric, mystical and mythic symbols of being, thought and action.

Dying, death and rebirth remain the core existential and metaphysical concerns of Hindus, Buddhists and Jains. In this respect, there are only individual differences between these viewpoints on the issue of death and survival beyond materiality. Otherwise, both of these traditions have a naturalistic, evolutionary and materialistic cosmology or theory about the origin of the universe and humankind.

The aim or purpose of existence for all three of these traditions is to achieve personal liberation from the cyclic nature of existence. The goal is realized differently in these philosophies although many of the practices may look similar on the exoteric or public level of experience. For example, all three recommend meditation, chanting and the purification of one's inner self, soul or consciousness. Also, there are fasting, eating and yoga practices that are quite similar and aimed at the control of the body, ego and mind for final or ultimate liberation from cyclic existence. Furthermore, although there are important doctrinal differences between these Indian philosophies, they view ordinary existence and the human form as ideal conditions for ultimate liberation from rebirth.

Perhaps ancient Indian philosophy is most noteworthy for its disciplines of spiritual development. Although many debatable assumptions in these religious philosophies exist, these three traditions of being, thinking and acting are grounded in discipline of self-control and self-realization that may predate each, called *Yoga* and particularly *Kundalini Yoga* theory and practice. The discovery and development of this viewpoint, practiced first by ascetics and mystics of ancient India, involved an integrative method of meditation, visualization and sound vibration theory—among other esoteric practices and theory. *Yoga* is an active form of experience, involving a disciplined process of movement, control and meditative awareness. The emphasis in most forms of Yoga is awakening the inner body, mind and Spirit of experience and less upon physical movement and the body than is usually practiced.

The aims and values of Yoga practice exist on many levels consistent with an adequate theory of human nature. Briefly this means integrated and holistic control the body, mind, and spiritual self for the purpose of a full awakening to worldly wisdom, intellectual, aesthetic and spiritual enlightenment. The discovery and experience of *something* buried deeply within human identity has been the Perennial goal of humanity—*something* which is also the same phenomenon through nature, existence and the cosmos. We have many words and ideas of what the universal *something* is, but it is not the same as the words that only symbolize it. Some call it the Mystery, Being or Consciousness, of all forms and things, while others name it after a god or goddess in their native religion; but what is *Absolute* can only be named and intuitively experienced through a feeling or insight, but not really known, intellectually or conceptually.

Finally, *Kundalini Yoga* is the awakening of the Inner Body, the living secret energy of *Ishvara*, the god of the soul, time and eternity. It is the discovery of Life-energy or *prana*, the vital fluid of the soul that is more vital than the blood of the body. *Kundalini yoga* means the great mythic serpent that inhabits the atomic elements of the soul or the field of energy that is the Unity of everything. It is the stumbled-upon realized by ancient yogis or practitioners of *something absolute* that eludes all knowers but is within the power, vision and possibility of experience. *Kundalini yoga* is the vision and embodiment of what could be true within the heart, mind and soul of humanity if we acted with a disciplined sense of *being, thought and action* in the real world of the here-and-now.

One further note: Carvaka was a notorious skeptic and materialist in the ancient Indian world. His criticisms of the Hindus, Jains, Buddhists and other religious and philosophical groups were well-known and ill-received. The Carvakans and other skeptics of the ancient world *doubted* the truth or value of practically every doctrine, assumption or practice associated with religious traditions. They said that religion is a waste of one's life-time and is totally false or untrue. There is no afterlife, an immortal soul does not exist, and the aim of life is (or should be) pleasure—pleasure of the appetites, senses and emotions and that self-sacrifice is the way of the fool. Furthermore, religious teachers or leaders are frauds, hypocrites or self-deluded by their own words and emotions and lead others down the same wrong path; and they manipulate others through empty words, negative emotions and false promises.

Ancient Chinese Philosophies: Taoism, Confucianism and Buddhism

The *horse-of-a-different color* from most things Western and Indian; Chinese philosophy is not the dream of Heaven apart from or alienated from Earth but of Heaven-on-Earth—the ideal social order of things in a simplified, earthly existence with no gods or goddesses, afterlives or consoling illusions. Chinese philosophy was a Confucian dream about the Emperor who ruled over the uncultivated and uncouth majority; and the Emperor reigned in rich, silk clothing surrounded by courtly scholars and a harem of concubines in obedient attendance.

The genius, high moral and political ideals, and literary excellence of Confucius were never far away from the imperial dynasties of China. Born out of wedlock and raised as an orphaned child, Confucius sought favor and acceptance from others for much of his life. Basically, his anecdotal philosophy is politically conservative and morally radical since he wanted, above all, to persuade the rulers of his day to stop the internecine warfare against their neighbors and strive to establish peace and harmony in their own province. He genuinely believed that if rulers were excellent persons in their moral, aesthetic and intellectual abilities, the people would strive to emulate the Emperor and follow him in perfect loyalty out of admiration and respect; but it was a dream largely unrealized since China would not realize the kind of social harmony and political nonviolence until several hundred years after his life ended.

Confucius remains the patron saint of ancient history, philosophy and education in modern China. In spite of all the changes in twentieth century China, Confucius is promoted by the Chinese Communist government to heroic levels of praise. Yet the Western world has greater interest in reading Lao-tzu, Chuang-tzu and Lieh-tzu of the Taoists. Mencius is an exceptional Confucian expressing a strongly mystical attitude about human nature, original Goodness and change. The Confucian and Taoist traditions represent more literary and aesthetic developments in China than anything narrowly intellectual or even ontological. If there is metaphysics in Taoism, it remains without a God although *shen,* an energetic soul remains separate from the five elements of *Yin and Yang*. At the same time, although Confucius expressed great interest in Taoism and the *I Ching*, there is little to suggest that he had more than an idle curiosity in the obscurity of the *Tao* and related quasi-metaphysical constructions. For Confucius, at bottom, was an agnostic and a skeptic who probably harbored strongly atheistic convictions as well; but he was careful only to answer that he did not know the truth about religious matters when asked by his students—so as not to kill their curiosity.

Taoism was the dream of the simple, unadorned and uncorrupted life of flowing streams, fleecy clouds, leafy forests and endless visions of harmony, peace and balance within the perfect invisibility, infinity and eternity of a silent cosmos in the dynamic stillness of *Tao* or *Yin and Yang*. Taoism spoke from a timeless Heaven, *T'ien*, which is everywhere in nature, as Nature, embodied in all forms and movements and beyond it, at the same time. It is the philosophy of the impersonal, faceless, abstract Unity behind every religion that can promises everything and delivers nothing but what you can see, experience and feel attuned with, in the universal patterns of all passing forms. Taoism is the realization that Nature is the perfection of the invisible Tao on Earth and the modest capacity of humans to appreciate the beauty and perfection of Nature if they develop the capacity to experience an attunement with the Tao.

Confucianism, the 'ism' is a later, more philosophical development, commented upon and extended beyond the *Analects* of Confucius. As a system of thought, it is barely developed beyond its obvious ethics of altruism known as the *Golden Rule* worldwide. Yet there are the sagely sayings of wisdom, worldliness and aphoristic insight that seem timeless. As in Aristotle, Socrates, Jesus, Mohammad, Siddhartha, Mahavira and other famous thinkers, saints and prophets, it is virtually impossible to know where their own conscious thoughts ended and the knowledge of the editors, writers and commentators—who compiled their contributions to human thought and civilization— began.

The Taoist and Confucian traditions are in a dialectical relationship, with the Taoist hermit, the recluse and saint of the hills and valleys of Nature, at once extreme and the Confucian gentleman of civilization, learning and literary virtues, occupying the other extreme. The emperor-scholar lives in his luxurious silk clothing, occupying a great array of buildings where servants, residential scholars and monks, and other sycophants are below and out-of-sight to the masses except for the generals, their families and brutal armies.

Confucianism is a humanistic philosophy in its most ideal or moral form of remote; it has a cloistered study separated from the moral, psychological and physical slavery of the masses; and in the fields surrounding the Confucian study, schoolyard and imperial palace, the blood flows from the endless civil and tribal wars of the Warring States Period.

[Confucianism is the good face on the corruption and violence of Chinese society; the public relations campaigns of the apologists and publicists of old and new China have covered-up the conditions of slavery, poverty and misery with images of royal happiness, wealth and plenty. It is the perennial lie that every ruling class wants the next, younger generation to learn before the wisdom that often accompanies maturity and older age occurs.]

Buddhism was transplanted from India to China in the first century and at first was rejected and then accepted among Taoists; but among Confucians, the transcendental side of Buddhism was not accepted in the cultivated gardens of Imperial scholarship. Siddhartha was seen by xenophobic, suspicious and skeptical Chinese scholars as merely another incarnation of Lao-tzu, the reclusive Taoist of the *Tao de Ching*. Questions were raised: 'Why do we need another voice to add to our contentious chorus of philosophers? And who is this foreign upstart from the backward land to the South?' Judgments followed: 'He can add nothing to what we already know and understand about Heaven, Earth and humankind'—such was the initial attitude from the heartland of Han China.

Attitudes and values would change in time in China as they do everywhere; but it took almost five hundred years for the acceptance of Buddhism. China is the land of great natural abundance, congested cities and a violent history that follows over-population; only in China there is always something else to consider with its swelling population, mega-constructions, resource projects, the growth of cities, deadly air pollution and the income gap between the extremely poor and the super-rich (over 100 billionaires and the average income is around 4,000 US dollars, circa 2014).

The royal family of Siddhartha looks beyond its concepts, rituals and ideals to the momentary experiences of awareness. It is the immediate experience of the living self that matters like the senses that extend pure consciousness into the world of things, other persons, events and changes. Everywhere, in the present moment, consciousness is present, interpenetrating every sensation, emotion, memory and thought. Profoundly conditioned by time-space and the psycho-physiological conditions of the body and mind, no one can know what the next moment will bring.

A familiar recipe easy to recite by a child but practically impossible for adults to realize in a single life-time of suffering and dissatisfaction: the Four Truths or Facts of human existence: 1, existence is suffering, dissatisfaction and conflict in all stages of growth and development; 2, existence is casually related through experience, knowledge and change, and there are causes or reasons that give rise to pain and suffering, etc. 3, the free-will and intentionality make it possible to eliminate pain and suffering, to some degree, once we understand the truth about existence and reasons for suffering; 4, a Middle-Way between the extremes of existence—asceticism and hedonism, etc. is the Path of deliverance, redemption and salvation for the Buddhist (1—8): right or perfect understanding, intention, speech, livelihood, action, effort, mindfulness, concentration.

In the Buddhist perspective the aim of life is to mindfully live the moral life with meditative concentration for the sake of liberation. The precious, immeasurable self that no mind can completely know through causal reasoning alone, is our ground of immediate experience from birth, life, death and rebirth and continuously through the inconceivable complexity of eternal Being.

Rendered insignificant by the immensity of time, the universe and the ordinary world, an individual struggles to remain free in a sea of conditionals, contingencies and uncertainties. And each remains alone in solitude to interpret experience and live freely before Being.

v. Acknowledgements

I wish to thank many people who helped me along the way in the process of writing this book. First, there were many students who read and favorably commented on parts of this text since its original draft form in 2008. Second, there were several friends who encouraged me to get the text published and also favorably discussed the text with me. Among them are: Steve and Robin Rodman, Musoeng of the Barre Center for Buddhist Studies, Brayton and Suzanne Shanley of the Agape Center, and Susan Coles, my life-companion in the Eternal Now. Second, there is the Philosophy Department at Worcester State University where I have been a full time teaching member for over four decades. I am the last of the infamous five who started the Department to retire and I intend to continue teaching there on a part time basis. I leave behind Dan Shardin, Kristin Waters, Jose Mendoza, and Henry Theriault—all of whom have been supportive of my teaching courses in Asian Philosophies of India and China. The Department has been and will continue to be a necessary and unique part of a small, multi-purposed and distinguished University. Third, special thanks go out to Professor Kenneth Gibbs, who retired somewhat before me and gave me very valuable feedback and advice on the *Introduction* to the book. I have had wonderful conversations with Professor Gibbs and all the other people mentioned here, over the years, and I am eternally grateful for that privilege. Fourth, there are all those persons at Amazon's CreateSpace Publishing who prepared this book for its present edition, especially Gaines Hill and *team five*. It is with sadness in my heart and hope in my soul that I bid farewell to the past and say *hello to a new world* and the possibilities that it may offer me in the *Eternal Now*.

44592439R10324

Made in the USA
Lexington, KY
04 September 2015